MILITARY RULE IN POLAND

MILITARY RULE IN POLAND

The Rebuilding of Communist Power, 1981-1983

GEORGE SANFORD

ST. MARTIN'S PRESS
New York

Library of Congress Cataloging-in-Publication Data

Sanford, George.
    Military rule in Poland.

    Bibliography: p.
    Includes index.
        1. Poland — Politics and government — 1980-
2. Communism — Poland. I. Title.
DK4442.S26 1986   943.8′056   86-15427
ISBN 0-312-53257-1

CONTENTS

LIST OF TABLES

TO ADRIANA

ABBREVIATIONS AND GLOSSARY OF POLISH TERMS

The original initials for Polish terms are normally retained
in this study.

AK	ARMIA KRAJOWA (Home Army)
AKTYW	Literally central core of active members of a party or organisation
CC	Central Committee
CKKP	CENTRALNA KOMISJA KONTROLI PARTYJNEJ (Central Party Control Commission)
CP	Communist Party
CPSU	Communist Party of the Soviet Union
ChSS	CHRZEŚCIJAŃSKIE STOWARZYSZENIE SPOŁECZNE (Christian Social Association)
DiP	DOŚWIADCZENIE i PRZYSZŁOŚC (Experience and Future)
DzU	DZIENNIK USTAW (Bulletin of Laws of the Polish People's Republic)
GDR	German Democratic Republic
GUS	GŁOWNY URZĄD STATYSTYCZNY (Main Statistical Office)
ICPA	Information Centre for Polish Affairs (London, News Bulletins, 1982-1983)
IW	INSTYTUT WYDAWNICZY (Publishing Institute)
KIK	KLUB INTELIGENCJI KATOLICKIEJ (Catholic Intelligentsia Club)
KiW	KZIĄŻKA i WIEDZA (Book and Knowledge Publishing House)
KOK	KOMITET OBRONY KRAJU (Committee for the Defence of the Country)
KOS	KOŁA OPORU SPOŁECZNEGO (Social Resistance Circles)
KOR	KOMITET OBRONY ROBOTNIKÓW (Workers' Defence Committee)
KPN	KONFEDERACJA POLSKI NIEPODLEGŁEJ (Confederation of Independent Poland)
KPP	KOMUNISTYCZNA PARTIA POLSKI (Communist Party of Poland)
KW	KOMITET WOJEWODZKI (PZPR Provincial Committee)
KZ	KOMITET ZAKŁADOWY (PZPR Factory Committee)
LOK	LIGA OBRONY KRAJU (League for the Defence of the Country)
MO	MILICJA OBYWATELSKA (Citizens' Militia)
MON	MINISTERSTWO OBRONY NARODOWEJ (Ministry of National Defence)
MSW	MINISTERSTWO SPRAW WEWNĘTRZNYCH (Ministry of Internal Affairs)
MSZ	MINISTERSTWO SPRAW ZAGRANICZNYCH (Ministry of Foreign Affairs)
ND	NOWE DROGI (New Roads)
NIK	NAJWYŻSZA IZBA KONTROLI (Supreme Control Chamber)
NSZZ	NIEZALEŻNE i SAMORZĄDNE ZWIĄZKI ZAWODOWE (Free and Self-Governing Trade Unions)
PAN	POLSKA AKADEMIA NAUK (Polish Academy of Sciences)

Abbreviations and Glossary

PAP	POLSKA AGENCJA PRASOWA (Polish Press Agency)
PGR	PAŃSTWOWE GOSPODARSTWA ROLNE (State Farms)
POP	PODSTAWOWA ORGANIZACJA PARTYJNA (Basic Party Cell)
PPR	POLSKA PARTIA ROBOTNICZA (Polish Workers' Party)
PREMIER	Colloquial usage for Chairman of the Council of Ministers
PRL	POLSKA RZECZPOSPOLITA LUDOWA (Polish People's Republic)
PRON	PATRIOTYCZNY RUCH ODRODZENIA NARODOWEGO (Patriotic Movement of National Rebirth)
PWN	PAŃSTWOWE WYDAWNICTWO NAUKOWE (State Academic Publishing House)
PZKS	POLSKI ZWIĄZEK KATOLIKÓW SPOŁECZNYCH (League of Polish Social Catholics)
PZPR	POLSKA ZJEDNOCZONA PARTIA ROBOTNICZA (Polish United Workers' Party)
OBOP	OŚRODEK BADANIA OPINII PUBLICZNEJ (Centre for Public Opinion Research of Polish Radio and TV)
OBS	OŚRODEK BADAŃ SPOŁECZNYCH (Centre for Social Research, Solidarity's Mazowsze region)
OCK	OBRONA CYWILNA KRAJU (National Civil Defence)
OKO	OGÓLNOPOLSKI KOMITET OPORU (Solidarity's National Resistance Committee)
OKON	OBYWATELSKIE KOMITETY OCALENIA NARODOWEGO (Citizens' Committees of National Salvation)
OTK	OBRONA TERYTORIALNA KRAJU (Defence of National Territory)
RFE	Radio Free Europe
SD	STRONNICTWO DEMOKRATYCZNE (Democratic Party)
SDP-PRL	STOWARZYSZENIE DZIENNIKARZY-PRL (League of Journalists of the Polish People's Republic)
SSS	SPRAWOZDANIE STENOGRAFICZNE SEJMU (Stenographic Report of Sejm Proceedings, Sejm Hansard)
TKK	TYMCZASOWA KOMISJA KOORDYNACYJNA (Solidarity's Provisional Co-ordinating Committee)
TL	TRYBUNA LUDU (Tribune of the People)
TU	Trade Union
UB	URZĄD BEZPIECZEŃSTWA (State Security Organisation)
WKOK	WOJEWÓDZKI KOMITET OBRONY KRAJU (Provincial Committee for the Defence of the Country)
WRON	WOJSKOWA RADA OCALENIA NARODOWEGO (Military Council of National Salvation)
ZBoWiD	ZWIĄZEK BOJOWNIKÓW O WOLNOŚĆ i DEMOKRACJĘ (League of Fighters for Freedom and Democracy)
ZLP	ZWIĄZEK LITERATÓW POLSKICH (League of Polish Writers)
ZOMO	ZMOTORYZOWANE ODWODY MILICJI OBYWATELSKIEJ (Mobile Units of the Citizens' Militia)
ZSL	ZJEDNOCZONE STRONNICTWO LUDOWE (United Peasant Party)

Introduction

THE CAUSES AND COURSE OF THE POLISH CRISIS OF
1980-1981. SIGNPOSTS TO THE ACADEMIC DEBATE

This study seeks to explain why it was possible
for the Polish Military to take power in December
1981.   It then examines how this was done and with
what consequences.   It is one of the oldest truisms
in politics that force solves nothing.   But the use
of force has been known to resolve situations.   The
declaration of the State of War in Poland in December
1981 and the use of mass repression to suppress Polish
society and Solidarity was a major event in postwar
European history.   It was more significant than
superficially comparable developments like 'Normalisation' in Hungary after 1956 and in Czechoslovakia
under Husak.   The Polish Generals aimed to reassert
the priority of the Soviet connection and to rebuild
the political framework and social bases of Soviet-
Leninist power in their country.   The result was
to dampen down the great hopes of 1980-1981 and to
aggravate the State-Society split which at various
times since 1944 had seemed to divide the Poles into
two great and irreconcilable camps.   But military
communist rule did not establish a permanent Army-
State.   It rebuilt the political institutions and
the mechanisms of the Party-State, recruited new
directing personnel and attempted to revivify
Marxist-Leninist ideology and to produce a new and
reliable supporting party membership.   Basic social
and economic problems were not resolved in any systemic way but a long-term political base was created
for Jaruzelski and the political officers who had
displaced a section of the civilian party functionaries.   The experience of the State of War in
1982-1983 sheds a powerful light on the problem of
reconciling Reform, Pluralisation and Democratisation processes with the Soviet definition of the
leading role of the Communist Party.   Crucial
questions about the nature of the communist system

1

and its capacity to respond to crisis, the interchangeability of its constituent apparats in producing varied forms of communist government, the
novel political role of the communist Officer Corps
and the clash of rival personalities and policy-
alternatives in the Developed Socialist State are
examined in this book.   But, as with my earlier
volume, Polish Communism in Crisis, this is a political study whose main focus is on the communist
powerholders.   It therefore makes no claim to
comprehensive economic, sociological, cultural and
international coverage.
     The Polish Crisis of the 1980s burst into the
open with a Workers' Revolt in Summer 1980.   The 16
month long confrontation between the Communist State
and Polish Society, represented by Solidarity and
the Roman Catholic Church, was then transformed
qualitatively by the imposition of the State of War
in December 1981 [1].   Martial Law was suspended in
December 1982 and lifted in July 1983.   Its primary
initial purpose was to bring the curtain down on
the independent social forces and reform hopes of
1980-1981, to administer a severe psychological
shock to the Poles and to halt the processes of
political contestation, social unrest and economic
collapse.   Solidarity and all opposition were to
be repressed, while unreliable individuals were to
be purged by the Jaruzelski régime from the party
and from directing positions in all walks of life.
But the longer term aim was to rebuild the communist
system on a new basis and with fresh personnel
within the ideological-political framework set out
by the Ninth Congress in July 1981.   The PZPR
Central Apparatus (CPA), the so-called beton (cement),
had remained remarkably firm under Kania's leadership;   it had, however, proved unable to cope with
the challenges of a restless and disillusioned
grassroots party membership and the efforts of its
pro-Solidarity working-class members to wrest an
autonomous form of Self-Management at the expense
of the PZPR factory committees.   As a result, the
directing civilian party functionaries were replaced
by a more determined hard-core of political officers
headed by Jaruzelski.   The Military carried through
the repression of Solidarity and society.   They then
proceeded to rebuild the communist party and state
within their own ideological terms of reference
with the prime aims of restoring the communist
hegemony and rehabilitating the economy.
     The two strands of suppression of opposition and
the rebuilding of viable communist political mechanisms

will be examined in detail in Section Two. But
this study's underlying purpose is also to assess
its long-term prospects and its significance for
the World Communist Movement. To this end I trace
out the rise of the political military to power
in postwar Poland. Either by accident or design,
for reasons elucidated in Chapter Two, the Kremlin
after 1956 favoured the emergence of a professionally
capable and reliably pro-Soviet cohort of native
Polish officers headed by Jaruzelski to replace the
large directing core of seconded Red Army officers
symbolised by Rokossowski who were swept out in 1956.
The Jaruzelski cohort won out eventually against the
more domestic resistance and partisan tendencies of
the Gomułka-Spychalski-Moczar period. The Polish
Officer Corps under Gierek gained full autonomy and
expanded its role in society; but above all a new
type of personally capable and educationally and professionally well trained political officer was produced during the 1970s. Their numbers went well
beyond what was needed for purely military purposes
and for the exercise of PZPR control over the Army.
If anything, Gierek and his supporters had to accept
the intramural criticisms of the military wing headed
by Jaruzelski, who took over unquestioned control
of the Officer Corps after the purges of 1967-1971.
Gierek was also constrained by the reliably pro-
Soviet (and Second World War military political commissar) Premier Piotr Jaroszewicz. These developments have to be considered within the framework of
a vast academic literature on civil-military relations, both comparative and communist, and the
theories of bureaucratic pluralism which have been
produced to explain the dynamics of communist decision-making. The replacement of civilian by military functionaries at the top and the pioneering of
new communist forms of government by Jaruzelski and
his military junta during the State of War in 1982-
1983, however, made it possible to revert to more
traditional forms of communist party rule thereafter. The institutional processes gradually returned to the communist norm with the key difference
that the Polish communist party-state, which never
quite became an army-state, retained a significant
proportion of the military influx of 1981-1982
into leading positions. The system has undoubtedly
been stabilised on this basis. This is not to deny
the depth of social and psychological discontent and
the gravity of the economic problems which faced
Poland in the mid-1980s. But the former aspects
constitute the long-term historical significance of

the State of War examined in this study while the
latter are part of the cyclical ups and downs of the
postwar state-society relationship in Poland.

E.H. Carr's maxim that history is about winners
should not lead us into a Whig view of history, but
neither should it be forgotten. This is sufficient
justification for my emphasis on the party-military-
élite dimensions in this study. The academic debate
about the causes, course and likely outcome of the
crisis has, however, suffered from the continuing
political sensitivity of the issue. Initially, at
least, it was difficult to present balanced, value-
free explanations which did not pay obeisance to
the 'heroic' character of the social struggle.
After all one man's bread riot is another's struggle
for freedom. The Western mass media and the earlier journalistic accounts, as well as the Polish
publications, both régime and émigré, were often
rationalisations for competing political interests
and programmes; they also reflected the political-
ideological conflict between East and West. The
Polish Crisis certainly produced new and more vigorous values for the latter against the former.
One should therefore establish the multifaceted
and complex nature of Polish reality at the outset.
This inevitably conditions assessments and even the
validity of issues and of areas to be studied [2].
An understanding of the fundamental, although not
always openly avowed, disagreements amongst analysts
concerning the various individual layers and dimensions of the causes of the crisis is an essential
prerequisite to a clear understanding of subsequent
developments. The initial starting-off point
naturally conditions judgements on the course of
the 1980-1981 crisis and interpretations of the
range of possible outcomes,including the inevitability, or otherwise, of martial law. Some of these
controversies are long-running disagreements about
the highly specific features of Poland's history and
political culture, while others centre on the special
circumstances of the 1980-1981 events. Yet others
are part of a wider debate in communist studies on
the nature of communist political power, the conditions for political legitimacy and the consequences
of its absence, social conflict and the socio-
economic dynamics of modernisation and nationalism
and religion in the developed 'actually existing'
socialist state. The main areas of controversy may
best be identified under the following headings,
which pinpoint the underlying areas of dispute and
which challenge some popularly held orthodoxies.

The Causes of Crisis
i)   A historically based Polish political culture. How historically specific to Poland was the 1980 crisis?

It has often been noted that the Poles have a
historically based political culture and that they
are obsessed with interpreting their past [3].
Attitudes towards such events as the reasons for
the Partitions, the 1791 constitution, the 1831 and
1863 Uprisings, the regaining of independence in
1918 and its loss in 1939 and the 1944 Warsaw Uprising are fraught with significance for reactions
to current problems and political values.   It is
hardly surprising that the State-Solidarity conflict
in 1982 centred around the battle to commemorate
differing national and communist anniversaries.
Given the strength of the traditional agents of
socialisation in Poland, the family and the Roman
Catholic Church, the demographic, cultural and
psychological conditions were right in the 1980s
for the Poles to behave in historically familiar
ways, to ape past experiences and even to resurrect
old labels, and to repeat almost traditional mistakes.
   Other commentators have suggested that external
factors have dominated Poland's domestic politics
and the national mood since the eighteenth century.
As the Poles were neither large nor strong enough
to ensure their Great Power independence or small
enough to accept client status, happily the result
was a cyclical historical pattern which superficially seemed to swing between two diametrically
opposed standpoints [4].   In practice there was a
genuine disagreement about how best to preserve the
Polish nation.   Political Realism (as in
Wielopolski's policy before 1863), 'Organic Work'
and most periods of postwar communist rule until
the late 1970s emphasised the priority of national
survival until better times.   Political Idealism
(as in the chiliasm of the nineteenth century re-
volutionaries, or in the interwar Piłsudski-ite self-
confidence) stressed the open aspects of the Polish
struggle for independence and the psychological importance of acts of national will.   Bromke therefore argues that 1980 was caused largely by 'a rebirth of political idealism' [5].   Such explanations in terms of underlying historical traditions
and national psychology emphasise Polish nationalism
and its identification with Roman Catholicism.
These are useful introductory statements but they
are pitched at too general and too determinist a
level to have more than post hoc explanatory value

5

about the timing, forms and particular conditions
of specific outbursts.

The sociological counterpoint to the above high-
lights a consequence of foreign domination and pressure which has led to a highly unintegrated and conflictual relationship between State and Society.
There has always been a potential, and often an
outright, split which has fuelled the Polish propensity for social autonomy and contestation [6].
One standpoint has been to regard this as worsening
the PZPR's lack of political legitimacy along with
all the other factors [7]. Another has been that
this has created the necessary conditions for the
emergence of a 'counter-community' [8]. The Polish
opposition and its Western supporters developed
a rounded-off conception that 1980 signified 'the
rebirth of civil society' which crowned the success
of the late 1970s' strategy of 'Independent Social
Movements' [9]. This built on the self-serving
critique of the likes of Kołakowski that the post-
1956 intellectual currents of revisionism and posi-
tivism were bankrupt as a result of the 1968 developments [10]. The argument that socialist states
could not reform themselves was cast in systemic
terms. This, along with the post-Helsinki emphasis
on human rights and the alleged lessons of Dubcek's
failure, produced the theory of 'the Self-Limiting
Revolution'. Soviet domination and interests in
Eastern Europe and the leading role of the PZPR
would not be challenged openly; but the formation
of Solidarity, which effectively was billed as a
national confederation of ten million adult Poles,
would bypass open confrontation. The Solidarity,
KOR and Church leaders were confident that such a
massive force would compel the communist system to
adapt and to co-exist with it; the cost of suppression was believed to be too high as it was normally
presented in terms of a Soviet invasion which would
provoke a horrendous Polish Uprising.

ii) The oddities of the 1956-1980 system in com-
     parative communist terms
The above historical, sociological and ideologically motivated explanations of the admitted weakness and instability of communist rule in Poland
all lost sight of the crucial significance of 1956.
'October' was an ambiguous and unstable compromise
between the national and reform aspirations of Polish
society and Gomułka's peculiar brand of domestic-
communist authoritarianism; but it undoubtedly marked
a qualitative and permanent change in the system as

well.   Its most notable features were the private
peasant ownership of about 80% of the land, the
independence of the Roman Catholic Church, a liberal
cultural policy and the legitimisation of most of
Poland's national symbols and traditions.   The revised relations with the USSR also gave the Polish
communist élite greater freedom of domestic manoeuvre
and a greater capacity to follow its own self-interest than in the rest of the Soviet bloc.   A tri-
angular balancing act between the forces of Soviet
power, the Polish élite (composed of both the
Nomenklatura communist functionary core and the
supporting stratum of university educated profes-
sionals) and Polish society thus emerged.   Different
alliances and balances were struck at different
times.   Although the Kremlin and the Polish functionary group were always close, the Polish leadership made concessions to the intellectual service
stratum and managed to maintain sufficient common
ground with society in general to prevent a fundamental challenge to the October 1956 system until
workers' discontent broke it in 1980.
     Although much maligned by both reformers and
hardliners after 1980 the historical truth is that
the 1956-1980 political system was an ideologically
hybrid form of authoritarianism which allowed what,
by Soviet standards, was a considerable degree of
social and even political pluralism.   It attempted
to reconcile Poland's pluralism, which had not
been subjugated by the relatively shortlived and
moderate period of Stalinism from 1948 to 1955 with
the inherent authoritarianism of the PZPR.   Régime
political scientists in the 1960s even argued that
it was a dominant hegemonic not monopolistic system
of CP rule [11].   The important consequence was
that informal mechanisms were established to prevent the recurrent confrontations between the PZPR
and the Roman Catholic Church and other social groups
from getting out of hand [12].   Even what looked
like a general crisis in 1968-1970 had a functional
character.   It unblocked the system by producing
Gierek's new and revivified leadership.   The year
1968, in particular, needs to be seen in perspective.   It did not mark a break,as some have
claimed;   only an important caesura.   The system
itself did not change in fundamentals;   only in
leadership personnel, and styles and some policies.
It is therefore a travesty of the facts to contrast
a 'good' Gomułka with a 'bad' Gierek as both the
Jaruzelski régime and its Western opponents have
done in order to justify their political purposes.

It is hardly surprising that the imperfections of
the centralised system of communist rule by political and economic directives and traditional Soviet-
type Nomenklatura methods in Poland have been held
responsible for social discontent [13]; but one
should juxtapose this factor against the rather obvious facts of PZPR weakness and incapacity either
to dampen down or suppress the overwhelming demands
of a free and, in many respects, irresponsible
society [14]. In terms of pure economic rationality
Polish society blocked an evolutionary, reformist
development through its veto on increased food and
other price rises from 1970 onwards. The Western
and domestic Polish recipe for making Polish society
a full and responsible partner to the state was democratisation. But the term has vastly different
meanings to the various interested parties and
Yugoslav practice has shown the long drawn out difficulties involved in implementing such a process.

iii)   The Gierek question;   individual responsibi-
       lity or systemic causes?
     Edward Gierek, the PZPR First Secretary from
December 1970 to September 1980, was held univer-
sally to blame for the crisis, both in Poland and
outside, when it broke out. I swim against the
tide on this by arguing that, while Gierek's political and economic mistakes were catastrophic ones
which more than justified his belated removal, that
responsibility should be spread more evenly to
include society. A perfectly reasonable case can
be made out for the 1956-1980 system as an original
halfway house with numerous checks and balances
which, in comparative communist terms, provided
much personal liberty and social autonomy. This
truth was forgotten in the onslaught on it from
diametrically opposed extremes following Gierek's
fall. One could argue that it was overthrown because of its good-natured cynicism and slightly
corrupt weaknesses, not because of its strengths.
The criticisms levelled against its centralism,
bureaucratism, heavy industry priorities and inefficiency are valid enough,but they fade into insig-
nificance when contrasted in comparative terms with
the Soviet, Albanian or any other less sophisticated
communist system.
     The Gierek régime was undoubtedly responsible
for the major economic crisis which resulted from
excessive foreign indebtedness ($20,000 million in
hard currency alone by 1980), the failure to use
imported Western technology to optimal effect and

mistaken investment priorities favouring some prestige heavy industry projects [15]. But the main
error was the fanning of excessive expectations in
the accelerated consumer boom of 1972-1974.
Gierek faced near insuperable political and psychological problems when the economic downturn set in
during the mid-1970s. He could not use Stalinist
terror for the reasons already outlined. He had
missed his best chance to introduce Hungarian pricing disciplines at the Sixth PZPR Congress in
December 1971. The latter mistake was repeated
after his climb-down over the attempted food price
increase in 1976. Once again he failed to learn
from the Hungarian experience and to enforce
socialist market disciplines and rational pricing
policies on the Poles. The result was a massive
Distribution Crisis in 1980 which was every bit
as important as the absence of political legitimacy
and ideological commitment. Subsidised consumption, excessive expectations, real hardship for
certain strata, personal envy of others' success
and quite unrealistic comparisons with the West
inevitably produced a state of national schizo-
phrenia about economic matters. In theory
society's purely extractive attitudes would have
been tempered by democratic involvement and responsibility. The failure of the post-1976 Economic Manoeuvre was, however, caused primarily by
social obstruction and the conservatism of the
state rather than the party bureaucracy. An
additional problem was that uneven distribution of
the economic improvement of the 1970s and the failure to evolve socially acceptable and economically
rational distribution methods fostered patterns of
unequal consumption, which heightened feelings of
social injustice, especially among manual workers,
poorer peasants and the old. Gierek fell between
many stools. He failed because he did not produce
sharp enough leadership and as a result of the
classic dilemmas diagnosed by de Tocqueville.
The beneficiaries of the system often compared
themselves with Western levels (partly because of
the open door to Westerm films, plays and publications) and therefore only noticed the remaining
Polish shortcomings. Those who were left out, even
if only in relative terms, naturally felt aggrieved,
peculiarly enough, even more than when a rough
equality of misery and some idealistic belief in
the socialist future prevailed during Stalinism.
Gierek's programme had been one of technocratic
management and consumer prosperity with prospects

of meritocratic advance for all. He fell victim
to the falling -off in the rate of social mobility,
the blocking of opportunities for advancement which
had first made themselves felt in 1968 and the
psychological effect of the disappointment of the
hopes for prosperity.
There is little question of Gierek's specific
political and economic mistakes after 1972. But
there is considerable academic debate about the
merits of the modernised, second generation corporatist socialism which he claimed to be working
towards. This issue is relevant to this study to
the extent that it impinges on the question of the
alleged bankruptcy of pre-August 1980 civilian alternatives. The balanced judgement by a fiercely
intelligent, critical Polish sociologist, whose
convoluted style reflects the complexity of the
Gierek era, renders it its due for its tension
management capacities. It can be counterbalanced
by the PZPR Ninth Congress programme of Socialist
Renewal, Lewis' dissection of its considerable institutional incoherence and the opposition critique
of its authoritarian and irresponsible character.
Staniszkis declares that 'the most absurd solutions
were abandoned, albeit informally, quasi-institu-
tional forms of conflict-regulation emerged ... in
the shape of corporative networks of relations between government and society. The ruling group
learned to take advantage of its power of allocation
in order to redistribute tensions in the system'
[16].
The issue of the personal responsibility of
Gierek's own team and his leadership generation was
used by many communist politicians after August
1980 to support their argument that the socialist
system was basically sound but that the deformations
of the 1970s needed to be put right. This theme of
the 'Settlement of Accounts' was propounded most
strongly by Tadeusz Grabski and Mieczysław Moczar
in 1980-1981. It led to the great leadership
turnover in the period before the Ninth Congress,
the trials of the most corrupt and compromised officials and the protracted charade of the setting
up of the State Tribunal in 1982-1983.
One of the major critiques of the Gierek leadership after its fall was that not only its political
and economic mistakes but also its faulty leadership
style and methods were prime causes of the 1980
outburst [17]. There was nothing new in this as
both Gomułka and Gierek had said as much about their
predecessors. Many commentators, both Western and

domestic and émigré Polish radicals, however, went
much further. They sought systemic causes for
social apathy, leadership irresponsibility and mistakes and centralised directive rule which acted as
a brake on the country's economic potential [18].
It was argued that Stalinism was only halted, not
demolished, in 1956. The time was now ripe for
another qualitative leap forward. Perhaps the
newly formed Independent and Self-Managing Trade
Unions would provide the much yearned for 'institutional guarantees' that the cycles of high hopes and
half cock reforms, then stagnation followed by popular outbursts which had characterised both the
Gomułka and the Gierek periods, would not be repeated.
This was heady stuff. It is, however, unproven
that the introduction of real economic and social
self-management, democracy within the PZPR and
economic decentralisation with self-managing, self-
financing enterprises was possible as long as
Solidarity refused to accept the PZPR's leading role
and resisted incorporation into the system. On
the other hand, critics point to Czechoslovakia 1968
to justify their case that such reforms introduced
by a radical PZPR leadership would have precipitated
a Soviet invasion. But the 1956 model of an apparently reform-nationalist Polish communist leadership gaining sufficient social support to discourage
the Kremlin from such a step can be adduced, especially
if the reforms were to be introduced in a long-term
and gradual manner as in Yugoslavia or Hungary after
1961. Was Gierek right in diagnosing economic
prosperity as the sole key to the Polish morass, or
did the 1980 reformers have a case in transferring
the problem to the political and psychological spheres?
    Gierek had presided over Poland's full emergence
as an international actor and the Poles also cured
themselves of some unnecessary national inferiority
complexes during the 1970s. If anything, they then
moved on to a degree of megalomania and lack of objective balance about their comparative economic and
political capacities. The election of Cardinal
Karol Wojtyła of Kraków as Pope John Paul II in 1978
fuelled the mood of excessive national optimism which
ran completely counter to the objective facts of
the late 1970s' economic downturn. The absurd consequence in Summer-Autumn 1980 was that the Poles believed that an act of national will like the negotiation of the Social Agreements of Gdańsk, Szczecin
and Jastrzębie and the formation of Solidarity would
suffice to resolve their economic problems and to
transform their strategic political situation [19].

As often happens in Polish history, maximalist demands then built up and undercut what little chance
there was of a realistic, if less exciting, reformism,
particularly as Wałęsa and his lieutenants failed
to co-ordinate their initiatives with the discontented grassroots PZPR membership. Everybody
talked of compromise and national understanding in
1981; in practice all this talk went past interlo-
cutors and was mainly directed at personal consti-
tuencies. All the Poles' effort at the end of
the day, partly because of Solidarity's bad timing
in not risking a showdown at Bydgoszcz, merely produced a classic Thermidorian counter-reaction and
a far worse situation than even total inaction would
have done.

iv)   The stresses of a developed socialist society;
      class struggle or distribution crisis?
     Gierek's favourite slogan had been that Poland
was a developed socialist society and that all that
was required was 'further improvement' [20]. This
theory along with his conception of corporatist
socialist unity was demolished by the 1980 outburst.
PZPR theorists conceded that the non-antagonistic
antagonisms of the 1970s had been replaced by open
class struggle. One should therefore ask some
searching questions about the nature of Polish
society and examine whether sociologists have given
adequate answers. Firstly, one needs to ask what
sort of ruling élite emerged in the 1970s? Can
one identify a political élite drawn from the PZPR
Nomenklatura against which Polish society rebelled
in 1980? Or did the workers revolt against the
excessive favouring of the professional service
élite derived from Higher Education? Was Konrad
and Szelenyi's general theoretical analysis that
this was becoming the dominant social group in the
1970s valid, and if so how did it tie in with the
traditional role of the creative intelligentsia
as a rebellious standard bearer of society's discontents [21]? Secondly, what sort of differentiated working class emerged? Was the Workers' Upsurge mainly a blue-collar manual workers' protest
against the privileges of the political and professional élites as argued by Western Maoists? Or
did it represent a qualitative maturing of a skilled
working class which developed the political demands
for free TUs and the right to strike in order to
gain social autonomy and to wrest control in the
enterprises from the PZPR committees and the party-
dominated managers [22]? Thirdly, apart from

traditional Polish idiosyncrasies such as the aping
of gentry manners and values and the adoption of
Catholic symbolism as well as wartime forms and
names, there are two other factors to be considered.
The first of these is the argument popularised by
Staniszkis that Gierek's corporatist and non-par-
ticipatory methods of political rule drove Polish
society, especially the workers, into a justified
revolt against the methods and privileges of the
communist apparatus and its hangers-on [23]. This
backed up the prevalent half-baked Western and opposition argument of the time that the political responsibility of the rulers to the people would auto-
matically produce the conditions for resolving the
socio-economic crisis. The second factor is that
the relative egalitarianism of Polish society was
offset by a drastic levelling up of aspirations
partly because of the dominance of traditional
gentry, bourgeois and intelligentsia values over
socialist ones. What had been an acceptable
social advance for millions of the first postwar
generation no longer contented the second generation.
The paradoxical situation expressed in highly
impressionistic terms was that, while a section
of the manual working class was worked like beasts
in the 1970s, and while a small stratum had considerable privileges by any standards, the remaining two-thirds or so were locked in a Hobbesian
war of all against all; they aspired to the most
desirable second generation, white-collar occupations such as academics, journalists, engineers,
foreign trade workers and the like either for themselves or their children, at the very time that
opportunities were beginning to dry up. The
younger workers with semi-Higher Education qualifications competed equally bitterly for the super-
visory, technical and junior management grades.
Only the younger peasants, who largely left the
land for the urban fleshpots, were still attracted
by first generation advance jobs like waiters, shop
assistants and hairdressers; the paradox in the
1980s was that there was a plethora of unfilled
jobs of this sort in the big cities at a time of
acute difficulty in maintaining full employment in
spite of Government sanctions against excessive
labour mobility and so-called social parasitism.
The system in the 1970s, therefore - a mixture of
politocracy and educational meritocracy skewed by
personal influence - as well as going adrift with
its pricing policies thus failed to develop the
appropriate mechanisms for controlling access to

the most desirable posts and occupations: hence the
social protest against PZPR Nomenklatura methods
during 1980-1981. In sum there was a Distribution
Crisis in the 1970s over access to desirable posts
and consumer goods and a total absence of accepted
criteria for the distribution of scarce resources.
Western critics and the domestic Polish opposition
claimed that this merely reflected the immorality
and anarchic inefficiency of the totalitarian communist system. This is partly true but it also
reflects its decomposition. The fact also remains
that the system suited most Poles who preferred the
possibility of 'fixing' things more than any East
German model of labour and social discipline. The
traditional faults of society, however conditioned
and excused by historical factors, reinforced those
of the post-1956 communist system. The fact was
decried by moral purists in 1980 but few had ob-
jected earlier. At the end of the day one of the
problems was that the Poles demanded socialist
egalitarianism at an American level of prosperity.
    Industrialisation, urbanisation and postwar
modernisation created a materialist, consumer-minded
society whose values nevertheless remained strongly
Roman Catholic and Polish nationalist. A high
birth rate produced an extremely young society
(about two-thirds were under 35 in 1981) who had
not experienced wartime and Stalinist rigours; its
dominant features were an incredible hotchpotch
of political naïvety, material envy, personal
cynicism and unrealistic comparisons with the West.
The régime, as Staniszkis points out, had turned
its youth into masters of the art of camouflaging
personal egoism with fine idealistic-sounding slogans.
These characteristics, as demonstrated by Paul
Neuburg in his fine study of East European youth,
were by no means unique to Poland and had evolved
much earlier [24]. But the crucial factor was
that the relatively weak post-1956 Polish state,
unlike the neo-Stalinist conservative stabilisers
in Bulgaria or the GDR, could barely succeed in
balancing between social groups. It had great
difficulty in maintaining ideological fervour and
political loyalty even within the PZPR membership.
Polish society was never properly disciplined, let
alone socialised into communist values and ways of
doing things. Hence it remained fairly autonomous
and family-based. Krzystof Jasiewicz, however,
follows Stefan Nowak in arguing that the late 1970s
saw a dramatic shift away from local particularisms
to national self-identification by the Poles [25].

This reinforced society's capacity to act in a traditional anti-state, counter-community manner in times of crisis; this occurred with the explosive development of Solidarity,which in September-October 1980 was nothing more or less than a classic Polish Confederation writ large.

The Course of the Crisis
v)   The failure to achieve a national compromise. Could Solidarity have been incorporated into the system?   Could the PZPR have been reformed sufficiently to respond to social demands?
     Two main general explanations of the course of the crisis were produced.   In Poland the post-Gierek leadership of Stanisław Kania argued that the Summer 1980 events were a justified workers' revolt designed to purify socialism and to rectify Gierek's political-economic mistakes and his deviations away from Marxism-Leninism.   What was needed was a Socialist Renewal (Odnowa).   The PZPR should be democratised on Leninist lines.   Gierek's élite should be made to settle their personal and political accounts in a rozliczenie and be dismissed or punished as appropriate.   Party-led reforms, especially of the economy, should be introduced.   The PZPR would attempt to collaborate with the workers', non KOR-political, wing of Solidarity led by Wałęsa and with the cautious Roman Catholic hierarchy.   Kania's Sixth Plenum, October 1980 diagnosis was rounded off in its fullest form in the Ninth Congress programme [26]; some of the systemic critique survived into the Kubiak Report of Autumn 1982 [27].
     The most prevalent Western view also came to mirror the foregoing; the Workers' Upsurge represented the sharpest expression of a general systemic crisis of developed socialism; the main bugbear was the Soviet type of authoritarian, centralist-bureaucratic system of rule through political and economic directives by an unrepresentative and irresponsible leadership [28].   The false corollary was then drawn in 1980-1981 that only two alternatives existed: either the advance to a democratised, self-managing higher form of socialism which would, in some miraculous manner, unite the Poles and mobilise them into producing an economic miracle; or continuing social unrest, punctuated by various outbursts eventually leading to hardline repression, probably through a Soviet invasion.   The ways in which Solidarity could be accepted by the communists were not thought through, nor were the consequences of a failure to do so.   The Leninists' determination

and capacity to hold on to their political hegemony
was underestimated in 1980 and overdemonised as pre-
cluding any evolutionary political settlement later
on. Solidarity and Western apologists for the
Polish August rightly considered that the costs of
Soviet invasion were so horrendous as to render
it a last resort, but they strangely neglected the
option of domestically applied repression. Warnings
that the most likely outcome of the destabilisation
of the 1956-1980 system, at a time of total economic
and consumer collapse, favoured the hardline endea-
vours to subjugate Polish society, which had been
shelved in 1956 in favour of more subtle methods,
were also rejected far too cavalierly.

Was it possible for the PZPR to accept Solidarity
and, if so, on what terms? After all almost a
million PZPR members, 70% of them workers, out
of just over 3 million, joined Solidarity at peak.
Many of the grassroots and professional members
also became radicalised. For a while workers and
intellectuals united in a Horizontal Movement
designed to bypass the vertical control of the CPA
[29]. The keys to the PZPR's fate, however, lay
in Kania's success in preventing real communist
reformers committed to living with Solidarity, like
Tadeusz Fiszbach, the Gdańsk province PZPR First
Secretary, from taking over the Politburo and
Secretariat. Kania, abetted by the harder and
more orthodox leaders like Olszowski, Moczar and
Grabski, managed to postpone the Extraordinary Ninth
Congress of the PZPR until July 1981. They controlled the renewal and democratisation of the party
in the run-up to the Congress by decentralising power
to a lower level of unknown, but reliable, party
militants [30]. Only over Bydgoszcz in late March
1981 did it look possible that Solidarity pressure
might force the Leninist pragmatic-centrists and
hardliners to give way to a more radical leadership
[31]. This might have created the conditions for
a re-run of October 1956 without a 'providential
leader' like Gomułka to complicate the issue.
Failing this, the most that the PZPR could offer
was its own democratisation on Leninist lines, some
party-initiated reforms, a greater degree of social
consultation in the revised National Front arrangements and long years of economic austerity.

One of the great debates is whether Solidarity's
'radicalisation' and 'politicisation' in 1981 was a
valid description and, if so, whether it was tactically justified [32]. But the controversy over
Solidarity's political or TU character is largely

irrelevant.   Its original sin was that the free
TUs in September and October 1980 organised themselves in a vast national federation and not on
an individual factory, regional or industry-wide
basis as the régime wanted and on the lines on which
it organised them initially in 1983.   Solidarity,
after August, inevitably became the spokesman of a
wide range of contestatory social groups and of
the whole of the Polish counter-community against
the communist order.   This fact was only partly
camouflaged by Wałęsa's hand-to-mouth policies of
organising the movement and of attempting to grow
into the system while refusing to become incorporated within it.   As it was, Solidarity's failure
either to overthrow, break, transform or come to
terms with the pragmatic, but essentially Soviet
type, Kania leadership and central committee left
Jaruzelski facing a number of bleak alternatives
in Autumn 1981.   His eventual resort to domestically applied repression was facilitated by the
predictable refusal of the Catholic hierarchy, under
both Wyszyński and Glemp, to commit the Church to
a fundamental confrontation with the communist
system [33].
    It is significant that both the official régime
and Western opposition schools of thought share a
positive analysis of the Summer 1980 Workers' Upsurge.   They then part company in interpreting the
course of the crisis before December 1981.   The
Martial Law régime argued that Solidarity started
out on the right lines of socialist renewal.   It
then fell increasingly under the influence of
counter-revolutionary political groups, notably
KOR and KPN, who provoked the strikes and confrontations which led Poland into a pit of political
anarchy and economic collapse from which it was
only saved by the State of War [34].   The Kania-
Jaruzelski 1981 view, which re-emerged after the
lifting of martial law, was that the PZPR had
hoped that its Leninist democratisation and the
vast renewal of its directing personnel at every
level would suffice to quieten society down.
They wanted to rebuild a slightly looser hegemony
for the PZPR in society and in the factories and
to incorporate Solidarity within a Front of National
Understanding.   This programme, ratified at the
Ninth Congress, failed for two major reasons:
firstly,because of popular discontent with the
economic disaster and Solidarity's refusal to accept
responsibility for unpopular measures of economic
rehabilitation without receiving fundamental

political concessions in return. Secondly,
Solidarity produced a new synthesis at its Congress
in September 1981. Some of its branches (notably
the radical Mazowsze in Warsaw) then presented more
strident demands for a referendum on workers' self-
management, for free elections to People's Councils,
a worker-controlled Second Chamber in the Sejm,
and for genuine organs of social consultation and
control. Although it is not clear,there is also
evidence that the PZPR aktyws within the factories
were not only challenged by the alternative 'Sieć'
(Network) but were on the point of collapse, especially after the Fourth Plenum ordered workers to
choose between their PZPR and Solidarity memberships
in October 1981. The basically orthodox and
unreconstructed PZPR leadership, then, had little
choice, given its ideological blinkers, but to cede
power to the military in order to carry out the
domestically applied repression of Polish society
[35]. The alternative was to accept the gradual
transformation of Poland in at best a Yugoslav, and
possibly Eurocommunist, direction, as a result of
the PZPR-Solidarity confrontations that seemed to
be building up for early 1982. At the same time
it would be impossible to carry through the long
years of economic austerity needed to stabilise
the economy, irrespective of whether it was being
run on Soviet centralised-directive or self-managing, self-financing lines. Is it really any
wonder that the tanks rolled on 13 December 1981?

vi)   External factors. Did the Kremlin veto the
      necessary domestic reforms and render social
      compromise impossible?
   The role of the Soviet leaders was simultaneously
demonised and misinterpreted in the West in 1980-
1981. The mass media falsified the picture by
playing up the possibility, almost the inevitability,
of Soviet invasion throughout the crisis. The
reality, however, was that the Kremlin and Kania,
representing the CPA*,in Poland, were in general
agreement on the need to play Solidarity along, to
gain time, to wear it down and hopefully to split
it. The disagreements over the handling of political prisoners, the printers and distributors of
anti-Soviet tracts as well as the re-introduction
of harder policies were largely tactical. But
the Kremlin intervened politically on, at least,
two occasions (early December 1980 and early June
1981) in order to nip in the bud attempts to introduce genuine reformists into the PZPR leadership.

This neglected aspect of the Kremlin's Nomenklatura
control over top leadership changes will be examined
in Section One. Here one can endorse Andrzej
Korbonski's judgement that the Kremlin's spoiling
tactics were successful in bolstering up the Kania-
Jaruzelski leadership at key moments in the run-up
to the Ninth Congress [36]. This prevented the
emergence of reformists like Fiszbach or Dąbrowa or
even Rakowski, who might have had more credibility
in seeking national support for a Historic Compromise with Solidarity.

Conclusion

Ray Taras has shown how the changing official
interpretations of Poland's postwar crises reflected
the varying leadership personnel, policy and ideological responses to current situations [37]. The
live and contentious character of official historiography was best illustrated by the political debate
over the Kubiak Report. Its final, and much
attenuated, 1983 draft revealed the mature assessment by the Jaruzelski régime of the general
character and determinants of the 1980 crisis.
The system's fundamentally sound ideological and
operative principles were confirmed. The conser-
vatives thought it sufficient to salvage this bed-
rock by conceding Gierek's functional policy and
implementation mistakes as well as his voluntaristic
errors in style and individual decisions and his
wholly catastrophic handling of the social consciousness. But Kubiak and the radicals wanted to go
further than the foregoing stock martial law analysis of 1982 and to include a critique of the system's
structural-institutional failings. Kubiak also
admitted that Gierek's faulty social policies promoted class antagonisms. The Report explained the
gravity of the 1980 crisis as being the consequence
of the unresolved character of the earlier ones in
1948-1956-1970-1976 which had built up cumulatively
to a social explosion which revealed all the system's
structural, functional and voluntaristic defects.
The implicit inference was that the situation demanded sweeping reform but the conclusion was muted
down to desirable theoretical aspirations rather
than concrete proposals. The Jaruzelski concensus
was therefore to accept the Ninth Congress type of
analysis but not to develop and to build on the Kubiak
reform recipe in practice: 'The cause of the social
crises in People's Poland was not the principles of
the socialist system, but exactly the deviations,
insufficiencies and mistakes in the method of

implementing its principles in a specific balance
of class forces, and especially mistakes in the
methods of exercising power' [38]. The problem,
as pointed out by critical political scientists
like Wiatr, was how to salvage the PZPR's leading
role by limiting its monopolistic tendencies and
by producing institutions to provide 'warning
signals' to prevent the state-society split from
building up to future outbursts [39]. The radical
Warsaw University state lawyer, Wojciech Lamentowicz,
placed the PRL's troubled history in a broader de-
velopmental perspective; the postwar crises were
functionally necessary to resolve contradictions and
comparable to the nineteenth-century growing pains
of High Capitalism and early liberal-democracy [40].

Notes

1. The following English language studies covering the
    1980-1981 period, either wholly or in part, have ap-
    peared so far: Nicholas G. Andrews, Poland 1980-1981.
    Solidarity versus the Party (Washington, D.C., National
    Defense University Press, 1985). Neal Ascherson, The
    Polish August (Harmondsworth, Penguin Books, 1981).
    Timothy G. Ash, The Polish Revolution. Solidarity
    (London, Coronet Books, 1985). Jack Bielasiak &
    Maurice D. Simon (eds.), Polish Politics. Edge of the
    abyss (New York, Praeger, 1984). Martin Myant, Poland.
    A crisis for socialism (London, Lawrence & Wishart,
    1982). Peter Raina, Poland 1981. Towards socialist
    renewal (London, George Allen & Unwin, 1985). George
    Sanford, Polish Communism in Crisis (London, Croom Helm,
    1983). J.B. de Weydenthal,B.D. Porter & K. Devlin,
    The Polish Drama, 1980-1982 (Lexington, Lexington Books,
    1983). Jean Woodall (ed.), Policy and Politics in
    Contemporary Poland (London, Frances Pinter, 1982).
2. Hostile reviewers of Polish Communism in Crisis almost
    seemed to deny the existence of the 'free play' of
    political conflict between personalities even during
    the 1980-1981 Solidarity period. I freely concede ,
    though that what Stanislav Andreski called 'the tedious
    parleys of sour apparatchiks' is a less gripping sub-
    ject than the 'heroic' endeavours of Solidarity and
    opposition activists (Times Literary Supplement,
    4 May 1984). The problem though is that the former
    decided, and continue to decide, the fate of the nation.
3. Cf. George Kolankiewicz & Ray Taras, 'Poland; Socialism
    for everyman' in A. Brown & J. Gray (eds.), Political
    Culture and Political Change in Communist States
    (London, Macmillan, 1977), pp. 101 ff.

4. Adam Bromke, Poland's Politics; Idealism versus
    Realism (Cambridge, Mass., Harvard U.P., 1967).
5. Adam Bromke, 'The revival of political idealism in
    Poland', Canadian Slavonic Papers (December 1982).
6. Cf. David Lane & George Kolankiewicz (eds.), Social
    Groups in Polish Society (London, Macmillan, 1973).
7. Paul Lewis, 'Obstacles to the establishment of poli-
    tical legitimacy in communist Poland', British Journal
    of Political Science, XII (1982), pp. 125-144.
8. Jadwiga Staniszkis, Poland's Self-Limiting Revolution,
    edited by Jan Gross (Princeton U.P., 1984). Peter
    Raina, Independent Social Movements in Poland (London,
    Orbis, 1981).
9. See Jerzy Holzer, Solidarność 1980-1981. Geneza i
    Historia (Paris, Instytut Literacki, 1984). Jan Józef
    Lipski, KOR (London, Aneks, 1983; also published in
    English translation by the University of California
    Press, 1986). Alain Touraine et al., Solidarity.
    Analysis of a social movement (Paris, Fayard, 1982).
    The KOR strategy on social movements is outlined inter
    alia in Adam Michnik's 'The new evolutionism', Survey,
    XXII, No. 3-4 (Summer-Autumn 1976), and in Jacek
    Kuroń's Zasady Ideowe (Paris, Instytut Literacki, 1978).
    The debate on Civil Society featured prominently in
    the left wing journal Telos; cf. Andrew Arato, 'Civil
    Society versus the State', Telos, No. 47 (Spring 1981).
10. Jacques Rupnik, 'Dissent in Poland, 1968-1978; the end
    of Revisionism and the rebirth of Civil Society', in
    R. Tokes (ed.), Opposition in Eastern Europe (London,
    Macmillan, 1979).
11. Jerzy J. Wiatr, 'The hegemonic party system in Poland'
    in Studies in Polish Political System (Wrocław,
    Ossolineum, 1967), pp. 108-123.
12. Cf. Jan Gross, 'Thirty years of crisis management in
    Poland' in T. Rakowska-Harmstone (ed.), Perspectives
    for Change in Communist Societies (Boulder, Col.,
    Westview Press, 1979). Dennis Pirages, Modernisation
    and Political Tension-Management (New York, Praeger,
    1972).
13. The institutional and social pluralism of the 1970s
    inevitably produced blockages and confused decision-
    making. These have been analysed by Paul Lewis,
    'Institutionalisation and political change', in
    Neil Harding (ed.), The State and Socialist Society
    (London, Macmillan, 1984). The classical study of the
    concept of pluralism, in both liberal-democratic and
    socialist terms, is Stanisław Ehrlich, Oblicza
    Pluralizmów (Warsaw, PWN, 2nd rev. edn., 1985).
14. George Sanford, 'Polish People's Republic' in
    B. Szajkowski (ed.), Marxist Governments, Vol. 3
    (London, Macmillan, 1980), pp. 553-588.

15. See George Blazyca, 'Comecon and the Polish crisis', World Today, 37, No. 10 (October 1981). Jan Drewnowski (ed.), Crisis in the East European Economy. The spread of the Polish disease (London, Croom Helm, 1981). D.-M. Nuti, 'The Polish crisis; economic factors and constraints' in The Socialist Register (London, Merlin Press, 1981).
16. Jadwiga Staniszkis, 'Martial Law in Poland', Telos, No. 54 (Winter 1982-1983), p. 93.
17. Kania's Sixth Plenum speech, ND (October-November 1980), pp. 9-32.
18. Cf. Leszek Kołakowski in Abraham Brumberg (ed.), Poland. Genesis of a Revolution (New York, Random House, 1983).
19. For the relevant documentation and a mainstream-liberal commentary on the Social Agreements, Anthony Kemp-Welch (ed.), The Birth of Solidarity. The Gdańsk Negotiations, 1980 (London, Macmillan, 1983).
20. See Woodall in J. Woodall (ed.), Policy and Politics, ch. I. On social dynamics, Alexander Matejko, Social Change and Stratification in Eastern Europe. An interpretative analysis of Poland and her neighbours (London, Praeger, 1984).
21. Georg Konrad & Ivan Szelenyi, The Intellectuals on the Road to Class-Power (Brighton, Harvester Press, 1979).
22. Alex Pravda, 'Poland 1980. From "premature consumerism" to labour solidarity', Soviet Studies, XXXIV, No. 2 (April 1982), pp. 167-199.
23. Jadwiga Staniszkis, 'The evolution of forms of working-class protest in Poland', Soviet Studies, XXXIII, No. 2, (April 1981), pp. 204-231.
24. Paul Neuburg, The Hero's Children. The postwar generation in Eastern Europe (London, Constable, 1973).
25. Krzystof Jasiewicz, 'Przemiany świadomości społecznej Polaków 1979-1983', Aneks, No. 32 (1983), pp. 125-139.
26. For the PZPR Programme, IX Nadzwyczajny Zjazd PZPR, 14-20 lipca 1981r (Warsaw, KiW, 1981), pp. 101-158.
27. Sprawozdanie z prac komisji KC PZPR powołanej dla wyjaśnienia przyczyn i przebiegu konfliktów społecznych w dziejach Polski Ludowej, ND (October 1983); hereafter 'Kubiak Report'.
28. Cf. Bronisław Misztal (ed.), Poland after Solidarity. Social movements versus the state (New Brunswick, Transaction Books, 1985).
29. See Kolankiewicz in Woodall, Policy & Politics ..., ch.4.
30. Sanford, Polish Communism in Crisis, ch. 6.
31. Ash, Polish Revolution, pp. 147-166; Andrews, Poland, 1980-1981, pp. 113-135.
32. Cf. Raina, Poland 1981, ch. 15. A useful collection of Solidarity and opposition material for the 1980-1981 period is Stan Persky & Henry Flam (eds.), The Solidarity

Sourcebook (Vancouver, New Star, 1982).
33.   See Bogdan Szajkowski,Next to God ... Poland (London, Frances Pinter, 1983).
34.   J. Bielecki, Co wydarzyło się w Polsce od sierpnia 1980r (Warsaw, KiW, 1982).
35.   George Sanford, 'The Polish communist leadership and the onset of the State of War', Soviet Studies, XXXVI, No. 4 (October 1984), pp. 494-512.
36.   Andrzej Korbonski, 'Soviet decision-making in Poland', Problems of Communism (March-April 1982), pp. 22-36. Weydenthal et al., The Polish Drama, chs. 4, 5, 9, 10.
37.   Ray Taras, 'Official etiologies of Polish crises; changing historiographies and factional struggles', Soviet Studies, XXXVIII, No. 1 (January 1986), pp.53-68. For a similar exercise on 1956, George Sakwa, 'The Polish "October"; a reappraisal through historiography', Polish Review, XXXIII (1978), pp. 62-78.
38.   Kubiak Report, p. 72.
39.   J.J. Wiatr, 'Sejsmografy Kasandry', Polityka, 20 October 1984.
40.   Wojciech Lamentowicz, 'Adaptation through political crises in postwar Poland', Journal of Peace Research, XIX, No. 2 (1982), pp. 117-131.

*CPA = Central Party Apparatus.

Chapter One

THE ARMED FORCES AND COMMUNIST POLITICS

Military forces intervene in politics in various
ways, at different levels and for dramatically different reasons and purposes. The enormous literature on military coups and military régimes has, for
understandable reasons, been largely concerned with
traditional regions of military intervention in Latin
America, the Middle East and the developing countries
of Africa and Asia. Attention has also been paid
to the interwar Eastern European and transitional
Mediterranean cases. The former provide particularly interesting examples of mixed civil-military
rule; the latter of how the military's exit from
power has been accompanied by the establishment of
democratic political systems [1]. The study of
civil-military relations under communism has, however, developed in a compartmentalised way. It has
not been integrated in the wider subject nor fertilised
fully by the concepts which have been pioneered in
other non-communist fields. The communist experience of party relations with the military is
undoubtedly a very special one. But it is not
entirely unique and sui generis. I therefore introduce this study with a broader view and some
generalisations distilled from the wider literature
[2].
S.E. Finer recognises four levels of military
intervention in his classic study [3]. Soldiers
may influence, blackmail, displace or supplant the
civil government. The modes of intervention may
range from normal constitutional action, collusion
or competition with the authorities leading to
intimidation or threats, mounting up to either a
failure to defend the civilian power or ultimately
the use of force against it [4]. The military
régimes, which are the outcome of the latter, may
take the indirect form of a nominally civilian

24

government, but one which is in practice blackmailed,
controlled or displaced by the military   Alter-
natively, military rule may be exercised directly
through a military leader or junta or less openly
through a mixed civil-military puppet government.
The intermediate case, which is of greatest interest
to the present study, is that of the mixed 'dual
régime'.   Here the military leadership, either in
an individual or collective form, leads both the
Army and the civil government [5].   Typical examples
are those of Peron in Argentina or the interwar
Royal Dictatorships in Romania, Yugoslavia and
Bulgaria [6].   Piłsudski's régime in Poland after
the coup of May 1926 was essentially similar [7];
but the Marshal partly camouflaged his rule by ap-
pointing civilians as his Prime Ministers until 1930
and only then did he turn to his famous 'Colonels'.
The problem of the military's exit from power was
demonstrated by a degree of re-civilianisation of political and administrative offices after his death in
1935 [8].   This was, however, mainly due to the weak
political personality of Edward Śmigły-Rydz,
Piłsudski's successor as Commander in Chief, and to
divisions within the Sanacja (Moral Renewal) ruling
group.   The 1935 to 1939 period in Poland therefore
was a far cry from the dramatic and complete return
to democratic party and parliamentary politics in
Spain, Portugal and Greece in the 1970s
     The traditional popular image of the military
coup is still perhaps that of an Officer Corps,
staffed and recruited from reactionaries, who put
the lid on social revolution,as Pinochet did in
Chile in 1974.   The Army was also the main support
of both the Franco and Salazar régimes as well as
of the Greek Colonels   But this Latin American and
Iberian image of the Army as the main prop of Right-
wing authoritarian and threatened socially conservative régimes was always too simple, as evidenced by
the Mexican and Peruvian cases.   The military in
the post-colonial and developing states of the Third
World, recruited from the native peasantry and cleri-
cal-intelligentsia strata, have been a fundamentally
different force.   They became associated with the
ideals of national independence, post-colonial state-
building and economic development and were often dominated by socially radical, populist ideologies [9].
This vast topic is not central to our concerns in
this study but we now need to examine the following
two questions.   Why do military governments face
such huge difficulties in carrying out their self-
assigned tasks of government and how do they attempt

to rule? Secondly, what criteria should be applied in assessing military claims that they are acting genuinely as Guardians of the National Interest or established goals which have been endangered by inefficient, corrupt and quarrelsome civilian party politicians or social strife and paralysis?

My personal answer to the second question is that it can only be a purely pragmatic and relative one. Some Military Governments of National Salvation are more credible and progressive, given their specific historical backgrounds and political circumstances, than others. The criteria for individual judgements are bound to be somewhat subjective. While a political scientist can take a dispassionate view, he is bound to be accused of bias by involved participants with their own axes to grind. The cases at the extreme may be straightforward enough to categorise. Such cases as the Ataturk tradition in Turkey, or, in lesser degree, of the military governments in Pakistan and Brazil, are in a different category, qualitatively, regarding motivation and the possibility of a return to the rule of law than purely repressive régimes such as those of Pinochet in Chile, Stroessner in Paraguay, or Amin in Uganda, to mention some obvious extreme cases. In practice, all Military Governments, including the more credible National Salvation type, face similar governmental and administrative problems; but they do not all encounter the same degree of difficulty in establishing their authority and legitimacy.

The issue of the power-seeking or altruistic character of the military therefore justifies the emphasis on the reasons for, and the goals of, military intervention [10]. One should remember that Marx himself was aware, from the experience of the two Napoleons in France, that a General, or a military group, could easily take advantage of a stand-off between conflicting social classes in order to seize and build up an autonomous power [11]. Engels expressed this thought far more concisely and plainly than the master in a famous passage in The Origin of Family Private Property and the State: 'Periods occur in which the social classes balance each other so nearly that the state-power, as ostensible mediator, acquires for the moment a certain degree of independence of both ... Such was the Bonapartism of the First, and still more of the Second French Empire which played off proletariat against the bourgeoisie, and the bourgeoisie against the proletariat' [12]. One should also note that the images of Thermidor (conservative reaction against revolution)

and Brumaire (seizure of power by the military)
were deeply ingrained in the folk-consciousness of
the European revolutionary Left. It was a potent
force in the minds of the Russian Marxist-Leninists.
Their often exaggerated and irrational fear of
Bonapartism undoubtedly contributed to Red Army
Commissar Trotsky's failure to take power in the
mid-1920s. It perhaps hastened Marshal Zhukov's
political demise as Soviet Minister of Defence and
Politburo member in 1957. This sentiment eventuated
in the classic Maoist dictum that 'Politics is
controlled by the barrel of a gun ... the party controls the gun and the gun will never be allowed to
control the party' [13]. But Marx also expressed
the ambiguity of the Napoleonic tradition; although
associated with authoritarian rule and military
aggrandisement it also confirmed many of the political
and social gains of the French Revolution.

The term 'Military Government' is almost invariably
a misnomer in one respect. Military régimes inevitably have to depend very heavily upon civilian skills
and personnel. The literature on the actual functioning of military régimes as a governmental type is
noticeably sparser than the studies of military coups
and their exits from power. There is general agreement that military régimes last longest in socially
or ethnically divided societies where they can act
as the sole unifying or arbitrating force [14].
The actual mechanisms of military rule are very
varied. It is rare for soldiers to monopolise the
main offices for more than a short period. This
stage of rule by the purely Military Council is,
however, often bypassed. What Perlmutter terms
the Praetorian State is, therefore, defined as 'a
régime dominated on the whole by the military or by
coalitions of soldiers, bureaucrats, technocrats
and civilian politicians' [15]. Feit argues that
such a régime often attempts to build up 'cohesion
without consensus' by balancing discordant interests
[16]. It then attempts to legitimise itself by
gaining mass support for its promised national renewal . But by doing so it runs the risk of politi-
cising itself and of jeopardising the cohesion of the
balance struck between various conflicting social
forces in the earlier stage. This brings about its
downfall either by replacement again by the professional military in control of the Armed Forces
or by an abdication of its power through elections,
as in Turkey in 1960, to the old political parties.
According to democratic theory the latter are better
qualified to integrate differing forces into a wider

political consensus in a peaceful and negotiated
manner.   One of the few exceptions to such cycles
has been the very instructive case of Mexico.
There the original 1910 revolution established a permanent system by incorporating all crucial groups
including the military into the Party of Institutionalised Revolution [17].   It also survived by
pioneering novel techniques for dealing with the
thorny question of political succession.   The executive President nominates his successor after a
wide consultative process has taken place within the
élite.   This basically civilian type of pluralist-
authoritarian rule corresponds very closely in its
end effects to systems, such as the Algerian, Chinese
and Yugoslav, where armies built up wide and permanent
social bases of popular support through wars of
National Liberation.   A specialist has also drawn
attention to the complexity of civil-military relations, the importance of cross-cutting alliances
between the various military and civilian groups
and the role of politicised Army officers in
Thailand in the transitional institutions between
military rule and civilian democracy [18].   Similar
comments have been made about Turkey, where the Army
assumed a clear Guardian role with mixed results [19].
     The dilemma of military rule is that the condi-
tions of political, social and economic conflict
which foster military intervention normally raise
insuperable obstacles to long-term military rule
Repression may work in the short-term;   but the cost
of maintaining terror and of eliminating opposition
is that support cannot be mobilised for desirable
national or social goals.   The façade of national
unity is a very shaky one.   It is based increasingly
on the uncertain foundations of the military either
eliminating, balancing between or co-opting various
social groups.   The dilemma is that control is best
attained by exclusion but that the building up of
legitimacy is best achieved by inclusion.   It has
also been argued that the central problem in advanced
societies is that the military by themselves just
cannot run a complicated modern state.   If they co-
opt civilian technicians, or if too many of their
top officers devote themselves overmuch to purely
political tasks of government, then splits will inevitably occur with the remaining purely professional
soldiers who remain in operational control of the
military forces.   The result is either replacement
of the former by the latter and then the cycle begins
anew, or abdication of power to the civilian politicians and a return to barracks, as has often

happened in Latin America and in different ways in
Spain and Greece [20]. This study will examine
the issue of whether the Communist military are
structured in such a way as to avoid these pitfalls.
The third, and rarer, outcome, mainly in newly
established, ex-colonial states like Egypt, is for
the military to succeed in achieving a civil-military symbiosis of a permanent type. Franco and
Salazar did so earlier in a right-wing, corporatist
manner in Spain and Portugal [21]. Different types
of corporatist-authoritarianism have evolved, ranging
from, and often alternating between, military-bureau-
cratic and semi-competitive, military controlled
populist rule [22]. One can, however, accept Jean
Blondel's conclusion that military men have not proved
to be 'a genuine alternative to party leaders' in
running governments or in establishing distinct and
viable military-type governmental structures [23].
But over a third of the countries in the world have
had recent, or currently have, experiences of military government, although only a fifth were of the
purer, not notably civilian influenced, form of military government. Blondel's statistics demonstrate
conclusively their short-term and transient character
[24]. As S.E. Finer says: 'Phrases such as "military régime" or "military government" are terms of
art, not scientific categories' [25]. Both the
classical-liberal and communist political models
posit the subordination of the military to the civilian power. We now turn to examine whether the
latter's practice of civil-military relations has
eschewed the problems outlined above.

Civil-military relations under communism

The Western study of communist systems has been
marked by a methodological debate, which has now been
going on for over a quarter of a century; what theory
or approach should replace or supplement the Totalitarian model? The latter was propounded most authori-
tatively by Carl Friedrich and Zbigniew Brzezinski
and was then defended in revised forms, most notably
by Leonard Schapiro [26]. The undoubted evidence
of growing pluralism in the Soviet world, after
Stalin's death in 1953, encouraged the development
of a school of interest and social-group theory.
A plethora of other approaches centred on such ideas
as Industrial Society, the Administered-Managerial
state, Elitist or New Class theory and associated
Neo-Marxist critiques also found varying degrees of
favour at different times [27]. But, above all, the
earlier leadership and Kremlinological studies such

as Robert Conquest's or Michel Tatu's evolved into a
much more subtle and complex approach which did justice to the interplay and conflicts between communist
institutions [28]. Bureaucratic Pluralism, as the
key to understanding communist decision-making and
governmental processes, appeared to be gelling into
a new orthodoxy by the late 1960s. Such events
as the invasion of Czechoslovakia in 1968, then,
changed the psychological climate. The Western academic field broadened out in a more eclectic fashion
with greater interest in social, economic and micro-
aspects, as well as such global themes as Legitimacy,
Opposition, Distribution, budgetary priorities and
the like. Bureaucratic pluralism was still propagated, most notably by Jerry Hough [29]; but the
approach, although inherent in the work of Merle
Fainsod, Alfred G. Meyer, H.G. Skilling and R.V.
Daniels, was perhaps developed most fully in the
field of communist defence and international studies
by scholars such as Thomas Wolfe, Jiri Valenta,
Martin Halperin and Alexander George. It was given
its initial impetus by Graham Allison's study of the
Cuban Missiles' Crisis of 1962. Here Allison established an 'analytical paradigm' which defined communist governments as being composed of 'semi-independent, quasi-sovereign' bureaucratic organisations
with their own distinctive skills, tasks, interests,
operations and even weltanschauung [30]. The interplay of their conflicts within the general organisational framework set by the Communist Party produced
more than mere pseudo-politics. The eventual decisions and policies, ratified by the top authorities,
reflected the balances struck between the various
apparats. The emphasis on the primacy and autonomy
of the component parts ran counter to the prevalent
orthodoxy that the various congeries of bureaucracies
were controlled strictly by the Communist Party's
Central Apparatus, notably its Politburo; this, at
the very least, played off one interest against
another and used one apparatus to parallel, check
up on and limit the functioning of another [31].
The truism of the party-controlled, centrally directed nature of communist decision-making was difficult
to shake. The general view is now that such apparats
have a varying, but never dominant, influence on the
CPA. The key question concerns not only their functional weight in the sytem, but mainly their possibilities of access to the formal decision-making core
which has been identified increasingly with the
Politburo in the Soviet context [32]. The contrary
school of thought is that a communist government is

composed of numerous functionally distinct, Party
(Politburo, Secretariat, Central Committee Departments) and State (Council of Ministers, its Presidium, Head of State bodies, National Assemblies and
their commissions) components [33]. These units,
although animated by a common desire to defend and
further the interests of the socialist system, form
an informal political arena for the debate and resolution of specific issues and especially for discussion of the optimal methods of implementing actual
decisions. But they also reflect the various interests within the communist system and are highly
susceptible to pressures from the various bureaucracies. The strengths of such an institutional approach in elucidating the process by which an aggre-
gative consensus is built up within an apparat and
between that organisation and the Central Party
authorities is demonstrated by Edward Warner's revealing study of the political role and organisation
of the Soviet military [34]. The clichés about
Communist Party monopoly control remain valid but
they have now assumed a significantly different meaning from the denial of politics implied by the transmission belt propounding leftovers of the Totalitarian
concept. 'The Soviet military establishment is an
active institutional participant in the politics of
the Soviet Union' but the controversies concern its
relative weight and the specific forms of that
influence [35].

Civil-military relations in communist states have
been characterised by the following paradox. On the
one hand the Red Army, in particular, has been glorified as the main force which consolidated and then
maintained (and extended) Soviet power against internal and external foes. On the other hand the CPSU
has viewed it with great suspicion for long periods
as a potential competitor. At one and the same time,
it has been the main support of the Soviet régime
since the Civil War, and also the greatest single
potential threat to the civilian party. Its organisational capacities, professionalism, esprit de corps
and power resources far outrun those of the police
or trade union apparats. It therefore had to be
kept in check. The Soviet State developed various
ideological and socialisation, special police,
screening and personnel-control mechanisms. They
were based on high percentages of party affiliation
and exercised by various types of political commissars [36]. As well as these sticks, which in its
most extreme form included the decimation of its
higher leadership ranks during the Great Purge (3 out

31

of 5 Marshals, all 11 Deputy Ministers of Defence,
60 out of 67 corps commanders and 136 out of 199
Brigade Generals perished), the officer caste was
also flattered and favoured with a whole range of
material and pecuniary rewards [37].   In addition
Soviet society and the economy was 'militarised' in
various ways and has remained so to the present day
through such factors as conscription, civil defence,
Second World War memories and the privileged role of
the military scientific-industrial complex. The
paradoxical relationship between the CPSU and its
essential military support has always, in practice,
been more complicated than the military subservience
implied in the previously cited Maoist dictum about
the party controlling the gun and never allowing it
to control the party.

It is often considered that one of the major
factors affecting the evolution of communist systems
is the specific form of power takeover.   In
Yugoslavia, China and Vietnam power was seized through
a partisan war of National Liberation which was followed organically by the political and social revolution [38].   Here the first stage of communist
rule was marked by a party-army symbiosis.   The
leadership personnel was an undifferentiated poli-
tico-military one.   The military commissars, few
of whom had originally been professional career
officers, quickly filled the whole range of directing positions in political and social organisations,
the police, factory-management and so on, and retained them for a whole generation.   In addition the
Army in Yugoslavia always remained the guarantor,
not just of the socialist order, but of the South
Slav federation.   It demonstrated this role both in
Tito's use of Military Intelligence to dismantle
Ranković's police apparat in 1964 and in the Croatian
Crisis of 1972 [39].   The People's Liberation Army
(PLA) was the prime factor in restoring order after
the chaos of the Great Cultural Revolution in China
during the 1960s; but it had always played a crucial
role in Chinese politics [40].   The old revolutionary generation saw no clash betwen being Red or expert but their younger and more professional successors who emerged in the 1970s introduced a much
greater potential for both intra-military and civil-
military conflict [41].   William Leogrande also confirms that, given the absence of a revolutionary
party in the early years of the Cuban Revolution, the
vanguard role was played by the rebel army, however
peculiar its original composition.   It performed all
the tasks of a Leninist party in the initial phases

of the socialist revolution 'in running the new
government - administration, socialising the
economy, mobilising popular support and in con-
stituting the organisational core around which the
foundations of a new political system were laid'
[42]. This civil-military fusion continued right
through into the later phases of Cuba's development;
many still consider that the country is run by
'civic soldiers' [43].

But the significance of the military in founding
communist systems in Yugoslavia, China, Vietnam and
Cuba is only a matter of degree as compared with
the USSR and postwar Eastern Europe. The differences have also been eroded with their subsequent development. As in the above-mentioned cases, the
Red Army soldiers who fought in the Civil War of
1918-1921 naturally assumed key directing roles in
Soviet life; later on they were also assigned
crucial organistional tasks in carrying through the
collectivisation of agriculture. The same was true,
after a certain time-lag, because of the irregular
character of the Stalinisation processes of 1948-1954
for members of the Soviet sponsored Eastern Front Army
in Poland, and for similar Soviet formed military
corps in the other Eastern European countries. But
Stalin, because of his rivalry with Trotsky and his
general dictatorial ambitions, established a long
tradition of communist party and police control over
the Red Army in order to obviate the threat of a
possible Bonapartist putsch. The Officer Corps was
purged intensively and put under the control of compliant, Stalinist stooges, a new breed of political
officer typified by Kliment Voroshilov. The techniques of party control over the military, the system
of politruks and zampolits, supervision by special
police units, intense ideological indoctrination,
strong socialisation and high degrees of party affiliation and screening of the Officer Corps, as well
as their simultaneous flattering and rewarding, was
then perfected [44]. Such methods assured military
loyalty and subordination even during the Great
Patriotic War when many of the outward symbols of
professional autonomy and nationalist identity were
restored. These techniques were then exported
wholesale to the East European satellites from the
end of the war onwards. They were extremely successful in eliminating the possibility of any outright military revolt. Huntington's generalisation
that 'no communist government in a modernising country
has been overthrown by a coup d'état' remained
unchallenged until December 1981 [45]; but even in

the Polish case the degree of PZPR supplantation by
the Army remains as an issue for later consideration.
The only known significant attempt at a military coup
within the Soviet sphere was the obscure revolt of
the Sofia Military Garrison in Bulgaria in 1965, which
has still not been explained satisfactorily [46].
But positive and reliable military support for the
civilian communist power in dealing with the eight
cases of local uprisings, or major civil unrest in
postwar Eastern Europe, was always doubtful according
to Ivan Volgyes [47]. On the other hand, the
loyalty of the Soviet occupying forces in suppressing
East European eruptions was evidenced very clearly
in East Berlin in March 1953, Hungary in October-
November 1956 and Czechoslovakia in August 1968.
    The dominant image of the Stalinist phase in
civil-military relations is one of total Army subservience and subordination to the Communist Party,
which controlled it through transmission belts just
like any other apparat or social organisation. But
after Stalin's death the Red Army played a crucial
role in helping civilian politicians like Malenkov
and Khrushchev to disarm the police apparat and to
liquidate its chief, Beria. Under Khrushchev and
Brezhnev the Soviet military establishment became
more autonomous and more functionally differentiated
with a growing emphasis on its professional integrity,
skills and standards. It also increased its weight
and influence as an actor within the system very
dramatically. Perlmutter draws attention to how
a communist Army inevitably gets drawn into party
politics in fulfilling its function of protecting
the party's hegemony [48]. Roman Kolkowicz has
shown how it developed into a powerful lobby, interest group and even political actor after 1953.
From being strictly controlled by the CPSU it became
a well represented and highly influential force acting on the central political leadership. Kolkowicz
stressed, however, that at the end of the day the
party's watchdog role over it still remained the decisive element. The Red Army's voice carried great
weight in decision-making; its political, social
and economic priorities such as the balance between
investment in heavy industry as against consumption,
central planning methods and the inculcation of
Great Russian, nationalist, military and Leninist
values in both educational establishments and society
came close to being a veto at times. In 1957 the
Army led by Marshal Zhukov intervened to save
Khrushchev against the so-called Anti-Party-Group.
In 1964 they abetted his downfall. On the other

hand, Khrushchev was able to implement dramatic cuts
in the size of Army infantry and to impose a major
shift in favour of strategic rocket forces.
Kolkowicz's final conclusion that 'in the internal
politics of the Soviet Union, especially under a
collective leadership, the military is a formidable
institution, whose needs and demands must be considered' if anything underestimates the position [49].
The foregoing considerations led Timothy Colton to
view the military as qualitatively more than just
a mere lobby, however powerful. He also challenged
Kolkowicz's interpretation of the civil-military relationship as being essentially a conflictual one.
The military had become an integral part of the system.
Their values and interests were absolutely congruent
with it, so dynamic and changing balances of accommodation could be achieved with the Central Party
Apparatus (CPA). He argues that the traditional
emphasis on 'party mechanisms for penetration and
control of the military command' produced a one-
sided view. It no longer explained satisfactorily
why the Soviet military did not intervene politically
more often and more forcefully [50]. In effect he
agrees with R.V. Daniels' characterisation of the
Soviet system as 'a participatory bureaucracy' which
can best be explained in terms of the bureaucratic
pluralism discussed earlier [51]. In the early
1980s the emphasis on 'rationalised repression' increased the standing of the military in the USSR
more than that of the, then, divided and slightly
compromised police-apparat, even during the rule
of the ex-KGB chairman Andropov [52]. It is true
that the Minister of Defence from 1976 to 1984,
Dmitri Ustinov, was originally a civilian-political
appointee, initially concerned with war-industry,
unlike his professional predecessors, Malinovsky
and Grechko and his successor Sokolov; but Ustinov
had a dominant voice in representing the military
interest in the highest leadership circles and in
stating the latter's view back to the military.
He also played a kingmaker's role in the Andropov
and, possibly, the Chernenko successions The absence of obvious sources of civil-military discord
and the growing weight of the military, evidenced
by the Czechoslovak and Afghanistan invasions, then
made it fashionable to talk in terms of William
Odom's 'symbiotic-congruence' model; although I
would adapt it considerably away from the 'totalitarian' version originally propounded by that author
[53]. Whether one accepts Kolkowicz's interest
group argument, Colton's participatory model or

Odom's symbiotic congruence paradigm. it is agreed
that a considerable blurring of the distinction
between civil and military functionaries has occurred
at the top political level [54]. This does not
contradict the evidence of growing professional
autonomy in all communist armed forces once the
original, revolutionary leadership generation had
passed away [55]. In the USSR, as in Eastern
Europe, the Marshals and the Generals have come to
share in the final decision-making with the dominant
part of the CPA [56]. In this respect the original
distinction between the Soviet and East European
pattern and the Yugoslav, Chinese, Vietnamese and
Cuban cases has now largely faded away. The con
vergent formation of a symbiotic civil-military authority forming its own consensus, although disputing
individual issues, was encouraged by Soviet ideological and organisational ossification in the late
Brezhnev era [57]; its contours had emerged in the
Soviet world even before military-communist rule
was established in Poland in December 1981. This
generalisation holds true in spite of the apparent
ups and downs of military influence as symbolised
by the differing personal-political weights of
Ustinov and Sokolov.

Communist academics have been quite clear in admitting the twofold character of the functions of a
socialist army and the changing balance between them
over time. 'Externally it is an instrument for the
defence of the independence and the interests of
the socialist state, whereas internally it is an
instrument for safeguarding the socialist system'
[58]. In a major enunciation Jerzy Wiatr considered that the socialist army was integrated into
the political life of the state through the complete
identity of military and Communist Party aims and
experience in establishing and in building socialism,
through the political socialisation of the military
cadres and through the army's everyday involvement
in civil society. Even in the early 1960s Wiatr
discerned that the tasks of the political apparat
were not merely to ensure the CP's leading role and
control over the military but to guarantee that the
Army would fulfil its two great functions mentioned
earlier [59]. The threat of Bonapartism was rendered negligible by correct policies of social recruitment into the socialist army. After a while
the CP-military relationship becomes a far more
organic and autonomous one. 'The Army is not
placed outside the reach of the leading role of the
party, but that leading role is implemented in a

rational way inside the Army, by the military political apparat which is linked at the highest level
with the party leadership, by the leaders who are
tied to the Party and finally by Party organisations
within the military.' [60]. Wiatr's rather optimistic conclusion that civil-military relations, therefore, did not constitute 'a difficult problem' in
socialist systems was over-influenced by the Polish
experience of smooth civil-military Communist harmony
in facing up to a hostile Polish society after 1944.
    The USSR is a self-contained Great Power capable
of taking its own decisions without being directly
affected by external factors. The same naturally
applies to the Red Army establishment. But this
is not true of the five Eastern European states
which have remained closely within the Soviet fold
(Poland, Czechoslovakia, Hungary, Bulgaria and the
German Democratic Republic). Since 1961 Romania
has been a semi-independent case [61]. Christopher
Jones in his major, but highly controversial, study
argues that the main, almost the sole, real purpose
of the Warsaw Pact is the following:

> Soviet influence in Eastern Europe depends
> on Soviet control over appointments to the
> upper echelons of the East European party
> leaderships and on the preservation of a
> Soviet capability for military interven-
> tion to prevent either the capture of the
> local party hierarchies by Communists
> with domestic bases of support or the
> destruction of the party control system by
> local anti-communist forces. Moscow and
> its protégés in the Eastern European par-
> ties together prevent the defence minis-
> tries of the loyal East European states from
> adopting military strategies which would
> greatly limit the Soviet capability for inter-
> vention against either a rebellious faction
> of an East European party or against local
> anti-communist forces. [62]

He therefore concludes that autonomous communist
states like Yugoslavia and Romania, and in lesser
measure Albania, survived mainly because they organised a strategy of national territorial defence
against possible Soviet military intervention.
Leaders like Tito and Ceausescu, and possibly
Gomułka in 1956, who mobilised their native natio-
nalisms against the Russians, survived [63]; but
those who, like Dubcek in 1968, remained purely on

37

the level of ideological differences and reform proposals were overwhelmed. The point is confirmed by
Ross's argument that the propensity for risk-aversion
in Soviet decision-making 'could only have prevented
the invasion if the Czechoslovak Reformers had raised
the probable costs by demonstrating a stronger will
and capacity to resist' [64]. Otherwise the interplay of Soviet bureaucratic politics was highly
likely to produce a coalition in favour of intervention, as has been shown by Valenta [65]. Jones is
quite right to emphasise the crucial significance
of the factor of Kremlin confidence in their East
European allied leaderships. The post-1968 Brezhnev
Doctrine effectively established an implicit Soviet
Nomenklatura over top East European appointments.
Neither ideological nor policy changes are significant if the Kremlin can be guaranteed that their
political and military supremacy will remain unchallenged by fundamentally reliable leaders. Hence
the notable deviations away from Soviet practice
which have been permitted: Kadar, Gomułka and
even Zhivkov and Ulbricht (Bulgarian agro-industrial
complexes and East German technocratic tendencies
in the 1960s). On the other hand Dubcek's renewal
of the Czechoslovak party-state with personnel
unconfirmed by the Soviets, and the setting of a
date for an early Congress to complete the process
in early September 1968, clearly set a deadline
before which the Soviet invasion had to take place
[66]. Dubcek would undoubtedly have received Soviet
permission to clear out the discredited Novotny-ites
and to promise reform and a new start if he had
collaborated with the Soviet agencies and representatives and had had his new appointments vetted by
them. But this would naturally have undermined
the popular credibility of his new programme and
was expressly designed to do so.
    Since 1968 the Warsaw Pact has set up new poli-
tical committees and held more numerous and more
integrated joint exercises; it has continued with
the traditional methods of producing a reliable
pro-Soviet Officer Corps in the five bloc countries
[67]. But, as we shall see from the Polish case,
Jones has overstated his argument. His paradigm
of either total Soviet personnel control or intervention is not borne out by normal practice. As
David Holloway argues: 'The Pact is more than a
mechanism for transmitting orders from Moscow to
the East European capitals. It has a political
life of its own' [68].
    The issue of the reliability of the Warsaw Pact

Armed Forces emerged as a major subject for Western academic debate in the 1980s [69]; this perhaps overshadowed the questions of economic defence-burden sharing and priorities raised by Holloway. Ivan Volgyes has distinguished four analytical categories for examining the political role of the individual Warsaw Pact armies. The headings of External-Defensive reliability in the event of a NATO attack and External-Offensive reliability in support of a Warsaw Pact offensive against Western Europe seem self-explanatory; but they also cover the thorny issues of reaction to a possible Soviet or Warsaw Pact invasion of one's own country, or the attitude to such an invasion of another Warsaw Pact partner, or of a communist neutral like Yugoslavia which had fallen foul of the Kremlin. These highly important issues are, however, less central to our concerns than the Internal-Defensive repressive capacities of the communist military, which Jones argues is one of the main purposes of the Warsaw Pact and which will be examined more fully in the Polish context in this study. Volgyes' third heading, Internal-Offensive reliability, covers attempted military coups such as Bulgaria (1965), the Sejna Affair in Czechoslovakia in early 1968 and the General Sorb Affair in Romania in 1971. It also covers the military's role as a pressure group within the system. Internal-Defensive reliability concerns the most relevant issue for our purposes. Would the communist military defend the civil party against internal threats, notably the social uprisings in Poland as in Poznań (1956), the Baltic Seacoast in 1970 and, more arguably, in 1976 and 1980? The key points here, which will need to be amplified in the Polish context, are the balances between the Officer Corps and the conscripted section of the Army, the loyalty of both groups, the role of special armed security units and the legitimacy and popularity of the civil authorities. Volgyes concludes his examination of the seven postwar internal East European crises, before Poland 1980-1981, with a challenging, and certainly iconoclastic, view: 'The armed forces consistently refused to support the régimes when confronted with a serious internal disturbance' [70].

One needs to conclude this introduction with some obvious political science points. There is a single classificatory category termed the 'communist system' just as there is a family genus of bourgeois liberal-democracy; but the important point is that both have assumed a variety of governmental forms at

different times and in different national contexts.
One fruitful approach may be to develop Ghita
Ionescu's long-established insight that communist
politics is mediated by the institutional interplay
between its constituent apparats, of which the most
important are the party, state, military, police,
economic planning, local territorial, youth and
women's bodies [71]. The Central Party Apparatus
(CPA), defined as being composed of the Politburo,
Secretariat, and Central Committee Departments and
associated institutes, is normally dominant most of
the time in most communist systems. But it certainly strikes varying balances of power with the
other apparats at different times. An obvious
example would be the party-state equilibrium symbolised by the Brezhnev-Kosygin tandem for some years
after 1964. The theoretical permutations are considerable but the four major apparats in contention
have almost invariably been the CPA, state administration, military and police. This is most dramatically evidenced by the Soviet Stalinist period
in the 1930s when the CPA, not to mention the grassroots membership, was not only terrorised but was
displaced by Stalin's tyranny which was implemented
by the state and police organs. We have also mentioned the dominant role of the PLA at the close of
the Chinese Cultural Revolution. The Army takeover
in Poland is therefore not quite so unique when
viewed in a wider historical and comparative perspective. This is not to deny that the institutional-
governmental approach has to be tempered with a
sociological analysis of the forces in play and the
issues of force and power have to be counterposed
against the considerations of ideology, values and
even morality. As with all great historical events,
the imposition of martial law had features that
were absolutely specific to Poland; but the Polish
experience also needs to be assimilated into the
wider debate about the possibility of the reform of
communist states, the nature of present-day socialist
society and its dynamics, and above all on the role
of force in maintaining communist power. Some
writers, like J.F. Brown, go as far as to argue
that 'the Polish experience may have begun a gradual
shift in power-relationships within the communist
system' by revealing that 'in the last analysis
the system's salvation rests not with the party,
but with the forces of coercion and repression'
[72]. The contrary view, which will be elucidated
in this study, is that Brown's prognosis of such a
secular long-term trend may only be true for the

short-term periods of the rebuilding of communist
power, as in Hungary after 1956 or in Poland after
1981. The communist system has not only produced
intra-system reformers like Khrushchev and Gorbachev,
who have tried to revitalise it after periods of
conservative stagnation; but a recent study also
reminds us of the dynamic and vital character of
the challenge of internal party democracy [73].
This goes back to the very beginnings of Soviet rule
and offers a major hope, however forlorn it may seem
at present, of the progressive transformation of
communism in the future.

Notes

1. Cf. Geoffrey Pridham (ed.), The New Mediterranean
   Democracies. Régime transition in Spain, Greece
   and Portugal (London, Frank Cass, 1984).
2. See Stanislav Andreski, Military Organisation and
   Society (Berkeley, University of California Press,
   1968). Samuel Huntington, The Soldier and the State,
   The theory and politics of civil-military relations
   (New York, Random House, 1964). Morris Janowitz,
   Military Institutions and Coercion in the Developing
   Nations (Princeton U.P., 1967). Eric A. Nordlinger,
   Soldiers in Politics. Military Coups and Governments
   (Englewood Cliffs, N.J., Prentice-Hall, 1977). Amos
   Perlmutter, The Military and Politics (New Haven,
   Yale U.P., 1977).
3. Samuel E. Finer, The Man on Horseback. The role of the
   military in politics (London, Pall Mall, 1962), pp.86-87.
4. Ibid., p. 140.
5. Ibid., pp. 164 ff.
6. On the latter, Robert L. Wolff, The Balkans in our Time
   (Cambridge, Mass., Harvard U.P., rev. edn., 1974), ch.
   6. C.A. Macartney & A.W. Palmer, Independent Eastern
   Europe (London, Macmillan, 1966).
7. The standard English language study is Anthony Polonsky,
   Politics in Independent Poland, 1921-1939. The crisis
   of constitutional government (Oxford U.P., 1972). For
   the pro-Piłsudski-ite Polish émigré interpretation see
   Władysław Pobóg-Malinowski, Najnowsza historia polityczna
   polski, 1864-1945 (Paris & London, 3 vols., 1953-1967).
8. Andrzej Ajnenkiel, Polska po przewrocie Majowym. Zarys
   dziejów politycznych Polski, 1926-1939 (Warsaw, Wiedza
   Powszechna, 1980). Andrzej Micewski, Z Geografii
   politycznej II Rzeczpospolitej (Warsaw, Znak, 1964),
   pp. 203-289.
9. Robert E. Dowse, 'The military and political development'
   in Colin Leys (ed.), Politics and Change in Developing
   Countries (Cambridge U.P., 1969).

10. The Pakistani case is illustrative.   Western comment
     on the high motives of Ayub Khan and Zia ul Huq is
     particularly striking.   Cf. Herbert Feldman, Revolution
     in Pakistan. A study of the martial law administration
     (Oxford U.P., 1967).
11. J.B. Sanderson, An Interpretation of the Political Ideas
     of Marx and Engels (London, Longmans, 1969), p. 64.
     Karl Marx, The Eighteenth Brumaire of Louis Napoleon
     (Moscow Progress Publishers, 1967).
12. Marx-Engels, Selected Works (Moscow, Foreign Language
     Publishing House, 1962), Vol. 2, pp. 320-321.
13. Mao-Tse-Tung, Selected Military Writings (Pekin, Foreign
     Language Press, 1963), p. 272.
14. Cf. Edward Feit, The Armed Bureaucrats. Military-admi-
     nistrative régimes and political development (Boston,
     Houghton-Mifflin, 1973). H. Bienen & D. Morrell (eds.),
     Political Participation under Military Régimes (London,
     Sage, 1976). Finer, Man on Horseback, op. cit., ch.12.
     Samuel P. Huntington (ed.), Changing Patterns of Mili-
     tary Politics (New York, Free Press, 1962). Eric A.
     Nordlinger, 'Soldiers in mufti; the impact of military
     rule upon economic and social change in non-Western
     states', American Political Science Review, Vol. 64
     (December 1970), pp. 1131-1148.
15. Amos Perlmutter in Roman Kolkowicz & Andrzej Korbonski,
     Soldiers, Peasants and Bureaucrats (London, George Allen
     & Unwin, 1982), p. 310.
16. Feit, Armed Bureaucrats, op. cit., p. 3.
17. Cf. Edwin Liewen, Mexican Militarism (Alburquerque,
     University of New Mexico Press, 1969). Leon V. Padgett,
     The Mexican Political System (Boston, Houghton-Mifflin,
     1966). Robert E. Scott, Mexican Government in Transition
     (Urbana, University of Illinois Press, 1957).
18. D. Morrell, 'Alternatives to military rule in Thailand'
     in Bienen & Morrell, Political Participation under
     Military Régimes, p. 20.
19. Clement H. Dodd, Politics and Government in Turkey
     (Berkeley, University of California Press, 1969). Ergen
     Ozbudan, The Role of the Military in Recent Turkish
     Politics (Cambridge, Mass., Harvard University Center
     for International Studies, 1965).
20. Cf. Stanley G. Payne, Politics and the Military in Modern
     Spain (Stanford U.P., 1966). Robert A. Potash, The Army
     and Politics in Argentina, 1928-1945 (Stanford U.P.,
     1968). Philippe C. Schmitter (ed.), The Military Role
     in Latin America (London, Sage, 1973).
21. Among the best studies on Egypt are: Anour Abdel-Malek,
     Egypt. Military Society (New York, Random House, 1968).
     Payanotis J. Vatikiotis, The Egyptian Army in Politics
     (Bloomington, Indiana, U.P., 1961). P.J. Vatikiotis,
     The Modern History of Egypt (New York, Praeger, 1969).

22. This case is argued by Philippe C. Schmitter in Interest
    Conflict and Political Change in Brazil (Stanford U.P.,
    1971).
23. Jean Blondel, The Organisation of Governments (London,
    Sage, 1982), p. 96.
24. Only Pakistan (15 years), Nigeria (13 years) and Peru
    have had the purer form of military rule for over a
    decade since 1945: ibid., pp. 126-134. Blondel in
    World Leaders (London, Sage, 1980), p. 153, also esti-
    mates that only 12% of top leadership positions were
    held by military men.
25. Finer, 'The morphology of military régimes' in Kolkowicz
    & Korbonski, Soldiers, Peasants and Bureaucrats, p. 301.
26. Carl Friedrich & Zbigniew Brzezinski, Totalitarian Dic-
    tatorship and Autocracy (Cambridge, Mass., Harvard U.P.,
    1956). Leonard Schipiro, Totalitarianism (London,
    Macmillan, 1972).
27. For a useful guide to the literature: Valerie Bunce &
    John Echols, 'From Soviet studies to comparative politics',
    Soviet Studies, XXXI (January 1979).
28. Michel Tatu, Power in the Kremlin (New York, Viking Press,
    1969). Robert Conquest, Power and Policy in the USSR
    (London, Macmillan, 1961).
29. Jerry F. Hough, 'The Soviet system; petrification or
    pluralism?', Problems of Communism, XXI (1972), pp. 25-
    45. Cf. A. Groth, 'USSR. Pluralist monolith', British
    Journal of Political Science, IX, No. 4 (October 1979),
    pp. 445-464. Stephen White, 'Communist politics and the
    Iron Law of Pluralism', British Journal of Political
    Science, VIII, No. 1 (January 1978), pp. 101-118.
30. Graham T. Allison, Essence of a Decision. Explaining
    the Cuban Missile Crisis (Boston, Little-Brown & Co.,
    1971), pp. 7, 32, 82.
31. Maria Hirszowicz, The Bureaucratic Leviathan (Oxford,
    Martin Robertson, 1980).
32. Karen Dawisha,'The limits of the bureaucratic politics
    model', Studies in Comparative Communism, XII, No. 4
    (Winter, 1980), pp. 300-326.
33. George Sanford, 'Fused or separate party-state insti-
    tutions?', unpublished paper presented to the Annual
    Conference of the Political Studies Association,
    Manchester University, April 1985.
34. Edward L. Warner, The Military in Contemporary Soviet
    Politics. An institutional analysis (New York, Praeger,
    1977).
35. Ibid., p. 268.
36. Zbigniew Brzezinski, Political Controls in the Soviet
    Army (New York, Columbia U.P., 1954).
37. Cf. Mervyn Matthews, Privilege in the Soviet Union
    (London, George Allen & Unwin, 1978). Ellen Jones, Red
    Army and Society (London, George Allen & Unwin, 1985),
    pp. 83-84.

38.   See Thomas H. Hammond, The Anatomy of Communist Take-
      overs (New Haven, Yale U.P., 1975). John Gittings, The
      Role of the Chinese Army (Oxford U.P., 1967). William
      Whitson, The Chinese High Command (New York, Praeger,
      1973). Ying-Mao Kau, The People's Liberation Army and
      China's Nationbuilding (New York, International Arts &
      Science Press, 1973).
39.   Robert W. Dean, 'The Yugoslav army' in J.R. Adelman
      (ed.), Communist Armies in Politics (Boulder, Col.,
      Westview Press, 1982). A.R. Johnson, 'The role of the
      military' in Kolkowicz & Korbonski, Soldiers, Peasants
      and Bureaucrats, op. cit. Robin A. Remington, 'The
      military in Yugoslav politics' in D.R. Herspring &
      I. Volgyes (eds.), Civil-Military Relations in Communist
      States (Boulder, Col., Westview Press, 1978). Milija
      Stanisić, KPJ u izgradni oruzania snaga revolucije,
      1941-1945 (Belgrade, Vojnoizdavacki Zavod, 1973).
40.   Ellis Joffe, Party and Army. Professionalism and Poli-
      tical Control in the Chinese Officer Corps. 1949-1964
      (Berkeley, University of California Press, 1977).
      E. Joffe & Gerry Segal, 'The Chinese Army and profes-
      sionalism', Problems of Communism (Nov.-Dec., 1978).
      William Whitson (ed.), The Military and Political
      Power in China in the 1970s (New York, Praeger, 1972).
41.   Harlan W. Jencks, 'China's civil-military relations,
      1949-1980' in Morris Janowitz (ed.), Civil-Military
      Relations. A regional perspective (London, Sage,
      1981), p. 155.
42.   William M. Leogrande, 'A bureaucratic approach to civil-
      military relations in communist political systems; the
      case of Cuba' in Herspring, op. cit. See also Louis
      A. Perez, 'Army politics in socialist Cuba', Latin
      American Studies, VIII, No. 2 (November 1976), pp.251-271.
43.   Jorge I. Dominguez, 'The civic soldier in Cuba' in
      Catherine Kelleher (ed.), Political-Military Systems.
      Comparative perspectives (London, Sage, 1974), pp. 20,
      209-239.
44.   See Roman Kolkowicz, The Soviet Military and the Commu-
      nist Party (Princeton U.P., 1967). John Erickson, The
      Soviet High Command. A military-political history,
      1918-1941 (New York, St. Martins, 1962).
45.   Samuel Huntington, Political Order in Changing Societies
      (New York, Yale U.P., 1968), p. 8.
46.   Cf. J.F. Brown, Bulgaria under Communism (New York,
      Praeger, 1970),p. 175. Some commentators would also
      add General Jan Sejna's failed attempt to organise
      a coup to save the conservative Novotny régime in
      Czechoslovakia in early 1968. H.G. Skilling,
      Czechoslovakia's Interrupted Revolution (Princeton U.P.,
      1976). The Natolin coup in Poland, if it had taken place
      in Summer-Autumn 1956, would, however, have been more of

a police than a military operation on the lines of
Mamula's similar strivings in Prague in 1967-1968.

47. Ivan Volgyes, 'Military politics of the Warsaw Pact
Armies' in Janowitz, Civil-Military Relations, op. cit.,
p. 200. Volgyes discusses Plzen 1953, East Berlin
1953, Poznań 1956, Budapest 1956, Prague 1968-1969,
Gdańsk 1970 and he mistakes Warsaw and Łódź for Radom
and Płock in 1976. To these seven cases one should also
add the Baltic seacoast in August 1980.

48. Amos Perlmutter, 'Civil-military relations in socialist,
authoritarian and Praetorian states' in Kolkowicz &
Korbonski, op. cit., p. 323.

49. Kolkowicz, Soviet Military and the Communist Party,
p. 349.

50. Timothy J. Colton, Commissars, Commanders and Civilian
Authority. The structure of Soviet military politics
(Cambridge, Mass., Harvard U.P., 1979), p. 279.

51. Robert V. Daniels in John Strong (ed.), The Soviet Union
under Brezhnev and Khrushchev (New York, Van Nostrand-
Reinhold, 1971), p. 22. Cf. Michael Dean, Political
Control of the Soviet Armed Forces (New York, Crane-
Russak, 1977).

52. Notably the Tsvigun scandal and the disgrace and suicide
of ex-Minister of the Interior, Scholokhov.

53. William E. Odom, 'The party-military connection; a
critique' in Herspring & Volgyes, op. cit., pp. 54-78.

54. Jonathan R. Adelman, 'Toward a typology of communist
civil-military relations' in Adelman, Communist Armies
in Politics, pp. 1-13.

55. Cf. David Holloway, Technology Management and the Soviet
Military Establishment (London, Institute for Strategic
Studies, 1971).

56. The intertwined, almost symbiotic, character of the top
Soviet civil-military decision-making is, in my judgement,
confirmed by such studies as Jiri Valenta and William
Potter (eds.), Soviet Decision-making for National
Security (London, George Allen & Unwin, 1984).

57. For the thesis that the USSR was developing into an
increasingly military dominated, post Communist Party
hegemony, system pre-Gorbachev, see Roman Kolkowicz,
'Military intervention in the Soviet Union - scenario
for the post-hegemonial synthesis' in Kolkowicz &
Korbonski, Soldiers, Peasants and Bureaucrats.

58. Jerzy J. Wiatr, 'Niektóre problemy socjologiczne armii
socjalistycznej', Studia Socjologiczno-Polityczne,
No. 14 (1963), p. 23.

59. Ibid., pp. 32-33.

60. Ibid., p. 41.

61. For the application of the Kolkowicz thesis to Romania
within the framework of Soviet power, see A. Alexiev,
Party-Military Relations in Eastern Europe. The case of

Romania (Los Angeles, University of California Press, 1979).

62. Christopher D. Jones, Soviet Influence in Eastern Europe. Political autonomy and the Warsaw Pact (New York, Praeger, 1981), p. 1.

63. The point will be amplified in Chapter Two but one might note here the significance of General Wacław Komar's appointment as Commander of the Home Defence Corps (KBW) just before Gomułka's return to power in October 1956. These troops played a crucial role in countering pro-Soviet activities and troop movements during the crisis which on the surface appeared to be primarily a dispute over the sacking of Rokossowski at the Eighth Plenum. Konrad Syrop, Spring in October (London, Weidenfeld & Nicolson, 1957), pp. 83-89.

64. Dennis Ross in Valenta & Potter, op. cit., ch. 10.

65. Jiri Valenta, Soviet Intervention in Czechoslovakia, 1968 (Baltimore, Johns Hopkins Press, 1979).

66. Karen Dawisha, The Kremlin and the Prague Spring (Berkeley, University of California Press, 1984).

67. Laurence Caldwell, 'The Warsaw Pact; Directions of change', Problems of Communism (Sept.-Oct. 1975). Robert W. Clawson & Laurence Kaplan (eds.), The Warsaw Pact. Political purpose and military means (Wilmington, Scholarly Resources, 1982). Malcolm Mackintosh, The Evolution of the Warsaw Pact (London, ISS, Adelphi Papers, No. 58, 1969). William J. Lewis, The Warsaw Pact. Arms, doctrine and strategy (New York, McGraw-Hill, 1982). Robin A. Remington, The Warsaw Pact. Case-studies in conflict resolution (Cambridge, Mass., MIT Press, 1971).

68. David Holloway, 'The Warsaw Pact in transition' in D. Holloway & Jane O. Sharp (eds.), The Warsaw Pact. Alliance in transition (London, Macmillan, 1984), p.192.

69. Daniel Nelson (ed.), Soviet Allies. The Warsaw Pact and the issue of reliability (Boulder, Col., Westview Press, 1984). A.R. Johnson, R.W. Dean & A. Alexiev, East European Military Establishments. The Warsaw Pact northern tier (Santa Monica, Rand, 1980).

70. Volgyes, 'Military politics of the Warsaw Pact Armies', pp. 194-215.

71. Ghita Ionescu, The Politics of the European Communist States (London, Macmillan, 1967), ch. 2.

72. J.F. Brown in Holloway & Sharp, Warsaw Pact in Transition, p. 209.

73. Richard Sakwa, Soviet Communists in Power. A study of Moscow during the civil war, 1918-1921 (London, Macmillan, forthcoming).

Chapter Two

THE DEVELOPMENT OF THE COMMUNIST ARMED FORCES
IN POLAND

Military values and historical episodes have
traditionally played a great role in the Polish
consciousness. The twentieth-century Pole has
been weaned from childhood in the belief of his
nation's martial qualities. A whole mess of dis-
jointed episodes - the victory over the Teutonic
Knights at Grunwald in 1410, Sobieski's defeat of the
Turks at Vienna in 1683, the Polish Legions in
Napoleonic times, Piłsudski's defeat of the Russians
before Warsaw in 1920 and the 'heroic' character of
the Polish resistance to the German Nazis on the
various fronts of the Second World War, symbolised
by the defence of the Westerplatte and Warsaw garri-
sons in September 1939, the storming of Monte
Cassino, the Warsaw Uprising of Summer 1944 and the
taking of Berlin in 1945 - have through a variety
of sources, official and private, strengthened this
belief from an early age [1]. Perceptions have
naturally changed postwar and there are significant
generational differences in attitudes. The communist régimes after 1956 unashamedly adopted all
the above national experiences (bar the 1920 war);
these were particularly glorified during the Partisan
offensive of the mid-1960s [2]. Somewhat later,
in the 1970s, even the thorny question of Piłsudski's
military régime was tackled gradually in public,
notably through the major historical works of Andrzej
Garlicki [3]. The national-patriotic role of the
Army in maintaining Poland's interwar independence
was rehabilitated. The anti-Soviet aspects naturally
continued to be condemned,as did its domestic-repres-
sive role in upholding the semi-authoritarian Sanacja
system. The prewar Army leadership's endorsement
of Piłsudski's maxim, practised by the Foreign Minister
Józef Beck from 1932 to 1939, that Poland's 'two
enemies', Germany and the USSR, were equally dangerous

47

to her independence, which could only be assured by
internal unity and alliances with Western Europe,
especially France, also came under fire [4].
Gomułka, in particular, derided the latter as 'moon
alliances'. His political aim was to demonstrate
that only alliance and friendship with the USSR could
save Poland and her postwar Oder-Neisse frontiers
from German revanchism [5]. Régime propaganda reinforced the realist political attitudes of the 1950s
and 1960s,which led to a marked swing away from the
Romantic-Idealist perception of Poland's history
[6]. A 1962 survey showed that the Poles rated
more recent military exploits about twice as highly
as earlier historical episodes. The responses to
the question concerning the most glorious battles
were: 20% pre-Partition times, 16% the nineteenth-
century insurrections, most surprisingly (or reveal-
ingly about the accuracy of the poll) only 1% distinguished the 1920 victory over the Russians, while
14% praised the September 1939 campaign and 8% the
1944 Warsaw Uprising; 23% gave the palm to the
battles, such as Monte Cassino in the West, while
19% rated the 1944-1945 campaigns of the Soviet-
sponsored Army on the Eastern Front the highest [7].
On the other hand, the Polish Army has always
benefited from a high degree of public regard. A
poll carried out by the Public Opinion Research
Centre of Polish Radio and TV (OBOP) in May 1981
showed that the Army ranked third in the population's
degree of trust. 89% of respondents trusted it
compared with 94% for the Church, 91% for
Solidarity while the PZPR was ranked seventh with a
mere 32%. A poll of Solidarity members carried out
by the Centre for Social Investigations (OBS) in
the Mazowsze region gave it 68% of support compared
with 93% for the Church, 95% for Solidarity and 7%
for the PZPR [8].

The Polish Army, unlike its French or British
equivalents, has not had an unbroken historical development. The break was particularly sharp with
the emergence of the Communist Armed Forces. But
the Second World War experience was not an entirely
novel one either. After the regaining of independence in 1918 the Polish Army had to be welded together out of various disparate elements. The bulk
of the Officer Corps was drawn from the old Austro-
Hapsburg Army, and in rather lesser measure from
the ex-Russian-Tsarist forces, while some significant individuals hied from the Haller Army which
had fought for the Western Allies on the Western
Front [9]. The most influential leadership group

was eventually drawn from Piłsudski's Riflemen
Legions who had originally fought on the Austrian
side until 1916. Many were then interned along
with Piłsudski for refusing to take a loyalty oath.
Piłsudski's control over the Army was, however,
challenged after the Polish victory in the 1920
war by hostile civilian-parliamentary politicians.
Officers opposed to him increasingly dominated the
Ministry of Defence during the democratic-parlia-
mentary period up till the military coup of May
1926. After that, however, Piłsudski had unchallenged control over the Polish Army, both as
Minister of War and its General-Inspector (GISZ).
Piłsudski naturally favoured his own supporters
drawn from the Legions to the detriment of the hostile and the lukewarm like Sikorski and Anders.
Piłsudski unfortunately came to power too late. He
proved too geriatric and too much of a military
dilettante to modernise the Polish Army or to work
out the strategic-operational plans for the future
war which he thought would be more likely to be with
the USSR than with Germany. In addition, many of
the top officers were withdrawn from active service
and became the political-administrators running the
Sanacja system [10]. Numerous superficial parallels
between the structures, although not the content, of
the Piłsudski and Jaruzelski régimes naturally come
to mind but such comparisons are inevitably highly
controversial. The key feature in both cases concerns the interplay between an authoritarian state
and a 'free society'. By the time Piłsudski died
in 1935 insufficient time was left for his successor as General-Inspector, Marshal Śmigły-Rydz, who
ruled Poland in tandem with the Foreign Minister
Józef Beck and with a team of civilian politicians
headed by President Ignacy Mościcki to mobilise
Poland economically and militarily. Poland's defeat in September 1939 was inevitable given the
obvious factors of strategic isolation and demographic and technological inferiority to the Germans.
One should also not forget France's craven failure
to unleash a full-scale offensive with the bulk
of her forces on the Western Front within 15 days
of the outbreak of hostilities, as laid down in
general terms in the Franco-Polish Alliance and
Military Convention of 1921 and confirmed by the
Gamelin-Kasprzycki protocol of May 1939 [11].
      The September 1939 defeat, again as in the Par-
tition and First World War period, caused the splin-
tering of the Polish Armed Forces. A large part
went into German and Soviet captivity after the

latter from 17 September 1939 occupied the half of
Poland allocated to it under the secret protocol of
the Ribbentrop-Molotov Pact. But a substantial part
escaped, mainly through the Balkans, and re-organised
in France and, after her May 1940 defeat, in Britain.
The losses of the Officer Corps, which totalled
19,731 in 1939, were particularly heavy. Zawodny
and de Sola Pool estimate that about 17,000 died or
became prisoners of war and that about half of this
total perished in the USSR [12]. Those sections of
the Officer Corps in Soviet captivity who escaped
massacre at Katyn, Kozielsk and Starobielsk, totall-
ing about 75,000 soldiers, were eventually evacuated
out through Persia to form the Anders Army in the
Middle East loyal to the London-based, Sikorski Government-in-Exile. These troops fought alongside
the Western Allies in the Desert and Italian campaigns and by the end of the war totalled about
200,000. The bulk, along with a considerable percentage of the officers and soldiers freed from
German captivity, decided to stay in the West at the
end of the war. A large-scale military resistance,
the Home Army (AK), loyal to the London Government,
was also formed in Poland from early on; at peak it
may have totalled as much as 400,000. The tragedy
of the Warsaw Uprising was its political and military
swansong [13]. A break in continuity between the
prewar and postwar Army then occurred. It was not
quite total but, especially at the leadership levels,
it was immeasurably greater than that which had taken
place in the First World War.
    With the emergence of a new communist party, the
Polish Workers' Party (PPR), to replace the KPP dissolved by Stalin in 1938, the domestic communist
leadership led from 1943 onwards by Gomułka and
Spychalski established its own resistance movement,
the People's Army (AL) and the People's Guard (GL);
Autonomous Peasant Batallions (BCh) were also formed.
But with the breaking-off of London Polish-Soviet
diplomatic relations in Spring 1943, following the
discovery of the Katyn graves, Stalin began recruit-
ing a Polish Army on Soviet soil out of the ranks of
the remaining Polish soldiers in his prison camps.
In May 1943 the First Infantry Division named after
Tadeusz Kościuszko was established, ostensibly on
the initiative of the League of Polish Patriots in
the USSR led by Wanda Wasilewska [14]. This has
come to be known colloquially as the 'Berling Army'
after its first commander. General Zygmunt Berling
was a prewar Polish Army Officer who agreed to collaborate with the Russians fairly early on. But he

was personally too independent-minded to be really
trusted by the Soviets and was sidetracked at the end
of the war [15]. The division, made up of 11,444
men, lacked sufficient officers and NCOs and was
blooded at Lenino in October 1943. After its brave
fight there, it was reported as having suffered 614
dead, 786 vanished in the bogs without trace and
1,333 wounded [16]. By April 1944 when it entered
Polish territory it had swelled to Corps size, totall-
ing 45,684. Reformed as the First Polish Army, it
was commanded by Berling for a short time with
Aleksander Zawadzki taking over as Political Commissar from Włodzimierz Sokorski. As the bulk of prewar officers were either dead, in captivity or even,
at one point, serving as rankers in an 'Officers'
Legion' in the Middle East, these Eastern Front formations suffered from a genuine shortfall in officers.
In October 1943, for example, the First Army only
had 38% of the required officer complement in infantry, 40% in artillery and 49% in tanks. Crucial
command and training roles therefore had to be performed by officers seconded from the Red Army. It
was not purely a matter of exercising Soviet control.
Those who were of Polish origins linguistically or
culturally, or who had originated from prewar Polish
territory now incorporated in the USSR, often (re-)
polonised themselves. It is therefore a difficult
task to distinguish such individuals of Ukrainian or
White Russian stock from entirely ethnic Poles. Be
that as it may, an official Polish publication admits
that 1,465 Soviet officers, the lowest possible
figure, were seconded in the initial phase from May
1943 to March 1944 out of a total Officer Corps which
had swollen to 4,124 by March 1943 [17].
    Concurrent with the establishment of the Polish
Committee of National Liberation (PKWN) in Lublin in
July 1944 the Berling Army was united with the AL in
the new Polish Armed Forces (Wojsko Polskie-WP) [18].
With additional recruitment on Polish territory the
First Army totalled 77,000 by August 1944. The new
Commander was General Michał Żymierski (pseudonym
'Rola') with Berling as his deputy. Zawadzki re-
mained as Political Commissar. These forces fought
very bravely in the final battles right up to the
capture of Berlin in Spring 1945 [19]. A Second
Army commanded by Karol Świerczewski was formed in
early Autumn 1944 and a Third Army soon afterwards.
Their numbers swelled to 400,000 by the end of the
war as a result of conscription, about double the
size of the regular Army forces in the West.
Korbonski endorses the estimate that 16,400 out of

40,000 officers were drawn directly from the Red
Army as of July 1945 [20]. General Włodzimierz
Sawczuk, the GZP Head in the 1970s, supplied authoritative figures that there were 19,000 Soviet
officers and 13,000 NCOs seconded to Poland at the
end of the war [21]. The People's Army adopted
Red Army equipment, organisation, regulations and
strategy. But, most important for the future,
it adopted the Soviet form of political apparatus
staffed by political officers from the very outset.
Their primary purpose was to ensure the indoctrination, loyalty and reliability of the Polish military and to socialise them as agents and supporters
of the new political order. Army estimates, produced in the early 1970s, revealed that about a fifth
of the Officer Corps, roughly 5-6,000 individuals,
were politruks of one sort or another [22]. These
were the men who helped to establish communism in
Poland and then made glittering careers postwar in
all walks of life. Taking the previously mentioned
First Army Commissar Włodzimierz Sokorski (born
1908) as a typical example, we see that he was the
Stalinist Minister of Culture from 1948 to 1956,
then Chairman of the Radio and TV Committee from
1956 to 1972, a CC candidate-member from 1948 to
1976 and Sejm Deputy from 1947 to 1976, ending up
as ZBoWiD chairman in the 1980s [23].

Two major problems faced the Polish Armed Forces
with the ending of hostilities. Firstly, the new
Army had to be welded together out of the five disparate elements of the Eastern Front Armies, the
AL, the ex-AK,which was dissolved officially in
January 1945, soldiers released from German PoW
camps and those Poles in the West who were courageous
enough to return to their Soviet-dominated homeland
after the war. The PKWN expansion and amalgamation
of the new Armed Forces was presided over by Berling's
successor Żymierski,who was supported by First deputy
Minister of Defence Spychalski. Secondly, even
before the war with Germany ended, the PPR began its
long drawn-out drive for total power, which was not
completed until 1947, and some would argue not until
its merger with the PPS in December 1948, which
formed the PZPR.

The main military concern of this period, apart
from contributing to economic reconstruction, reset-
tling the Western Territories and driving out the
residual Germans, was a major, but until recently
half forgotten,civil war. It was waged mainly
against ex-AK supporters and not just against its
extreme, semi-Fascist NSZ wing, UPA Ukrainian

nationalist and sundry bandit bands, as claimed by
official propaganda. It continued right up till
1948, and sporadically for even longer, in the
Carpathian foothills [24]. Jaruzelski had his own
reasons for playing up the fear of civil war in
February 1982; he claimed that domestic conflict in
the 1940s had cost 30,000 lives [25]. He was
genuinely scarred, however, by his experience as a
young officer in these conflicts. Forty years
later in his first New Year's address as Head of
State Jaruzelski reminisced how he had spent New
Year's Eve 1945 in action against a Ukrainian terrorist group near Hrubieszów on the south-eastern
border with the USSR (TL, 2 January 1986). A
French specialist claims that Jaruzelski's services
in this repression gained him the backing of Soviet
Counter Intelligence and the patronage of Marshal
Nikolai Ogarkov, who eventually became Soviet Chief
of Staff. Was there a 'Polish dimension' to
Ogarkov's fall in 1984, one wonders?(Pierre de
Villemarest, Le Monde, 9 August 1982).

   Tadeusz Walichnowski, the Home Affairs Academy
Rector (ASW),claimed that 12,000 soldiers and militia
and 10,000 PPR members and sympathisers died at the
hands of the opposition underground, of whom about
8,000 were killed (TL, 20-22 July 1985). About
70,000 were arrested and 23,000 sentenced by Military Tribunals. The brunt of repression was carried out by the UB and MO, the 30,000 strong Internal Security Corps and the Reserve Militia (ORMO)
recruited in 1945 from ex-People's Army soldiers [26].
The Army also undertook full-scale operations, notably in Spring 1946. The most striking régime loss
was that of General Karol Świerczewski (pseudonym
'Walter'), the commander of the Dąbrowski Brigade
during the Spanish Civil War and of the Second Polish
Army. He was serving as deputy Minister of Defence
when he was killed, apparently by Ukrainian nationa-
lists, in the Bieszczadach in March 1947. The affair
has never been clarified satisfactorily and has continued to cause controversy. Was Świerczewski disposed of by the Muscovite communists as he was too outspoken and independent an individual and being slated
as Żymierski's replacement? The real dilemma of
participants in this hopeless struggle against the
new Soviet-supported socialist power has been conveyed most graphically in films such as Andrzej
Wajda's 'Ashes and Diamonds', starring Zbigniew
Cybulski as the symbolically doomed hero. The subject was also dealt with most sensitively in the
liberal Gierek period in Kazimierz Kutz', 'Droga do

Nikąd' (Road to Nowhere). The topic finally came
out completely into the open after Gdańsk 1980 when
the danger of renewed fratricidal,civil war was expounded by ex-communist partisans such as Mieczysław
Moczar and then by Jaruzelski himself with increasing
vigour during 1981-1982. What should also be noted
in the light of the developments of the 1980s is that
the People's Army played an important political role
in the struggle against Mikołajczyk's Peasant Party
(SL), the main legal opposition. From late 1946
onwards in the run-up to the 1947 elections the pre-
cursors of the Territorial Army Groups of the 1980s
were organised in the form of 'Protection and Propaganda Groups'. About 30-40% of the Army's manpower
was directed towards organising and controlling mass
meetings of the population, while the police arrested
and harassed opposition leaders and activists [27].
A well informed ex-participant, now in the West, has
stressed the importance of the military counter-
intelligence organisation called Informacja in these
processes [28].

The postwar Polish Armed Forces represented
fundamentally new socialist revolution and pro-Soviet
values which were in basic conflict with those of
their interwar and wartime predecessors. But for
the ordinary soldiers who found themselves in Soviet,
and not German, captivity or who were conscripted in
1944-1945 it was largely pure chance and circumstance
that they fought on the Eastern Front and thus gained
a foothold and increasingly a stake in the new system
[29]. Sociologically the Army also changed dramatically. Although some authorities consider that
in 1947 about half of its senior officers had been
prewar career officers compared with about a third
who were seconded Soviet officers, most of the former
were cashiered, dismissed or persecuted in the
Stalinist period [30]. The interwar Officer Corps
was largely recruited from the gentry and professional strata with a slight influx from the more
popular classes under Sikorski in the West. As one
would expect, the communists ideologically favoured
individuals of peasant or working-class origins
and the remnants of the interwar KPP,the PPS-Left,
Comintern agents and such progressive organisations
as OM TUR and, later, 'Wici'. But the individuals
who served as Political Commissars in the Eastern
Front Armies were of varied social origins. As one
would expect, they later went on to become the most
prominent communist leaders, especially up till 1956
but not only till then. We have already noted the
typical case of Sokorski, who was of minor gentry

kresy origins, a Warsaw University graduate (1930) and literat to boot before becoming the Assistant Stalinist Gauleiter of Culture to Jakub Berman. Among the other most important names one can mention are Zawadzki, Ochab, Zambrowski, Matwin, Jaroszewicz, Jędrychowski, Szyr, Putrament and Pszczółkowski. Individuals with AL backgrounds like Spychalski played important roles in 1944-1948 and again after 1956. The partisan exploits of the likes of Moczar and Szlachcic were much publicised in the 1960s. The best estimate of officer cadre origins in 1948 concludes that 63.2% had come up from the People's Army from 1943 onwards, 28.7% had belonged to the prewar Army (a marked drop from Frontczak's figure for 1947), while 7.7% were admitted as Soviet advisers, a clear underestimate [31]. These inconsistent and contradictory figures revealed at different times for different motives have to be treated with caution.

The Hoover study by de Sola Pool of communist military élites published in the mid-1950s emphasises the extent to which a new Officer Corps, dominated by professional Red Army officers, was produced by 1945. It concludes that the prewar professional career officer was never very prominent and quickly discarded or shunted into harmless byways postwar unless he was an exceptionally pliant tool like Żymierski. Dynamic Polish and Russian 'muzhik generals' of KPP, interwar Red Army, Spanish Civil War or Second World War Eastern Front pedigree played crucial roles in establishing the WP and in running it for the first decade or so; but their lack of military-technical expertise meant that they had to be supplemented by the direct import of large numbers of Red Army officers. After 1956 the latter were almost entirely removed, apart from the genuinely polonised, while the former Polish Political Commissars had already largely moved on to key posts in running People's Poland. Both categories were therefore replaced by about 1960 by a new type of entirely Polish career officer symbolised by Jaruzelski and his co-evals. It was the extent and directness of Soviet control at the leadership level which led Stalin to build up the Polish Army so rapidly after 1948 into such a powerful force.

Prewar career officers like Boruta-Spiechowicz, who returned from the West, were sidetracked with the ending of hostilities, although Boruta came back into public prominence as a prominent dissenter in the 1970s. Others, like Generals Gustaw Paszkiewicz and Jerzy Kirchmayer, were dismissed in 1948, with

the onset of full Stalinisation, in spite of having
served the communist state devotedly in suppressing
AK opposition.   The extent of the post-1949 purge
of the military is difficult to quantify.   Kirchmayer
himself was sentenced to life imprisonment along with
Franciszek Herman and Stanisław Tatar in the first of
the show trials in the early 1950s designed to dis-
credit the Spychalski military wing of the Home Communist Gomułka faction.   Soon afterwards 19 senior
prewar career officers were executed.   Chęciński
cites reliable evidence that military counter-intelligence alone organised 48 trials between 1950 and
1955, which produced 37 death sentences and long
prison sentences for dozens of others [32].   The
effect of these purges was to eliminate the prewar
officer caste and to intimidate national-communist
inclinations.

The most notorious prewar survivor was General
Michał Rola-Żymierski who, although a prewar career
officer and Piłsudski-ite Legionary, had suffered
various personal misfortunes and scandals.   In
1927 he was sentenced to five years' imprisonment
for allegedly taking bribes and dishonourably dis-
charged from the Army.   After fighting on the communist side in the Spanish Civil War, Żymierski became a GL commander and in 1944 emerged as Commander
in Chief and Minister of Defence until 1949.   But,
even before being replaced by Rokossowski, Żymierski
had become a compromised figurehead bypassed by the
Soviet Generals who filled the key commands and the
more anonymous Soviet agents who conveyed Stalin's
commands.   Created a Marshal in 1945, Żymierski
claims in his official biography (in Kto jest kim
w Polsce, p. 1170) that he was unjustly accused and
imprisoned 1952-1955,but he certainly came back
into public, although not military, prominence after
1956.   He was much publicised in honorary positions
by the Gomułka, Gierek and Jaruzelski régimes if only
in view of his incredible longevity (born 1890).
The Ninth Congress even made him a CC member with
much fanfare.

Although many prewar career officers were rehabilitated in 1956 they played no significant role
thereafter.   One might also note that, unlike the
Palffy-Oestreicher 'family connection' of interwar
officers in Hungary, there was not even the slightest
hint of an ex-Piłsudski-ite network in 1944-1948
Poland.   The main political significance of the
military purges was therefore to eliminate the Home
Communists and Spanish Civil War veterans whom Stalin
considered unreliable and expendable after 1948.

Until 1956 the Polish Army was dominated completely
by Red Army officers who took over the key commands.
Chęciński has revealed the key role of Semyon Davidov,
the Head of all Soviet advisers in Poland and 'the
KGB's real viceroy' [33]. He has also shown how
Polish military counter-intelligence, headed openly,
after 1949, by two Soviet agents, Voznesensky and
Skulbashevsky, was directly answerable to Stalin's
closest KGB advisers, Beria and Abukamovic. They
often bypassed the nominal Polish Politburo bosses,
Bierut, Berman and Mazur, in mounting the Polish
purges. They came within an ace of organising the
anti-Home Communist-Zionist show-trial that would
have eliminated Gomułka, Berman and Spychalski on
Slánsky lines.
    Although the extent of Soviet direct control
over the Polish Army is unquestioned it was complicated by the fact that many Red Army officers had
loose ethnic, family, linguistic or territorial links
with Poland, which did not affect their general
loyalty to the USSR but which rendered them liable
to polonisation and hence to fall victim to Stalin's
paranoia.   There is a Polish minority of about a
million in the USSR and this number swelled after
the annexation of Poland's Eastern Territories.
One should draw a distinction between complete outsiders and Russified Poles who eventually became
polonised Russians like the two Chiefs of Staff,
Korzyc and Bordziłowski; Korzyc was even reported
as having been withdrawn and accused of having succumbed too much to the Warsaw atmosphere.
Rokossowski himself had been born in Warsaw in 1896
but these childhood experiences were the best of
his direct contacts with Poland.   He joined the
Bolsheviks and the Red Army in 1918.   Imprisoned and
almost purged in the 1930s, he was by 1946 a Soviet
Marshal, Supreme Soviet Deputy and deputy Minister
of Defence.   What was unusual about his appointment
as Polish Minister of Defence in November 1949 and
member of the PZPR Politburo in May 1950 was the open
blatancy with which a Soviet Marshal (who inter alia
had to change citizenships) assumed command of a
satellite Army preparatory to its final purging and
building up on reliable pro-Soviet lines. Rokossowski
behaved quite honourably as a military technician but,
although he did not soil his hands personally in the
Terror of the early 1950s, he must carry political
responsibility.   Equally blatantly on his return to
the USSR in October 1956 he reassumed his Soviet
citizenship and his erstwhile post of deputy Defence
Minister, which he retained until his death in 1968.

The USSR Supreme Soviet passed a decree in 1945 allowing Soviet officers to renounce Soviet citizenship
in favour of Polish and on that basis quite literally
thousands were infiltrated into Polish commands. Another prominent 'Russian' commander was Stanisław
Popławski,who had taken over the First Army from
Żymierski, and had become Second deputy Defence
Minister and operational commander of the land
forces on Świerczewski's death. Popławski was to
command the forces which suppressed the Poznań uprising in 1956. Most of the military districts and
sections were commanded by a succession of Soviet
Generals between 1948 and 1956: the Navy
(Szylingowsky, Cherekov), the Air Force (Romeyko,
Turkel) and the Artillery (Czerniawski). We have
already noted the less clear cases of the two successive Chiefs of Staff, Władysław Korzyc (a muzhik
General) and Jerzy Bordziłowski, a Red Army Brigade-
General by 1942 and eventually commander of the
Polish sappers. Both were ethnically and linguistically from the 'borderlands' so their post-1943
polonisation was credible enough, but all their
careers and loyalties had been tied up with the Red
Army. Bordziłowski remained as a 'guarantor' that
the Polish Army under Gomułka would remain loyal to
the USSR as late as the mid-1960s. In this respect
he played a similar role to Emil Bodnaras in Romania.
When he died in April 1983 his MON obituary eulo-
gised him as 'a symbol of Polish-Soviet friendship
and soldierly brotherhood of arms' (TL, 7 April 1983).
The main Polish figures of the takeover period
like Świerczewski did not survive much post-1948.
Świerczewski, popularly still known as 'Walter',
was a major figure in operational control of the
ground forces at the time of his death. It has
always been rumoured that a PPR faction was backing
him as Żymierski's replacement as Minister of Defence. To this day many Poles suspect that the
Soviets liquidated an independent-minded, potential
national communist. There is some evidence that,
while 'Russians' occupied most of the command positions where technical-professional qualifications
were required, they ceded non-command posts such as
the Quartermaster-General's and the GZP to native
Poles. Piotr Jaroszewicz was the first incumbent
of the former post after having been an AL Chief of
Staff and then a Berling Army politruk. He became
a deputy Minister of Defence before moving on to
political matters to become deputy Premier in 1952
and eventually Premier from 1970 to 1980. The
Quartermaster's post was taken over in 1950 by

General Wacław Komar, a Świerczewski associate, as
'Colonel Wacek' in the Spanish Civil War, who postwar was in charge of the sensitive area of Army
Intelligence.   By 1953 though Komar was purged and
imprisoned.   He was rehabilitated in 1956, along
with others like Kirchmayer, and played a key role
as KBW commander.   Polish political officers
(notably Spychalski, Wągrowski, Naszkowski and
Witaszewski) controlled the GZP in the decade before
1956, and all bar the second made important political careers after 'October'.   Witaszewski ('General
Gaspipe') was recalled in 1959 to become CC Administration Department Head which dealt with Army matters.
Naszkowski was Rapacki's First Deputy at the Foreign
Ministry for many years.   Spychalski had been both
GL and Berling Army Chief of Staff, although his
training had been as an architect   not as a professional officer.   A PPR Politburo member and close
Gomułka associate, he was purged, imprisoned and tor-
tured after Gomułka's fall.   After 1956 Spychalski
became Minister of Defence but he failed to consolidate his hold over the Army.
    While the political significance of the con-
flicts between native Poles, 'Russians', Home Communists and Muscovites should not be overemphasised,
they do provide some keys to an understanding of the
political control of the Polish Army up till 1956.
What is clear is that the Polish Army in this period
was the satellite army which was most directly offi-
cered and controlled by officers seconded from the
Red Army.   Prewar career officers generally only
played roles until 1947.   Native Poles, Spanish
Civil War veterans, interwar KPP individuals and even
Poles trained in wartime Russia were screened very
carefully and purged on the slightest suspicion.   Of
the wartime Eastern Front group, those who survived
were the most reliable pro-Soviet political officers
like Jaroszewicz, Zawadzki and Ochab.   They shared
political power with the resurgent Home Communists
after 1956.   The 'Russian' Red Army officers provided
both loyalty to the USSR and technical, military professionalism up till 1956.   But this was always meant
as a stop-gap measure.   The absorption of the Polish
by the Red Army was never a serious possibility even
at the height of Stalinism.   As de Sola Pool wrote
so perceptively in 1955:   'The Russians intend eventually to replace the present officers by a new
generation of Soviet trained Poles' [34].   They
would combine political loyalty to the USSR with the
professional military training and skills picked up
in Polish and Soviet Military Academies after 1948.

Pool even put a date, 1961, to the process. Although one cannot blame him for not foreseeing the events of 1956, which led to the open departure of Rokossowski, he predicted the general drift of events remarkably correctly. It is Jaruzelski's historical significance to be the embodiment of this new Soviet-trained military leadership which took over wholesale by the early 1970s after the hiccup of the partisan interlude. Jaruzelski's rapid promotion must have been accelerated by 'October'. It is symbolic that he was appointed Poland's youngest General in 1956 at the age of 33. Only four years further on he headed the GZP, thus uncannily fulfilling Pool's prediction. Five years later when he took over the General Staff his generation of military leadership was clearly replacing the Bordziłowski transitional type at all levels. The Jaruzelski cohort, however, faced transient challenges both from the wartime resistance, less military-professional clan headed by Spychalski after 1956 and then, in a different manner, by Moczar in the mid-1960s.

Andrzej Korbonski, taking a long look at the Polish Army's postwar political development, distinguishes four distinct stages - co-optation (1944-1948), subordination (1948-1956), accommodation (1956-1968) and participation (since 1968) [35]. We have already discussed the dynamics of the first period but we should also note that the Army was then reorganised on a new basis. A General Staff, new military districts, the Internal Defence Corps (KBW), the Border Defence Guard (WOP) and the Polish Navy all emerged during 1945. Military training was taken in hand by the General Staff Academy (1947), the Military-Political Academy (1951), the Military-Technical Academy (1951) and in due course another eleven specialised Higher Schools were established. The Army was then brought under direct Soviet-Stalinist control during 1948-1955. Rokossowski became the symbol of Soviet domination, although he was a straightforward career officer. He was so unhappy with his appointment that he 'literally fell on his knees and begged Stalin not to send him to Poland' [36]. The police and security organs, both Polish and Soviet, dominated the military establishment at this time and controlled it through classic Soviet techniques. In common with the general Polish experience though the military purge was probably less extensive than in Czechoslovakia and Hungary. It achieved its aims, however, of liquidating the remnants of the

prewar officer cadre, any dubious Home Communists
and Spanish Civil War veterans and even demoted or
sidetracked some of the Eastern Front recruits in
favour of Red Army personnel, most of whom were
later thanked and sent home in 1956.
     The balance of Soviet control, however, tilted
away from Moscow during the New Course of 1953-1955.
It changed decisively in favour of Warsaw as a result
of the great political crisis of 1956 which opened
with PZPR First Secretary Bierut's death in Moscow
and Khrushchev's Secret Speech at the Twentieth CPSU
Congress in March 1956. In spite of official
mystification it seems clear that the local Army
units in Poznań, drawn from the Military Academies,
initially proved unreliable. A special KBW unit
under deputy Defence Minister Popławski, a Red
Army officer who left along with Rokossowski in
October, had to be rushed in from Warsaw. The
Poznań Uprising of 28 June 1956 was suppressed at
the cost of 74 deaths and 575 severely injured, a
much higher death toll than any of the subsequent
Polish disturbances [37]. A crucial factor then
proved to be the appointment of the recently rehabilitated Komar to head the Internal Security
Corps (KBW). He frustrated the machinations of
the pro-Soviet military elements supporting the
Natolin faction and ensured that Soviet military
movements were counteracted. He was supported by
the Navy Chief of Staff, Jan Wiśniewski, and by an
Air Force General, Jan Frey-Bielecki. Khrushchev
admits in his memoirs that Komar's forces 'were used
against the Soviet Union' and that the pro-Soviet
forces controlled by Rokossowski would have been
insufficient to quell an uprising without external
Soviet assistance [38]. Soviet pressure, culminat-
ing in the descent of Khrushchev and most of the
CPSU Politburo on Warsaw, proved insufficient to
prevent Gomułka's return as First Secretary, by
political means [39]. For the moment the lack of
sources does not permit us to come to a definitive
judgement about the seriousness of the possibility
of a military coup in favour of the pro-Soviet
Natolin faction. One of the most popular slogans
though had been 'Rokossowski go home' and he now
went back along with 32 Soviet Generals who were
thanked publicly while many hundred other officers
returned more quietly. Rokossowski's dropping from
the Politburo on the surface appeared to be the main
issue in contention at the Eighth PZPR Plenum where
23 out of 75 CC members voted for his retention [40].
The legal embodiment of the political changes of

'October' regarding the native Polish communist
élite's control over its foreign policy and armed
forces was the Moscow Declaration and the Treaty of
17 December 1956 on the stationing of Soviet forces
in Poland [41]. These documents conceded the principle of sovereignty and equal rights within the
socialist community,which has rightly been described
as moving from an Empire to a Commonwealth. The
Treaty regarding the legal status of Soviet troops in
Poland led to the disappearance of the Red Army from
public view, the holding of its garrison at the
30,000 strong level in Legnica in Silesia and the
control of Soviet troop movements within Poland by
the Polish authorities who had to be kept informed.
    Gomułka's new team in charge of military mat-
ters was headed by Spychalski, who became Minister
of Defence on 13 November 1956, a Politburo member
at the Third PZPR Congress in March 1959 and Marshal
in 1963. General Janusz Zarzycki, another close
Gomułka supporter, also became GZP Head in 1956,and
various other key positions, such as the post of
deputy Minister of Defence, went to the national-
communist General Zygmunt Duszyński, who became the
first Chief Inspector of Training in 1959. On the
other hand, powerful figures like Bordziłowski remained to guarantee the Polish Army's loyalty to
Moscow. Gomułka never made more than a shortlived,
and not very determined, effort to subordinate the
Soviet-controlled intelligence and police agencies
to his own control. His rapid consolidation in
1957 and increasing attack on so-called Revisionism
cut away the ground for a full-scale offensive on
Soviet-controlled mechanisms in Poland, which were
limited in a number of significant ways in 1956 but
never to the extent of allowing Gomułka to do what
Gheorgiu-Dej achieved later on in Romania. Two
parallel political trends therefore dominated the
military-political situation in the 1960s. On the
one hand the USSR adopted looser and more subtle
methods to protect its hegemony. This meant the
gradual replacement of older cadres in the Army by
the postwar-trained, PZPR committed officers of the
Jaruzelski cohort. On the other hand, a joker in
the pack appeared in the ambiguous form of the
nationalist and authoritarian police chief Mieczysław
Moczar; he presented a challenge to both the
Gomułka-Spychalski wing and the new postwar-trained
professional officer class. It is still highly
controversial whether Moczar had potential Romanian-
type anti-Soviet inclinations as well. The Partisan
offensive of the 1960s used anti-Zionism quite

cynically as a tool with which to remove most of
the remaining communists of Jewish origins.   This
was used as a front for destroying any potential
liberal-reform communist movement of a Dubcek type
as well as for a massive provocation in March 1968
which intimidated the Polish intelligentsia and student community [42].   Whether Moczar did this at
Moscow's behest in order to weaken Gomułka, or
whether he had wider personal ambitions, which he
abandoned when he returned to play a major political
role again in 1980-1981, is still contentious.
My own view is that the dynamic, ruthless and oppor-
tunist Moczar started off as a licensed Gomułka
agent (by CC Secretary Ryszard Strzelecki) to discipline the liberal intelligentsia.   He then became
something of a Sorcerer's Apprentice.   His Partisan
faction not only controlled the police but also had
a strong appeal to sections of the political élite
and the Officer Corps, including ZBoWiD.   This explains why Brezhnev saved Gomułka in 1968 when he
was down and, bar the invasion of Czechoslovakia,
right out.

Spychalski had managed to place a number of his
supporters of AL and GL background in command positions for a while between 1956 and about 1960.
Bielecki and Wiśniewski were rewarded with the commands of the Air Force and Navy, a victim of
Stalinism, Józef Kuropiejski, became commander of the
Warsaw Military District, Korczyński took over Military Intelligence while another Home Communist resistance General, Jerzy Fronkowicz, took over MON's key
Personnel Department.   After that, however, Gomułka
went along with the Moscow-encouraged policy of
favouring the return of ex-Natolin personnel in order
to carry through the struggle against Revisionism.
In the military sphere, an important role in purging
national autonomy seeking officers of the Duszyński
type was then played by General Teodor Kufel, who
remained as Head of Military Counter-Intelligence
(WSW) until as late as 1979 [43].   The result of
all these intrigues was first to weaken, then to
isolate and finally to overthrow Spychalski.
He ceded the Defence Ministry to Jaruzelski in
Spring 1968, although he survived as Chairman of the
Council of State until swept away with Gomułka.
Spychalski never became a complete non-person during
the 1970s and his historical role was discussed quite
objectively by the time he died in 1980.

Korbonski's characterisation of the third period
in the Polish Army's development seems to have been
borrowed far too mechanically from the literature on

Soviet politics to be entirely accurate in the Polish
context. But it may be relevant enough to intra-
Army developments,where the percentage of PZPR membership in the Officer Corps increased to well over
two-thirds by the time of the 1968 upheaval, while
the criteria for recruitment changed from socio-
economic class origins and political loyalty to those
of educational qualifications and technical capacity.
Various Generals such as Tuczapski, Molczyk, Chocha
and Korczyński were closely identified with Moczar's
Partisan and ZBoWiD faction. Grzegorz Korczyński
was appointed the first Inspector for Territorial
Defence (OTK) in 1965. He turned the OTK into a
Partisan stronghold while the GZP also came under
strong Moczarite influence, especially after Chocha
took it over in 1968. But the purge of officers of
Jewish origins in 1967-1968 was an extremely complex
affair. The 200 odd remaining Jewish officers were
forced to sign loyalty oaths after the Arab-Israeli
War of 1967. Most were purged within a year, whatever their attitudes. The Air Defence Forces (WOPK),
which had been reorganised on Soviet lines as an independent service, in 1962 paradoxically became a
haven for critics of the static Soviet military doctrine as compared with the dynamic Israeli strategy.
Gomułka reacted to such criticism during the Six Day
War by giving the green light to the Partisans. The
result was a complete purge of all the WOPK commanders. Johnson estimates that 14 Generals and
200 Colonels, only some of whom were of Jewish origins,
were caught up in the military purge of 1967-1968
[44]. Spychalski's removal from the Defence Ministry
did not, however, signify the victory of the Polish
authoritarian national-chauvinist, covertly anti-
Russian officer group seeking to emulate the
Romanian example. Had Moczar taken over the party
Korczyński would have become his Defence Minister.
Instead Jaruzelski's appointment, according to
Korbonski, 'symbolised the emergence in its right
of the professional Officer Corps' as an autonomous
and distinct force [45]. This élite group showed
its hard-nosed realism in supporting the Warsaw Pact
invasion of Czechoslovakia. The invading Polish
contingent was led by General Florian Siwicki, the
commander of the Silesian Military District. He was
Jaruzelski's Chief of Staff from 1973 to 1983 and
then his successor as Minister of Defence. In 1986
he was also the only other Four Star General [46].
Jaruzelski endorsed Gierek's replacement of
Gomułka. He was rewarded by being made a Politburo
candidate straightaway in December 1970 and a full

member at the Sixth Congress in December 1971. The blame for the officially admitted 44 deaths and 1,164 injured was laid at the door of deputy Defence Minister Korczyński, who was shunted out of his military posts [47]. Jaruzelski purged the OTK of Partisan influence in 1971, although Czapla maintained it in the GZP during 1971-1972. After that Jaruzelski's supporters cleared out the remaining Partisans. The 1970s,then, became a time of very marked personnel stability in the military sector.

The myth of the Army's and Jaruzelski's lack of involvement in the Baltic seacoast repression was thus maintained. Jaruzelski refused to save Gomułka in 1970 and Gierek in 1980 because he was loyal to the communist system,not to individuals. He was determined and powerful enough to prevent the Army from being used as an outright tool of repression when political solutions were still available in the form of personnel change and policy concessions [48]. This explained his reserved role on both those occasions and, one presumes, during the June 1976 riots. He thus built up his prestige and indispensability to the system and maintained public respect for the military as a patriotic, national force. The price for this autonomy was that,with the growing demoralisation and near collapse of the civilian party during 1981,the CPA leadership of Kania, Barcikowski and Moczar increasingly found it necessary to tie the Army down by co-opting Jaruzelski into key positions: firstly as Chairman of the Council of Ministers in February 1981 and then as PZPR First Secretary as well in October. The Army thus assumed its underlying role as Guardian of the communist system quite openly. It moved in to destroy the opposition as a viable political alternative by imposing the State of War in December 1981.

Korbonski is therefore correct in tracing out how the discredited and divided Polish Army of the 1940s was subordinated in the Stalinist period [49]. Its development after 1956 mirrored that of the Red Army in spite of the Partisan and other cross-currents introduced by Soviet pressure. Kolkowicz's model of the Army as a key pressure-group applies quite well up till 1970, while after that Colton's autonomous actor and participation model is more relevant. The scale of the post-1980 crisis though and the very different local Polish circumstances, however, support the argument that something close to a CPA-military élite symbiosis occurred in personnel terms from 1981 onwards. The thesis of

the professional autonomy of the Polish Officer
Corps, developed by Herspring and Korbonski, is,
however, another side of the coin.   It will now
have to be examined critically in the light of
some vital and somewhat neglected considerations
about the role and the character of the political
apparatus of the Polish Armed Forces and the way in
which it defined its role under cover of the 1967
Law on Universal Defence Obligation.

Professional Capacity and Party Loyalty
        Dale Herspring has argued that a number of fac-
tors have tended to make the Polish Armed Forces
more independent of detailed party control than most.
His thesis that the higher the technological level
went up, from the 1960s onwards, the lower the degree
of direct civilian control and the greater the degree
of Officer Corps' professional autonomy seems convincing at first sight [50].   It appears to supply a
partial explanation of the Army's reserved and non-
committal role during the crises of 1970 and 1980
and why it was fiercely loyal to the communist system
but agnostic about the fate of any particular leadership team.   It also became increasingly a competitive alternative.   Herspring's ideas also serve as
the beginning of an elucidation of why the military
had the capacity to move into the political vacuum
left by the party in 1981.   The Polish programme of
technological modernisation which started in the mid-
1950s and accelerated in 1963 soon left the GDR far
behind.   Herspring concludes that it was accompanied
by a high level of professional and technical autonomy
in Poland as well as by a low degree of politicisation: this in spite of the increase of PZPR membership among the Officer Corps from a mere 15% in 1945
to a peak of 85% by 1975.   Does Herspring equate
politicisation too much with ideological commitment
on the GDR model, and does he underestimate the dimension of deep officer involvement in all walks of the
Polish communist system?   It is true that the Polish
Army faced considerable difficulties with its processes of ideological and political indoctrination
in spite of the institution of party cells at
increasingly lower command levels [51].   The PZPR
structure in the Armed Forces has, however, remained
relatively unchanged since the major 1961 reorganisation.   This unified the party-GZP organs by making
the latter's political officers superior to POP Secretaries.   Military leaders confirmed that it worked
well, even during the 1967-1968 and 1970 upheavals
[52].   The paradox was that the Polish Army under

Jaruzelski was remarkably successful in projecting
its traditional image as the guarantor of Poland's
national independence, values and security. Without overtly challenging party supremacy in Gierek's
time, indeed partly by default, it achieved a degree
of institutional integrity, and even autonomy, that
held a potential challenge to the orthodox Soviet
Leninist concept of party control of the military
which the USSR had foisted on its East European satellites at the end of the Second World War [53]. Was
this also the paradoxical consequence of the potential ideological-political distance between the
liberal national-communist régimes of 1956-1980 and
the increasingly pragmatic, although fundamentally
pro-Soviet, military élite? It is also significant
that the problem of civil-military relations almost
vanished from public discussion in Poland in the
1970s. Few Western commentators, either then or
now, considered the possible Soviet interest in destabilising the unreliable and unorthodox Gierek
form of communism.

The increase in the political weight of the Army
apparat in communist politics was not, however, accompanied by a corresponding increase in the military's social status. Army officers had ranked
highest in terms of occupational prestige in prewar
Poland. This fell considerably postwar with the
recruitment of officers of proletarian and peasant
origins. One study ranked them 20th out of 28 in
1958, 13th out of 27 in 1975 but 10th out of 21 in
rural areas [54]. An earlier study placed them 13th
out of 18 in terms of occupational prestige and 9th
out of 18 in terms of material benefits [55]. The
drop in officers' prestige, which fell even below
that of office workers in a 1958 poll of Warsaw
secondary schoolchildren, caused considerable re-
cruiting difficulties in the decade after 1956, but
the profession's ranking picked up with modernisation.
The decline in military prestige was because the
postwar Army became one of the main agents promoting
social mobility. In 1963, 49% of all officers were
of working-class origins, 33% of peasant and 11% of
white-collar intelligentsia background [56]. Up
till the late 1960s the junior and middle rank officers tended to have a lower level of satisfaction
with their profession and its prospects than prewar
or after 1970 [57].

The Polish Army is now the largest Warsaw Pact
Army after that of the USSR. In 1981 it ranked in
size in Europe after the West German, French and
British [58]. With 319,500 under arms it was widely

regarded as an extremely powerful, well equipped and
well organised force.   Its 15 divisions included
élite airborne-assault and sea-landing formations.
Its equipment was reportedly above the East European
average.   The Military Balance for 1981-1982 estimated that its ground forces had 3,560 tanks (including 30 T-72s and 130 PT-76s) while the Air Force had
705 combat aircraft.   Sadykiewicz points out that
prewar the ratio of the regular service cadre to
conscripts was about one to six, whereas nowadays
it is two to three, not one to one as he loosely
claims [59].   Table 1 shows that the conscript
element in 1982 in the whole of the Polish Armed
Forces was 59% of the total.   But, as one would
expect, it was much lower in the specialised arms,
only 27% in the Navy, and 31% in the Air Force as
compared with 74% in the Land Army.   Overall there
were 130,000 regulars to 187,000 conscripts. Article
92 of the constitution states that 'the defence of
the Fatherland is the most sacred duty of every
citizen'.   The obligation of military service falls
on all males aged between 18 and 50 (up till 60
for officers).   It lasts 24 months in the infantry
and 36 months in the specialised Navy, Rocketry and
Communications branches.   Military service can be
deferred while educational studies are pursued, but
other exemptions, even medical ones, are hard to
obtain;   conscientious objection does not meet with
much sympathy.   The French concept of the Nation of
Arms has been given its full expression in People's
Poland.

     The crucial factor, however, is that there was
only one officer to 18 soldiers in 1939 compared with
the current ratio of about one to five.   For the
same size of Army there were just under 20,000 officers in 1939, but Malcher estimates that the 1980
figures were 64,000 officers and 66,000 NCO equivalents [60].   Śmigły-Rydz had 438 Colonels in 1939
but by the 1970s Jaruzelski disposed of 3,500 Colonels
as well as over 200 Generals.   These figures fuel
the suspicion that there are far more officers than
are needed for purely military functions.   What
have all these apparently redundant officers, a
common sight on the average Warsaw tram in the
1970s, been up to?   The most convincing answer is
Malcher's that a very large and, until martial law,
fairly militarily redundant class of senior 'political officer' was produced in Poland from the 1960s
onwards;   their numbers went beyond what was necessary just to exercise political control over the
military.   He argues that Jaruzelski's mission was

Table 1

Size of the Polish Armed Forces (Net figures in thousands)

Year	Total Forces	Con-scripts	ARMY Total	ARMY Con-scripts	NAVY Total	NAVY Con-scripts	AIR FORCE Total	AIR FORCE Con-scripts	Re-serves	Total Para-mili-tary	Border Guards WOP	Inter-nal Defence Troops	Citizens' Militia MO/ORMO	LOK (Active Estimate)
1981	319.5	187 58.5%	210	154 73.3%	22.5	6 26.7%	87	27 31%	605	72	16	56	350	250
1982	317	187 59%	207	154 74.4%	22	6 27.3%	88	27 30.7%	605	85	20	65	350	250
1983	340	190 55.9%	230	157 68.3%	22	5 22.7%	88	27 30.7%	500	85	20	65	350	250

Sources: Military Balance for 1981-1982, 1982-1983, 1983-1984 (London, International Institute for Strategic Studies, 1981-1983). Of the 65,000 Internal Defence Troops about 25,000 were ZOMO who are controlled by the MSW. Out of 30 Soviet divisions stationed in Eastern Europe in 1981 two were based in Poland at the Northern Group HQ in Legnica. But 67 Soviet divisions were stationed in the USSR's European Military Districts (Military Balance, 1981-1982, p. 12).

to ensure the political reliability of the Polish
Army as a component part of the Warsaw Pact.
Directly linked with this was the need to prepare
the Army for an internal role, for the defence of
the system should 'the Communist Party lose control
during one of the recurring Polish crises' [61].
The two issues are interlinked. They impinge on
the wider issue of a non-Soviet controlled defence
capacity for an independence seeking local communist
leadership, which has already been touched on in
connection with 1956. It is admitted officially
that Poland's Armed Forces are, in practice, divided
into external and internal sections. The former
are the operational troops, closely integrated into
the Warsaw Pact, which are designated for external
military operations. The degree of military integration accelerated with the Warsaw Pact's greater
activity and institutionalisation after 1967.
Jones estimates that Polish forces participated in
about 25 WTO exercises between 1961 and 1979, of
which 7 were wholly on Polish territory, 7 wholly
outside and 11 partly in Poland and Czechoslovakia
or the GDR [62]. In personnel terms integration
was helped on by the fact that the cream of the
Polish Officer Corps have almost invariably spent
a year or two in mid-career at a Soviet military
academy. The high fliers normally went to the
Voroshilov General Staff Academy in Moscow, as in
the cases of Nowak (1954), Jaruzelski (1956),
Siwicki (1956), Hupałowski (1956), Tuczapski (1957),
Sawczuk (1964), Oliwa (1965) and Użycki (1973).
The more technically specialised (like Piotrowski)
went to the Engineering Academy (1956) or the Tank
Training Academy, as in the case of Rapacewicz (1954).
     The only attempt to halt, or at least to re-
fashion, this close integration within the Soviet
framework came after 1956. Jones accepts the evidence of Michał Chęciński, a Jewish, ex-Polish
Intelligence Officer now in the West (Israel), that
the more autonomy-seeking wing of the Gomułka-
Spychalski faction led by deputy Defence Minister
Zygmunt Duszyński viewed the Rapacki Plan as an
opportunity for some disengagement and disentagle-
ment from the maws of the Red Army. The intention
was to form 'a separate, compact, well defined "Polish
Front" intended as an exclusive theatre of operations
for the Polish Armed Forces' [63]. The wider political implications were, however, secondary to the
development by Polish military theorists of a coalition doctrine based on the premise that a European
conflict would be nuclear and against NATO forces

[64]. Polish forces were to unleash 'a dynamic offensive' on an 'external front'. In Duszyński's more nationalist version the Poles hoped to maintain direct and independent control over their three Armies fighting alongside their Warsaw Pact allies, especially if a domestic defence industry could be built up. The interesting corollary was the concept of the 'defence of the national territory' expounded by Bolesław Chocha, the Partisan Chief of Staff [65]. The political implications, as with everything about the Partisans, were unclear; domestic Polish military control over the non-operational part of the Army linked it with the domestic repressive capacities. In the event the Civil Defence against nuclear attack aspects failed to produce a programme of national mobilisation of the civilian population, as in Yugoslavia, because of the obvious range of Soviet and other restraints. On the whole these inclined the 1960s' leadership to curtail its full blooded development. The OTK framework was established between 1962 and 1965 and was institutionalised in the 1967 Law,about which more later [66].

The post-'October' initiatives for a distinctive Polish military doctrine, national defence system and armaments industry bore some limited fruit but were largely abandoned by Gomułka after 1960. They were suppressed by cunning Soviet political pressures,by their sponsorship of the joint exercises and joint educational training already mentioned and, above all, by the rapid promotion of Jaruzelski and his Eastern Front military generation. These factors, if nothing else, are an additional explanation of Jaruzelski's reserve towards, and political distance from, Home Communist civilian leaders like Gomułka, Kliszko and Spychalski - not to mention his police faction rival, Moczar. Jaruzelski may also not have had much in common emotionally with Gierek,who after all had spent the war in Western Europe. Gierek seems to have been carefully cordoned off from military matters during the 1970s by Jaroszewicz, Jaruzelski and Kania. But the corollary is not proven that Jaruzelski was a mindless Soviet stooge. If he were a Muscovite of sorts he was fundamentally a more intelligent and flexible one than the earlier generation of Bierut, Berman and Zambrowski and Generals like Rokossowski, Korzyc, Popławski and Bordziłowski. The émigré equation that a Soviet ally equals hardliner equals Soviet stooge is far too simple in Jaruzelski's case. The evidence is also that

Jaruzelski's primary links before 1981 were with the Red Army establishment and not with the civilian party apparatus; in the 1980s his most regular Soviet 'contact man' was Warsaw Pact Commander Kulikov. All this reinforced Jaruzelski's temperamental inclination against getting involved in the political infighting which would inevitably have made him more susceptible to various pressures and reduced his national standing.

Command and Organisation of the Armed Forces

According to Article 41, Clause 10, of the 1952 constitution the Council of Ministers 'exercises general direction in the sphere of the country's defence and in the organisation of the armed forces of the PRL' [67]. The Law of 21 November 1967 on the Universal Obligation to Defend the PRL established the National Defence Committee (KOK) as the body entrusted with this task [68]. This grew out of the Military Council established in MON in February 1957 to oversee the various military branches. Although chaired by the Premier, KOK was in practice run by its deputy chairman, the Minister of Defence, who was charged with strategic defence matters. In addition the Army Chief of Staff was later to become the committee's secretary while the Council of Ministers formally nominated the remaining, mainly military members. The 1967 Law, based on the very similar Soviet document of April 1967, obligated all Polish citizens, organisations and factories to defend the Socialist Fatherland. These tasks were spelt out in even greater detail by a 1979 Law. The Armed Forces were, again, entrusted with ensuring Poland's sovereignty in terms which allowed the Army to have access to, and to penetrate into, all civilian sectors. On this basis KOK established provincial defence committees (WKOKs) in all of Poland's post-1974 provinces and lower-level ones in many of the largest cities and factories. The WKOKs were chaired by the Wojewoda but were, arguably, really under the influence of the Head of the local military staff who was usually of, at least, Colonel rank. This countrywide, alternative network of state-military government, designed to cope with national emergencies, internal and external, was activated by KOK and given its fullest dimension during the State of War. Premiers Józef Cyrankiewicz (1954-1970) and Edward Babiuch (February-August 1980) seem to have had little influence over KOK matters; but Premier Piotr Jaroszewicz (1970-1980) may well have been nominated by the Soviets with the primary purpose of giving Jaruzelski a free run in preparing and training the Polish Army for its repressive tasks [69].

The main body dealing with the specific implementation and co-ordination of the policy decisions of the Council of Ministers, which originated substantively from the top levels of the CPA, is MON, the Ministry of National Defence, which naturally also exercises operational command over the Armed Forces. It is sub-divided into a number of central institutions (IC MON), notably the General Staff, the Main Political Department (GZP), the Training Inspectorate, the Main Territorial Defence Inspectorate, the Main Quartermaster's Office and the Personnel Department, most of which are usually headed by a deputy Minister. The Minister of Defence, in addition to his other strategic and political functions, is also the operational Commander-in-Chief in Poland. He is supported by the Chief of the General Staff, the commanders of Poland's three military districts (currently Warsaw, Pomerania and Silesia), and the naval, air force, air defence and other subsidiary branches who answer to him directly. Jaruzelski, backed politically by Jaroszewicz, was largely left to himself by Gierek, although MON published the First Secretary's speeches concerning military matters [70].

Jaruzelski took over untrammelled control of KOK when he became Premier in February 1981. One presumes that the final details of the martial law preparations were then perfected. In November 1983, when Jaruzelski ceded the Ministry of Defence to Siwicki, KOK was revamped and he was formally appointed its Chairman and Commander-in-Chief. At about the same time the first open suggestions for an executive Presidency on Tito's Yugoslav lines, to encompass the military-command function, were floated [71]. In the event Jaruzelski became Chairman of the Council of State in October 1985. The issue was also linked with the ticklish question of whether Jaruzelski would take a Marshal's baton like his predecessors as Ministers of Defence, Żymierski, Rokossowski and Spychalski. The only other Marshals of Poland have been Piłsudski and Śmigły-Rydz interwar, parallels which Jaruzelski perhaps preferred to avoid. Rokossowski had also been a Soviet Marshal, while Prince Józef Poniatowski, who perished at the Battle of Leipzig in 1813, was a Marshal of the French Empire. Jaruzelski was pressed to become a Marshal by political and social organisations; most notably

by the unwontedly obscure PZPR First Secretary in
Katowice, Bogumil Ferenstein, in May 1985 on the
occasion of the fortieth anniversary of the ending
of the war in Europe. But it is indicative of
Jaruzelski's long-term civilian-political ambitions
and a measure of his balanced realism that he refused
publicly. Ferenstein was rewarded soon afterwards
with very belated promotion in the CC; it would seem
that the question of the Marshal's baton has been
put into cold storage until Żymierski's death, at
least.

The third name after those of Jaruzelski and
Siwicki on the list of WRON members was that of
Corps-General Tadeusz Tuczapski, the main Inspector
of Territorial Defence, KOK Secretary after 1971 and
deputy Defence Minister since 1968. From 1972 onwards he also doubled up as the main Inspector of
Civil Defence (OCK), a role formalised by the Council
of Ministers' resolution of 18 May 1973 on the Civilian Defence of the Country. Tuczapski therefore
commanded a vast system for the Territorial and Civil
Defence of the Country. It covered not only the
forces required to defend the country against air
and nuclear attack, but also the special troop units
available to maintain internal order or to put down
uprisings like those in Poznań or the Baltic seacoast towns. It is significant that the KBW was
transferred by Gomułka in 1965 away from the Moczar-
controlled MSW to the Spychalski-headed MON. They
are now known as Internal Defence Troops (WOWewn)
and are about 14,000 strong according to Malcher,
who disputes the muddled and composite figures for
domestic security formations presented by The Military
Balance [72]. Although official sources do their
best to camouflage the fact, much of the expansion during the 1970s went into this sector at a
time when overall Polish military spending was
claimed officially to have been cut down from 4.4%
in 1967 to 3.5% (1974). Expressed in terms of GNP the
figure for 1975 was 3.1%-6.7% of the State Budget,
but these figures are obviously too low.

Although most of the actual physical repression,
both during martial law and earlier, was carried out
by specialised security corps, formal control over
them has been shared by the MSW and MON in different
balances ever since their formation in 1944 [73].
Unlike other communist states, though, one can hazard
the generalisation that the Army and the police apparats have been more supportive than competitive in
Poland; they have collaborated because of the scale
and longevity of social opposition, although the

normal Polish factional conflicts affected them, especially in the 1960s. Personnel tended to inter-change fairly freely at the top levels, as witness the rather odd and ambiguous career of the Partisan Minister of the Interior (1964-1968) and CC Secretary (1968-1971), Mieczysław Moczar. Kania continued, and possibly renewed, the older tradition of mili-tary-police collaboration, after the Moczar inter-lude, during his spell as CC Secretary in the 1970s in charge of both. The policy was, if anything, deepened by Minister of the Interior (1980-1981) and CC Secretary (July 1981-1985), Division-General, Mirosław Milewski. But the most significant step occurred when a Soviet-trained pragmatist of the Jaruzelski cohort, Corps-General, Czesław Kiszczak, who had been deputy Intelligence head to Kufel (1972-1979) and then Chief of all intelligence services, took over the Interior Ministry in July 1981. The ascent of this subtle and senior political officer symbolised the final subordination of the police to the Army apparat, in spite of police rumblings which were most dramatically revealed by the Popiełuszko affair.

Apart from the WSW and the WOWewn, already men-tioned, the other internal defence formations directly subject to the Army are the 18-20,000 strong Border Defence Guards (WOP). Their functions go far beyond border defence proper and they have been used to combat anti-socialist opposition. They,like the KBW, were transferred from MSW to MON control in 1965. It is also apparent that particularly reliable military units, like Jaruzelski's old command, the Twelfth Mechanised Division in Szcecin (1957-1960), were assigned especially sensitive repressive tasks during martial law. Finally, Territorial Army Groups (TGO), modelled on the rough and ready military intervention teams of 1946-1947, and drawing on the experience of military involvement during the tumul-tuous popular-religious celebrations to mark Poland's Millenium in 1966, were organised in Autumn 1981. About 2,000 such 5-6 strong teams were sent into towns and communes in late October 1981. Somewhat more high-powered urban TGOs were sent into the 100 largest provincial centres and cities in late November and some Army Inspection Groups even des-cended on industrial enterprises for the first time. Their role was camouflaged under the attack on spe-culation, corruption and mismanagement which were popular themes under the conditions of consumer col-lapse in 1981. It was, however, primarily to pre-pare the terrain for the establishment of martial

law; their leaders then became key figures in the
new military administration as KOK plenipotentiaries
at the lower and middle levels in every sector. But
most of the dirty work of actual physical repression
was carried out by the MSW security formations, notably the 25,000 strong Motorised Units of the Citizens' Militia (ZOMO) supported by the reliable part
of the Volunteer Reserve Citizens' Militia (ORMO),
which had earlier been re-organised as the ROMO and
which was used as the back-up to the repressive ZOMO
spearhead. Lastly, the ordinary police, the Citizens'
Militia (MO), variously estimated as 70-100,000
strong, were used mainly for everyday policing, although their detailed local knowledge was drawn on
by the other bodies. The local MO commander, for
example, drew up the internment lists in 1981-1982.
Significantly Army reservists were not used directly,
although the most trustworthy had previously been
incorporated in the ROMO. The ZBZZ war veterans
competitor to ZBoWiD was given improved pensions and
promised greater opportunities for action within LOK
and its reserve-officer clubs. It helped the regular forces with sentry and propaganda duties during
martial law and its chairman, the retired Colonel
Roman Leś, became a member of WRON and then a Sejm
Deputy in 1985.

The three aspects of civil defence, territorial
defence and internal policing and counter-subversion
activities by the military have been interlinked very
ambiguously in Poland since 1956. The aspect of
territorial defence is particularly important as it
gives the domestic communist leadership the capacity
to suppress uprisings, which go beyond police capacities, without the need to call on external Soviet
or Warsaw Pact assistance. But, in theory, it could
also give nationally-minded communist leaders an
autonomous military capacity, directly controlled by
them and not by the WTO, with which to bargain, or
even to stand up to the Russians, as Gomułka did in
1956. This is a highly controversial issue as the
dominant Western tendency is to view military agencies as Soviet-controlled, régime transmission belts
and indoctrination and socialisation agencies.
What one should note in the Polish case is that a
variety of social and sub-para-military mass organisations, such as the League for the Defence of the
Country (LOK), the Aeroclub, the Maritime League and
the League of Volunteer Firemen (ZOSP), as well as
preparing for civil and territorial defence against
a Western enemy also have a potential organisational
capacity for resistance, under Hungarian 1956 type

circumstances, to a Soviet or WTO invasion. On
paper this organisational network goes far beyond
that of any other East European country except
Yugoslavia, Albania and Romania [74]. The Soviets,
however, warned by 1956 events, counteracted autono-
mist tendencies very strongly during the 1960s.
The evidence suggests that the anti-Soviet and
national-communist potential of such bodies was emas-
culated but at the price of often leaving them largely
as leadership-controlled husks.

Creating the 'Political Army'
     The educational and technical quality of the
Polish Officer Corps improved very considerably after
che December 1957 Law on Officers' Conditions of
Service. Poland now has a very developed network
of five Military Academies - the Świerczewski General
Staff Academy (ASG), the Dzierżyński Military-Poli-
tical Academy (WAP) and the Military-Technical
Academy (WAT) are based in Warsaw, while the Higher
Naval School (WSMW) is in Gdynia and the Military-
Medical Academy (WAM) is in Łódź. These can grant
degrees right up to the Habilitated Doctor level.
There are also 11 branch technical-specialist Higher
Officer Schools (WSOs) as well as schools for the
equivalent of NCOs. The evidence is that the Polish
Officer Corps has, over the last quarter of a century,
developed into a highly trained, highly qualified and
highly educated body in contrast to the pre-1957
generation, which has now been almost entirely pen-
sioned off. One should also note that the
Jaruzelski leadership cohort was born in the 1920s
and was therefore just old enough to experience the
Second World War and to commit itself to the new
postwar Polish order from the outset,but young enough
to be trained properly. The military educational
system, especially in medicine and engineering, is
held to be superior to its civilian equivalents,
while the Army has also formed its own School of
Social Sciences as a direct competitor to the civilian trend. Such figures always need to be viewed
with care but the percentage of the Officer Corps
with higher educational qualifications increased
from 12% in 1953,to 17% in 1958,to 25% in 1963, to
30% in 1968, to 40% in 1973 and was claimed to be
about 80% in 1980.
     As in all Eastern European Armies, though, tech-
nical military proficiency, skills and leadership
capacity have had to be combined with a strong ideological commitment to socialism. Malcher is right
to stress that two of Jaruzelski's most popular

77

slogans during the 1970s were 'Every officer a
.rained Marxist' and 'Every officer an expert in
political military matters'. Political Commissars
were originally trained at the Łódź Political-Edu-
cation School and its successors. It lost its central monopoly when a political stream was established
in the 8 main WSOs from 1970 onwards. The new
military graduates have combined military command
and political duty functions since then and rounded
off the post-1961 trend. This unusual development
has lessened the importance of the traditional forms
of civilian-party control which developed out of the
earlier Soviet-Leninist experience. Is this further
evidence in support of my argument that the Kremlin's
distrust of the post-1956 civilian party had paradoxical results in strengthening the autonomy of the
military arm? But the Polish officer's fundamental
loyalty to socialism and to the Soviet alliance was
guaranteed at the same time. The cream of the
Political Officer élite were the 9,000 odd postwar
WAP graduates. The curriculum was widened in the
1970s to include more Social Science studies in
economics, politics and sociology. It was also
made available as a conversion course for command-
technical WSO graduates with some line experience
who wished to turn themselves into fully fledged political officers. The conclusion one has to draw
is that the Army Academies produced a much larger
number of graduates than were required not just for
purely military purposes (the ASG and the specialised
schools would have sufficed), but even for the political control of the Armed Forces. One can only
speculate whether this was conscious policy designed
to produce a large pool of directing personnel who
would be available to run society as the USSR and
its orthodox Leninist allies had justified doubts
whether Gierek's PZPR could fulfil this function.
Or was it pure accident with an interest group ex-
panding and taking full advantage of circumstances?
At all events the model of the well educated, culturally broad-minded and technically able, but at the
same time committed Marxist-Leninist, Political
Officer with a capacity for political training and
party-political work and an insatiable desire to
work for socialism in walks of life outside the purely
military one emerged during the 1970s. It has been
estimated that over 33,000 soldiers had been seconded
to non-military jobs and occupations, such as local
councils, the National Unity Front, scientific establishments, youth and social movements, just before
martial law [75]. Large numbers of retired Army

officers also succeeded in making alternative careers
so the weight and penetration of the military into
all walks of Polish life was substantial even before
the crisis. As competitors with the graduates of
party schools and universities this new breed of
Major Magister (MA), Colonel Docent Doctor and even
General Professor, Doctor Habilitated felt self-
confident of their own capacities and a great con-
tempt for the mistakes and muddles of civilian
competitors.

As in all communist armies, there are two main
columns of political control, the political apparatus
and the party organisation, and a minor supporting
one composed of youth and other socialist organisations. The political apparatus is headed by the
Main Political Department (GZP) which, as well as
being a CC Department for all practical purposes, is
also controlled directly by MON. It is in fact
one of its Central Institutions. It is always given
second ranking after the General Staff, although it
may well have become the more influential body during
the last decade. The GZP is invariably headed by
a deputy Minister of Defence who eventually achieves
Corps-General rank. It came into its own during
Jaruzelski's tenure (1960-1965). Since then it has
been occupied by major military figures such as
Urbanowicz and Sawczuk. The post was occupied from
1980 to 1985 by the intellectually able and up and
coming General Doctor Habilitated Józef Baryła, who
was listed ninth in WRON membership. In late 1985
he became only the second Polish General, after
Jaruzelski, to enter the PZPR Secretariat when the
GZP post was taken over by his First Deputy, Tadeusz
Szaciło. The GZP controls all the Army's political,
cultural, social and external activities through a
number of functional directorates. It oversees
the political directorates in the three military
districts and in the service branches. It also
has a huge empire of facilities at its disposal;
the Military-Historical Institute (WIH), the largest
publishing house in Poland Wydawnictwo MON, the
academic quarterly Wojskowy Przegląd Historyczny,
the monthly Wojsko Ludowe, the weekly Żołnierz
Polski, the daily Żołnierz Wolności and a vast regional and specialist press. Through LOK and the local
political directorates it also controls a mass of
training, sporting, leisure, propaganda and social-
cultural facilities which reach into most walks of
Polish life. The GZP's main general task is to
inculcate in the Army the values of technical proficiency, Socialist Internationalism and pride in

the WTO, patriotism, socialist interpersonal rela-
_ions and to extend the military's relations with
society, especially into working-class, cultural and
intellectual circles,as well as to participate and
assist in the work of state bodies [76].

PZPR committees exist down to the regimental
level, while POPs are normally at the battalion level.
They are therefore quite large as they total about 80
members each. Party penetration of the Officer Corps
has increased from the low of 15% in 1945, 40% in
1949, 50% in 1953, 67% in 1958, 73% in 1963, 79% in
1968, up to its peak of 85% in the mid-1970s. It
was 83% in 1980 and was reported as falling back to
a questionable figure of 64% after the martial law
verifications and purges. What this means, in practice, is that all Generals and Colonels and most
Majors are PZPR members and have been so since the
1960s. The percentage of PZPR affiliation among
the regular soldiers reached 60% by 1972 and the
figure was even higher in the specialised branches.
The Navy in 1978 had 90% officer affiliation and a
staggering 70% of the entire regular section were in
the PZPR. The figures were a touch higher in the
artillery and rocketry branches and a bit lower in
the Air Force[77].But the paradox is that this high
degree of party penetration of the military has not
since 1968 resulted in the orthodox party control
which Kolkowicz and Brzezinski have described in
the Soviet case.   Officially the PZPR military is,
of course, a section of the party as a whole.   As
such it obeys Politburo and CC resolutions,which are
then amplified by MON and the GZP.   Jaruzelski was
the main military spokesman in the Politburo during
the 1970s.   The evidence is that Stanisław Kania,
the CC Secretary in charge of military matters in
the Administration Department, was an amenable collaborator and a bridge through his original patron,
Babiuch, to Gierek [78]. It was no doubt Jaruzelski's
support and advice to the Kremlin which gained Kania
the First Secretary's post on Gierek's fall.

The People's Army held four major National-
Ideological Conferences, attended by the whole of
the top military leadership, in 1973, 1976, 1978 and
1982 in order to define its ideological-educational
response to new political situations.   Ideological-
Education was given a very wide-ranging definition
in 1973 by GZP Head, Sawczuk.   It covered not only
national defence but also the country's political-
ideological education and the military's contribution to science and the economy.   Jaruzelski's
three priorities were loyalty to the PZPR, the

inculcation of socialist ideas and closer links
with the WTO and the Red Army. The Army's internal
role in protecting the domestic socialist order was
highlighted as being as important as its functions
of external defence against West German revanchism
and American Imperialism. The concept of the Army
as the School of the Nation quite literally training
thousands of soldiers as drivers, electricians,
mechanics and in other specialised trades was significant but another task was more important; this was
the schooling of both the soldier and the nation in
a hybrid patriotic, socialist internationalism. The
latter extended into inculcating military values and
traditions, discipline and respect for the socialist
order into young people, especially by incorporating
military training into the school and the university
curricula [79]. Jaruzelski always emphasised how
deeply rooted the Polish soldier was in society:
'He participates actively in the country's development processes, he stands in the front line of education and training, the economy and science in technology and culture' [80]. The overriding aim was to
define the Universal Obligation of the Defence of the
Fatherland in such a way as to enable the military
to maintain its internal cohesion and discipline and
to obey the orders of the PZPR officer cadre in the
event of its being needed for the repression of domestic subversion or of an uprising. Jaruzelski rejected a purely technical-military role for the Army.
Since the postwar civil war it had been 'an active
and committed agitator for the cause of socialism'
and for 'shaping the consciousness of society'. He
considered that 'the specific forms of the participation of the army of a new type in the life of the
nation, in building socialism, is dependent in equal
measure on the social-political situation in the
world and in the country and on the degree of internal development of that same Army' [81]. One can
only endorse Malcher's judgement that after the
Jaruzelski wing had repelled the Korczyński-Czapla
Partisan tendency by 1971-1972 every effort was
directed towards providing 'an excuse for unlimited
political indoctrination and justification for maintaining in the Army a huge political machine for
eventual use outside the Army' [82]. The Polish
military thus became a Frankenstein's monster as far
as the civilian party élite was concerned. They
needed the military in 1981 but could not be happy
that the shift in directing positions did not prove
as temporary as they had hoped. But the myth of
Jaruzelski's non-political involvement misled even

Table 2
Incumbents of the Main Military Posts

a. Ministers of National Defence

Żymierski, ('Rola'),		
Michał	1890-	1944-1949
Rokossowski, Konstanty	1896-1968	1949-1956
Spychalski, Marian	1906-1980	1956-1968
Jaruzelski, Wojciech	1923-	1968-1983
Siwicki, Florian	1925-	1983-

b. Chiefs of Staff

Spychalski, Marian	1906-1980	July-Sept.1944
Korzyc, Władysław	1893-1966	1944-1954*
Bordziłowski, Jerzy	1900-1983	1954-1965
Jaruzelski, Wojciech	1923-	1965-1968
Chocha, Bolesław	1923-	1968-1973
Siwicki, Florian	1925-	1973-1983
Użycki, Józef	1932-	1983-

* Korzyc was Chief of Staff in August 1944 and again from
December 1944 onwards. The post was filled by Bronisław
Połturzycki and Bolesław Zarako-Zarakowski in between.

c. Heads of Main Political Department (GZP)

Zawadzki, Aleksander	1899-1964	1944-1945
Spychalski, Marian	1906-1980	1945-1946
Kuszko, E.	?-1984	1946-1948*
Wągrowski, Mieczysław	1902-1967	1948-1950
Ochab, Edward	1906-	Jan.-June 1950
Naszkowski, Marian	1912-	1950-1952
Witaszewski, Kazimierz	1906-	1952-1956
Zarzycki, Janusz	1914-	1956-1960
Jaruzelski, Wojciech	1923-	1960-1965
Urbanowicz, Józef	1916-	1965-1971
Czapla, Jan	1925-	1971-1972
Sawczuk, Włodzimierz	1925-	1972-1980
Baryła, Józef	1924-	1980-1985
Szaciło, Tadeusz	1925-	1985-

* The 1944-1950 situation is unclear. Some sources claim
that Spychalski remained as the Head of the then Main
Political and Educational Deprtment until 1948, when
Kuszko took over.

acute commentators like Johnson into believing that
'the élite security units apart in the 1970s the
utility and the reliability of the military institution as an instrument of domestic repression appeared
to be quite low' [83]. Johnson, like Herspring,
discerned the modernisation tendencies which encouraged
political autonomy; but he regarded the political
officer in traditional terms as an instrument of
party control over the military, whereas in the 1970s
he became an autonomous actor and force. The reason
why the Polish military got away with it was because
they were the Soviet's best friend in Poland. They
gained considerable leverage within Gierek's régime,
which was only partially trusted by the Kremlin and
only tolerated by the Polish people after December
1970 for as long as it was mortgaging the country's
future in exchange for the consumer manna of the
early 1970s.

We now need to identify the main military leadership élite and to assess its political weight in the
civil-military relationship prior to martial law.
For peculiarly Polish reasons none of her major postwar leaders before Jaruzelski (Bierut, Gomułka and
Gierek) had any deep interest in military matters.
Ochab and Kania did but they proved to be political
stop-gaps. This factor facilitated the de facto
control of the Minister of Defence. Rokossowski
and Jaruzelski were more powerful figures than the
Home Communist Resistance leader, Spychalski, whose
lack of formal military training weakened his position in relation to his professional subordinates,
particularly as he was never fully trusted by Moscow.
His Marshal's baton was the butt of the normal round
of Warsaw jokes. A now half-forgotten figure,
Bordziłowski counterpoised him along with the likes
of Kufel, before Jaruzelski took over their roles
as the Guarantor of the Polish Army's loyalty to
Moscow.

As Table 2 shows, there have only been five
postwar Ministers of National Defence, seven Chiefs-
of-Staff since 1944 but a larger number of GZP Heads,
although only six since Jaruzelski took over in 1960.
Apart from Jaruzelski, who had his position as
Commander-in-Chief and KOK chairman confirmed in
November 1983, operational control of the Armed
Forces is, in practice, exercised by the Chief-of-
Staff,firstly Siwicki (1977-1983),and after that
Użycki. An important role has also been played
since 1971 by Corps-General Eugeniusz Molczyk as
deputy Defence Minister, Chief Inspector for Training
and Poland's WTO representative. The main military

Table 3
Deputy Ministers of Defence since 1970

Incumbent	Term	Other Posts
Chocha, Bolesław (b. 1923)	1968-1973	Chief of Staff 1968-1973. CC* 1968-1975.
+Tuczapski, Tadeusz (b. 1922)	1968-	Chief Inspector of Territorial Defence and Head of Civil Defence 1971-. CC* 1968-
Urbanowicz, Józef (b. 1916)	1968-1983	First deputy Minister 1971-. CC* 1968-1971. CC 1971-. SD 1965-1985. Ambassador to Mongolia 1983-.
+Molczyk, Eugeniusz (b. 1925)	1972-	Chief Inspector of Training 1972-. CC* 1971-.
+Siwicki, Florian (b. 1925)	1973-1983	Chief of Staff 1973-1983. Minister of Defence 1983-. CC* 1969-1975. CC 1975-. SD 1981-.
Sawczuk, Włodzimierz (b. 1925)	1975-1982	GZP Head 1972-1980. CC 1975-1981. SD 1976-1985.
Nowak, Zbigniew (b. 1926)	1976-	Chief Technical Inspector 1974-. CC* 1980-.
Obiedziński, Mieczysław (b. 1920)	1976-	Main Quartermaster-General 1970-. CC* 1980-.
+Baryła, Józef (b. 1924)	1980-1985	First deputy GZP Head 1972-1980. GZP Head 1980-1985. CC* 1975-1980. CC 1980-1981. CC* 1982-.
+Użycki, Józef (b. 1932)	1983-	Commander Pomeranian military district 1978-1983. Chief of Staff 1983-. SD 1980-.
Jasiński, Antoni (b. 1927)	1984-	First deputy Chief of Staff. SD 1985-.

Key: CC = Full Central Committee member. CC* = Central Committee candidate. + = WRON member. SD = Sejm Deputy. Date in brackets = date of birth.

leaders invariably become deputy Ministers of Defence.
The eleven since 1970, including the seven who were
still incumbent in 1985, are set out in Table 3.
Jaruzelski's main lieutenants in running the
Army have been Siwicki as Chief-of-Staff and now
Minister of Defence, Tuczapski as Head of Territorial
and Civil Defence and Molczyk as Inspector of Training. More recently, Baryła rose to prominence as
GZP Head and then CC Secretary. The main autonomous
figure was Sawczuk, the GZP Head in the 1970s, while
an increasingly lone figure from another historical
period is Quartermaster-General Obiedziński, who is
a rehabilitated victim of the 1950s' purges.
Jaruzelski's éminence grise and informal deputy in
the 1970s was Józef Urbanowicz, who was of Latvian
and Red Army background, and a decade older than
the Jaruzelski cohort. Whether his appointment as
ambassador to Mongolia in 1983 represented an
honourable form of semi-retirement is unclear.
The contemporary Generals like Kiszczak, Hupałowski,
Piotrowski and Oliwa, not to mention the mass of
Colonels, who played key roles in running the communist system since 1982, on the other hand owe
everything to Jaruzelski. They are representative
of a fairly homogeneous Officer Corps, about four-
fifths of whom claimed to be of worker or peasant
background and only 2% of whom, by the early 1970s,
had any prewar military experience (Polityka, 29
April 1972).

Only Spychalski and Jaruzelski have held all
three of the main military posts in People's Poland
(see Table 2). But the latter's tenure of all three
was longer and firmer and this certainly gave him
an unquestioned range of experience and authority.
Allied with his prestige gained by his role during
the State of War, the KOK institutional arrangements
and his balanced leadership style in both civilian
and military spheres, one cannot expect a credible
military rival to emerge in the foreseeable future
[84].

If we now turn to the question of military representation on party and state bodies we find that
Jaruzelski and Baryła have been the only serving
officers to enter the CC Secretariat. Only
Rokossowski, Spychalski and Jaruzelski have become
full Politburo members, while Kiszczak and Siwicki
have become candidate members. At the 1981 Ninth
Congress the military, who had 125 out of 1,964
delegates, ended up with four full CC members plus
Żymierski and five candidates. This did not differ
markedly from the five full and six candidate members

elected in February 1980, the four full and five
candidates elected in 1975 and the three full and
six candidate members elected in 1971.   Between five
and seven Generals were elected to each Sejm between
1957 and 1976; the military Deputies re-elected
in 1980 were Jaruzelski, Urbanowicz, Sawczuk, Siwicki,
Oliwa and Admiral Janczyszyn, while the newcomers were
military district commanders Rapacewicz and Użycki.
In the Sejm elections of 13 October 1985 the Generals
got amongst the lowest personal votes on the National
List of fifty.   Kiszczak (96.89%) had the lowest
vote after Rakowski, Barcikowski and Gucwa, Jaruzelski
had the sixth lowest personal vote (97.25%), while
Siwicki had only a touch better [85].   The other
Deputies were elected in 74 multi-member constituen-
cies with each 'favoured' candidate being opposed by
another.   The military representatives to emerge
were Jerzy Skalski (Warsaw MD Commander, 96.3%),
Baryła (94.68%), Janczyszyn (91.66%), Łozowicki
(96.97%), Jasiński (94.45%), Paszkowski (Katowice
Wojewoda, 97.25%) and Łukasik (Poznań PZPR First
Secretary, 94.83%).

Although many military men had entered the
state administration,at both local and national
levels, immediately postwar, serving officers were
largely restricted to MON in the 1956-1980 period.
An exception at ministerial level was the WAT Com-
mandant, General Professor Sylwester Kaliski, who
headed Science, Higher Education and Training from
1974 to 1977.   The Warsaw Military District Commander, General Zygmunt Huszcza, was nominated as
deputy Minister of Education in 1972 in order to
strengthen the military's role and values in the
educational system.   In due course he was replaced
by ex-GZP Head Jan Czapla, another Partisan, who
had previously been an Under-Secretary of State in
the MSZ.   Another early 1970s deputy Minister was
the ex Air Force commander Jan Raczkowski at Transport.
From 1981 onwards more Generals were appointed to
head Ministries: notably Kiszczak at the Interior,
Piotrowski at Mining, Hupałowski at Territorial
Administration and then NIK, after which his former
post was taken over by Oliwa.   Various military men
naturally became deputy Ministers and Departmental
Heads and Wojewodas during martial law [86].   The
military infiltration into party posts was not as
marked as into the state administration, though.
According to the Head of the CC Cadres Department, a
mere 103 serving officers had been given leave of
absence during martial law, in order to take over
directing positions - six in the Council of Ministers,

two as KW First Secretaries, ten as Wojewodas, 14
as large factory managers and 22 as CPA functionaries
(General Dziekan, Polityka, 19 November 1983).
These low and misleading figures naturally underestimate the influence of reserve officers, of KOK
plenipotentiaries and the crucial weight of
Jaruzelski and the WRON hardcore.

The system of military rule and the rebuilding
of the PZPR are examined in Chapters Four and Five.
This survey of the postwar development of the communist armed forces in Poland leads to the following
conclusions: The replacement of the direct control
of the Polish Army through seconded Red Army officers
during the 1943-1956 period began in 1956. The
Jaruzelski cohort finally won out against its more
Home Communist and resistance rivals by the early
1970s. This group of professionally capable military specialists, then, also gained a striking degree
of political autonomy. Jaruzelski and the new type
of political-military functionary effectively replaced the traditional politruk role of being the
party's watchdog over the Army with a major function
of political socialisation which turned into a full-
blown Guardian role over the system after 1980. The
latter had developed from 1967 onwards and was cast
in terms of the Law on the Universal Obligation to
Defend the Country. It provided the basis for the
KOK framework and for the internal-defensive capacity of the Army centred around the OTK-OCK and the
para-military formations. The Polish military was
thus endowed with a fearsome capacity for internal
intervention and repression which it utilised effectively during the State of War from December 1981
onwards. But the term 'political officer' by the
1970s came to have a meaning that went far beyond
its original politruk connotations. Sufficient of
the 60,000 odd Polish officers, particularly of the
200 Generals and 3,500 Colonels, were not directly
needed for operational-military purposes in the
'external' section of the Army assigned to the WTO
to play crucial political and administrative roles
within the system. The Partisan legacy was that
Jaruzelski co-opted its drive to socialise the Poles
in its hybrid form of military-nationalist and
socialist-internationalist (i.e. pro-Soviet) values.
By the time of the 1980-1981 crisis the effective
collapse of the PZPR outer ring undermined Kania's
CPA and opened up the way for the replacement of
discredited civilian, with more effective and determined military, functionaries. The soldiers in
1982 both took over party-state posts directly and

Communist armed forces in Poland

provided a new directing layer of control through
the WRON-KOK and military commissioner system.   This
Army-State proved temporary but it broke the opposition, came to terms with the Church, gradually rebuilt the old CP system and developed a new National
Front framework of Patriotic Renewal.   With the lifting of the State of War in Summer 1983 there was a
general reversion to normal Soviet-Leninist methods
of party rule,even though the state-society split
remained as wide as ever.   Jaruzelski and a significant number of military functionaries remained
embedded as key figures in the new system.   This
demonstrated, in an extreme form, the capacity of
the political apparatus of communist armies to
produce a hardcore of ideologically reliable and professionally capable functionaries.   They could act
as an alternative set of politico-administrative
leaders to the civilian apparatchiks if this were
functionally required by the communist system.

Notes

1.   Cf. J.J. Wiatr, 'The public image of the Polish Mili-
     tary' in C.M. Kelleher (ed.), Political-Military
     Systems. Comparative perspectives (London, Sage, 1974),
     pp. 199-207.
2.   I can confirm the point from personal experience during
     my year of postgraduate studies at Warsaw University
     in 1965-1966, and subsequently.
3.   Andrzej Garlicki, U źródeł obozu belwederskiego (Warsaw,
     PWN, 1979) and Przewrót Majowy (Warsaw, Czytelnik, 1979).
     See also Andrzej Ajnenkiel, Polska po przewrocie Majowym.
     Zarys dziejów politycznych Polski 1926-1939 (Warsaw,
     Wiedza Powszechna, 1980).
4.   George Sakwa, 'The Franco-Polish Alliance and the Re-
     militarisation of the Rhineland', The Historical Journal,
     XVI, No. 1 (1973), pp. 125-146; 'The "Renewal" of the
     Franco-Polish Alliance in 1936 and the Rambouillet
     Agreement', Polish Review, XVI, No. 2 (Spring 1971),
     pp. 45-66; 'The Polish Ultimatum to Lithuania in March
     1938', Slavonic & East European Review, LV, No. 2 (April
     1977), pp. 204-226.   Beck was not as emotionally com-
     mitted to the French Alliance as his predecessor, Auguste
     Zaleski.   His attempts to 'balance' were much resented
     by the French.   This does not mean that he took Poland
     into the German camp, as claimed by his domestic oppo-
     nents and some communist historians.
5.   Władysław Gomułka,Przemówienia 1959 (Warsaw, KiW, 1960),
     pp. 412-418.
6.   Bromke, Poland's Politics, Part Two.

Communist armed forces in Poland

7. J. Gęsek, S. Szostkiewicz & J.J. Wiatr, 'Z badań opinii społeczeństwo o wojsku', Studia Socjologiczno-Polityczne, No. 13 (1962), p. 121.
8. 'Społeczne zaufanie do instytucji politycznych, społecznych i administracyjnych' (Warsaw, OBOP, May 1981). See D.S. Mason, Public Opinion and Political Change in Poland, 1980-1982 (Cambridge U.P., 1984), p. 118.
9. Wiatr estimates that 2 Army-Generals, 10 Lieutenant-Generals and 33 Major-Generals originated from the Austrian Army. The proportions of those of Russian Army origins were 0-5-32, the Legions' proportions were 1-3-7, while the German Army's figures were a mere 0-1-1: J. Wiatr in J. Van Doorn (ed.), Armed Forces and Society (The Hague, Mouton, 1968), p. 232.
10. See Piotr Stawecki's study of military penetration of the interwar state-administration in Wojskowy Przegląd Historyczny (1965, No. 3).
11. For texts, Józef Beck, Dernier Rapport. Politique Polonaise, 1926-1939 (Neuchatel, La Baconnière, 1951), pp. 329-330, 345-346.
12. The figure excludes reserve officers. Ithiel de Sola Pool, Satellite Generals. A study of military élites in the Soviet sphere (Stanford U.P., 1956), p. 57.
13. Jan Ciechanowski, The Warsaw Rising of 1944 (Cambridge U.P., 1974).
14. Fryderyk Zbiniewicz, Armia Polska w ZSSR (Warsaw, MON, 1963).
15. Cf. Jan Nowak, 'Sprawa Generała Berlinga', Zeszyty Historyczne, No. 37 (Paris, 1976), pp. 39-60.
16. Wacław Jurgieliewicz et al., Ludowe Wojsko Polskie 1943-1945 (Warsaw, MON, 1973), pp. 36-37, 69.
17. Ibid., p. 88.
18. Gomułka's 1943-1945 speeches are full of praise for the PPR inspired AL resistance effort against the Germans. Artykuły i Przemówienia, Vol. 1 (Styczeń 1943-grudzień 1945), (Warsaw, KiW, 1962).
19. For an interesting reassessment of the role of the Communist Resistance in relation to the Eastern Front Army, see Zygmunt Duszyński & Jan Zamojski, 'PPR organizatorem walki zbrojnej narodu Polskiego w wojnie wyzwoleńczej' in W. Góra (ed.), PPR w walce o niepodległość i władzę ludu (Warsaw, KiW, 1963). See also Zbigniew Załuski, Finał 1945 (Warsaw, MON, 1963).
20. Korbonski, 'The Polish Army' in J. Adelman (ed.), Communist Armies in Politics (Boulder, Col., Westview Press, 1982), p. 125.
21. Krasnaya Zvezda, 11 May 1975.
22. Wojsko Ludowe, No. 9 (1973), p. 42, and No. 4 (1977), p. 74.
23. Kto jest kim w Polsce (Warsaw, Interpress, 1984), pp. 898-899.

Communist armed forces in Poland

24. Maria Turlejska, Z walk przeciwko zbrojnemu podziemiu 1944-1947 (Warsaw, MON, 1966). Tadeusz Walichnowski, U źródeł walk z podziemiem reakcyjnym w Polsce (Warsaw, KiW, 1975 & 1985).
25. VII Plenum KC PZPR, 24-25 lutego 1982r (Warsaw, KiW, 1982), p. 18.
26. Leszek Grot, 'Działania Ludowego Wojska Polskiego przeciwko zbrojnemu podziemniu w latach 1944-1947', Wojskowy Przegląd Historyczny, XVIII, No. 3 (July-September 1973), p. 496. M. Leczyk in Wojsko Ludowe (1982, No. 3), p. 65.
27. Wojsko Ludowe (1973, No. 9), p. 58. A Bliss Lane, I saw Poland betrayed (Indianapolis, Bobbs-Merrill, 1948). Stanisław Mikołajczyk, The Pattern of Soviet Domination (London, Sampson Low, 1948).
28. Michał Chęciński in J. Adelman (ed.), Terror and Communist Politics (Boulder, Col., Westview Press, 1984), pp. 21-23.
29. Cf. Zbigniew Załuski, Przepustka do Historii (Warsaw, MON, 1967).
30. Kazimierz Frontczak, Siły Zbrojne Polski Ludowej (Warsaw, MON, 1974), pp. 333-335, 366.
31. Józef Graczyk, Problemy socjologiczne Ludowego Wojska Polskiego (Warsaw, MON, 1972), p. 73.
32. Chęciński in Adelman, Terror and Communist Politics, p. 27. See Mieczysław Szerer, 'Komisja do badania odpowiedzialności za łamanie praworządności w sądownictwie wojskowym', Zeszyty Historyczne, No. 49 (Paris, 1979), pp. 71-160.
33. Chęciński, op. cit., p. 25.
34. Pool, Satellite Generals, p. 69.
35. Korbonski, 'Polish Army' in Adelman, Communist Armies in Politics, pp. 104 ff.
36. Krushchev Remembers. The last testament, trans. & ed. by S. Talbott (London, Penguin, 1977), p. 218.
37. Kubiak Report, pp. 28-29.
38. Cf. Marian K. Dziewanowski, The Communist Party of Poland (Cambridge, Mass., Harvard U.P., 2nd rev. edn., 1976), pp. 272-274.
39. Syrop, Spring in October. The story of the Polish revolution 1956, op. cit. Zenobiusz Kozik, PZPR w latach 1954-1957 (Warsaw, PWN, 1982).
40. ND, 10/88 (October 1956), p. 157 for the voting figures, pp. 145-150 for the debate.
41. See communiqué in TL, 19 November 1956, for the main principles later embodied in the Treaty. Stosunki Polsko-Radzieckie w latach 1945-1972 (Warsaw, KiW, 1974), pp. 338-344. Also Paul Zinner, National Communism and Popular Revolt in Eastern Europe (New York, Columbia U.P.,1956), pp. 306-313.

42. George Sakwa, 'Jews and the Polish power struggle', Soviet Jewish Affairs, XI, No. 3 (1981), pp. 72-76.
43. Chęciński, op. cit., pp. 43 ff.
44. A. Ross Johnson, A.R. Dean & A. Alexiev, East European Military Establishments. The northern tier (New York, Crane-Russak, 1980), p. 46. Josef Banas, The Scapegoats. The exodus of the remnants of Polish Jewry (London, Weidenfeld & Nicolson, 1979), pp. 86 ff.
45. Korbonski, 'The Polish Army', p. 117.
46. Confusion easily arises between British and American practice in describing the various grades of General. I have therefore adopted the East European practice in this study, however odd it might strike Anglo-Saxon readers: Brigade-General (One Star), Division-General (Two Star), Corps-General (Three Star, General Broni), Army-General (Four Star) and Marshal.
47. Kubiak Report, pp. 39-44. Korczyński very conveniently died as ambassador to Algeria soon afterwards.
48. Cf. Ivan Volgyes, 'Military policies of the Warsaw Pact Armies' in Morris Janowitz (ed.), Civil-Military Relations. Regional perspectives (London, Sage, 1981).
49. A. Korbonski & S. Terry, 'The Military as political actor in Poland' in R. Kolkowicz & A. Korbonski, Soldiers, Peasants and Bureaucrats (London, Allen & Unwin, 1982).
50. Dale R. Herspring, 'Technology and Civil-Military Relations; the Polish and East German cases' in D.R. Herspring & I. Volgyes (eds.), Civil-Military Relations in Communist Systems (Boulder, Col., Westview Press, 1978), pp. 123-124.
51. Richard F. Staar, Poland. Sovietisation of a captive people (Baton Rouge, University of Louisiana Press, 1962), pp. 134-138.
52. Jaruzelski in Włodzimierz Sawczuk (ed.), Ludowe Wojsko Polskie (Warsaw, MON, 1974).
53. A. Ross Johnson, 'Soviet military policy inEastern Europe' in Terry, Soviet Policy in Eastern Europe, p. 269.
54. M. Pohoski, K. Słomczyński & W. Wesołowski, 'Occupational prestige in Poland', Polish Sociological Bulletin (1976, No. 4), pp. 70-75.
55. Adam Sarapata, 'Iustum pretium', Studia Socjologiczne (1962, No. 3), p. 106.
56. Wojciech Jaruzelski, 'Ludowe Wojsko Polskie' in XX Lecie Polskie Ludowej (Warsaw, 1964), p. 205.
57. Roman Budny in J. Wiatr (ed.), Z badań nad zawodem oficera (Wrocław, Ossolineum, 1966).
58. See Military Balance, 1981-1982 (London, IISS, 1981).
59. Michael Sadykiewicz, 'Jaruzelski's War', Survey, XXVI, No. 3 (Summer 1982), pp. 19-20. On the prewar Polish Army, Eugeniusz Kozłowski, Wojsko Polskie 1936-1939 (Warsaw, MON, 1964), p. 323.
60. Malcher, Poland's Politicised Army, p. 20.
61. Ibid., p. 9.

62. Jones, Soviet Influence in Eastern Europe, p. 120.
63. Ibid., pp. 94-95.
64. See Wacław Stankiewicz, Socjalistyczna myśl wojenno-ekonomiczna (Warsaw, MON, 1972). Henryk Michalski, 'Polska socjalistyczna myśl wojskowa 1942-1973', Wojsko Ludowe (October 1973), pp. 28-34.
65. B. Chocha, Obrona Terytorium kraju (Warsaw, MON, 1965 & 1974).
66. Johnson, East European Military Establishments, pp. 29-32.
67. Konstytucja PRL (Warsaw, KiW, 1976), p. 32. For the legal-constitutional framework, see Wacław Dawidowicz, Zagadnienia ustroju administracji państwowej w Polsce (Warsaw, PWN, 1970), pp. 155-158.
68. DzU, 1967, No. 44, pos. 220. It was publicised in a mass run with accompanying commentary, O Powszechnym Obowiązku Obrony PRL (Warsaw, MON, 1968).
69. Jaroszewicz had after all been the main Political Commissar of the First Polish Army in 1944 and a deputy Minister of Defence 1945-1950 before becoming deputy Premier from 1952 to 1970. He achieved Division-General's rank in 1950. As well as being Premier he was the ZBoWiD chairman in the 1970s. Such a man need have no qualms about being interned in 1982. See Kto jest kim w Polsce, pp. 334-335. Incidentally, was Jaroszewicz the irremovable minister protected by Soviet influence in Stefan Kisielewski's (Tomasz Staliński, pseud.), Widziane z góry (Paris, Instytut Literacki, 1967).
70. Edward Gierek, O Wojsku i Obronności (Warsaw, MON, 1974).
71. Cf. Jerzy Muszyński, Wojsko Ludowe (1983, No. 5), pp. 45-46.
72. Malcher, Poland's Politicised Army, p. 164.
73. Chęciński in Adelman, Terror and Communist Politics, pp. 21 ff.
74. Mały Rocznik Statystyczny 1982 (Warsaw, GUS, 1982), p. 20, gives the following membership figures: LOK ran sports, shooting, para-military training and driving instruction clubs. It claimed a fantastic, and one suspects largely inert, membership of 1.98 million. One also blinks at the thought of 4.84 million Poles leaving their queues to support the Red Cross! More credibly, ZOSP had 547,000 and ZBoWiD 651,000.
75. S. Malinowski, Wojsko Ludowe (1981, No. 5), p. 60.
76. Doroba, Wojsko Ludowe (1976, No. 3), pp. 55-59.
77. Malcher, op. cit., p. 44.
78. Kto jest kim w Polsce, p. 368; TL, 17 April 1971 and 20 July 1981, for Kania's official biographies. Kania had been CC Administration Department Head in charge of Military Questions from 1968 to 1971. At that time Jaruzelski was still outside the Politburo, the only time in the PRL's history when a Minister of Defence was

in this isolated position.   One can speculate whether
Kania thus effectively became Jaruzelski's tame political
spokesman and linkman with the CPA run by Gierek's main
lieutenant and Kania's original patron, Babiuch.

79.   Walerian Magoń, 'Funkcje Sił Zbrojnych w budownictwie
      rozwiniętego społeczeństwa socjalistycznego' in
      M. Michalik (ed.), Budownictwo rozwiniętego społeczeństwa
      socjalistycznego (Warsaw, MAN, 1979).
80.   Jaruzelski, 'Trzydziestolecie zwycięstwa', Wojsko Ludowe
      (1975, No. 6), p. 10.
81.   Jaruzelski, 'Istota klasowa i nowa rola armii w
      społeczeństwie socjalistycznym', Problemy Pokoju i
      Socjalizmu (1975, No. 7), pp. 38-39.
82.   Malcher, op. cit., p. 52.
83.   Johnson, East European Military Establishments, p. 55.
84.   See G. Sanford, 'Poland', in M. McCauley & S. Carter
      (eds.), Leadership and Succession in the Soviet Union,
      Eastern Europe and China (London, Macmillan, 1986),
      pp. 62-63.
85.   'Obwieszczenie Państwowej Komisji Wyborczej z dnia 15
      października 1985r', TL, 16 October 1985.
86.   In 1983, apart from the usual six Generals in MON only
      the perennial Czapla at Education, Kołatkowski at Trans-
      port, the Generals in the MSW and Janiszewski in the
      Government Bureau were military deputy Ministers.
      There were also three Generals as Director-Generals in
      the Planning Commission, Administration and the Govern-
      ment Bureau while, hardly surprisingly, a General headed
      the War Veterans Office.   The military Wojewodas
      were in Warsaw City, Elbląg, Gdańsk, Kalisz, Katowice,
      Koszalin, Radom, Siedlce, Tarnobrzeg and Zielona Góra.

Chapter Three

THE MILITARY AND THE 1980-1981 CRISIS

The prevalent view is that the Army, especially
its Officer Corps, remained largely untouched by the
social and political unrest of the Solidarity period
of 1980-1981. Quite the contrary: along with the
police and the Procuracy, it was regarded as Solidarity's main enemy and critic. The crisis, however,
unleashed considerable internal criticism and what
seemed to be a political and generational conflict
within the Officer Corps. There are therefore two
large topics for discussion in this chapter. Firstly,
how was the Army affected internally by the Solidarity period? Secondly, what was the role of the
military leadership in the politics of the period?
Malcher suggests that a conflict arose during
1980-1981 between line officers and the party-military wing. He also speculates about whether the
latter were in favour of the military repression of
Solidary while the former were opposed, if only because they would actually have to do the dirty work
[1]. Both suggestions stretch the evidence more
than is warranted. What happened in the military,
as in the civilian,POPs was that the ordinary grassroots members found themselves licensed to criticise
the ideological, organisational and personal shortcomings of the political committees, executives and
functionaries of the Gierek period. The balance of
Democratic Centralism therefore shifted as a result
of the official acceptance of the slogan of Socialist
Renewal. As always in post-1956 Poland, the element
of job-seeking and of straightforward letting off of
steam against authorities was very strong, even in a
normally disciplined body like the military.
Numerous party meetings and conferences were held
by the PZPR military groups between Gdańsk and the
Ninth Congress. As in the civilian party, a wide
range of postulates for change and reform was

presented. The GZP and the General Staff after weeding and collating them down drastically presented 1,685 to a Co-ordinating Committee within MON [2]. Most demands were concerned with bread and butter aspects of the Army's organisation, remuneration and advancement prospects,personnel matters (about 20%) or the covert line-officer protest against having technical duties interrupted by political-ideological training and demands. But a significant number paralleled the civilian party slogan of the return to Leninist norms. Guarantees were demanded against deformations. So was a settlement of accounts with the mistakes and personnel of the Gierek era. What was required was a greater degree of accountability and freer discussion in future. Such pressures should logically have affected the incumbent military leader of the 1970s. Jaruzelski himself had, however, carefully maintained his public distance from Gierek. The main attack was therefore diverted against the 1970s' GZP Head, Włodzimierz Sawczuk, who was replaced by the intellectually more flexible Józef Baryła in 1980. In late 1985 Baryła became only the second Polish officer to become a PZPR CC Secretary. Suggestions for splitting the military-party organisation away from its civilian counterpart and for establishing a separate Political Committee for the Army were mooted but rejected. All this reflected the Army's determined attempt to dissociate itself from the mistakes of Gierek's civilian wing. It was also an implied form of blackmail that a hardline alternative to the party CC would always be available if the latter became too reformist. The top military hierarchy, however, succeeded in directing the sharp edge of criticism against such harmless aspects as the inadequacies of ideological education and propaganda in the Army. A samokrytyka by military propagandists was carried out at a Warsaw conference in May 1981 [3]. But the 1980-1981 mood, inevitably, also produced attacks on internally bureaucratic arrangements such as the excessive use of competitions, directives and instructions from the top. Such internal pressures within the Armed Forces were therefore genuine enough and potential causes of volatility and instability. But Jaruzelski managed to co-opt the drive for Socialist Renewal to his own purposes. He re-established internal discipline in the campaign against Solidarity and the anti-socialist opposition after the Ninth Congress. By September 1981 the classical distinction between constructive and negative criticism had been re-introduced. The mistakes of individuals such as Sawczuk within the GZP for supporting Gierek's 'propaganda of success' were very carefully distinguished from the soundness of the institution itself [4].

To say that the Army was affected by Socialist Renewal to the extent of questioning individuals in party-political functions and some of its internal arrangements is a far cry from arguing that it caught the Solidarity virus in any way. Long years of ideological and political training, military discipline and temperament and sheer self-interest rendered the Officer Corps, particularly senior and middle levels, largely immune. The military aktyw heard Baryła formulate the welcome thesis, at the GZP Ideological-Theoretical Conference of late January 1981, that the Army had already put its own house in order in the 1970s. It had remained in a good Marxist-Leninist condition and avoided deformations, by implication because of the vigilance of the Jaruzelski leadership; so Socialist Renewal had a very limited meaning for the Army, unlike what was necessary for the party and the state. There was no need for any basic structural overhaul of the military. All that was required was the improvement of existing procedures and organisations [5]. The political officers' counter-attack pointed rather smugly to the Army's successful promotion of ideological and political work among soldiers during the 1970s; this enabled it to maintain its unity, discipline and morale during the difficult days of 'August'. The general self-congratulatory message from the top was that only the civilian party, not the military, had deviated from the PZPR's Sixth Congress line formulated in December 1971, although some minor shortcomings needed to be put right. On the other hand, there was also no doubt that most officers had learnt from the dramatic changes in official line following all Poland's upheavals since 1956 not to commit themselves too deeply until the situation had definitely clarified itself. The mass of the Army was therefore, arguably, passive and dominated by a wait-and-see attitude until after the Ninth Congress, in spite of the official pronouncements of its spokesmen. This perhaps explains Jaruzelski's search for allies elsewhere, notably among War Veterans. The establishment of an Association of ex-Army Officers (ZBZZ) in February 1981, which was expanded into a regional network with 22,000 members by the Summer, offset the more police, ex-partisan and nationalist dominated ZBoWiD. Information about the loyalty and the state of

mind of the conscripted section of the Army is much
more difficult to elucidate. The Autumn 1980 intake was inevitably affected, both as participants
and observers. It was conceded officially that
passionate slogans and ideas had thus entered the
Army barracks and that fresher, more realistic
political-instruction methods were necessary. Although it was possible to quarantine conscripts from
general developments to some extent, it was difficult to impose discipline at a time of Socialist
Renewal when criticism was sponsored from the very
top. Fears that the Autumn 1981 intake would be
completely unmanageable as they, both workers and
peasants, might have become Solidarity and Rural
Solidarity members and would certainly have participated in anti-PZPR demonstrations and strikes
were expressed at the Warsaw Military District's
plenary session in August 1981 [6]. The political
officers were therefore directed to pay particular
attention to the problems of newly inducted conscripts. In the event the term of service of
existing conscripts was extended by three months in
Autumn 1981. The problem could only be postponed,
however; the extent to which the 1982 intake had
succumbed to religious and Solidarity influences
and their distrust of the martial law authorities
was admitted intra muros by the commander of one of
the Army's best formations, the Twelfth Mechanised
Division [7]. In the nature of things conscripts
reflected the characteristics of their age-cohort.
As such about half must have belonged to Solidarity.
Polls carried out amongst soldiers in 1979 and 1980
also confirmed the high degree of religious belief
amongst both conscripts and regular lower-level
ranks and the general inefficacy of atheist propaganda [8].
     The military's role in the political events of
Summer 1980 to December 1981 was monopolised by a
small group of political Generals headed by Jaruzelski.
Their activities can be divided into two sub-periods,
before and after Jaruzelski became Chairman of the
Council of Ministers in February 1981. In the first
phase the military tended to react to events and
issues as they arose. In the second phase they
played an increasingly more active role,which culminated in Jaruzelski's appointment as PZPR First
Secretary in mid-October 1981 and in the State of War
two months later.
     Jaruzelski played a crucial role in two of the
key decisions of August to September 1980. The evidence is that the Polish Army ruled out the possibility

of military repression of the Baltic seacoast
Workers' Upsurge. They endorsed a peaceful,
negotiated outcome which confirmed the Social
Agreements at the PZPR Fifth Plenum. The main
considerations were not so much a patriotic refusal
to risk civil war or ethical morality but a hard-
headed awareness of the scale and intensity of opposition, the likely costs involved in suppressing it,
and even the uncertainty of what the conscripts or
junior line officers might do in such a situation.
The military also hate to embark on any enterprise
which has not been thought out carefully and prepared for beforehand; the fear that events might
escalate and that they might get out of hand spon-
taneously was paramount. The second main decision
concerned Gierek's dismissal and replacement by Kania.
The latter had to some extent been the military's
spokesman within the CPA proper. He was now endorsed
by Jaruzelski as his candidate against the livelier,
more intelligent, more determined and more unpredictable Olszowski [9].

Jaruzelski did not declare himself openly at
these party forums until the renewed Sixth Plenum in
early October. He declared that the Army was doing
a difficult job and stressed that the soldiers would
maintain their traditional unity with the nation.
He rejected attacks against the Army for its alleged
privileges. But the important issue for him as a
soldier was the protection of Poland's frontiers and
independence. Both depended on domestic stabilisation and Soviet support [10]. The initial military
line was therefore to accept the justified character
of the workers' protest against deformations and the
need to rebuild the state's authority by remedying
mistakes and abuses [11]. The military leaders kept
a very low profile during the Autumn on specific
issues such as Solidarity's registration. But the
military press was full of warnings about the threat
to Poland's international position and alliances caused
by anti-socialist elements who were taking advantage
of the ferment. The full military line only emerged
publicly at the PZPR Seventh Plenum of 1-2 December
1980. This took place at a time of rumours of imminent Soviet invasion following the Naroźniak crisis.
By then the Polish military leaders had had time
to consult with the Soviet Marshals. The sole military spokesman at the Seventh Plenum was GZP Head,
Baryła. He led an official counterattack on the
negative and destructive aspects of the Autumn crisis.
The priority was to rebuild the PZPR's leading role
so that it could lead the Socialist Renewal. The

military were not prepared to accept the critical
attitudes within the civilian party. They were
most concerned by the collapse of its morale.   It
was as though the PZPR membership 'had lost the feeling of its historical and political raison d'être'.
For Baryła the time had now come for an open 'political struggle with the opponents of the system,
with irresponsible extremists, about the socialist
direction of our country's renewal'.   A particularly
important sector was the ideological one.   The attempt to eliminate Marxist philosophy from the teaching of University Social Sciences should be resisted;
the mass media should be disciplined.   But the long-
term significance of his speech was, not so much
the stock warnings against NATO subversion and the
attempts to dismantle the socialist state from
within, as the priority which Baryła ascribed to
maintaining the Army's combat readiness defined in
terms of the universal obligation to defend the
country. 'The ideological-political activities
undertaken by us serve the many sided improvement
of the armed forces, the basic unit of the country's
defence.   We are particularly sensitive about this
matter.   We are especially aware of the fact that
shaking the stability of our socialist state, its
economic balance, anarchy, chaos and lawlessness
may create the threat of a counter-revolution, a
danger to the country's defence capacities.   No
soldier can be neutral in regard to such phenomena'
[12].   Baryła therefore served notice on
Jaruzelski's behalf to both the PZPR and society
that the anti-Soviet Leninist tide must be stemmed.
     Baryła's battlecry at the party forum was then
transmitted downwards by the party committees of the
service branches and the military districts during
December.   The Navy meeting considered that, while
military orders were sacrosanct, what was also needed
was more concern for the sailors' problems and conditions of service.   So was more accurate information and a more direct and less hectoring style at
party meetings in order to narrow the distance between
the leadership and the ranks.   The briefing in the
Silesian military district highlighted four main
areas of struggle.   The first was to expose the
anti-socialist and counter-revolutionary threat.
Soldiers' resistance to hostile propaganda should be
built up by emphasising how the Soviet alliance
served Polish raison d'état.   An ominous stress was
also placed on the role of the Army Security Service
and the MO.   The second was to develop the awareness
of Poland's frontier and security interests and again

to spell out how they were protected by Soviet support and the WTO. Thirdly, the military pledged its support to the PZPR programme of Socialist Renewal. Lastly, any ideological and political indiscipline was to be stamped on but all legitimate work grievances were to be alleviated promptly and in full [13].

It is significant that the PZPR Eighth Plenum on 9 February 1981 confirmed the military hardline. But Western journalists fell into the Polish misinformation trap; they tended to present Jaruzelski's appointment as Premier as 'a masterstroke putting the cap on the failure of the alleged hardline offensive to capture the CPA and to overawe society' [14]. Grabski's hardline call for the PZPR to halt antisocialist developments, especially in the TU sector, was balanced by Barcikowski's emphasis on the need to implement reforms and to fulfil the Social Agreements. The Plenum resolution declared that the main reasons for the insufficient implementation of the Sixth Plenum line of Socialist Renewal was that it was 'threatened mainly by the forces of the enemies of socialism and our party, by the destructive activities of extremist and anarchisant elements and also by the attitudes of self-preservation which have revealed themselves in the party ranks' [15]. What appeared as a struggle at this Plenum between the reform and the hardline counterattack groups really reflected more of a division of labour. The debate at this, and the following two Plena, really was over what personnel had to be sacrificed and over the degree of intra-party democratisation which was required to appease society. It is significant that there was no speech by a military spokesman at the Eighth Plenum. Jaruzelski maintained the calculated ambiguity of his position. Although he was willing to scourge the PZPR his main priority was to defend the socialist order. This set limits to how meaningful or extensive the dialogue could be with society about the implementation of political, although not necessarily economic or social, reforms. All this was not understood so clearly at the time. Jaruzelski's emergence as Premier was interpreted as an important psychological warning to society to settle down after the turmoil of the January events. The Kania-Barcikowski-Moczar party pragmatists then utilised the military's power and prestige to push through the PZPR's renewal on their own terms in the run-up to the Ninth Congress. Jaruzelski's replacement of the (weak and uniformly unsuccessful) Pińkowski also brought a capable administrator

to galvanise the government and to impose a strong
arbitrating hand on the warring state agencies.
A firmer line by the authorities on the use of force
was likewise presaged.

In nominating Jaruzelski as Premier in the Sejm
Kania hailed him as an outstanding party and state
activist who, as a result of 'the new and socialist
interpretation of the role of the armed forces, was
inextricably bound up with the nation's life and
work'.   As military commander Jaruzelski had protected the country's defence and its revolutionary
transformations;   he had developed Poland's role in
the Warsaw Pact coalition.Kania presented Jaruzelski
as a key proponent of 'the course ot political settlement and agreement' [16].   Jaruzelski's programmatic
theses committed him to Socialist Renewal and the
struggle against deformations;   but 'the creeping process which undermines the country's stability must
be halted'.   His Government had the means and the
constitutional obligation 'to bar the road to those
people and processes who aim to push the circle of
history to counter-revolution' [17]:   plain speaking which was brushed off too lightly at the time.
But the immediate problem for Jaruzelski was the
social unrest, the economic collapse and the use of
'the strike pistol' to paralyse the Government.
He therefore called for a 90 day strike moratorium
during which the economy could be stabilised, an
economic reform prepared and a social dialogue with
the TUs and other social organisations initiated.
A new Economic Committee of the Council of Ministers
was set up to tackle a ten point economic recovery
programme.   As usual Jaruzelski concluded with his
stock appeal to Polish raison d'état.   Economic collapse, foreign indebtedness and social unrest weakened the country's international position.   But
Poland would remain committed to the Soviet Alliance.
He claimed, most unjustly, that the opposition was
willing to exchange the Western Territories for a
new social order.   Jaruzelski replaced seven ministers straight away.   His most important new appointment was that of Mieczysław F. Rakowski, the longtime liberal Editor of Polityka, as deputy-Premier
in charge of the Council of Ministers' Committee for
Relations with Solidarity and the TUs.   The new
Government's brisker style soon brought results with
agreements terminating unrest among students and
peasants and a lull in the strike situation [18].

The new Polish party-state leadership was soon
told 'to reverse the course of events'.   The Soviet
leaders warned that,if they proved incapable of doing

so, then the Brezhnev Doctrine would be applied
against them, at the end of the Twenty-Sixth CPSU
Congress, on 4 March. Was this just a form of
Soviet pressure calculated to keep the Polish leaders
up to the mark, or was it aimed at preventing the
pragmatic Poles from making too many concessions in
order to stabilise their domestic situation?
Korbonski considers that the Kremlin's spoiling tactics were designed to prevent a genuine PZPR compromise from being achieved with Solidarity [19].
It is undoubtedly true that Soviet interventions
contributed to the repeated cycles of confrontation-
compromise-polemics which sabotaged all agreements
during the 1980-1981 period; by maintaining social
discontent they, therefore, eventually moved the
communist authorities towards martial law. But,
contrary to Western and Polish-liberal hopes, it is
not proven that Jaruzelski and the military really
needed much pushing. As Gelman has shown, a very
centralised and limited top Soviet political-military leadership developed under Brezhnev [20].   It
is likely that Jaruzelski had secret channels of
communication with it which were denied to Kania and
the civilian apparatus. It is also possible that
Jaruzelski was more concerned to prove the competence
of the military as a potential supplanter of the
civilian party during 1981.

The effect of Soviet intervention was confirmed
by the Bydgoszcz incident, which would appear to be
a straightforward police provocation at first sight.
But the military's knowledge of, or involvement in,
the incident remains shrouded in mystery. Everybody, including the critical Stefan Bratkowski, accepted the explanation that it was a hardline attempt designed to sabotage the promised Jaruzelski-
Kania reforms, but it could also have been a 'try on'
by the police boss, Milewski. He was summarily but
unobtrusively stripped of all his Politburo, Secretariat and even CC posts, but not until as late as
mid-1985 after the Popiełuszko murder. Soviet
military pressure manifested itself in March-April
1981 in the Soyusz manoeuvres and in direct pressure
to save Olszowski and Grabski at the Ninth Plenum.
But the Plenum set a date (20 July) for the holding
of the much delayed Extraordinary Congress. The
Tenth Plenum at the end of April also endorsed the
decision to carry out a full-scale personnel renewal
and the democratisation of the PZPR in the pre-
Congress Election campaign by unleashing the weapons
of free elections and debate against Gierek's party
incumbents.

All this suggests that Jaruzelski went along
with the Kania-Barcikowski reform consensus.
Whether he banked inwardly on the PZPR's rejuvena-
tion or collapse is, however, another matter for
speculation.   Baryła, the only military spokesman
at the Ninth Plenum, blamed the economic collapse
and the political crisis on Solidarity.   He excoria-
ted the anti-socialist and destabilising activities
of KOR and its allies.   His stock Polish raison
d'état theme was that all this caused Poland's
allies great concern and threatened a European conflict.   Baryła informed the CC that the Armed Forces
under Jaruzelski's command were 'politically united
and ideologically mature, well trained and disciplined'.   The party and youth organisations which
supported the Army's combat readiness·had been
strengthened.   He went on to issue yet another
warning that the Army was always ready 'to defend
socialism as well as Poland's independence' [21].
Jaruzelski himself spoke at the Tenth Plenum.
Starting off in his role as Premier, he reported
on Governmental activities, especially in the economic sector.   But he then set out his political
credo.   The PZPR's hegemony and internal health
and its promotion of reform was the only way out of
the crisis.   'Without the leading role of the party
there is not any socialism.   Without any socialism
there is not an independent and secure Poland based
on beneficial frontiers.'   The Social Agreements
would be fulfilled but Jaruzelski threatened that
his Government would defend the socialist order very
firmly.   His main thoughts were about the sort of
united Marxist-Leninist Party which, having re-
asserted its identity at the Congress, would then be
in a position to collaborate with the outside world.
He gave the green light to a justified degree of
change within the PZPR.   As usual, he concluded with
an attack on 'the politically disastrous, economically harmful' consequences of anti-Sovietism.
This he considered 'morally base' in view of the
600,000 Red Army soldiers who, he claimed, were
buried in Poland as a result of liberating her from
the Nazis in the joint Polish-Soviet effort which
had given the country the Oder-Neisse and Baltic
frontiers [22].
The election of delegates to the Ninth Congress
took place at the same time as that of party committees and Executives in the military cells and sections in late May to June.   The latter led to
changes which were as sweeping statistically as in
the civilian part of the PZPR.   All First Secretaries

in the military districts and service branches were
replaced as well as 80% of those at division level
[23].   In the Air Force 70% of the committee members
and 66% of the Secretaries were new.   90% of the
Pomeranian District Secretaries were new [24].   The
elected PZPR organs of the Polish Army therefore
underwent a sweeping transformation in personnel in
Summer 1980.   But control remained firmly centralised at the top.   The new men could not conceivably
be reform radicals under military circumstances.
They were largely people who gained promotion by
catching the tide of permitted criticism of past
deformations in order to attack and replace incumbent office holders.   The military changes compared
well with the civilian election of 22 out of 49 new
KW First Secretaries, the replacement of between 75
and 90% of provincial committees and 50% of POP
committees.   A total of 125 military delegates to
the Congress was elected, 83 by military district
and 42 by provincial conferences.

The pace and sweeping character of the personnel
renewal through free elections caused the Kremlin to
take fright.   It intervened to slow the process.
The CPSU CC letter to the PZPR CC in early June
charged that the Polish leaders had not done enough
to halt the wave of nationalism, anti-Sovietism and
counter-revolution which was sweeping the country
[25].   The Eleventh Plenum on 9-10 June saw a hardline offensive by CC members and officials who were
slated for dismissal at the Congress.   The reformers
rallied, however, and Kania, in effect, won a vote
of confidence by 89 votes to 24.   The ex-GZP Head
in the 1970s, Corps-General Włodzimierz Sawczuk,
made his political swansong with a blistering attack
on the anti-Soviet and anti-socialist forces which
had been tolerated by Kania's weakness.   He even
suggested that the Congress would open up the way to
a takeover of power by the opposition if the PZPR
did not take the advice contained in the Soviet
Letter [26].   Jaruzelski, as was his wont, kept out
of sight during the unresolved conflict but his
speech, which was written into the protocol, identified four major tasks.   Firstly, the priority was to
save the unity, strength and Marxist-Leninist character of the party.   Secondly, the state machinery
had to be stabilised at all levels.   Thirdly, the
economy had to be reformed in order to alleviate the
consumer disaster.   Lastly, the confidence of friends
and allies had to be rebuilt.   For the first time
he specifically threatened firm police action and
declared that the Army remained loyal and would do

its duty in spite of painful insults [27]. The official military line that social unrest was weakening Poland's alliances and that it was being produced by NATO subversion was expressed by Chief of Staff Siwicki [28]. The official protocol stated significantly that the CC's military members expressed their full support for Kania and Jaruzelski. The Soviets had therefore pushed as hard as they could but, for the moment, Jaruzelski's control over the military was an unquestioned fact; this meant that he would remain as Premier while Kania would continue in office until the Congress, at least. More importantly, the tide of potential reform and national communism within the PZPR was suppressed with fateful consequences for the credibility and social appeal of the Congress.

In Summer 1981 Jaruzelski concentrated on running Poland while Kania and Barcikowski prepared the Congress. In the Sejm on 12 June Jaruzelski, once again, called for social discipline and respect for law and order. He threatened severe action against anti-socialist and anti-Soviet activities. This was more than a smokescreen designed to keep the Soviets happy. He also announced that economic reforms and measures such as rationing to contain the consumer crisis were in the pipeline. Soon afterwards Jaruzelski was elected as a Congress delegate by 238 votes out of 241 present by the Warsaw Military District's PZPR electoral report conference. The soldiers confirmed their leader's thesis that the main danger was now socio-economic anarchy. Anti-socialist opposition activities were preventing the PZPR from renewing itself properly so that it could lead the reform process [29]. This self-serving argument may strike the Western reader as nonsense but it was believed quite genuinely by the Polish communist élite; it struck a responsive chord with those sections of society whose life experiences of war and uncertainty predisposed them in favour of stability and Law and Order at all costs. The soldiers also expressed bitter indignation at the desecration of Soviet War Memorials which had begun a few weeks earlier.

In late June more Polish-Soviet manoeuvres in Silesia were announced. Whether this was yet another warning to Polish society or to potential PZPR reformers and autonomists is unclear. What is probable, however, is that Jaruzelski and his Generals were manoeuvering in their own interest. Warned by Dubcek's fate Jaruzelski (and one might add the rest of the Polish communist élite, except that section slated for removal) wanted to do everything possible to avoid Soviet invasion. Unlike Rakosi's polarisation of alternatives in Hungary in 1956, Jaruzelski wanted to renew the PZPR; he was therefore extremely flexible on such issues as personnel change, the Settlement of Accounts with the Gierek era and Economic Reform. Hence the paradox of the Ninth Congress is easily explicable. The Congress endorsed a radical new programme and statute and promised reform by accepting a radical diagnosis of the causes of the crisis [30]. The key was, however, that what Westerners would call genuine reformers of the Fiszbach type were kept strictly in check on the new committees. All this confirms Jones' argument that the Kremlin is always most concerned with reliable personnel and not with the declamation of reform slogans. The fiercely realpolitik Polish communist élite understood this basic fact very clearly; this was one of the main lessons which they had drawn from the Czechoslovak débâcle. Kania was re-elected as First Secretary while Jaruzelski, Barcikowski and Olszowski were the only other old faces on the 16 strong Politburo. But both it and the democratically elected and 90% new CC were to prove reliable Soviet Marxist-Leninists, albeit in the flexible Jaruzelski way. Jaruzelski, in his Government Report to the Congress, outlined the measures and reforms designed to cope with the massive economic crisis and the social chaos which he painted in bleak terms [31]. His political message was that reform had to be party-led and approved by Poland's allies and that the PZPR would now counter-attack. The growing influence of the military on the Government, and the expansion of its control and inspection functions, was not reflected in any dramatic increase in military representation on the new CC, which merely went to nine out of 278. The four full members were Jaruzelski, Kiszczak, Siwicki and Urbanowicz, plus the venerable figure of Marshal Rola-Żymierski, while the candidates were Janczyszyn, Molczyk, Nowak, Obiedziński and Tuczapski.

In retrospect Jaruzelski's message during the Summer and Autumn was very clear. If the PZPR could change its leading ranks and renew itself morally and ideologically, and if it could persuade the NSZZs and the independent social movements to accept its leading role, and if a degree of social discipline could be re-imposed by political means, then well and good. But if the PZPR failed in these tasks then the military would gradually extend its influence at the leadership levels and become more active in checking up on the economic and state administrations. Above all, the military in collaboration with the police apparat would prepare for a full Army takeover based on the KOK framework. Such plans for emergency conditions had always been available ever since the postwar domestic conflicts, but they were given a new shape after 1967. There is no doubt that the Polish Generals activated them immediately after Gdańsk and with increasing vigour from December 1980, when the USSR gave every indication of being on the brink of invading. All this evidence of close contact between Jaruzelski and the Red Army does not, however, disprove the thesis that the General had his own autonomous aims and policy. As we have seen, he was never a Rokossowski-like Soviet political stooge and even less a Żymierski-type rubber stamp in the political conflicts in the year up till the Ninth Congress.

It was apparent within a few days of the Congress that it had failed politically as far as quietening the domestic situation was concerned. Kania and Jaruzelski, in their mid-August holiday with the Soviet leaders in the Crimea, therefore finally accepted the Soviet thesis that Solidarity was an anti-socialist force which had to be destroyed. But Jaruzelski was in no hurry and Kania only accepted the Soviet thesis as a theoretical proposition. The result was that Solidarity was allowed to hold its Congress in September. Its Address to the East European Workers occasioned another angry Soviet Letter demanding an immediate State of Emergency [32]. Jaruzelski, however, decided to give the civilian party led by Kania, Barcikowski and Olszowski one last chance to negotiate a Front of National Understanding (FPN) with the Church and the independent social forces. During this time he could finalise his military-police preparations under various guises. The hardline populist worker and Politburo member, Albin Siwak, actually spilt the beans in September that Jaruzelski had established a high level, six man Crisis Staff to plan and carry through the suppression of Solidarity[33]. My own feeling, for which I have been criticised most notably by Paul Lewis, is that Jaruzelski would have preferred a negotiated solution [34]. But he hoped that the Solidarity leaders would understand that, although his offer fell hugely short of what they wanted, it was the best that they could get. To many Western minds this naturally smacks more of a demand for near capitulation using the threat of force than a compromise. Moralists may decry this analysis but it is rooted in Eastern European realities. It implies no judgement on the ethics of the case or the desirability of the political solutions being proposed. The military view that Solidarity may have been a positive workers' TU movement at the outset,but that it had now turned into an opposition political organisation planning to take over power on the advice of anti-socialist experts and dissidents, was stated by General Professor Dr. Habilitated Norbert Michta as early as September [35]. One should note that the popular military press, the daily Żolnierz Wolności and the weekly Żolnierz Polski, were always a touch sooner and a bit more strident than the rest of the media in their condemnation of KOR and KPN, their infiltration into Solidary and their alleged 'collaboration' with Western subversion agencies like the CIA, RFE and the Paris Kultura.

At the Fourth Plenum of 16-18 October 1981 Kania proved unable to save himself by enforcing the resignation of PZPR members from Solidarity. He had hoped to face down the hardline demands for a more assertive policy, as he had done earlier in the Spring, but this time the CC accepted his resignation by 104 votes to 79. Given the near collapse of the PZPR grassroots membership, the chances of a new civilian leader like Olszowski, or even Kania's alter ego, Barcikowski, were very slim. One can suppose that Jaruzelski had full Soviet support and that this was now the key factor. The CC turned to a saviour in uniform and elected him as First Secretary by 180 votes to 4. The mood of this Plenum was caught by Professor Marian Orzechowski's maxim that the anti-socialist forces should now be dealt with 'not only with the force of argument but with the argument of force'. The Plenum resolution criticised the previous leadership's failings and weaknesses. It 'considered it essential that the highest authorities of the PRL should, in the event of a supreme need, reach out for their constitutional rights with the aim of defending the most vital interests of the state and the nation' [36]. Olszowski argued that Solidarity had been taken over by the political opposition. Painting the political,social and economic crisis in the blackest colours, he lauded the Army's political balance and social maturity, its contributions to the economy, to maintaining Law and Order and its ideological-political activities [37]. His fulsome praise of it as 'the mainstay of the socialist state' immediately suggested, given the rules of internal communist politics, that he must have led the civilian party opposition or, at least, expressed

reservations about Jaruzelski's nomination.
Jaruzelski merely stated that his goal was to overcome the crisis and postponed all policy and personnel changes.   The Fifth Plenum on 28 October simi-
larly marked time, although it co-opted Jaruzelski's
closest lieutenant, Corps-General Florian Siwicki,
the Chief of Staff, as a Politburo candidate.   The
threatened Emergency Powers Bill was also left suspended at the Sejm session of 30 October.
    Did Jaruzelski's appointment signify that the
USSR had now found a leader who would suppress the
opposition?   The answer must be in the positive,
although Jaruzelski agonised for another six weeks
over whether a more limited form of Emergency Powers
might be a substitute for the full-scale State of
War.   In the event, we now know that the November
negotiations for the FPN came to nothing.   There was
no improvement in PZPR morale and organisation.
The spontaneous swelling up of a wave of Solidarity
workers' protests and demands also indicated that
the situation was building up to another full-scale
confrontation between Solidarity and the authorities.
That it would be even more serious than the Bydgoszcz
crisis was apparent, very late in the day,after the
forcible suppression of the strike in the Warsaw
Firemen's School.   The tenor of the Solidarity KPP
decisions and statements at Radom, and in lesser
measure Gdańsk, also provided fuel for the authorities' propaganda, although the Solidarity leadership, except in Mazowsze, was barely beginning to
organise itself for the coming confrontation.
Szymanski exaggerates in claiming that 'had the
Polish Army not intervened to end the deepening
crisis in Polish society the most likely outcome
would probably have been the radical disruption of
socialist institutions' [38].   His scenario of a
return to capitalism and parliamentarianism or to the
interwar forms of East European right-wing authoritarianism is far-fetched as it ignores the external
Soviet constraint and the possible growth of a reform
tendency within the PZPR in response to polarisation
during 1982.   Be that as it may, the die was cast
on the night of 12-13 December 1981.   Like all great
decisions of this sort, and the invasion of
Czechoslovakia before it was the best example, it had
built up incrementally and was postponed until a
late moment [39].   Jaruzelski revealed his frame of
mind at the PZPR's Sixth Plenum on 27-28 November.
His main preoccupation was with the destabilisation
of socio-economic life and the economic collapse
with its attendant need for large price rises to

soak up the 'inflationary overhang' (<u>nawis inflacyjny</u>)
as a preliminary to the Economic Reform. As the
party was determined to stand firm he saw only two
ways ahead : either confrontation, total chaos and
collapse or a process of gradual stabilisation to be
built on a National Understanding within the socialist constitutional framework. But he warned that
the present state of dissolution could not be allowed
to continue: 'Otherwise it would inevitably lead to
confrontation, to a state similar to that of war'
[40]. The Kremlin had been saying this since August.
One can therefore endorse Larrabee's judgement that,
although martial law was approved by the Soviet leaders, 'the timing of the crackdown, however, appears
to have been a Polish decision and dictated by Polish
events' [41]. Deputy Defence Minister Molczyk
stressed that 'we took the decision to introduce the
State of War in a sovereign way entirely on our own
responsibility, being directed by the superior interes
of the nation and state' (<u>TL</u>, 14 May 1982).

There is widespread agreement that 'the army takeover from the party was all but inevitable' because
of 'the near collapse of the effectiveness, if not of
the very structure',of the PZPR [42]. The balance
of opinion considers that the Army gradually replaced
the PZPR in influence with its agreement during
Autumn 1981; but there is disagreement about the
actual declaration of the State of War. Paul Latawski
goes as far as to claim that 'the Polish Generals
staged what may be considered the communist world's
first successful military <u>coup</u>' [43]. André Fontaine
called it 'the Eighteenth Brumaire of General
Jaruzelski' (<u>Le Monde</u>, 15 December 1981). Ross
Johnson developed the same theme. The State of War
was 'a Bonapartist challenge to party rule from the
military'; the latter 'in effect superseded the
party apparatus as the primary instrument of rule'
[44]. One can also regard December 1981 as a
straightforward counter-revolution if one accepts
the arguments by Nowak and Kurczewski that there was
a revolutionary restructuring of Polish society and
politics away from an authoritarian base to a
pluralist-participatory one during 1980-1981 [45].
It has therefore been argued that martial law represented a classical Thermidorian counter-revolution
and was supported by the social forces threatened
by the 1980-1981 processes. Szajkowski declares
that 'the Polish military had in effect carried out
an internal invasion' [46]. The official réplique
by the military was that 'a sort of liberation has
taken place today' (<u>Żołnierz Wolności</u>, 13 December

1981). Such views fed the unconfirmed rumours that
the bulk of the PZPR Politburo had been sent out of
Warsaw on the night martial law was proclaimed [47].
Even if this were true it would prove little. The
hardening-up process included the PZPR Secretariat's
'Instrukcja' of 10-12 December 1981 suspending the
Party Statute by freezing its key provisions for
inner-party democracy. In effect it returned power
to the presidias as against the grassroots membership.
Other factors one should also remember are that PZPR
hardliners had wanted repression much earlier.
Jaruzelski had held on because he felt that too early
a crackdown, under such unfavourable circumstances
as Bydgoszcz, for example, would spark off a domestic
uprising which the communist authorities might not be
able to cope with; the result might then be a
Hungarian 1956 process of decomposition, threatening
a breakdown of communist power and the inevitable
Soviet invasion. As it was, the State of War was
so successful initially because the sporadic resistance had been isolated by careful planning and was
too local and shortlived even to begin to affect the
conscript and non-officer sections of the Army. In
addition, the careful logistical preparations for
repression ensured that the Army only played spearhead and back-up roles which the breaking up of most
of the resistance was entrusted to the ZOMO.
    The timing of the imposition of martial law was
conditioned by the following factors:

1.   The economic collapse and the need to intro-
      duce massive price rises as a preliminary to
      the Economic Reform.
2.   The need to suppress a potential wave of strikes
      and to restore industrial discipline and pro-
      ductive order.
3.   The fear that the political situation could
      only worsen as Solidarity presented new demands
      for real political and economic democratisation
      and self-management. These would inevitably
      have led to a real showdown in early 1982 over
      the demand for a national referendum on support
      for the authorities; conditions would have
      become increasingly unfavourable for the com-
      munist bunker.
4.   The dread that the outer ring of PZPR intel-
      lectual-professionals would rally to support
      Solidarity demands and use the Ninth Congress
      Statute to produce reformist leaders and poli-
      cies. The workers' PZPR membership, on the
      other hand, had either decamped or been totally

demoralised by Autumn 1981, especially by the
ban of bigamous PZPR-Solidarity membership.
5. The new intake of 1982 draftees into the Army
would have been influenced by Solidarity views
and activities. To that extent the conscript
base of the Army would have become less reliable.
It was only possible to defer one single intake
in   Autumn 1981.

Why the USSR supported Jaruzelski's option of
domestically applied repression is obvious enough.
Poland's strategic importance in the crucial Northern
Tier of the Warsaw Pact, allied to her demographic,
economic and military resources, always made Kuroń's
argument that the USSR would be glad to concede
Finlandisation if the Poles made too much of a nui-
sance of themselves absolutely incredible.   Solidarity
and the emergence of NSZZs did more than threaten
Soviet defence interests.   The Workers' Upsurge posed
an ideological, democratisation and national autonomy
challenge which went far beyond anything that had
actually occurred in the Prague Spring.   The various
challenges may have remained somewhat inchoate until
Autumn 1981.   They were clearly understood and taken
in deadly earnest by the Soviet leadership right from
the very beginning.   This paradoxically, quite apart
from Kania's skilful trimming and tacking, explains
the relative quiescence of the Soviet mass media [48].
The basic Soviet quarrel was always with Polish
society, not with the Polish party after 1980, so the
form of dialogue and pressure had to be somewhat different from the Czechoslovak 1968 case.   Such evidence as there is suggests that the Russians prepared
for a whole range of outcomes [49].   Building up
their Silesian garrison, perfecting communications
networks, practising landings on the Polish and
Lithuanian seacoast and joint manoeuvres with the
GDR and Czechoslovak armies were actual preparations
for the worse case outcome of direct invasion.
Soviet pressures and interventions were mainly directed towards ensuring that the PZPR retained its
Soviet-Leninist character.   As long as the PZPR
then maintained its leading role in society, as understood in Soviet terms of near-monopoly control rather
than Eurocommunist Gramscian ideas of hegemony, the
Kremlin was agnostic whether the best outcome was a
politically negotiated settlement and a Gomułka-type
1957-1959 stabilisation or the full-blown scenario of
domestically applied repression.   The Soviet and
Polish leaderships were in agreement on basic aims
but differed over methods and timing.   This is

evidenced by the various informal and secret tutorials which various levels of political leaders, functionaries and academics took part in during 1980-1981, mainly in the USSR, on how best to contain, then to push back and eventually to overcome the opposition forces and the social ferment which had burst out in Summer 1980.

The State of War's domestic dimension has naturally gained most scrutiny but it also had a crucial significance for the external Polish-Soviet relationship. Firstly, Jaruzelski and the Polish military retained their autonomy and general control over the domestic normalisation processes in a way which was not true for Husak after 1969 or for Kadar from 1956 until the early 1960s. Secondly, the Polish Army's takeover of the country's administration weakened its contribution to the Warsaw Pact and entailed corresponding adjustments by its Soviet and other allies to fill the gaps which had been left. But it also increased direct Polish control over those forces which had been disengaged and redirected to the domestic Polish front. Without going as far as to claim that the State of War prevented a Soviet takeover, one can argue the more limited case that it allowed the Polish military to retain the initiative, and not only in relation to Moscow and its Warsaw Pact allies. Its main internal purpose of destroying Solidarity and organised forms of opposition as well as of administering a sharp psychological shock to Polish society was fairly successful in the short term. But the long-term effects of military penetration or supplantation of the PZPR may prove to have a more important historical significance for the evolution of the Government forms of the communist system.

Notes

1. Malcher, Poland's Politicised Army, p. 111.
2. Walczuk, Wojsko Ludowe (1981, No. 4), pp. 52-56.
3. Wojsko Ludowe (1981, No. 8), pp. 59-69.
4. Ibid., pp. 45-46.
5. See Wojsko Ludowe (1981, No.4), pp. 22-23.
6. Wojsko Ludowe (1981), No. 10.
7. Brigade-General Szumski, Wojsko Ludowe (1983, No. 2), pp. 50-52.
8. Józef Czerwiński, Argumenty, 18 April & 6 December 1982.
9. The military dimension has been wholly ignored by most studies. Cf. Howard E. Frost in Bielasiak & Simon, Polish Politics, ch. 13.
10. ND (October-November 1980), pp. 146-149.

11. Michalik, Wojsko Ludowe (1981, No. 7), pp. 13-19.
12. ND (January-February 1981), pp. 47-50.
13. Wojsko Ludowe (1981, No. 2), pp. 7-11.
14. Sanford, Polish Communism in Crisis, p. 130.
15. ND (March 1981), p. 36. Barcikowski, pp. 26-35; Grabski, pp. 7-25.
16. Debata Sejmowa, 11-12 lutego 1981r (Warsaw, KiW, 1981), pp. 6-7.
17. Ibid., p. 23.
18. See Raina, Poland 1981, ch. 2.
19. Korbonski in Terry, Soviet Policy in Eastern Europe, pp. 82-84.
20. Harry Gelman, The Brezhnev Politburo and the Decline of Détente (London, Cornell U.P., 1984).
21. ND (April 1981), pp. 112-115.
22. ND (May-June 1981), pp. 141-144.
23. Wojsko Ludowe (1982, No. 3), p. 3.
24. Wojsko Ludowe (1983, No. 1),pp. 45-47.
25. ND (July 1981), pp. 29-32.
26. Ibid., pp. 38-41.
27. Ibid., p. 135.
28. Ibid., pp. 115-117.
29. TL, 16 June 1981.
30. IX Nadzwyczajny Zjazd PZPR, 14-20 lipca 1981r (Warsaw, KiW, 1981), pp. 100-158 for programme; pp. 169-211 for statute. The latter is available in my translation in W.B. Simons & S. White (eds.), The Party-Statutes of the Communist World (Martinus Nijhoff, The Hague, 1984), pp. 333-361.
31. IX Nadzwyczajny Zjazd, pp. 76-100.
32. TL, 18 September 1981.
33. KPA 1/82 of 10 January 1982. First reported in Agencja Solidarność, No. 44, 26.9-12.10.81.
34. Paul Lewis, 'The PZPR Leadership and political developments in Poland', Soviet Studies, XXXVII, No. 3 (July 1985), pp. 437-439. See my réplique, 'Interpreting the Polish Crisis', in Soviet Studies (October 1985), pp. 542-543.
35. TL, 15 September 1981.
36. IV Plenum KC PZPR (Warsaw, KiW, 1981), p. 161.
37. Ibid., p. 35.
38. Szymanski, Class-struggle in Poland, p. 149.
39. Compare Karen Dawisha, Kremlin and the Prague Spring.
40. VI Plenum KC PZPR. Przezwyciężanie kryzysu (Warsaw, KiW, 1981), p. 146.
41. F. Stephen Larrabee, 'Soviet crisis management in Eastern Europe' in D. Holloway & J. Sharp (eds.), The Warsaw Pact, p. 133.
42. Z.A. Kruszewski in Bielasiak & Simon, Polish Politics. Edge of the abyss, p. 261.
43. P. Latawski in Ibid., p. 278.

44.   A.R. Johnson in Terry, Soviet Policy in Eastern Europe, p. 279.
45.   Leszek Nowak, Kontakt (1984, No. 3). Jacek Kurczewski, Sysyphus, Vol. 3 (Warsaw, 1982).
46.   Szajkowski, Next to God, p. 157.
47.   R. Spielman, 'Crisis in Poland', Foreign Policy, No. 49 (Winter 1982-1983), p. 32.
48.   Weydenthal et al.,The Polish Drama, ch. 4.
49.   See Roger E. Kanet, 'The Polish Crisis and Poland's "Allies"' in Bielasiak & Simon, Polish Politics, ch. 14.

Chapter Four

WAR AGAINST THE NATION. IMPOSING, APPLYING AND LIFTING MARTIAL LAW

       Both the interwar Polish constitutions of 1921
and 1935 differentiated between the declaration of a
state of war (stan wojenny) and a peacetime state of
emergency (stan wyjątkowy).   The 'Little Constitution' of February 1947 carried over this prewar distinction.   The current constitution of 22 July 1952
was, however, less clear in its original Article
28,which remained unchanged after the 1976 amendments as Article 33.   Section One lays down that
the Sejm or, when it is not in session, the Council
of State, can proclaim a State of War in the event
of armed aggression on Poland or in order to fulfil
allied obligations.   Section Two goes on to declare that 'the Council of State can institute a
State of War (Stan Wojenny), on either the whole or
part of the territory of the PRL, if this is required by considerations of the defence or the
security of the state' [1].   The crucial phrase
is underlined.   The military authorities used it
as their constitutional justification for the State
of War and the Council of State's promulgation of
the Decrees of 12 December 1981.   The Sejm later
confirmed all the legal regulations in a procedure
which had been standard postwar Stalinist practice
but which had dwindled dramatically after 1957 [2].
The PZPR leadership had thus decided long ago that
states of emergency would be cast within the framework of the Defence of the Country, against both
external and internal foes; a special role, depending upon circumstances rendering normal police
action insufficient, would be played by the military.
       Official propaganda justifying the State of
War emphasised the following themes in 1982.
Solidarity had arisen out of a justified workers'
protest but it had turned into a destructive opposition political movement.   It aimed to 'take over

state power and to change the Polish state's political orientations' [3].   The case was documented,
step by step, in official diaries of the 1980-1981
events, which can be summarised under the following
headings [4]:

1.   Political: The growing strength of Solidarity
      extremists working to overthrow the legal so-
      cialist order and its officials threatened con-
      frontation [5].   The Solidarity decisions in
      Radom and Gdańsk in December 1981 regarding
      strikes, steet protests and student demonstra-
      tions opened up the possibility of a bloody
      civil war.   Demands for a workers' referendum
      and for 'free elections' to the Sejm and
      People's Councils indicated their anti-socia-
      list programme.
2.   Economic: The state's security was threatened
      by political struggles within the workplace,
      growing industrial anarchy and strike activity
      and the use of emergent self-management bodies
      against the authorities.   Solidarity was ac-
      cused of trying to throw the PZPR committees
      and their supporting aktyws out of the factories
      in Autumn 1981.   The State of War also saved
      the economy from final collapse and total dis-
      aggregation.   Its price rises and anti-infla-
      tionary measures opened up the way to finan-
      cial stabilisation and Economic Reform.
3.   International: The further development of the
      above situation would have weakened Poland's
      position, both in the socialist community and
      in the world.   Financial dependence and poli-
      tical stalemate would have led to her being
      treated as a helpless object.

The official conclusion was that 'as all other
means of resolving the conflict had been exhausted,
above all the road of understanding proposed by the
PZPR, the introduction of the State of War was the
only way out in accord with the legal-constitutional
bases of the state' [6].   All this may, to Western
eyes, have had little contact with reality, but the
historian should record it as the official perception.   These pronouncements established the myths
and justifications for martial law which have remained current, although with decreasing stridency.
      In his 23 minute long radio and TV speech at
6.0 a.m. on 13 December 1981 Jaruzelski claimed that
Poland stood on the brink, 'not days but hours' away
from a national catastrophe (TL, 14 December 1981).

117

He painted a bleak picture of strikes, protests, political struggles and psychological demoralisation. His efforts to achieve national understanding had been torpedoed by Solidarity, which had prepared mass demonstrations in Warsaw which might have set the country alight. His Government, and he did not mention the PZPR once in his speech, therefore refused to stand idly by and await the confrontation being prepared by Solidarity: 'In this situation failure to act would be a crime against the nation.' He announced that the Council of State had decreed a State of War as of midnight according to Article 33, Paragraph 2, of the constitution. We now know that PAX Chairman Reiff voted against its introduction while doubts were expressed by Jan Józef Szczepański, who eventually agreed. A 21 strong Military Council of National Salvation (WRON) to be chaired by Jaruzelski had been constituted. It included almost all the major military figures - Generals Siwicki, Tuczapski, Molczyk, Kiszczak, Hupałowski, Piotrowski,Baryła, Oliwa, Użycki, Rapacewicz, Łozowicki, Janiszewski and Jarosz, Admiral Janczyszyn, Air Force Commander Krępski, as well as Poland's only cosmonaut, Mirosław Hermaszewski. The remainder were Colonels Makarewicz, Garbacik, Leś and Włosiński. General Zygmunt Zieliński, who had been the MON Personnel Department Head since 1968, was later co-opted as its Secretary. The most significant omission was deputy Defence Minister Józef Urbanowicz, whose Latvian and Soviet CP background suggested that he was one of the few 'Russians' to survive from 1956. Jaruzelski denied that the military were carrying out a <u>coup</u> or establishing a military dictatorship. Nor were they supplanting the party-state authorities, although KOK had appointed plenipotentiary military commissioners at all levels of the state administration as well as in the 190 most important economic enterprises which were militarised. Jaruzelski admitted that force could not provide a long-term solution; but WRON's aim was to save the country from crisis and disintegration by protecting the state's legal order and by creating 'executive guarantees' which would restore order and discipline. He promised that WRON would be dissolved and normal life resumed when stabilisation had been achieved (<u>Communist Affairs</u>, July 1982, pp. 689-693).

WRON's proclamation elaborated on Jaruzelski's speech, although it let slip that TUs were being suspended. WRON had been mandated by the Polish Armed Forces. It counted on 'the confidence and

support of patriotic and progressive forces' and
would 'operate until the situation is normalised'
(Communist Affairs, July 1982, pp. 694-696). The
Council of State's proclamation outlined the various
restrictions, bans and punishments laid down by
the State of War [7]. These were given legal form
by four decrees passed by the Council of State on
12 December - on the State of War, Special Procedures,
Special Powers of military courts and the Abolition
Decree. A whole stream of Ministerial regulations
and instructions followed. These were broadcast
repeatedly by the mass media. In sum, movement was
limited drastically. A curfew was imposed from
10.0 p.m. to 6.0 a.m., identity documents had to be
carried at all times, public rail and bus transport
was curtailed; permission had to be obtained for all
travel to a different town. TUs, Youth, Catholic
and other professional associations were suspended.
Schools and universities were closed. All public,
cultural and sporting meetings except religious services were banned; this applied, in particular, to
all strikes and demonstrations. Censorship was
tightened up by the military and extended to all
postal and telephone communications. Newspapers
and journals except Trybuna Ludu and Żołnierz
Wolności were closed. Radio and TV were limited to
a single programme dominated by military spokesmen
in uniform like Captain Górnicki. Arms and even
radios had to be handed in. Individuals were subject to labour conscription and particularly dangerous people were interned. A sweeping number of
penalties was threatened for any infringement of the
wide range of State of War regulations. KOK militarised the railways, buses, ports, postal services,
oil and building industries as well as major factories and organisations at the state level from
top to bottom.

The State of War had been carefully planned in
detail from December 1980 onwards, according to an
ex-military associate of Jaruzelski's [8]. It was
imposed in a meticulous bureaucratic manner in order
to heighten the shock effect which WRON wanted in
order to demonstrate the futility of resistance.
The country was closed down and shut off from the
outside world. Regions were isolated from one
another and the barrage of orders, instructions and
threats presented by the mass media strengthened the
impression of menace. Troops and police appeared
everywhere in the streets. It is hardly surprising
if the initial reaction to such ferocious shock
tactics was one of muted shock and disbelief;everyone

had been caught by surprise.   The first public
reaction was Primate Glemp's sermon on the Sunday
evening, which condemned the régime's resort to
force but which counselled against hopeless resistance and unnecessary bloodshed.

Resistance and Repression
There was widespread, although mainly local
and isolated, resistance, mainly in the form of
sit-in strikes and street demonstrations, during the
first fortnight of martial law.   All the main urban
centres were affected but the most bitter incidents
causing loss of life occurred in a number of coalmines.   The strikes were often broken by a direct
assault on the factory by Army tanks which would
break down the gates, while the actual hand-to-hand
repression was carried out mainly by the ZOMO with
their heavy riot gear.   The major attack of this
sort took place at the Wujek coalmine near Katowice
on the morning of 16 December.   About 2,000 miners,
attacked with tear gas, rubber bullets and water
cannon, fought back with red-hot iron bars, pick
axes and even Molotov cocktails [9].   Official
sources conceded that 7 miners were killed and 39
wounded, while 41 policemen were injured;   Solidarity
claimed that 4 of the ZOMO also lost their lives.
The most widespread street demonstrations and fighting, not surprisingly, occurred in Gdańsk on 16-17
December when the shipyard was stormed and pacified
with about 330 people being injured.   Similar incidents took place in other urban centres, notably
Warsaw, Wrocław and Kraków.   The strikes and factory occupations dragged on into the second week of
the State of War.   The most long drawn-out and
potentially most serious incidents took place in
the Ziemowit and Piast coalmines near Tychy.   About
1,200 miners stayed underground, warned by the
Wujek experience, protected by dynamite at the exits
in the former until Christmas Eve.   About 1,850 of
the workforce, dwindling to a few hundred, occupied
the latter from 14 to 28 December.   By then most of
the strikes and demonstrations had petered out nationwide and there was a gradual return to work even in
the Baltic Shipyards [10].
The official mass media naturally played down
reports of resistance in order to increase the feelings of isolation and the pointlessness of protest.
A stream of arguments presented their case for
martial law.   Poland had always needed a 'strong
state' throughout her history in order to protect
her independence and domestic development against

excessive local or sectional particularisms (Salecki, TL, 15 December 1981). Military rule meant that socialist renewal and the August Agreements could now be implemented in an orderly manner (Leszczyński, TL, 15 December 1981). Solidarity and KPN/KOR extremists were blamed for creating the ideological, political and economic chaos which they hoped would enable them to seize power. The radio and TV blared out the theme that the State of War had prevented the civil war threatened by Solidarity's Radom and Gdańsk decisions. They initially claimed that resistance had been local and easily suppressed, but after a few days admitted the scale of the protest in the major urban centres.

The impression that the military authorities were knuckling down to the task of running the country briskly and efficiently was put across right from the beginning. A whole stream of WRON decisions adapted administrative and economic life to martial law conditions. The Economic Committee of the Council of Ministers, chaired by Obodowski, met from the 15th onwards to tackle the problems of food distribution, the stopping of food exports and the preparation of price increases and the Economic Reform. The military takeover of the state and economic apparats started straightaway. Wojewodas in Katowice, Elbląg, Koszalin and Radom were dismissed on the 15th for not fulfilling martial law duties. They were replaced by Division-General Roman Paszkowski (ex-head of Air Defence and ambassador to Angola 1976-1980) and Colonels Urliński (see interview, Polityka, 29 May 1982), Mazurkiewicz and Wojciechowski. The first dismissals for incompetence, corruption, unreliability or opposition to martial law started with the sacking of the WSMW Rector and his deputy in Gdynia. They were followed by long daily lists of the dismissal of provincial officials, town and commune heads, industrial managers and officials in co-operatives and other organisations. Attacks on the 'false road' of autonomous movements like the students' NZS presaged its dissolution in early January. The military leaders attempted to rally and mobilise their supporters from the 16th onwards, when Orzechowski met the PZPR Warsaw aktyw, but most provincial ones were not assembled until just before Christmas.

The main priority until the New Year was repression and the breaking of all attempts to organise opposition. The initial pacification of the industrial and urban centres was backed up quickly by the legal apparatus of martial law. This swung

into play with daily communiqués by the Procurator-
General from the 19th onwards of the temporary arrests
and the accelerated, summary procedures dealing
with martial law infringements. But the régime also
mounted an intensive legal and propaganda drive against
speculators, black marketeers and corrupt officials
like Radio-TV chairman Maciej Szczepański, whose
trial opened at long last on 5 January. Breaking
what was billed as the crime wave of 1981 was backed
up by further appeals to the silent Law and Order
majority that resistance to martial law was hopeless.
Its rigours were blamed on the opposition leaders.
As much mileage as possible was made of the declarations of loyalty and appeals for calm by the handful
of Solidarity leaders, like Zdzisław Rozwalak of
Poznań, who accepted martial law.   All these themes
were summarised by a leading party publicist.   He
confirmed the official line on Solidarity's fomen-
tation of chaos as a preliminary to seizing power.
The priority now was to think in realistic state
categories about the need for a temporary period of
martial law; only 'a return to a realistic assessment of possibilities could hasten its withdrawal'
[11].   This article provoked an open clash between
civilian party and military viewpoints.   General-
Professor Norbert Michta, Head of the party school
(WSNS), was very happy to develop Siedlecki's thesis
that the State of War had saved Poland from civil
war and that it constituted the only real chance of
leading the country out of the crisis.   But he
polemicised with the implicit party argument that
the limitations of citizens' rights meant that no
basic political problems had been, or could be,
solved.   Michta stressed the extent to which KOR
aims and strategy had dominated Solidarity right from
the outset, irrespective of the good intentions of
ordinary renewal-minded workers.   He criticised the
PZPR for not carrying out a full Settlement of
Accounts in 1981 of those responsible for the crisis,
as the soldiers now intended to do.   Michta reflected a clear attempt by the military to distance themselves from the PZPR's failures in 1980-1981.   Not
only could there be no return to August 1980, but the
curtain had also come down for good on the pre-13
December situation.   The self-confident and uncom-
promising military hardline on the State of War came
through very clearly for the political cognoscenti.
Solidarity, KOR and KPN activities in 1980-1981
were 'the greatest political manipulation in the 36
year life of the PRL',designed to overthrow socialism
and to serve Imperialism by smashing the unity of

the socialist community.   Polish society must be convinced of this as a preliminary to the relaxation of martial law [12].

By the second week of the State of War the bulk of open industrial and social protest had been broken. The Solidarity call for 'passive resistance' allowed WRON to move the ZOMO around Poland to suppress the isolated and unco-ordinated protests, whereas a nationwide General Strike would have overtaxed their resources and brought the Army more directly into the task of repression with unpredictable consequences as far as the conscripts were concerned [13]. But, as usual, the Solidarity leaders did not take such a basic risk.   Their initial success allowed WRON to move on to break resistance within factories through the tried and tested methods of dismissal, arrest,beating up and general browbeating,which had been so effective in 1971 and 1976.   The curfew in all provinces except Katowice, Lublin, Elbląg, Gdańsk, Szczecin and Wrocław was shortened on the 19th and raised entirely for the Christmas period and New Year's Eve.   In order to heighten the picture of life returning to normal travel restrictions were lifted gradually;   by 5 January WRON felt strong enough to authorise the re-opening of schools and universities.   Stabilisation was the primary goal. It was repeated ad nauseam that the gradual withdrawal of the martial law restrictions,nationally or regionally, was solely dependent upon this factor.

The propaganda and psychological struggle to convince the Poles of the inevitability, if not of the necessity,of martial law and to win over key social groups continued apace.   On 23 December Jaruzelski, supported by Rakowski and Duraczyński, tried unsuccessfully to persuade a group of representative academics to support the military endeavour to lead Poland out of her political and socio-economic crisis.   Rakowski accused the intelligentsia of developing in 1980-1981 a totally destructive critique of everything that had been developed in People's Poland since 1945.   A messianistic and culpably irresponsible myth of a new European order had been propagated by Solidarity's intellectual advisers [14].   On Christmas Eve Jaruzelski addressed his credo to the nation over the radio and TV: 'In Poland's history there have, on occasion, been moments when one had to choose not between good and evil but between a greater and a lesser evil.   We made such a choice.'   There was no alternative to the State of War by 13 December but it 'would not be maintained for an hour more than would appear

necessary'.   He promised that the road of national
understanding was still open once troublemakers had
been dealt with.   He would soon present a programme
to that end (Przemówienia1981-1982, pp. 222-225).
     By the New Year the new military system was in
place.   The fear of the first few days was replaced
by a sullen form of outward acceptance.   The authorities continued the massive legal repression of
opposition and lists of heavy sentences appeared
daily from late December onwards.   Legal proceedings
were also promised against the defecting ambassadors,
Zdzisław Rurarz in Japan and Romuald Spasowski in
the USA.   But it was also announced that a State
Tribunal would be established to call Gierek, Szydlak,
Kaim and the other 1970s' leaders to account for
their responsibility for the crisis.   Much information was publicised about the legal proceedings
against the 540 odd officials accused of corruption
(TL, 31 December 1981).   On the other hand, the
propaganda drive against Solidarity's 'extremists'
and their 1981 activities was amplified.   The WRON
message of 'Law, Order and Work' was blazoned out
in spite of its Vichy Pétainist associations.   On
the surface political life gradually returned to
normal with Jaruzelski meeting Western diplomats.
Even the party machine began to stir at the top with
Kubiak summoning the provincial PZPR Secretaries to
Warsaw to prepare the re-opening of the schools and
universities.
     One of the most unusual features of the State of
War was the internment of about 5,000 individuals
during its first days.   The most intensive round-up
was on the night of 12-13 December but some prominent
leaders like Bujak, Frasyniuk and Lis evaded capture
and went underground.   The proscription lists had
clearly been prepared well in advance.   Not only
Solidarity, KOR and KPN activists and their advisers,
but also a wide range of intellectuals, workers,
peasants and social activists, including some absurd
cases, were hauled in.   The muddle, both in conception and implementation, is well illustrated by
the case of the two Solidarity activists who shared
a room in a Gdańsk hotel.   One set of militia arrested the first at 2.0 a.m. on 13 December, but a different set of militia did not arrive to carry out
their instructions to arrest the second one until
6.0 a.m., by which time he had naturally flown [15]!
The first published list of 32 names announced on
15 December was composed wholly of 1970s' figures
(Gierek, Babiuch, Łukasiewicz, Szydlak, Wrzaszczyk,
Jaroszewicz, etc.) plus other officials accused of

corruption (TL, 16 December 1981). The second list
of 57 major Solidarity and other political internees
included Michnik, Kuroń, Gwiazda, Geremek, Jurczyk,
Rulewski and their associates (TL, 17 December 1981).
But there were some revealing give-aways indicating
the mechanical application of long and carefully prepared procedures [16]. The list of prospective
internees included Seweryn Blumstajn, the 1968 Warsaw
University 'commando', KOR activist and Solidarity
Information Bulletin Editor. He had been in Paris
since the previous November and remained there during
martial law. Other proscribed figures like Mirosław
Chojecki and Wojciech Krupiński were also abroad.
     Internment, as one knows from Britain's Ulster
experience, is an exceptional administrative-penal
procedure designed to quarantine individuals considered dangerous by the authorities, over 17 in
the Polish case, who cannot be dealt with satisfactorily by normal legal processes. The preventive
measure of internment was laid down in Articles 42-45
of the State of War decree which was implemented by
the provincial MO commander. The procedures, set out
in an Order of the Council of Ministers of 12 December
1981, were not susceptible to any meaningful appeal,
although internees could object within a week of internment [17]. Individuals to be interned were those
whose behaviour indicated that they would not respect the legal order, or who carried on activities
endangering its internal and external security or
defence capacity. A total of 10,131 individuals
was interned during the course of martial law in
1982,but there were never more than just over 5,500
at peak; many internees were released after a few
weeks, while others were later put on trial and
imprisoned. First deputy Minister of the Interior
Bogusław Stachura told the Sejm Committees on Internal Affairs and Justice on 7 January 1982 that 5,906
people had been interned; of these 839 had already
been released, so the total stood at 5,076 (TL, 8
January 1982). Jaruzelski gave a figure of 4,549
and 1,760 released in his Sejm speech in late January.
Interior Minister Kiszczak stated that the total
stood at 4,095 and that 2,552 had been released as
of 26 February (TL, 1 March 1982). The obvious
inference is that an additional 1,561 individuals
had been interned between these two dates. Another
3,500 were to be interned between then and December.
The most prominent opposition leaders were interned
at Białołęka near Warsaw and Strzebielinek near
Gdańsk. Wałęsa himself was neither formally arrested nor detained but kept under house arrest firstly

near Warsaw, where he refused various offers to collaborate, and then at Arlamowo in south-east Poland
near the Soviet frontier.   Conditions in the 49 internment camps, which gradually settled at a figure
around two dozen, varied.   There were allegations
of maltreatment, beatings and bad health care and
food.   Romuald Bukowski, the only Sejm Deputy to
vote against the State of War Decree, presented a
Sejm Question in March.   He wanted the Government
to notify families and employers about individuals
who had been interned, to alleviate conditions in
the Białołęka camp and to stop attempts to force internees to emigrate.   He failed to get much satisfaction from Justice Minister Zawadzki, who merely
replied that conditions were in order and were being
improved all the time (SSS, 25 March 1982, Inter-
pellations,Cols. 20-22).   When internment was dis-
continued in December 1982 the main Solidarity and
KOR leaders had charges of conspiring to overthrow
Poland's socio-economic order laid against them.
Their status was changed from internees to that of
political prisoners under criminal investigation.
More second rank individuals, according to Solidarity
sources, were conscripted into the Army and forced
to serve in penal labour camps [18].
     The summary and accelerated court procedure
was directed initially mainly against offences in
the militarised workplaces.   Attempts to organise
strikes or even to carry on Solidarity activities
and any form of demonstration fell into this net.
The scale of legal repression can be gauged from the
statistics of those arrested by 5 January 1982:
1,274 had been arrested on serious charges,   529 had
been charged (339 in civil and 190 in military
courts) while 170 sentences had already been handed
down.   The police Tribunals for Misdemeanours had
dealt with 31,609 infringements of the martial law
regulations and had handed out 29,106 fines and
60 reprimands.   1,713 more serious cases had already resulted in 60 prison sentences.   Stachura's
body count was that 9 people had lost their lives,
245 civilians had been injured, of whom 45 were
still in hospital, as well as 222 policemen, 35 of
whom were still in hospital (TL, 8 January 1982).
     The legal regulations establishing and imple-
menting the State of War were a whole series of decrees passed by the Council of State on the night
of 12-13 December 1981.   Because of the wording of
Article 33 of the constitution and WRON's emergence
as an outgrowth of KOK, the 1979 successor law to
that of 1967 on the Universal Obligation to Defend

the Country became a key document (DzU, 1979, No. 18, pos. 111). So were the existing Criminal Code, the Code of Criminal Procedure and the Code of Misdemeanours [19]. The Council of State's Resolution of 12 December 1981 justified the State of War by referring to 'the threat to the vital interests of the State and the Nation, with the aim of working against the further breakdown of social discipline as well as to create more effective conditions for the defence of calm, harmony and public order, also to ensure the stricter compliance with legal regulations and respect for the principles of social cohabitation' (DzU, 1981, No. 29, pos. 155). The main Decree on the State of War constituted the general legal framework for martial law and was backed up by another three decrees on 12 December. Firstly, Emergency Procedure for dealing with Crimes and Misdemeanours regulated the accelerated and summary procedure during the period that the State of War was in force. Secondly, Special Powers of Military Courts widened their jurisdiction and changed their organisation. Lastly, the so-called 'Abolition Decree' wiped the slate clean on all offences arising out of political and social conflicts prior to the declaration of martial law (DzU, 1981, No. 29, pos. 154-158). A mass of orders and detailed implementing regulations was passed by other bodies. All these decrees, orders and instructions were sanctioned by the Sejm in the Law on Special Legal Regulations during the State of War on 25 January 1982, which also confirmed the main Council of State Decrees of 12 December 1981.

The main Council of State Decree of 12 December 1981 suspended a whole series of civil rights which had previously been guaranteed by the constitution or international agreements (DzU, 1981, No. 29, pos. 154). These concerned the rights to the inviolability of individuals and dwellings, secrecy of correspondence, the freedoms of organisation, speech, publication, assembly, movement and demonstration. Along with the curtailment of rights went new obligations in terms of work, defence of the country and obedience to the strengthened powers of the state administration and of the military commissioners. New offences going beyond what was laid down by the Legal Codes established penalties of up to five years' imprisonment for organising strikes and demonstrations, three years for what was vaguely described as activity in any suspended TU or organisation and 3-8 years for spreading information which might weaken the country's defence capacities.

Mere participation in a strike or protest carried a
penalty of up to 3 months plus a 5,000 złoty fine,
as did any unauthorised change of residence.   Prison
terms of up to a month plus 5,000 złoty fines could
be handed out for not carrying identity cards, failure to go to work or to practise agriculture, travel
violations or even carrying out water sports in a
border region!   Many of the offences against the
obligation to military service and to defend the
country laid down by the 1967 and 1979 Laws were now
extended,especially those concerning militarised factories and institutions.   This carefully prepared
and worked out legal framework gave the military
authorities the judicial-administrative Rechstaat
which most military juntas lack.   Along with verification, it assured them of the effective support
of the state administration in implementing it.
     The Council of State's Emergency Procedures for
dealing with Crimes and Misdemeanours laid down
three new forms of summary, simplified and accelerated
legal processes.   Summary procedure had been in
force from November 1946 until the introduction of
the Criminal Code in 1969.   Covering 87 different
types of offences, it could be applied either in
military courts or in civil ones composed of three
professional judges without the usual lay assessors,
in serious cases where the penalty ranged from a
minimum three years' imprisonment to the maximum of
death or 25 years.   The main aim, as with the simplified and accelerated procedures dealing with offences carrying up to three year sentences, was to
shorten the legal proceedings and to control the
rights of defence and appeal in order to get as many
cases dealt with as quickly as possible.   Normally
the court rejected the accused's appeal against summary procedure within 48 hours, the prosecutor completed his case within 15 days and the trial took
place within five days of the accused being formally charged.   Radio Warsaw revealed on 12 January
1982 that 394 cases had been dealt with in this way
during the first month of martial law.   Procurator-
General Franciszek Rusek gave a figure of 11,908
individuals being thus processed between 13 December
1981 and 22 October 1982, 2,369 being political infringements of the martial law regulations and the
remainder straightforward criminal offences.   The
most serious 'anti-state' offences were directed by
the Security Organs to the military courts run
directly by MON and the GZP.   Previously they could
only try civilians for espionage.   Their jurisdiction was now widened to include the catch-all

provisions of Articles 47-48 of the Martial Law
Decree and those which occurred in militarised enterprises, especially if the organisation of strikes,
protests, labour boycotts or the distribution of
leaflets were concerned [20].

The sheer extent of repression can be gauged
from the following figures covering the first six
months of martial law.   90,847 individuals had been
sentenced by civil courts, 5,504 for more serious
crimes by provincial courts.   By December 1982
about 3,616 sentences for politically motivated offences had been handed out (TL, 10 December 1982).
The majority of minor offences was dealt with by
the MSW Misdemeanour Tribunals, which also benefited
from the accelerated procedures.   They could impose
fines of up to 20,000 złoties or three month prison
sentences.   Up to the suspension of martial law they
dealt with about 100,000 cases, no less than 70,000
of which were for curfew and identity card violations.
The procedure, especially in cases of bystanders
caught up in Solidarity demonstrations, was highly
haphazard.   The sentences were very erratic and
judicial safeguards and appeal possibilities were
minimal.   Other forms of repression included the
ad hoc beating up of street demonstrators by the
militia, often including those who were subsequently
charged [21].   But, as in the 1970s in the Baltic
Shipyards and Radom, Ursus and Płock, the main form
of social control was applied in the militarised
factories.   The suppression of strikes, go-slows
and the imposition of strict labour discipline concerning respect for supervisors, pay and the length
of the working week were imposed by the punishment
of work absence, unauthorised changes of employment
and refusal to carry out orders.   Workers could be
re-assigned to less attractive jobs with less pay,
while their holiday and pension entitlements could
be curtailed.   In more drastic cases the worker
could be dismissed, losing all entitlements (housing
and family benefits) which he had accumulated over
many years and normally finding it impossible to
find alternative employment.   Local Arbitration
Commissions received 55,793 protests against unfair
dismissals in the first half of 1982 and only gave
the plaintiff satisfaction in about 16% of the cases
(Rzeczpospolita, 6 October 1982).   Only about 400
odd of the almost 4,000 appeals to the Labour Courts
from these commission decisions went in favour of
the worker.   One of the best informed estimates of
the statistical aspect of martial law repression is
that over 10,000 were interned, 30,000 imprisoned,

almost 4,000 to serious terms over three years, over
60,000 fined and tens of thousands dismissed from
their jobs [22].

Why no National Uprising broke out

Our examination of the mechanisms for imposing
the State of War gives a clear answer to the question why a national uprising did not break out.
The shift towards military rule and repression had
been very gradual during 1981. It was camouflaged
by the presentation of Premier Jaruzelski as a
guarantor of Socialist Renewal and National Understanding. Until the very last moment there was
complete ambiguity over whether the preparations for
Emergency Measures were tactical or whether they
had more sinister implications. The senior military and police officer cadres went ahead quietly
and secretly with these preparations unaware, except
at the very top, of the timing and full significance
of their work. Jaruzelski's takeover as PZPR First
Secretary signified that the communist leadership
accepted that the Ninth Congress programme could
not be effected through social agreement and negotiated means, only by force and from a position of
strength. Their other main fear was that Solidarity's
challenge in Spring 1982 would provoke a democratisation of the PZPR on Dubcek lines, which would make
a reality of the new party statute, thus removing
the option of domestically applied repression.

The key to the successful imposition of the State
of War was the breaking up and quarantining of the
whole country into individual regions. Resistance
was local and factory or street based so the security forces did not come under any significant pressure which might have tested their loyalty. The
ZOMO fulfilled its assigned tasks, as did the militia,
while the Army backed them up without getting too
directly involved in hand-to-hand repression. There
was no real occasion for the potential reticence of
the conscripts to be brought into play. Their role
was largely one of patrolling the streets and of
acting as sentries while crack units of proven reliability were used to break down factory gates and external defences. The Army Security Corps no doubt
nipped any incipient stirrings in the bud, although
there were rumours of the odd breakdown in discipline. Unconfirmed Solidarity reports claimed that
a whole unit, together with its officers, had mutinied
at Niepołomice near Kraków and had been arrested en
masse, that clashes between the ZOMO and the Army
occurred in Bydgoszcz and that a soldier had broken

down at Wujek and shot his officer [23]. What is clear, though, is that, in spite of some emotional outbursts, the main officer and regular NCO cadres and the military police units maintained sharp discipline. Thus there was no question of divided loyalties breaking out as the result of the decomposition of the situation and the presentation of alternative choices and nationalist anti-Russian reactions, as occurred in Hungary in 1956. Senior officers slotted easily, and with much relish, into their new appointments as military commissioners in charge of the administration, enterprises and other organisations or took over posts directly. They were then in a position to animate the less reliable apparats and subsidiary élites in breaking down social resistance.

The questions of how the State of War was imposed and why it succeeded, apparently so brilliantly in its technical and short-term aspects, therefore raise no real problems; although it is a valid criticism that many of the later problems can be traced back to some of the initial failures, like that of only catching about 80% of the Solidarity leaders. The controversial historical issue is why it was imposed when it would so obviously rule out of court all the negotiated Social Contract type of agreements and the democratic-pluralist relationships which Western opinion considered to be the only way of resolving the socio-economic crisis. The answer is, of course, that Marxist-Leninist values, interests and perceptions differ fundamentally from such Western and Polish opposition ones. Putting it bluntly, the communist power élite had an ideological view of history which justified the use of all means, including force, to preserve its system. Such ideological values were buttressed by the very real personal, political, social and economic interests of the communist Nomenklatura élite. It was not inclined to give up its privileges and position without a fight. Lastly, the values and interests of the Polish élite were very strongly supported by the parallel interests as well as the military-strategic-national and Soviet bloc leadership concerns of the USSR. The moral-political issue regarding the use of force need not detain us long, although its influence on world opinion as a factor in the East-West conflict can be noted. Our study merely has to explain why the option of domestically applied repression was preferred to that of external Soviet or Warsaw Pact invasion and why the former involved a qualitative shift in power from civilian party politicians to the military and the supporting police apparats.

The legal justification and framework for the State of War does, however, provide a revealing insight into the motives and the aims of its instigators. The broad argument was that all political systems have constitutional mechanisms, for what the noted Polish political scientist, Stanisław Gebethner, calls 'states of particular danger' (or 'imminent threat') [24]. But the Polish state lawyers, in spite of their wide range of comparative examples, had greater difficulty in getting round the fact that Article 32 of the constitution did not differentiate between martial law following a declaration of war and the situation occasioned by a domestic state of emergency. Gebethner argued that the real problem was that the length, conditions and safeguards regarding martial law periods had never been worked out in detailed constitutional form. This needed to be done in future. Deputy Edmund Osmańczyk later made the same point in the Sejm (SSS, 26 May 1982, cols. 150-158). The issue of guarantees against executive tyranny during such periods of 'Constitutional Dictatorship' was also addressed by the critical academic state lawyer, Professor Jerzy Stembrowicz. He was realistic enough to accept that legal guarantees could not heal a divided society; but he argued that the greatest check on the executive would always be its need to gain social support for its measures [25].

The rights and wrongs of the argument of 'higher necessity' cannot be resolved meaningfully. The thesis that the State of War prevented Civil War and a Solidarity takeover was no more than a short-term and ritualistic justification. The reality was that the military and their supporters refused to risk losing the initiative to Solidarity or the reform-minded and workerite PZPR grassroots during 1982. Zbigniew Kowalski, the Łódź Solidarity leader, claimed that 'the authorities were seized with panic' at the victory of the radical workers at the Solidarity Congress and the emergence of the new tactic of 'the active strike' [26]. Apart from that, it was obvious that the imminent political crisis of 1982 would prevent any economic improvement. This in turn would fuel the political and social crisis. Lastly, Jaruzelski and his team knew that a fundamental confrontation with Solidarity or a Dubcek-type evolution within the PZPR would either sweep them away or render them increasingly dependent on Soviet support; at best Soviet military invasion

would entail the loss of all their domestic autonomy enjoyed since 1956.

One should also not underestimate the lessons
which the communist power holders drew from Dubcek's
failure.   They considered that the Soviet's greatest concern, as pointed out by Christopher Jones,
was over the vetting of the new personnel to replace
the discredited Novotny-ites, especially in the
security, military and party apparats.   The trigger
for the decision to invade was Dubcek's failure at
Cierna and Bratislava to reassure the Soviet leaders
about the composition of the new CC and committees
to be elected by the forthcoming Congress.   This
therefore explains why Kania's CPA concentrated
lucidly, not on anything minor in their terms, like
resolving the socio-economic crisis or coming to
terms with Solidarity, but with preventing any major
infiltration of reform forces into the CPA and its
supporting military, security and mass media apparats.
At the end of the day they preferred the gradual
shift of power to the military in order to carry
through the option of domestically applied repression.   This held out the possibility of an eventual
return to classical Soviet Leninist forms of rule
while maintaining the relative autonomy which the
Polish élites had enjoyed since 1956.   Hard-nosed
political realism had enabled the Polish élite to
ride out crisis after crisis without ever becoming
prisoners of either the Kremlin or autonomous Polish
and social forces.   Dawisha has also shown that
the Soviets themselves drew very rapid conclusions
from the political failure of their invasion of
Czechoslovakia to produce a collaborating Workers'
and Peasants' Government [27].   Within a few days
they had to negotiate with Dubcek and to normalise
the situation for the first eight months through
the very individuals who had been slated for political, if not physical, elimination.   The Soviet
perception was therefore that, even if an invasion
of Poland were synchronised with the simultaneous
formation of a loyal, pro-Soviet Government,as
occurred with Kadar in early November 1956, this
would still be a much more costly and uncertain
outcome than the domestically applied repression
which they had been pressing on Kania ever since
late November 1980.

Verification and Purges

The State of War was not only imposed in order
to suppress independent social movements and
Solidarity and to intimidate the rest of Polish

society.   Its second, and almost as important, aim
was to verify directing personnel at every level of
every sector.   The central and local state administration, and the economic, intellectual, cultural
and judicial spheres as well as the party itself
were to be purged of individuals who had proved
unreliable by becoming too pro-Solidarity, democratisation inclined or lukewarm about the Soviet connection during 1980-1981.   The process started as
early as 17 December 1981 with General Janiszewski's
circular, issued in his capacity as Head of the
Bureau of the Council of Ministers [28].   Officials
were to be told to resign their Solidarity memberships.   They would be dismissed if they refused.
The process was to be completed with military brisk-
ness within four days at the central and six days
at the local levels.   Those who complied had in
addition to sign a loyalty oath accepting that
Solidarity was a counter-revolutionary force.   WRON,
at its 16 December meeting, also widened the verification process to include the dismissal of incom-
petent and corrupt officials, who at the local
level had been identified earlier by the TGOs.
Glemp wrote to Jaruzelski on 28 December protesting
against what he regarded as a violation of con-
science [29].
     Under cover of the State of War the military
verified and carried through a purge of the main
walks of Polish life.   The PZPR will be examined in
Chapter Five.   As far as one knows, there were no
pro-Solidarity feelings within the Army Officer
Corps.   Any stirrings among the conscripts were
contained within the barracks.   Although there had
been attempts to set up an independent police TU
in 1981 divisions within officers and men had no
significance in the polarised conditions of martial
law.   The Procuracy, given the character of its
function, intimate links with the security services
and Solidarity attacks, also remained solidly reliable to the régime out of vested self-interest.
Most surprisingly, though, about 900 of the 3,400
Judges are reported to have joined Solidarity, in
an attempt to wrest professional autonomy in 1981.
They, like all state officials, were summoned for
talks on the basis of Janiszewski's circular.
They had to resign their TU membership and to sub-
scribe to the loyalty oath.   According to Podemski,
26 were dismissed and 18 resigned in 1982 (Polityka,
28 May 1983).   Others took early retirement or had
their promotion prospects blighted.   This process,
which lasted during the Winter 1981-1982 and resumed

again in May 1982, was carried out centrally by the
Ministry of Justice [30]. Close liaison was established with the Presidents of Provincial Courts
about current cases and the sentences to be handed
down. The effect of the verification of central
and local state administrations is not clear, but
the state's huge capacity to exert pressure on its
employees must have led to the rapid suppression of
any stirrings. The most obvious changes were at
the top directing levels. By July 1982 over 65%
of Under-Secretaries of State and ministerial department heads had been in their posts for less than a
year. The state administration had been cut by
3,000 during the previous year and a further reduction
of 2,400 was planned. In the 18 months before
July 1982 50% of Wojewodas, 40% of Commune Heads
and 58% of directors of urban communes had been
changed [31]. The verification of the central state
administration was carried out by Janiszewski's
Bureau of the Council of Ministers. The provincial
and local state administration was checked by
General Tadeusz Hupałowski, the Minister of Local
Administration and Territorial Economy. 203 officials were dismissed during February, 60 at the central and territorial levels and 143 from the economic
administration. 68 individuals were recalled for
making use of their post for private gain. Others,
mainly Commune Heads, were sacked for incompetence.
Each Ministry published long lists of dismissals
(Dziennik Polski, 9 March 1982).
    Verification of the mass media, cultural and
educational fields proved more difficult. The main
social group to be normalised was the journalists.
The régime was less successful here as vast numbers
left the publications,which were restarted from late
January onwards. The Association of Polish Journalists (SDP) had elected the livewire Establishment
critic, Stefan Bratkowski, as its chairman at the
November 1980 Congress. The SDP played an important role in pushing for a liberal censorship law
and in enlarging the boundaries of debate in 1981.
But it soon came under official challenge backed up
by Soviet thunderbolts. The régime, animated by
Olszowski, successfully resisted its attempts to
limit or to raise censorship; Bratkowski was expelled from the PZPR. The December to February
verification of the journalists was among the most
intense of any sector. By March 1982 about 1,200
out of the 10,000 journalists had been dismissed or
had resigned in order to boycott the military
régime (Le Monde, 23 March 1982). About a dozen

of Polityka's 30 journalists left after intense and
public soul-searching, some (like Radgowski) breaking links with the journal that stretched back over
decades (Cf. Passent, Polityka, 20 February 1980).
The most dramatic departure was that of Dariusz
Fikus, whose protest against the curtailment of
civil liberties began a most peculiar evolution.
This Jewish erstwhile Secretary of the Journal's
PZPR cell adopted Catholicism flamboyantly and joined
the opposition [32].   Słowo Powszechne lost 20 journalists, while another ebullient journal, the SD
daily, Kurier Polski, saw 13 go.   The SDP itself
was dissolved on 20 March and replaced by a régime-
sponsored Association of Journalists of the PRL
(SD-PRL).   It accepted a new programme and statute
and elected Klemens Krzyżagórski as its chairman.
In a letter to Jaruzelski it pledged itself to work
'for the full normalisation and renewal of socio-
political life' (TL, 22 March 1982).   Bratkowski
in a fruitless gesture came out of hiding to protest
against the SDP's dissolution.   The press purge
was paralleled by a similar one in radio and TV.
By mid-March about 513 journalists had been dismissed
and another 40 suspended in this sector.   The
creative cultural workers like the writers, theatre
and film workers, sculptors, musicians and painters,
however, proved the most resistant sector of the
intelligentsia.   Their struggle to boycott the
martial law system will be discussed later, as will
the official moves to limit the student and academic
autonomy gained in 1981.

Jaruzelski's Winter, Jaruzelski's Spring
        January 1982 saw the emergence of the main post-
initial repression tendencies of the State of War.
The economic front was dominated by the Government
Economic Committee proposals on the forthcoming
price increases (TL, 29 January 1982).   The military
authorities attempted, at every level, to explain the
necessity for martial law and to rally support for
their programme of reconstruction.   From the second
week of January onwards great publicity was accorded
to the formation of District Committees of National
Rebirth (OKON).   The provincial PZPR aktyws were
summoned during January, as were the ZSL and SD
hardcores, in order to discuss their role and tasks
under martial law.   Jaruzelski and WRON met the
industrial workers' party aktyws on 13 January.   The
General indicated that the PZPR would have to wage
a hard battle in order to rebuild its presence within
the factories.   This conclusion had been drawn from

the Government meeting with managers of 30 leading
enterprises on 30 December which reflected 'an
atmosphere of gloom and lack of confidence'.   More
sober attitudes had followed the state of shock in
factories where the security forces had intervened.
Solidarity members believed that 'a return to previous conditions' would be possible after the emergency was over.   'Frustration and contestatory
attitudes' were prevalent, especially among the young,
because of the lack of prospects.   'Second, and
even third sets of Solidarity leadership' had appeared
under martial law but management remained solidly
loyal to the state.   The conclusion was that new
unions and self-management bodies were needed to fill
the void left by Solidarity (ICPA, 1/82, p. 20).
    The mass media heightened its anti-Solidarity
propaganda,claiming that it had been taken over by the
anti-socialist KOR-KPN opposition from the outset.
It still remained to be seen whether misled 'healthy
elements' could be won over (Kraszewski, TL, 15
January 1981).   There was also a spate of official
post-martial law versions of the 1981 conflicts, such
as Professor Hebda's account of the Radom WSI conflict provoked by his election as Rector.   The legal
repression of the opposition continued apace with
continual reports of the stiff sentences being handed
out by the courts.   These were counterpoised by the
widespread publicity accorded to the prosecution of
the corrupt officials of the Gierek era.   The trial
of Maciej Szczepański and his associates,however,
dragged on during January; as a result many of the
black and white certainties regarding his activities
became blurred.   The PZPR Cultural Department established contact, not too fruitfully, with representatives of the film, theatre, music and plastic arts
at a large meeting on 21 January.   Strenuous efforts
were made by the official media to popularise the PPR
period and to build up a cult of Gomułka, while
Jaruzelski's 1981 speeches were highlighted notably
just before important Sejm and CC sessions.
    The Sejm session of 25 January 1982 was the first
public ratification of the State of War [33].   It
confirmed the four Council of State decrees of 12
December 1981 establishing martial law and the draft
law on the Special Legal Regulations for the Period
of the State of War.   Only Romuald Bukowski from
Gdańsk voted against and there were five abstentions
(Karol Małcużyński and the PZKS Deputies).Jaruzelski
set out his political case and programme in his hour
and forty minutes' long speech (SSS, 25 January 1982,
cols. 7-32).   The stability and security of the state

had been saved by martial law which prevented civil
war and total economic collapse.   The State of War
was a bridge for the country to pass through a critical period.   Its repressive aspects would be
lightened as opposition abated and lifted once stability had been restored.   The worst would be over
within a year.   Economic balance might be achieved
within 2-3 years if work and order were maintained.
Jaruzelski presented the standard denunciation of
US economic sanctions and of attempts to use the
Polish Crisis to dismantle the postwar Yalta order.
He quashed rumours that internees would be forced to
emigrate,but said that they would be allowed to go
to a country of their choice if they so wished.   The
military would not allow a return to the pre-1980
corruption and incompetence.   He promised a merci-
less struggle against enemies of the socialist order.
The PZPR Ninth Congress programme would be implemented but a strong, honest and just state was necessary to introduce reforms and democratic guarantees
of social development.   In this way, Poland, in collaboration with socialist allies, would rebuild her
international position.   No decision had been taken
on the structure of the new TUs and all proposals
would be considered.   Economic Reform was a complex
matter but it would be pushed through determinedly.
The nation should work and maintain order and all
patriotic forces should join the OKONs in the task
of political and economic rebuilding.   Jaruzelski
hoped this would be supported by the Church.   The
Poles should understand that WRON and the State of
War offered the only way out of the crisis, albeit
at the price of some temporary restrictions and
privations.

     The Sejm resolution was again only opposed by
Bukowski.   The debate was naturally dominated by
Jaruzelski's supporters, notably Barcikowski and the
new PAX chairman, Komender.   Some significant critical voices were still raised.   Małcużyński, although interrupted repeatedly, asked some awkward
questions about what might follow the State of War.
He criticised its costs and euphoric media presentation.   He prophesied confrontation, especially
with the,young who composed 60% of the population,
if the authorities did not honour their pledges to
eschew revenge.   Zabłocki, the PZKS leader, described the State of War as a defeat for the policy
of dialogue and agreement.   He was not convinced of
the legal basis of martial law and would therefore
abstain.   Zabłocki repeated Glemp's theme about the
futility of political terrorism and economic

sabotage and called for the resumption of the Church-State understanding. Osmańczyk warned the Government against extremist policies which might cause an irreparable breach in Polish society. The Sejm moved on to more normal matters the following day and approved the Teachers' Charter unanimously. Jerzy Nawrocki, who had resigned as Minister of Education in opposition to martial law, was replaced by Benon Miśkiewicz, a hardline military historian and ex-Rector of Poznań University.

Crisis or not, it was announced that work would start on the Warsaw Métro in 1983 in order to put the capital on a par with Moscow, Budapest, Prague and Bucharest. It was to total 90 kilometres in length and to be based on Soviet technology and assistance. On 27 January the Council of Ministers confirmed the price rises for food, fuels and energy to be introduced on 1 February along with the compensations in pensions and other allowances. The massive price rises ranged from 100 to 400%. The following are illustrative examples per kilo with the old price in złoties in brackets: sugar 46 (10½), butter 240 (68), cheese 190 (50), ham 550 (180), chicken 130 (50), pork loin 360 (90), coal 2,200 (650). Gas, electricity and hot water prices more than doubled (TL, 28 January 1982). The net result was to raise food prices by 241% and domestic heating costs by 171%. This provoked a spontaneous demonstration in Gdańsk, mainly by young people, with 205 arrests and 13 injured. The authorities responded by lengthening the province's curfew. Their strengthened military and police presence ensured order and resigned acceptance, although strikes were reported in Wrocław, Ursus and the Lenin Shipyard.

Unlike his predecessors, Jaruzelski had every interest in painting the economic situation in dismal colours. But no embellishment was required of the GUS communiqué for 1981 (TL, 29 January 1982). GNP had fallen by 13% (following falls of 4% in 1980 [upped to 6% later] and 2.3% in 1979) and industrial production by 12.6%. Agricultural production had increased by 4.1% overall, but this was made up of a 20% increase in cereals and a 12% fall in livestock, as a result of the 1980 fodder shortage. Investment had fallen by about a quarter since 1978 and had returned to 1972 levels. Exports to the capitalist world had fallen by 20%, while imports had been cut by 30%. Money in circulation had risen by 27%, nominal wages by 30%; prices in the socialised sector had increased by a quarter, while free market prices had rocketed by 58%.

    In spite of the Gdańsk riots and a demonstration
before Mickiewicz' statue in Poznań on 13 February,
which resulted in 192 arrests, the late Winter saw
a gradual easing of martial law. Permission was
granted for public meetings and the activities of
religious, ethnic minority, cultural and voluntary
associations like the Red Cross. Various national
newspapers reappeared, notably the ZSL's Dziennik
Ludowy, the SD's Kurier Polski, the popular Życie
Warszawy, as well as a whole range of the provincial
papers and influential journals like Polityka, Życie
Literackie and Perspektywy. The régime also set up
a new daily Rzeczpospolita as its official mouth-
piece which somewhat downtoned the role of Trybuna
Ludu. Petrol was sold for private cars again, LOT
resumed international flights, communications were
extended and foreign travel restrictions were eased.
Alongside this normalisation the military régime
sought support wherever it could find it. The recalcitrant Reiff was replaced as PAX chairman by
Minister of Domestic Trade Zenon Komender, whose
meetings with the General were much publicised.
The PZPR provincial aktyws met again in February to
discuss the party's role and tasks under martial
law. The normal round of party-state meetings
picked up apace. WRON overviewed the political
and agricultural situation on 4 February, the Council
of Ministers on the 5th, the Politburo on the 6th,
while a national assembly of Wojewodas,Town Presidents and KOK Commissioners met in Warsaw on the 8th.
On 20 February the Government Committee on TUs issued its discussion paper theses on the evolution
of TUs, which laid down that they should co-operate
with the authorities in running the country but did
not specify how (TL, 22 February 1982). The police
carried out a massive two-day operation,'Spokój', in
mid-February to tighten up respect for the martial
law regulations which remained. The military continued to take over key positions with Division-
General Jan Dębicki emerging as Warsaw City President
in mid-February, following Brigade-General
Mieczysław Cygan's appointment as Gdańsk Wojewoda.
    WRON declared on 22 February that all the
rigours of the State of War had been adhered to.
It hoped that TUs and social organisations which
could fit into the constraints of the State of Law
would be licensed (TL, 23 February 1982). The trial
of the four KPN leaders (Moczulski,Szeremietiew,
Stański and Jandziszak) opened in the Warsaw provincial court on 22 February. It dragged on till early
October when 2 to 7 year sentences were handed down

to coincide with Solidarity's dissolution. The
authorities publicised a rare case of armed terrorism
when an MO sergeant, Zdzisław Karoś, was shot in a
Warsaw tram by a group of youths. They had set up
an amateurish armed league with the encouragement of
a priest, Sylwester Zych, who sheltered them in his
presbytery in Grodzisk Mazowiecki.

The PZPR Seventh Plenum met on 24-25 February
to discuss the strengthening of the PZPR's ideological
and political unity and how it could best regain
social confidence and lead Poland out of the crisis
[34]. Jaruzelski defined the aims, functions, justifications and duration of the State of War in his
long opening speech, which bears comparison with
Gomułka's 1956 and Gierek's 1971 Eighth Plena
speeches. Imperialism had attempted to use Poland,
'the temporarily weak link in the socialist system',
as a way of reversing the postwar balance of power.
The State of War by thwarting counter-revolution had
saved the peace and perhaps prevented the outbreak
of a Third World War. It 'was the last of our possible initiatives for avoiding the consequences of
incalculable confrontations'. All conspiracy and
opposition would be suppressed firmly but justly;
the long-term political battle would be to create
the correct political consciousness. 'The State of
War is not an aim in itself. We treat it as a
stage in regaining balance, in overcoming the most
difficult stage of the conflict.' Its rigours were
being eased but the process was being slowed by
social tension and opposition activity. The General
declared that he wanted to rebuild a strong, independent and self-managing TU movement. Such tactical promises helped to disarm opposition and maintain illusions on this score until Autumn Jaruzelski
claimed that US economic sanctions had caused heavy
losses to the Polish drugs industry and the Atlantic
fishing fleet, while the cutting of US grain imports
had caused the poultry industry to collapse. But
the Economic Reform would provide a way out in the
long term, even though the harsh price rises were an
essential preliminary to its introduction. Jaruzelski
claimed that the 4,500 OKONs which had already been
formed provided the intelligentsia and non-party
individuals with an alternative to 'internal emigration'. If everyone pulled together in the common effort of socio-economic rehabilitation Poland would be
back on her feet within 2-3 years.

Jaruzelski then told the CC what the PZPR's role
would be in these processes. It was 'at the beginning of a long and difficult road' of defeating

socialism's enemies,winning over the non-party mass
of the country and rallying its own ranks so that it
could implement the party's directing role in all
walks of life.   Its membership had admittedly
fallen to $2\frac{1}{2}$ million,but the PPR had had only 20,000
members and the PPS-Left 8,000 in 1944.   So the
party's real strength depended upon its quality
while its leadership personnel had been renewed by
between 50 and 80% in the run-up to the Ninth Congress.   Under martial law 311 provincial secretaries,
249 factory secretaries and 1,856 POP and lower
secretaries had been replaced.   These were the
greatest cadre changes in the party's history.
Although the 'process of democratisation is irreversible' this depended upon strong leadership and
party unity.   Jaruzelski made it crystal clear that
'there is no place for fractional activity.   In
this matter there must be absolute clarity.   The
party is neither a sect nor a discussion club.   The
party speaks with a single voice'.   Party resolutions would in future have to be carried out in full,
not selectively as in 1980-1981.   Jaruzelski's
hopeful answer to how this could be done, without
lapsing back to Gierek's deformations or full-
blooded Stalinism, was that socialism was a live and
adaptable ideology.   It 'was reformable in the best
sense of the word', in particular by working out the
right cadres policy.
      The CC had therefore not been summoned to hold
an inquest on its shortcomings which had necessitated the State of War but to begin the long-term
work of its ideological and organisational renewal.
CC Secretary, Marian Orzechowski, presented the draft
of the party's new Ideological Declaration entitled
'What are we fighting for, where are we heading?'.
CKR chairman Morawski called for a return to the
PZPR's working-class character and for its moral and
political cleansing.   Jerzy Urbański, who was
playing a crucial role in the party's verification
as CKKP chairman, echoed the theme that the PZPR's
moral and ideological health was the precondition
for regaining social and working-class confidence.
Other speakers stressed the importance of the party
statute and programme in this drive.   General Edward
Łukasik, soon to become the Poznań First Secretary,
denied that martial law had hindered the party's
functioning.   Kubiak had greater difficulty in
defending himself against charges of leftist revisionism and in explaining why he supported the
State of War as a Politburo member and CC Secretary
once it had been introduced.

The CC elected Czesław Kiszczak and Marian Woźniak as candidate members of the Politburo, the former receiving 179 votes out of 182 and the latter 178. The actual victims of martial law were very few. Only three left the CC, notably Marian Arendt, the Toruń Horizontalist, and Professor Jan Malanowski of Warsaw University, a DiP spokesman. The Plenum resolution ratified the establishment of WRON and the State of War. It confirmed Jaruzelski's ban on factions and called on provincial executives to establish full discipline by the end of March. Jaruzelski concluded by calling for a new style of party work and promised improvements for teachers and the young, especially in housing. Jaruzelski's cautious final word was that the Plenum marked 'the next step forward'. The opposition judgement on these proceedings banked on internal divisions forcing the junta to negotiate with them: 'The current leadership managed to paper over its differences without resolving them' [35].

The Sejm met immediately afterwards on 26-27 February to receive the resignations of the popular actor, Gustaw Holoubek, in protest against the internment of intellectuals and of the ex-Foreign Minister and CC Secretary, Emil Wojtaszek [36]. It passed unanimously seven Laws on the first day giving statutory body to the Economic Reform (cf. Szeliga, _Polityka_, 6 March 1982). The next day it established a State Nuclear Agency, and began work on the Constitutional and State Tribunals, replaced the Minister of Chemical Industry and promoted Krasiński to full Minister for Prices. Kiszczak, however, presented the real news of the day, in a newspaper interview, about the lifting of the remaining travel restrictions. The loosening up process and the release of internees depended entirely on domestic stabilisation. The counter-revolutionary forces, according to the Interior Minister, had been paralysed but the Special Regulations concerning internment, censorship and special judicial processes would be needed for a while longer (_TL_, 1 March 1982).

The Course of Martial Law

Polish foreign policy in this period was marked by the re-establishment of closer relations with Warsaw Pact allies and a propaganda drive against Western sanctions and protests. The MSZ protested in mid-March against the release of 10,000 balloons containing Solidarity appeals for passive resistance from the Danish island of Bornholm by a committee of

French intellectuals.   Jaruzelski had been invited
to Moscow just before the Seventh Plenum.   Unlike
Kania, he arrived in his own good time on 1 March
accompanied by a delegation which reflected the
novel constellation of power in Poland - Malinowski,
Kowalczyk, Czyrek, Messner, Siwicki and Obodowski.
They were received by all the key Soviet leaders.
Brezhnev and Jaruzelski exchanged compliments on their
primary concerns, the primacy of the Soviet alliance
and the suppression of anti-socialist opposition in
Poland, before haggling about the amount of Soviet
economic aid and the speed with which the PZPR would
resume its leading role.   The communiqué gave nothing away, stressing their common views and the tightening of mutual links (TL, 3 March 1982).   It later
transpired that, as a result of the Tikhonov-
Jaruzelski talks, the Soviets had granted aid worth
$1.7 milliards to follow the January credit of
$3.7 milliards.   The Politburo responded on 6 March
by declaring that friendship and alliance with the
USSR was the cornerstone of Polish foreign policy.
Their Warsaw Pact links were tightened when
Jaruzelski, flanked by Siwicki and Molczyk,met Kulikov
just before the Soviet-Polish-GDR 'Friendship 82'
manoeuvres in North-Western Poland in mid-March.
     From early March onwards Jaruzelski paid a series
of official party-state visits to re-establish 'fra-
ternal' relations with the leaders of Poland's
socialist neighbours.   Foreign Minister and CC Secretary, Józef Czyrek, became Jaruzelski's indispensible
right-hand man in external affairs and accompanied
him on all his trips.   Even before visiting Moscow
Jaruzelski had been to the GDR on 29 March.   He seems
to have received Honecker's promise of full support.
The Polish-GDR alliance was confirmed in the communiqué as 'an important factor of peace and stability
in Europe and an effective barrier to the forces of
revenge and reaction' (TL, 31 March 1982).   On 5
April the General sought economic and technological
assistance in Prague with moderate results.   A
friendlier reception greeted him in Budapest on 21
April.   CPSU Secretary Rusakov came to Warsaw on 17
May to discuss the tightening up of CPSU-PZPR organisational contacts.   Bulgaria and Zhivkov saw the
peripatetic General three days later and this particular round was completed with the visit on 4 June
to see Ceausescu in Bucharest.   On 8 June Jaruzelski
met Kadar, as well as Soviet Premier Tikhonov, at
the 36th Comecon Session in Budapest.   This intensive tournée of visits and contacts designed to rebuild the confidence of their neighbouring allies

and to solicit economic assistance in order to gain
time to resolve the political crisis culminated in
Jaruzelski's annual report to the Soviet leaders
in the Crimea on 16 August. Jaruzelski, no doubt,
stressed the beneficial changes brought about by
the State of War in order to forestall Kremlin criticism of the slowness and caution with which he
was re-asserting communist power. The official
communiqué stated that 'the process of bringing the
country out of the crisis was being hindered by the
counter-revolutionary underground whose activities
were inspired and backed from the outside, especially
from the USA' (TL, 17 & 20 August 1982). Brezhnev's
views on the domestic Polish situation were not
revealed except for his promises of economic assistance. Back in Poland, Jaruzelski responded to
the strictures about his leadership's lack of social
control by instructing the WKOKs to repress the
opposition under cover of a campaign against speculation, parasitism and other economically harmful
activity and to report back by 5 September.

After the Seventh Plenum the official stress
moved somewhat from the eradication of opposition to
combating 'internal emigration' and the neutral.
This drive was initiated by the Politburo document
on 'The tasks of party bodies and organisations' of
6 March (TL, 11 March 1982). The PZPR membership
and the educational, mass media and administrative
sectors, according to the Politburo directive, were
to be evaluated and brought to order within two
months. The aim was to rebuild the PZPR's leading
role. As Guetta remarked, however, this was a
largely theoretical proposition under martial law
conditions. Jaruzelski demanded support for WRON
decisions as a precondition of party membership; so
to that extent the PZPR was no more than a transmission belt for military decisions (Le Monde, 13 March
1982).

The tightening of the verification process started in early March soon made itself felt. Firstly,
the 200 teachers who attended the Ministry of Education's theoretical-political conference in Warsaw
on 12-13 March heard Rakowski tell them that there
was no place for anti-socialist teachers, especially
those who condoned contestatory activities by their
pupils [37]. Secondly, verification was at its
sharpest within the party arena. The CC Report on
the Implementation of the Seventh Plenum Theses
revealed that 59% of the 44,500 deleted from the PZPR
during March went for passivity. In the more
serious 4,223 cases of expulsion, 38% went for the

new crime of 'two facedness towards the party' (TL,
21 April 1982). The tempo of party activity picked
up after the stagnation of the early period of martial law; 100% of party cells in the opposition
stronghold of Wrocław as well as Krosno, 82% in
Częstochowa and 40% even in the lowest case of
Tarnobrzeg had met to assess the political situation
in their milieux. The régime also took the students' association in hand in late March. The
parallel drive to establish OKONs also seemed to be
making progress as far as structures were concerned
with a figure of 6,000 being claimed for late March.
Thirdly, as already noted, the SDP was dissolved and
a new Journalists' Association formed. The régime
set about trying to break the actors' boycott with
indifferent success and also attempted to discipline
the writers and other cultural workers (see CC
Culture Department Assessment, Kultura, Paris,
November 1982 , pp. 163-172). Lastly, the TGOs were
let loose against the peasants. The régime planned
to give the ZSL a much increased role. The Eighth
ZSL Plenum, attended by Jaruzelski, confirmed the
Workers'-Peasant alliance and ZSL support for the
State of War. The ZSL in its resolution aspired
to be 'the strong force' representing the professional interests of the peasants (TL, 1 April 1982).
    On 25-26 March the Sejm confirmed that private
peasant farms were a constitutionally accepted and
permanent factor. It raised the top legal limit
on their size from 20 to 100 hectares [38]. Minister
of Agriculture Wojtecki admitted that there would
be a shortfall of 600,000 tons of cereals to meet
Poland's current needs for flour. This aroused
fears that even bread would have to be rationed.
The general tenor of the debate was that the agricultural sector would be appeased by the military
régime, although there was no question of renewing
Rural Solidarity. The Sejm supported Czyrek's
statement on foreign policy and confirmed the Council of State decree extending the term of People's
Councils to March 1984. The Constitutional Tribunal
to check up on the constitutionality of all laws
and the State Tribunal to call Government members to
account were finally established; the latter met
with four abstentions and was only supported by
318 votes out of a possible 460. The Sejm also set
up a 120 strong advisory Economic and Social Council
chaired by Jan Szczepański. Joining in this proli-
feration of new bodies the Council of Ministers soon
afterwards set up a Consultative Economic Council
chaired by Professor Czesław Bobrowski.

Social unrest and opposition still continued and was still suppressed. Zawadzki let it be known that 275 individuals had been condemned for illegal political and industrial activity, through the accelerated procedure, by March and that another 50 cases were in train. Eight had received sentences of over 5 years, 40 between 3 and 5 years, 105 between 1 and 3 years and 148 had been sentenced to one year terms. Rakowski's and Kubiak's attempt to persuade 30 notable intellectuals to call off their boycott of official publications ended in an embarrassing public fiasco. The authorities, however, dismissed Henryk Samsonowicz, the liberal Rector of Warsaw University, and his three deputies in early April. They did likewise to the popular Rector of Gdańsk University at the end of the month. The profound split between state and society and the political isolation of the military régime was noted by both its friends and foes. The military daily decried the refusal of much of society to think in terms of reason of state. It characterised the continuation of the so-called struggle for honour and civil rights as defined by Reagan as 'irresponsible and anti-Polish' (Żołnierz Wolności, 5 April 1982). Chief Editor Morawski admitted the dilemma which the authorities faced in filling the void left by Solidarity and the impossibility of establishing a social dialogue (Życie Warszawy, 29 March 1982). Hardly surprisingly the Kremlin, encouraged by Polish hardliners like Kociołek, was most dissatisfied with Jaruzelski's continuing failure to suppress the social turmoil. Literaturnaya Gazeta even went as far as claiming that 43 communists had been murdered by opposition terrorists during martial law. Soviet displeasure was, however, for the moment less significant than Finance Minister Krzak's success in signing an agreement in Frankfurt on 6 April with five Western commercial banks over the rescheduling of $2,400 milliards worth of the Polish hard currency debt. Jaruzelski admitted that Poland needed a further $4,000 milliard loan for basic food and other necessities. His implicit threat was that he would worsen domestic repression if the West did not provide it, but conversely he offered the carrot that it would be abated if the West collaborated (Le Monde, 7 April 1982).

Western commentators struck by the depth of social discontent and anomie, underestimated the cold, calculated and long-term resolve with which the political officers were rebuilding the system step by step. Starting off with matters within

their control they set about reconstituting the
PZPR's ideological front.   CC Secretary Orzechowski
stated that the Ideological Declaration currently
under discussion by party organisations would provide the permanent synthesis of the work of the
Ninth Congress.   It would also act as the bridge
between the Congress Resolution and the PZPR's new
Perspective Plan (TL, 30 March 1982).   This was
the prologue to the PZPR's First Ideological-Theoretical Conference attended by about 400 participants
in Warsaw on 2-3 April (Bijak, Polityka, 10 April
1982).   Deputy-GZP Head, Division-General Tadeusz
Szaciło, explained the significance of the Patriotic
Movement of National Rebirth in providing an institutional framework for all social classes interested
in renewal and reform (ND, April 1982, pp. 119 ff).
He also gave his party audience an authoritative ex-
position of the military's role in these processes.
'Under conditions of the State of War the increased
role of the Army is in accordance with reality.   The
Army together with the domestic security organs
carried out the function of being the main organiser
and,in the first phase, enforcer of the State of
War.   It had a particular legitimacy to do this;
moral authority in society, one of the few institutions to face up to the crisis politically, as
well as the appropriate capacities' (TL, 3-4 April
1982).
     The Eighth Plenum on 22-23 April was devoted
largely to economic questions [39].   The rising CC
Secretary and Politburo candidate, Woźniak, in the
Plenum Report blamed the 13% fall in GNP in 1981 on
the Solidarity strikes and social tensions which had
broken the economy.   The overcoming of the economic
crisis, which he admitted would take two years longer
than envisaged in the original Government projects,
and the introduction of the Economic Reform were now
the main tasks of the party.   Deputy-Premier Obodowsk
then updated the Ninth Congress Report on overcoming
the economic crisis in the light of subsequent developments.   He presented the main lines of the
Three Year Economic Recovery Programme - strict control of raw materials, especially of fuels, cuts in
investment (minus 25% in 1981, minus 10% planned for
1982), increased exports, closer collaboration with
socialist allies and disentanglement from reliance
on the West, the introduction of self-financing,
self-investing criteria to encourage efficient enterprises and a selective social policy to cope with
the consequences of the drastic cuts in living standards brought about by the price rises which were

an essential component of the anti-inflation drive.
The Plenum then broke up into 9 specialised sub-
groups to which 157 speakers,including invited
guests and specialists, contributed.   Deputy
Defence Minister Obiedziński, a victim of the
Stalinist purges who was rehabilitated in 1956,
called for greater party and social discipline.
He reported on the TGOs' 'Spring 82' operations in
1,940 rural communes designed to prepare for the
harvest and to check up on milk and meat contract-
ing by peasants to the state.   The Plenum Resolution
declared that martial law 'opened up the possibility
of the normalisation of economic life';   'the political activity of the party had been rejuvenated'
since the Seventh Plenum.   This Plenum set the pattern for the worthy but increasingly dull and stodgy
character of its frequently held successors (24 by
February 1986) which contrasted dramatically with
the lively and unpredictable ones of 1980-1981.
    At its 28 April meeting WRON announced the li-
beration of 800 internees and the conditional free-
ing of another 200.   This meant that a further 2,000
still remained interned.   It achieved a notable success when Jan Kulaj, the young Rural Solidarity leader,
announced on TV, after being freed, that he now accepted the ZSL programme;   he was willing to work
within it.   WRON also raised the curfew nationwide
on 1 May, reopened some frontier crossings, restored
automatic inter-provincial telephone communications
and allowed licensed associations to meet without
prior permission, but maintained controls over meetings and lectures.   These measures gradually loosening up martial law controls were partly designed
to influence Western public opinion against the harder
US line on economic sanctions against Poland.   As
Jaruzelski told the Eighth Plenum, the most effective
incentive for the West to lift its economic sanctions
was 'the regaining of political, social and economic
balance in Poland' [40].
    On May Day Barcikowski celebrated the centenary
of the Polish Workers' Movement.   He justified the
State of War in terms of Poland's history and political culture.   But Jaruzelski's appeal for all
Poles to work together to extract 'our country as
soon as possible from the crisis, to ensure a normal
socio-economic rhythm' (TL, 3 May 1982), met with the
largest wave of disturbances since December.   The
Solidarity counter-demonstrations on May Day were
especially strong in Gdańsk, Warsaw and Wrocław,
where crowds of up to 30,000 demonstrators were
reported.   The main militia repression with water

cannon, tear gas and baton charges took place mainly
on 3 May, the anniversary of the 1791 constitution.
WRON met immediately on 4 May.   It restored the
curfew in the most disturbed provinces and made it
stricter for the under-21s.   In order to discourage
the Solidarity TKKs' call for a 15-minute work stoppage on 13 May, the anniversary of six months of
martial law, Urban issued a stiff public warning
that all public order disturbances 'would meet with
determined counter-measures' by the security forces
(TL, 11 May 1982).   The strike call was partially
heeded in Solidarity factory strongholds in Warsaw,
Gdańsk, Wrocław and Białystok, while the appeal to
stop traffic movement and to sound hooters for a
minute in support of the midday stoppage met with
a patchy response (Le Monde, 15 May 1982).   About
700 were arrested or interned as a result.   The May
disturbances represented a draw.   They demonstrated
Jaruzelski's failure to achieve a stable normalisation
but they also illustrated the limits of Solidarity's
support and the diminishing number of older people
with responsibilities willing to risk the consequences
     On 3-4 May the Sejm duly passed the Government's
Higher Education Law and the Resolution on National
Understanding but critical voices were still raised
[41].   Jan Szczepański demanded a Government statement on the disturbances and wanted to know 'how it
intended to react to this situation'.   Zabłocki set
out the Theses of the Primate's Social Council (see
Chapter Six) and reproached the authorities for their
vague concept of national union, which they only practised with their own supporters.   Osmańczyk demanded
a new legal framework for martial law which would
allow internees to be released and the State of War
proper to be ended.   As things stood there was no
way out.   Nobody knew whether the current situation
'would last another five months or five years'.
All this was more pertinent than Rakowski's attack
on Solidarity, the ritual appeals for support and
the setting up of yet more bodies - a National
Council for Culture and a Development Fund for
Culture.
     The hermetically closed off world of Government
continued as before.   The Council of Ministers met
on 10 May to discuss the disturbances and the Economic
Reform.   Only then did the Politburo meet to express
'support for the assessments and activities of the
Government in the situation which has arisen', not
vice versa as under normal communist conditions (TL,
12 May 1982).   Detailed reports by the Consultative
Economic Council on the economic developments of the

previous 18 months and on Government achievements
during the first five months of the State of War
appeared. They were read only by the committed
faithful and the occasional scholar in the West.
The debate on the future shape of TUs struck a
wider public chord, however. The 27th anniversary
of the Warsaw Pact allowed deputy Defence Minister
Molczyk to praise its value as a defensive alliance.
He reiterated that the State of War had been declared
in a fully sovereign manner by the Poles themselves
(TL, 14 May 1982).

Solidarity naturally responded in the first half
of May by showing that it existed, that it was
capable of canalising social discontent and that it
could hold up normalisation permanently. Its leaders hoped that this would force the more pragmatic
communist wing to come to terms with them, particularly as the Church continued to support dialogue and
the 1980 Social Agreements. But the Jaruzelski régime's flexible response of containing, but not suppressing, disturbances and strikes in a bloody manner
placed them in a quandary. Although the situation
appeared to be a stalemate the authorities' capacity
to grind down resistance was to prove stronger than
Solidarity's ability to mount bout after bout of
opposition, as was to be shown in August, October
and November. Guetta's argument that Solidarity had
a greater freedom of manoeuvre than its rival, especially because of Soviet displeasure, which was
communicated to Jaruzelski by Rusakov and Kulikov in
mid-May, was not justified (Le Monde, 11 & 19 May
1982). The Kulikov meeting, also attended by
Siwicki, was concerned with 'training problems and
the improvement of the combat readiness of the Armed
Forces', which naturally had a specific political
meaning against the canvas of the May disturbances
(TL, 20 May 1982).

Jaruzelski was not, however, deflected from his
course. On 26 May the Sejm indulged in the usual
symbolic sops to Soviet pressure by dismissing ex-
PAX leader Reiff from the Council of State; here
five Deputies abstained ostentatiously including
Sejm Vice-Marshal, Halina Skibniewska (SSS, 26th
sitting, Col. 96). His place, along with that of
a throwback to the Gierek era, ex-CRZZ chairman
Kruczek, and Szczepański's were taken by Alfons
Klafkowski, a noted International Law specialist,
Kazimierz Morawski, the ChSS chairman, and Stanisław
Kania, who was now expressly put in the political
reserves (17 Deputies against, 42 abstentions).
Adam Łopatka also replaced Jerzy Kuberski as

Minister of Religious Affairs.   On 12 June WRON attempted to cover up social discontent by stating,
rather smugly, that all the main tasks of the State
of War were well in hand (TL, 14 June 1982).
'Faisant bonne mine au mauvais jeu,' WRON claimed
that normalisation was proceeding.   It instructed
the MSW to alleviate the rigours of the State of War
even further.   Alongside the development of PRON
the military's concept of participation was publicised when WRON met women's representatives on 23
June.   Jaruzelski also let it be known that there
were 'objective conditions for increasing the role
of PAX in PRON' after meeting Komender; the development of PRON was now one of the régime's main priorities (TL, 21 June 1982).   The formation of
Professor Klimaszewski's committee to bring back
Sikorski's ashes from Newark, UK, for reburial in
the Wawel may not have been much compensation for the
price rises in alcohol, tea and coffee,but the Polish
football team's third place in the World Cup in
Spain certainly was.   There was, however, little
joy in the 1982 Budget, Economic Report for 1981
and the work on the 1983-1985 Three Year Plan passed
by the Sejm on 5-6 July (SSS, 23rd sitting).   Returning to the realm of the possible, the Sejm appointed the 28 members of the State Tribunal, headed
by High Court President Władysław Berutowicz, as
well as the 94 members of the Socio-Economic Council.
      Interior Minister Kiszczak made it clear in mid-
May that the State of War would be loosened up but
not lifted.   Social discipline and the overall situation had improved, but the lifting of martial law
restrictions depended entirely on the pace of 'the
stabilisation of the socio-political situation'
(Polityka, 17 July 1982).   There would be no general
amnesty.   The Government would, however, release
internees who promised to behave themselves.   It
would take a 'benevolent attitude' towards clandestine members of the Solidarity underground if they
gave up their activities 'which are destined to be
defeated'.   The Solidarity truce, calling off protest until the end of July, thus met with the official response that opposition individuals could
escape punishment if they abandoned the conflict
but that there could be no political settlement with
the underground (Rogowski, Żołnierz Wolności, 12
July 1982).   The régime pressed ahead with the
formation of its own structures.   The joint PZPR-
ZSL-SD collaboration committee met on 20 July with
PAX, ChSS and PZKS representatives to confirm the
PRON Declaration.   They announced that a provisional

PRON National Council would be established and this was done in the Autumn.

The Communist leadership was reported by the Western press as being divided between hardline and conciliatory wings. The political significance of the personnel changes at the Ninth Plenum of 15-16 July, ostensibly called to discuss the Youth Question, was, however, quite clear. The resignation as CC Secretaries of the liberal Kubiak and the conservative Olszowski was choreographed to symbolise the triumph of Jaruzelski's pragmatic centrism; in practice the shedding of these individuals indicated that the leadership would become more cohesive and even more dominated by Jaruzelski in future. The dropping of the other remaining 1981 reform figure, Łabęcki, from the Politburo and the arrival of Stanisław Kałkus, a simple Poznań worker, and Woźniak as full members and Bejger and Główczyk as candidates also confirmed this. The General's close aides, Główczyk and Manfred Gorywoda, also became CC Secetaries. The size of the residual pro-worker element in the CC could be gauged from the unusually high 31 votes against and 25 abstentions on Łabęcki's dismissal from the Politburo [42]. In the main Plenum Report Jaruzelski attempted to win over Poland's restless youth by promising them a key role in pushing through reform and in combating incompetence and corruption. But he stressed that, although a number of youth organisations were possible, they would have to fit into the political and ideological unity of the new system (Jaruzelski, Przemówienia 1981-1982, pp. 379-418).

On 20 July WRON ratified the decisions on the 'further normalisation of the socio-political life of the State' (TL, 21 July 1982). Jaruzelski announced them to the Sejm the following day, the eve of Poland's national day [43]. These determined the course of the State of War in the second half of 1982. Jaruzelski hoped for economic recovery, welcomed the Papal Visit in general terms and promised a rebirth of TUs while rejecting both the CRZZ and Solidarity frameworks. WRON considered that martial law could not be lifted as there was still active anti-revolutionary opposition, but sufficient progress had been made for 'a further easing of the rigours of the State of War'. The bulk of internees, including all women, would be released. Postal, telephone and foreign travel restrictions and the suspension of most of the remaining associations would be lifted. WRON was prepared to lift martial

law by the end of the year and to replace it with
new legal regulations and special powers for the
Government if the social situation and opposition
activities quietened down.   PRON would be open to
all Poles supporting socialism and the Soviet alliance.   Both the Sejm resolution and the Politburo
called on PZPR members and the nation to support PRON
to the utmost.   Rakowski's attack on Solidarity did
not, however, throw much light on the new TU structures which were under discussion.   Olszowski's
displacement away from the centre of power was confirmed.   He was appointed as Foreign Minister again,
after a six-year break, although this was opposed
by 9 Deputies and another 32 abstained.   Olszowski's
close ally, Tokarski, was also replaced by Bogdan
Jachacz as CC Press, Radio and TV Department Head soon
afterwards.   Among other changes Komender replaced
Ozdowski as deputy Premier; the latter became Sejm
Vice-Marshal in place of Andrzej Werblan, a controversial major figure who at last dropped out of
political life.   No dramatic changes therefore occurred in July.   The military authorities made sufficient concessions to ensure a reasonable press,
but they remained well in control in spite of the
social and industrial challenges mounted by the opposition.   The régime was now in a position to move
on to institute the PRON and the TU sections of
their long-term strategy.

August was a month of major anniversaries and
therefore of grave disquiet for the authorities because of their symbolic capacity to trigger off
protest.   That, on 1 August, of the 1944 Warsaw Uprising caused a manifestation against the Katyn massacre in the Warsaw Powązki cemetery.   The Solidarity
TKK announced that it would resume action as of the
13th (symbol of martial law because of its imposition on 13 December), while the Gdańsk committee
called protests on the 16th and 31st to commemorate
the beginning and the ending of the 1980 Lenin
Shipyard confrontation.

Developments within the opposition and the Roman
Catholic Church are examined in subsequent chapters.
One might note here that the former finally realised
that the military régime had only been playing for
time; it would not treat them as a negotiating power
unless the scale of social opposition was stepped
up.   The latter became increasingly preoccupied with
the Papal Visit.   The régime issued the usual warnings that it was determined to maintain public order
(Żołnierz Wolności, 12 August 1982).   Threats were
coupled with official claims that the PZPR was being

transformed for the better and that Poland was reformable in a socialist sense (Loranc, TL, 9 August
1982). The major wave of mid-August street demonstrations mainly in Gdańsk, Warsaw, Wrocław and
Nowa Huta were put down by the ZOMO and militia, but
they also demonstrated the capacity of the TKK to
embarrass the military régime. The scenes of confrontation and street violence were repeated in other
towns in the following days. Tension rose as the
major national conflict scheduled for the 31 August
anniversary of the signing of the Social Agreements
approached. All this led Jaruzelski, on his return
from the Crimea, to order the WKOKs to take the ne-
necessary counter-measures. The Politburo appealed
for social calm and discipline and parroted the
theme of the connection between tranquillity, reform
and the ending of martial law (TL, 21-22 August 1982).
Kiszczak continued the campaign of intimidation on
TV. He warned that the martial law authorities were
determined to break the wave of destructive anarchy
which could only be compared to that which had lost
Poland her independence for a century. Disturbances
would be crushed with a firm hand. 'The attempts to
delay stabilisation of life in the country and to
prolong the crisis can only have one outcome, that
the road will be longer and more difficult' (TL, 26
August 1982). WKOKs met to publicise the theme
that normalisation was continuing in spite of opposition which would be suppressed. PRON signatories
appealed for calm,while Jaruzelski told graduating
officers in Poznań that martial law was a dam against
counter-revolution. The usual announcement of joint
Polish-Soviet manoeuvres, this time unwontedly in
the Warsaw region, made its customary appearance.
The police presence was strengthened in all urban
areas. Some Western commentators considered that
these events showed the obstinate refusal of the
majority of the Polish population to be 'normalised'
and that a permanent underground structure was in the
making (Le Monde, editorial, 15-16 August 1982).
But as usual it was unclear whether this was a tribute
to the Poles' determined commitment to political
values or whether it was a spontaneous and desperate
social reaction to the fall of a quarter in real in-
come during martial law's first seven months. However, ordinary petrol appeared on free sale again
in late August to compensate for the rationing of
shoes, underwear and stockings which had been added
earlier in the month.
     The disturbances on 31 August-2 September were
as major as anticipated in the streets of the 4 main

trouble centres - Warsaw, Gdańsk, Wrocław and Nowa
Huta. Preliminary estimates were that 54 towns in
34 provinces were affected and that about 75,000
Poles took to the streets. As often happens, the
worst flashpoint occurred not in the main centres,
but in the coppermining town of Lubin, where at
least two people lost their lives. Wojciech
Markiewicz's account of indiscriminate shootings
and repression in Lubin was censored from Polityka
but appeared in the Underground press (ICPA, 19/82).
The officially admitted toll was 5 deaths, 219 injured, including 148 militia men, 6 firemen and 2
soldiers. The heightened police activity produced
a bonus for the authorities in the arrest of the
major KOR-opposition leader, Zbigniew Romaszewski.
The mass media claimed that 31 August was 'a normal
working day' above all else; they crowed over the
defeat of the Underground and its RFE paymasters
(Bielecki, TL, 1 September 1982). On 1 September
WRON welcomed 'the limited character' of the disturbances in spite of the long preparations. Kuroń,
Michnik, Lityński and Wujec were arrested, while
Lipski and Chojecki escaped this fate by being
abroad. The legal dossier against KOR was sped up.
The Politburo condemned the disturbances, regretted
the casualties and blamed the Americans. Their
message was that all plans to turn Poland into 'a
centre of tension and troubles' were doomed to defeat
(TL, 3-4 September 1982). The authorities had therefore weathered the worst that the opposition could
mobilise against them in the streets and had avoided
a blood bath. Their refusal to negotiate with the
Solidarity leaders and Wałęsa was now complete and
obvious to all. As Urban said, the demonstrations
were Solidarity's last throw and its 'funeral march'
(TL, 3-4 September 1982).
     Władysław Gomułka died of cancer in the early
morning hours of 1 September at the age of 77. Western comment was more reserved (cf. Bernard Féron,
'L'Inexorable décadence du héros',Le Monde,2 September
1982) than the homage paid to him by the military
authorities (see Polityka, 4 & 11 September 1982).
The eulogistic official obituary hailed him as 'the
most outstanding individual in postwar political
life'. It emphasised his merits in establishing
communism in Poland postwar, in 'giving the correct
sense to the concept of "the Polish Road to
Socialism"' and in correcting Stalinist deformations
after 1956 (TL,2 September 1982). The Politburo
set up an Honorary Funeral Committee headed by
Jaruzelski. After lying in state in the Sejm

building Gomułka was buried with full honours in the
Powązki Cemetery on the 6th.   Barcikowski's farewell
political tribute praised his achievement in creating
the KRN concept of broad alliance with all forces
willing to join in building socialism.   Gomułka's
close lieutenant and ex-CRZZ chairman, Ignacy Loga-
Sowiński, making his first public appearance since
1970, staked out Gomułka's position in history as
'the most important Polish resistance leader', as
the wise strategist who had adapted the universal
laws of building socialism to Poland's specific conditions and as the great realist who had based
Poland's postwar frontiers and independence on the
Soviet alliance (TL, 7 September 1982).
    The authorities claimed to uncover a Solidarity-
inspired terrorist group in Katowice in early
September.   It was therefore grist to their mill
when four Poles of unclear background occupied the
Polish Embassy in Berne from 6 to 10 September and
took hostages.   Claiming to represent a so-called
Army of the Interior (echoing the Second World War
organisation) they demanded the lifting of martial
law and the release of all internees.   Although
Solidarity spokesmen disociated themselves from this
act of violence, which ended peacefully, the Polish
mass media had a field day claiming that the opposition had opted for terrorism.   The shady background of the group's leader (pseudonym Florian
Kruszyk) and the modalities of the incident have remained obscure to this day.
    Foreign Minister Olszowski's task of reassuring
the Soviet leaders during his Moscow visit of 13-14
September about the military régime's controlled
response was not rendered easier by the usual recru-
descence of mid-month disturbances, notably outside
Wrocław Cathedral.   Śląsk Wrocław's UEFA Cup football
match with Moscow Dynamo not surprisingly also occasioned disturbances on the 15th.   Jan Józef Lipski
was arrested immediately on his return from London,
where he had been treated for a cardiac condition
after being released provisionally from internment.
The régime, however, went forward regardless in
setting up its new institutions with the PRON
Provisional National Council.   Kiszczak presented
the régime's considered reaction to the social unrest
(SSS, 16 September 1982, Cols. 8-15).   He claimed
that normalisation was taking place slowly and that
Solidarity was gradually losing support.   He admitted that street demonstrations had broken out
in about 66 towns in 34 provinces.   Serious conflicts had occurred in about 25, roughly 70% of the

participants being young people. 5,131 individuals were detained, of whom 67 were imprisoned under the summary procedure, 3,328 were directed to Tribunals of Misdemeanours who had imprisoned 263 and fined 2,821, while 228 had been interned. Four demonstrators had been killed and 89 injured, 14 seriously, as had 295 police. The authorities would defeat all Western-inspired attempts to keep Poland permanently in crisis as 'the sick man of Europe'. WRON would not be diverted 'from the road on which we have embarked of saving the socialist state, strengthening its independence and sovereignty, implementing the process of renewal, reform and democratisation, in order to bring about a rebirth of Poland'.

The last desperate attempt by Solidarity to force the authorities into negotiating with them had failed, although Kiszczak blamed Frasyniuk, Bujak and Lis for ignoring his April offer of conversations backed by 'special guarantees' by the Church. The mass media now made it clear that there would be 'no return to public life' either for Solidarity underground members or even for the name of Solidarity which was tarred with 'highly negative factors' (Rzeczpospolita, 22 September 1982). The demonstrations of August failed to prevent the final banning of Solidarity which the junta had probably decided on once the Underground had refused to come in after Easter 1982. On the other hand, the authorities and the Church negotiated a basis for the suspension of the State of War by the end of the year.

The three main strands of régime policy in this period were, firstly, the continued repression of the last attempts to organise mass open opposition followed by the banning of Solidarity, the political and judicial campaign against KOR and the building up of PRON. By late September it transpired that the legal basis for Solidarity's existence would be replaced by a severely amended form of the TU Law first presented in 1981 which would effectively de-legalise Solidarity, which had only been suspended up till now. Rakowski's attacks on Solidarity's attempts to dismantle the socialist state in 1981 and its failure to change its policies in 1982 also suggested that Solidarity would not be allowed to play any part in the new TUs [44]. The draft bill was produced by a Council of State committee, approved by the Sejm's committees on Labour and Social Questions and Legislative Affairs and the Politburo confirmed the final version on 6 October in spite of Glemp's

objections and John Paul's warnings.   The régime
was undeterred by the usual round of Warsaw, Gdańsk,
Wrocław demonstrations.   It mobilised its security
forces and went ahead regardless of Church and Western protests, like those of French Premier Mauroy in
the Senate on 7 October.

Jaruzelski stated his firm determination to
push through the programme of national rehabilitation in his own way in the Sejm on 9 October.   The
only concessions were the liberation of most internees and the easing of passport procedures.   The
General refused to commit himself to the lifting of
the State of War until it had achieved its purposes.
He warned both Church and society that national understanding could only take place within the developing
PRON framework.   The new TUs would be built up from
the lowest factory level upwards.   They could be
'independent and self-managing' as long as they were
socialist and restricted purely to representing workers' interests and the process of renewal!

The Law on TUs was published in full by the
mass media (TL, 9-10 October 1982; Communist Affairs,
July 1983, pp. 363-371).   All existing labour organisations, including both Solidarity and the branch
unions, were dissolved by the Law, which replaced
the 1945 and 1949 legislation, as well as the Laws
of May 1981 on Inter-Factory Organisations and
Peasant Unions.   The new unions would initially be
formed by Foundation Committees solely at the enterprise level.   They would have to accept the socialist constitution, the socialised means of production and the PZPR's leading role in their statutes,
which would be registered by the appropriate court.
All political activities and aims were banned, while
a long list of the bread-and-butter matters which
should concern them was enumerated.   All political
strikes were forbidden.   The right to strike was
conceded 'as a final resort' after a detailed arbitration procedure had been exhausted.   Even this
right was denied to workers in MON, MSW, defence
industry, educational, railway, communications,
energy producing and fire fighting establishments.
On top of all this, the Sejm could suspend the
right to strike if this were justified by the
critical state of the economy.   Article 53 set out
what appeared to be the optimistic programme that
bottom level enterprise TUs should be formed during
1983, nationwide unions during 1984 and that a
national TU organisation would be established in
1985.   The bill was opposed by 10 Deputies while
another 9 abstained [45].   The accompanying, and

less controversial, bill on peasant organisations
also met with 9 abstentions [46].   On 12 October the
Council of State decreed a National Consultative
Social Commission to co-ordinate and advise on the
formation of the new TUs.   It laid down the procedure for their registration in great detail (TL,
13 October 1982).   A model statute was published
to help the Foundation Committees with their work
(TL, 23-24 October 1982).

Solidarity's dissolution met with a spontaneous
outburst, a strike in its birthplace in the Gdańsk
Lenin Shipyard, and the calling of a regional strike.
The authorities broke it by militarising the shipyard on 12 October (Communist Affairs, July 1983,
p. 362).   The security forces and the Army sur-
rounded and then occupied the shipyard.   These developments gained Jaruzelski Soviet Defence Minister
Ustinov's assurance of 'full support' when they met
to celebrate the 39th anniversary of the formation
of the Polish Armed Forces.   On the other hand,
Western, especially French, opinion reacted bitterly.
President Mitterand outmanoeuvred the French communists by demonstrating that such repression was an
intrinsic fault of 'the communist system' (Le Monde,
15 October 1982).   Jaruzelski had therefore closed
the chapter headed 'Solidarity' without provoking an
explosion, even though it had taken him nine months
of cautious repression and the wearing down of the
opposition and of society to do it.   The Soviet bloc
was ample in his praise at a meeting of communist
Foreign Ministers in Moscow and during Kulikov's
Warsaw Pact Military Council visit of 22 October to
Warsaw.

The Jaruzelski régime avoided the option of the
bloody suppression of the workers and society.   The
possibility of mass political violence and terror
was never a serious one.   Its use and consequences
were aired in Wajda's film Danton, although any historical parallels were unclear and much disputed
(cf. Polityka, 5 February & 5 March 1983).   The
régime's political analysis now made KOR the scape-
goat for the anti-socialist activities of Solidarity,
thus providing an escape hatch for the avoidance of
legal sanctions against Wałęsa and the more quiescent
worker-leaders and activists.   The drive against
anti-socialist elements to please Soviet allies and
to maintain their ideological credentials could thus
be restricted to proceedings against an extremely
small gremium of the KOR and KPN individuals.   The
latter were sentenced symbolically on 8 October
(Kopka, Polityka, 16 October 1982).   Régime

publicists explained that skilful manipulation of
the country's real problems had allowed a small
group like KOR, which was basically a NATO subsidised
fifth column, to create a dangerous situation for
the state (TL, 20 October 1982).   It was also correct to describe KOR as 'a mini Solidarity' and
Solidarity as 'a maxi KOR'.   KOR leaders considered
that a revolutionary opportunity existed after Summer
1980 to limit the PZPR hegemony and to establish political and party pluralism.   KOR had objectively
become Reagan's Trojan Horse for fomenting anarchy
and self-destruction in Poland as a way of weakening
the Soviet bloc [47].   These rationalisations showed
the narrow ideological limits of Soviet-Leninism
even in relation to Eurocommunism.

Socio-economic discontent still fuelled residual support for the Solidarity Underground.   In practice, after facing down social protest in August
and October, the régime's internal return to ideological orthodoxy was matched by the rebuilding of
the institutional basis of its power through the
development of PRON, the new TUs and the rallying of
the party bodies.   The most serious immediate obstacle now became the continued intellectual and
cultural boycott.   The strength and bitterness of
the writers' boycott and opposition to 'collaboration' with the military authorities was shown in
the difficulty in launching new journals (TL, 25-26
September 1982).   Rakowski's efforts in mid-October
to win over the contestatory theatre workers also
failed (cf. Polityka, 13 November 1982).   On the
other hand, Culture Minister Żygulski, who had himself been imprisoned from 1944 to 1955 by the Soviets
for his AK activities in Lwów [48], announced in
the last week of October that all interned writers,
actors and artists would be released.   Jaruzelski,
Rakowski, Czyrek and Minister Faron had earlier
courted a group of 'deserving teachers' on 15
October.   The other main sector of régime disquiet
concerned the youth, who provided the troops for
most of the protests in the second half of 1982.
Jaruzelski summoned the youth organisation ideological aktyws to Warsaw on 13 October before their
Congress, but this was no more effective than the
preferential consumer and housing benefits for
newly-weds.   A survey of 740 Warsaw students and
200 schoolchildren showed that 51.5% considered that
the State of War had been declared merely to save
Poland's rulers.   Only a quarter accepted that it
had been imposed for justifiable national and raison
d'état reasons [49].   Repression continued with

severe sentences being handed down daily. These
were leavened by sensational corruption trials.
Bierut's biographer, Henryk Rechowicz, an ex-Rector
of the Silesian University, was sentenced to three
years for defrauding the university by having his
flat refurbished at its expense. Within the élite
the Kubiak Commission plodded on with its labours.
It was reported as having held 7 plenary sessions,18
meetings of its 4 sub-committees and as having com-
missioned 69 studies.
     In spite of meeting with social opposition and
partial boycotts the military proceeded with the
building of their new institutions. Initiating
Groups and Provisional Councils of PRON were formed
at different territorial and milieux levels from
September onwards. They were composed of the residual post-Ninth Congress PZPR aktyws, older national-
domestic communists of the Partisan generation and
such PAX, ChSS and SD figures as could be attracted.
The PRON Initiating Committee met amidst much publicity in Jaruzelski's presence on 15 September to
set up a Provisional National Council. It was
chaired by Jan Dobraczyński (born 1910), a PAX writer
who had been a member of the ZBoWiD and FJN Executives. The most prominent participants were either
party leaders like Malinowski, Kowalczyk, Komender,
Morawski, Ozdowski & Gertych,or writers and academics
like Tadeusz Hołuj, Halina Auderska, Kazimierz
Koźniewski, Janusz Reykowski and Mieczysław
Klimaszewski; even famous sporting personalities
like Irena Szewińska-Kirszenstein and the national
football team's coach, Piechniczek, were roped in
(TL, 16 September 1982). All in all, they were a
rather mixed and secondary group of worthies but
the best that the régime could muster. Sufficient
progress was deemed to have occurred for a second
session of the PRON Provisional Council to take
place in the Sejm on 4 October.
     The WKOKs met in late October to discuss the
state of society, public order and the anti-specula-
tion campaign. The Law on 'Work Shirking' was opposed in the Sejm by 12 Deputies and 22 abstained,
a dozen more than over Solidarity's demise. The
bishops had written asking for its rejection as it
was 'contrary to the interests of Polish society'.
Its provisions allowed any able-bodied male aged
between 18 and 45 to be directed to obligatory
labour or to be sentenced to terms of between three
months and two years of 'limited liberty'.
Małcużyński considered this an obvious Government
weapon against Solidarity supporters who had been

dismissed.   Zdzisław Auleytner (PZKS) regarded it
as a violation of international law (SSS, 27th sitting of 26 October 1982).   A motion by 100 Deputies
asking that Jaroszewicz,Wrzaszczyk,Pyka and Szydlak
answer to the State Tribunal was directed to the
Committee on Constitutional Responsibility.

The last of the liberal KW First Secretaries of
1981, Krystyn Dąbrowa, resigned in Kraków on 26
October.   He was replaced by City President Józef
Gajewicz, who had just suppressed the Nowa Huta
disturbances with the loss of a worker's life.   The
Ninth Plenum of 27-28 October then heard an extremely
gloomy Economic Report from the Planning Chairman.
Gorywoda admitted 'an unprecedented breakdown in
economic equilibrium' and a 40% cut in 1982 living
standards;   but he claimed some success in halting
the fall in industrial production.   He held out the
hope of 'modest improvement' in 1983-1985 to counter-
poise the threat of 'inevitable price rises'.
Hardly surprisingly the CC, after having broken up
into six problem groups, directed its fire against
Gierek's team responsible for the disaster.   This
Plenum was a very full and active one, with 22 plenary and 104 working party speeches plus another
26 written into the protocol, but all this speech
making merely emphasised the magnitude of the economic problem (Polityka, 6 November 1982).
Jaruzelski's announcement that he would seek more
Soviet economic assistance and the CC's resolutions
on the economic and fuel energy situations, on
maritime policy and on the rebirth of TUs merely
confirmed that life within the PZPR political fold
was becoming closed against social reality again
[50].

The real sensation occurred in the corridors
during the Ninth Plenum.   Ex-Politburo member
Tadeusz Grabski, a hardliner who disliked political
and economic muddle, but who was by no means a dog-
matist like Kociołek or an advocate of repression
for its own sake like Siwak, made public an Open
Letter, ostensibly directed to his POP in Poznań
(ICPA, 20/82, pp. 38-40).   Grabski blamed
Jaruzelski for the 'moribund' state of the party,
the 'explosive' social atmosphere and for allowing
the threats which had initially been suppressed by
martial law 'to reappear with new and incomparably
greater strength'.   The counter-revolution had not
been defeated.   Jaruzelski had tolerated 'the
creation of powerful clandestine structures capable
of menacing the security of the state'.   The party
had not been rebuilt but languished in 'a state of

marasmic and progressive atrophy'. Apart from
the Economic Reform there was no programme to prevent society from polarising because of the drastic
fall in living standards. PZPR membership had been
decimated and demoralised by martial law. The party
had lost its leading role in society. Nothing less
than 'the self-liquidation of the party' was taking
place. What was necessary was 'a revolutionary
purge' so that it could be consolidated around its
reliable Marxist-Leninist hardcore. The Church's
influence should be limited. Socialism could not
be built in Poland without a strong party. Working-
class support should not be alienated by being made
to bear the costs of the socio-economic crisis and
Jaruzelski's policy of reprivatisation (Le Monde,
31 October 1982). Grabski, who had always been associated with the more cautious Olszowski, thus
spoke out on behalf of the discontented sections
of the party apparatus; they had regrouped around
the weekly Rzeczywistość and its associated clubs,
which he chaired. Grabski had been slated to
become ambassador to the GDR but he was now punished
by being sent as a mere Commercial Counsellor.
His bid for Soviet support was too premature and
ill timed to embarrass Jaruzelski and the military
more than momentarily. Grabski's letter was circu-
lated to Western journalists by the MSZ in order to
demonstrate to Western opinion that much harder alternatives to Jaruzelski existed. Barcikowski, his
closest party lieutenant, then waded in against
Grabski accusing him of ambition. He demolished
Grabski's PPR parallel with the fantastic, although
inaccurate, admission that not even a reliable 50,000
strong hardcore existed now as in 1944-1945 (Le
Monde, 10 November 1982).
　　　Solidarity's eight-hour general strike call for
10 November was countered by a bitter official campaign against Western economic sanctions and support
for the internal opposition. A symptomatic indicator was Rakowski's violent diatribe against the
hail of Western criticism of Solidarity's de-legalisation [51]. All this did not deter Western banks
from agreeing to reschedule Poland's hard currency
debts in Vienna on 3 November. The Jaruzelski-Glemp
agreement in principle on 8 November on the date of
the Papal Visit for mid-June showed that the Pope and
Primate had decided to help the régime in stabilising the situation. This undermined the proposed
Solidarity strike to such an extent that the TKK
fell back to calling for demonstrations and symbolic
protests. Solidarity also suffered another major

blow when Piotr Bednarz, Frasyniuk's successor, and 18 other major activists were arrested in Wrocław. As usual the régime threatened reprisals. Jaruzelski met the Army leaders on 4 November and the WKOKs were summoned to make their preparations, as did the Politburo.

The first General Strike called by Solidarity under martial law proved an undisputed failure in spite of some work stoppages and demonstrations, which caused about 800 arrests. Urban immediately hoped that this opposition defeat might enable martial law to be lifted by the end of the year. The Third Session of the PRON Provisional National Council on 3 November had attempted to divert support away from the planned Solidarity protest of the 11th to mark the 1918 regaining of Poland's independence. A violent confrontation nevertheless occurred in Kraków but the more moderate ones in Warsaw and Gdańsk, centring around the slogan of Wałęsa's liberation, subsided when Warsaw Radio announced that this would take place. Wałęsa had written to Jaruzelski on 8 November suggesting a meeting to have a serious discussion 'to undertake steps towards agreement' on 'subjects of mutual interest'. The letter was signed 'Corporal Lech Wałęsa' (Le Monde, 13 November 1982). After being interviewed by Kiszczak Wałęsa was released. He returned in triumph to his first floor flat (17d Ulica Pilotów) in the Zaspa suburb about six miles from the centre of Gdańsk. There this 'symbol of the opposition' assured Western journalists that Solidarity would win; he was willing to negotiate but not on his knees. PAP, however, described him as 'a private person' and denied that there was any possibility of his meeting Jaruzelski (TL, 1 November 1982). On the other hand, Wałęsa's declarations and his comings and goings inevitably became the focus of intense Western interest. He became one of the principal actors on the Polish political chessboard. His meeting with Glemp on 20 November aroused speculation as to how far the Church would protect the interests of the Solidarity Underground in its bargaining with the régime over the price of its support for stabilisation.

Brezhnev's death on 10 November overshadowed these events for the Polish leaders. Jaruzelski had had excellent contacts with his military-political team, while Andropov was more of an unknown quantity. Accompanied by Czyrek and Jabłoński he attended Brezhnev's funeral in Moscow, meeting the Soviet leaders and Greek Premier Papandreou.

On his return the General,flanked by Barcikowski,
Siwicki and Baryła, presided over the Armed Forces'
Fourth Ideological Conference. From the 23rd onwards the TGOs descended on most communes to check
up on the local situations and to implement the tasks
set by their WKOKs. It was obvious that they were
preparing the disengagement from martial law. WRON
had intimated as much on 13 November by convoking
the Sejm for a month ahead. All this opened up the
way for PRON on 24 November to appeal to the Sejm to
lift martial law and release all internees.

Normalisation à la Polonaise

The 'after Solidarity' period opened what a
political commentator described as a complex and
long drawn-out chess game between four major actors - the authorities, the Church, Wałęsa and the
Underground [52]. Jaruzelski had smashed Solidarity
and separated the Church from it. He could now
begin a long-term, evolutionary process of stabilisation even though opposition hardcores still con-
spired and society remained a cauldron of psychological and economic discontent. But the party
barely existed in the factories. The minimum 15
safe workers needed to establish Foundation Committees had only been found in 1,300 of the 60,000
factories. Jaruzelski had maintained cohesion in
his leadership ranks but he still had not gained
the minimum social support required for economic
reconstruction. The Church's policy of mutual
compromises had prevented the resort to terror.
It had extracted concessions at crucial moments.
The Underground had suffered a massive defeat on
10 November and was now in a political impasse.
It would,however, continue as an important working-
class pressure group. Along with the Church it
would be one of Wałęsa's main cards, even though it
was expected that some of its leaders would now come
out of hiding. The real joker in the pack was
Wałęsa. Guetta considered that the ex-Solidarity
chairman had imposed himself quickly as 'the leader
of the opposition'. The authorities could not
silence him through police-judicial methods. At
the end of November the TKK called off the proposed December demonstrations. It declared that
'it was ready to subordinate itself to the decisions of Lech Wałęsa' and set out its minimum expectations from the lifting of the State of War (ICPA,
22/82, pp. 9-10). At the same time the Procurator
in Frasyniuk's trial demanded an exemplary ten year
sentence, although the verdict was seven years.

With the internees being released in batches
and with the reactivisation of the KIKs in sight
Glemp responded on 29 November by asking film and
theatre workers to call off their boycott.   In
early December ZASP was dissolved.   Culture Minister
Żygulski dismissed two celebrated theatre directors,
Gustaw Holoubek and Adam Hanuszkiewicz.   He brought
the National Theatre, the National Philharmonic and
the National Opera under his direct control.   A
pro-régime group started to undermine Wajda and
his film committee by accusing them of 'monopolising'
the film world.

On 3 December the Sejm heard Małcużyński inter-
pellate Żygulski about ZASP's dissolution and his
plans for the film world (SSS, 3 December 1982,
Cols. 93-97).   It also paid homage to Brezhnev,
considered the draft Budget and Economic Report for
1983 and debated changes in Housing Law.   Nothing
specific was revealed about martial law.   Jaruzelski
promised the Jastrzębie miners 'a great but, at the
same time, measured step towards complete normalisation' [53].   The Warsaw WKOK on 8 December considered
that all the aims of martial law had been fulfilled
and that the situation had improved in every sector
during 1982.   These panglossian chords were echoed
by the Sejm Committees on Justice and Internal Affairs.   The National PZPR-ZSL-SD Collaboration
Committee on 9 December confirmed the new legal
framework for the State of War to be passed by the
Sejm.   First deputy Interior Minister Stachura
announced that martial law had succeeded in its aims.
It still faced the challenge of a possible General
Strike in Spring 1983, threatened disturbances for
13-16 December and a permanent conspiratorial Underground was being formed.   The authorities had
liquidated 677 conspiratorial groups, 360 illegal
printing presses and 11 radio stations.   They had
confiscated 730,000 leaflets, 340,000 brochures and
4,000 posters.   10,131 individuals had been interned but by 8 December only 317 remained in the
camps.   3,616 had been arrested for political crimes
and 2,822 cases had been proceeded with.   15
demonstrators had been killed and 178 injured, as
had 813 soldiers and militiamen, 26 seriously.
Most of these figures underestimated the real position
but not too seriously.   Stachura's most questionable
assertion was that industrial action had only affected 150 workplaces and that a mere 21,000 out of a
socialised workforce of 12 million had been involved
(TL, 10 December 1982).

Wałęsa wrote to Jaruzelski on 4 December asking

for a reasonable compromise and an armistice for
all those interned or prosecuted for martial law
offences.   His key demand was the return to TU
pluralism: 'The rebirth of social effort and the
strengthening of Poland's world position would be
possible solely if reciprocal confidence were rebuilt between society and the authorities' (Le
Monde, 14 December 1982).   Jaruzelski in his broadcast of 12 December ignored these overtures.   He
intimated that 'conditions had arisen for suspending,
not lifting, the State of War by the end of the year'
(Contemporary Poland, January 1983, pp. 36-40).   Although 'the worst was behind us' opposition activity
still continued.   The authorities therefore would
maintain the regulations needed to ensure the state's
fundamental interests, law and order and economic
rehabilitation.   'The scope of the presence of the
Armed Forces in the life of the country will change.
WRON, moving on from the function of the Administrator of the State of War, becomes the Guarantor of
its safe transition from its suspension to its complete lifting.'   The rebuilding of institutions
would continue and the country's aspirations would
be channelled into PRON and the new TUs or not at
all [54].   Jabłoński presented the Council of
State's draft to the Sejm the following day [55].
This was a modification of the Special Regulations
of 25 January 1982 easing many of the martial law
controls over personal movement and association, as
well as abolishing internment, summary procedure and
the militarisation of the factories (cf. Podemski,
Polityka, 25 December 1982).   But the Council of
State could suspend or re-introduce Special Regulations according to need.   Barcikowski made it
clear that the authorities would respond flexibly
depending on the pace of normalisation, which depended entirely on the attitude of society.
Zabłocki regretted, on behalf of Polish society,
that martial law had only been suspended, not lifted
altogether.   He welcomed it as 'an undoubted step
forward' but criticised its limited and conditional
character.   He feared that the Special Regulations
would become permanent.   His diagnosis was that
the split between state and society had widened in
1982, even though open opposition was now being replaced by passive hostility.   The authorities
should, in collaboration with the Church, rebuild
social confidence.   Social control over the economy
should replace the military once they returned to
barracks.   Deputy Premier Komender's promises of
social justice and economic improvement failed to

counteract the feeling of let-down, expressed by
Zabłocki.   The impression was not improved when
Jaruzelski, Siwicki and Molczyk reported to Kulikov
during his Warsaw visit of 15 December, nor by the
Sejm Committee's on National Defence tribute to the
Polish military for 'saving Poland in 1982'.   In a
letter to Sejm-Marshal Gucwa Glemp opposed the
Special Regulations.   The state's survival should
not be based solely upon repression.   However, the
Sejm passed the Special Legal Regulations for the
period of the suspension of the State of War with
nine abstentions [56].   It also heard Siwicki's
tribute to WRON and the achievements of military
rule (SSS, 18 December 1982, Cols. 82-86).   The
Council of State Decree of 19 December then suspended
the State of War as of 31 December.   With all this
activity behind him and 1,661 TUs registered and
another 323 motions for registration in the pipeline
Jaruzelski, together with Czyrek, Jabłoński and other
party leaders, went off to Moscow to celebrate the
USSR's 60th anniversary and to consult with Andropov
and Kadar in particular.
     Although all the internees were released by 23
December and the camps closed down, the seven main
Solidarity leaders (Gwiazda, Jaworski, Jurczyk,
Pałka, Modzelewski, Rozpłochowski and Rulewski) were
formally arrested and criminal proceedings began
against them.   As there was no possibility of a
general amnesty for the 3,600 odd individuals sentenced for political offences the Council of State
instructed the Civil and Military Procuracy to exercise leniency towards requests for pardon.   The
Sejm passed the 1983 Budget and Economic Plan for
1983-1985 and heard the miserable news that Poland's
hard currency debt now stood at $28.5 milliards
(SSS, 31st Sitting of 28-29 December 1982).   WRON
assessed its martial law successes and failures
during 1982 and considered its future tasks during
its suspension.   Similar exercises were carried out
on 30 December by the Politburo which met with the
49 KW First Secretaries while the Council of Ministers assembled together with all the Wojewodas, City
Presidents and KOK plenipotentiaries.   Jaruzelski
intimated that political normality was returning but
that he would suppress all anti-socialist and destructive activities (TL, 1-2 January 1983).
Jabłoński's New Year message was that it depended
entirely upon society as to how long it would take
to get out of the crisis.
     However, the authorities started the New Year
with a campaign against Western journalists and their

Polish collaborators.   Ruth Gruber, an American UPI
journalist, was expelled for maintaining contacts
with the opposition.   Her agency was closed down in
early February.   Kevin Ruane's visa was not renewed.
Such reprisals could not mask the failure to establish a new TU as planned in each factory by the New
Year.   About 2,500 had been formed and another 4,000
were claimed to be in train, but the number of workers
contained in them was miniscule.   Only 300 out of
17,000 workers at Huta Warszawa and 200 out of
12,000 at the Ursus tractor factory had joined the
union.   It was estimated that national membership
was barely a third of a million.   It was obvious
that the Jaruzelski régime did not represent the
working class and had difficulties with even its
vanguard.   But, while Western commentators hailed
'the incredible tenacity' of 'the moral refusal' of
the Poles, the more realistic were aware of the
authorities' unshakeable resolve to wear this down
and at whatever economic cost (Le Monde, editorial,
5 January 1983).   The extent of Poland's reintegra-
tion within the Soviet bloc was soon demonstrated
by the presence of Jaruzelski, Czyrek, Olszowski
and Siwicki at the Warsaw Pact Political Consultative session of 4 January in Prague.   This did not
prevent the party-state leaders from congratulating
Glemp on his Cardinal's hat.   They also, rather
prematurely, proclaimed the Underground's demise as
one minor activist after another came out of hiding
and was released with much media fanfare after conversations with the MO.
    On 10-11 January, fortified by Jaruzelski's
communist bloc support received during his Moscow
and Prague visits, the Politburo met with the ZSL to
prepare their forthcoming Joint Plenum on agriculture.   The current habit of pooling PZPR-ZSL resources continued with a joint meeting of their committees for women's questions.   By mid-January
3,607 TUs had been registered, out of 4,986 motions
produced;   100 were being registered daily.   TU
Minister Ciosek admitted publicly, however, that the
new unions only included a small percentage of the
workers.   The problem dominated the conference of
KZ First Secretaries of the largest 207 enterprises
on 17 January.   Jaruzelski heard that unions were
developing in 'a most irregular way' and that a
political struggle over their rebirth was taking place
in the factories.   The pace then hotted up;   by
early February 5,097 unions had been registered,
the daily registration rate had picked up to 130, and
another 1,300 motions were in the pipeline.

Predictably the most registrations were in industrial provinces like Katowice (TL, 5-6 February 1983). Ciosek had earlier continued the official theme that Solidarity's greatest fault had been to foster the illusion that the Poles only needed to demand prosperity of the authorities without having to work for it. The current economic situation, revealed by GUS's January communiqué, was that the drastic pace of economic decline had, at best, only slowed down in late 1982 apart from the forced improvement in coal production. The only slight relief was that soap and soap powder were de-rationed in early February. Czyrek warned the CKKP that the real political problem was that the social consciousness still refused to accept that the country was living above its objective economic means. The last phase of the PZPR KW report conference campaign then got under way with the slogan that 'the party regains its authority through its activity'.

The Joint Eleventh PZPR Plenum with the ZSL Executive Committee generated an incredible amount of material on 20-21 January on the central problem of agriculture and how to achieve self-sufficiency in foodstuffs [57]. CC Agriculture Secretary Zbigniew Michałek's report stressed the significance of the Workers'-Peasant Alliance. He condemned the agricultural policy of the 1970s, which had achieved an 18 kilogram per capita increase in meat consumption by making the industry dependent upon grain imports; these had averaged 9 million tons p.a., but had now fallen to 5 million tons p.a. He assured the private peasant farmer that his holding was 'a permanent unit in our national economy'; régime policy was to integrate him in the national economy without formal ownership changes. The main problem was the existence of 2.8 million intensely cultivated private plots run by four million aging and badly educated farmers who had a low technological level and whose holdings, averaging 5.4 hectares, were too small and split up for efficient farming. The Plenum Resolution promised that 30% of national investment would go into agriculture and foodstuffs.

The problem of re-integrating opposition figures now became pressing as the alternative of forced emigration to the west was not taken up. Urban revealed figures that 5,165 had requested emigration facilities between 1 March 1982 and 20 January 1983 (1,429 internees, 396 opposition political militants). The authorities had agreed in 4,510 cases, 3,339 passports had been issued but only 1,070 had

actually left Poland. Sandor Gaspar, the chairman
of the Hungarian TUs, visited Warsaw in early
February and saw 'no reason to be optimistic'
(Polityka, 12 February 1983). In a Nepszabadsag
interview, however, Jaruzelski defended the achievements of martial law while admitting that major
political and economic problems still remained.
John Paul's visit would be 'an important event'.
Church-State relations were 'generally good', although complicated by the political activity of some
contestatory priests [58].

The régime felt confident enough to go strongly
over to the political offensive from early February
onwards. The PRON Provisional National Council met
on 10 February to work on its programme and statute
[59]. The CC Secretariat was brave enough to pub-
lish a massive report on the PZPR's activities during
1982, the year when arguably it had shrunk to less
than its 1944-1947 role [60]. The Council of
Ministers on the 11th defined Poland's main external
aims for 1983 as being closer collaboration with
socialist allies both bilaterally and within Comecon
and the Warsaw Pact. On the 15th the Politburo
assessed the party debate on the Ideological Declaration; 'it had led to the reactivisation of the party
organisations' and would be ratified by the Twelfth
Plenum. The following day Jaruzelski presided
over a party-state conference in the Party HQ de-
voted to social problems, while PRON published its
draft Declaration (TL, 17 February 1983). Jaruzelski
rounded off the series of PZPR KW report-conferences
with two important speeches. In Katowice on 21
February Jaruzelski expressed satisfaction that 'the
party is regaining its strength, is mobilising its
membership, is becoming the motor power in the process
of renewal and the strengthening of the socialist
values of the state and society'. But the political
enemy, encouraged by external support, was still
active, even though it 'did not have any historical
chance'. Jaruzelski blamed 'refined' KOR political counsellors for the disorientation of the
workers and the young. He promised that inflation
would be curbed; the 1983-1985 Plan would increase
GNP by 16% compared with 1982 and consumption by 11%.
He claimed that 60% of the largest factories now had
registered TUs or Foundation Committees and that $1\frac{1}{4}$
million workers had joined. The battle was now on
for the Polish social consciousness, but the General's
diatribe against American Imperialism and West
German revisionism would have done Gomułka proud.
The keystone of his raison d'état policy purloined

the opposition song, 'aby Polska była Polska [So
that Poland can be Poland] - she must be a socialist
state. Only such a state can count on the guarantees of our allies' [61]. His Warsaw speech attacked the indecisive attentisme of party members
and the intelligentsia, sections of which remained
hostile to his régime [62]. This put strong pressure on the still suspended ZLP to conform.
Barcikowski told a conference of 269 PZPR writer-
members that the ZLP had not carried out the required
leadership changes (i.e. replacement of Jan Józef
Szczepański) and internal purging of dissident writers
to justify its survival (TL, 26-27 February 1983).
This self-constituted body declared that no ZLP
decisions, resolutions or activities should be directed against the socialist state and its alliances.
Jaruzelski was warned at the Warsaw conference that
economic hardship 'could provoke an explosion of
dissatisfaction' (Le Monde, 2 March 1983). The
strained atmosphere caused by the overall increase of
105% in prices in 1982 and of between 300% and 500% in
some items led to bitter attacks on Prices Minister
Krasiński. He seemed to enjoy his job too much
for popular comfort.
     The CC Secretariat met KW First Secretaries to
assess the PZPR Report Campaign while Rakowski had
a predictably difficult exchange with the PZPR aktyw
in the Lenin Shipyard. The Council of Ministers
passed the Three Year Economic Plan while the Committee
on Economic Reform confirmed its Report, which
would be published after being considered by the
Government and the Sejm. The official campaign to
bring back Sikorski's ashes for reburial in the Wawel
continued. It provoked bitter Polish émigré opposition which eventually frustrated the scheme.
The mass media, more uncomfortably,tried to ridicule
Western speculation about Bulgarian involvement in
the plot to kill the Pope. Rumours of similar plots
against Wałęsa's life in 1981 were denied. But the
official success was that the pace of union registration had hotted up and reached 7,890 with 1,478
motions in the pipeline and 1.7 million workers signed
up. Huta Warszawa was reported as having unionised
1,200 out of its 9,500 workers and the metal workers
now had about 10-12% union membership (Kowalski,
Polityka, 16 April 1983). Rural organisations had
a strong vested interest in registration and 9,063
Agricultural Circles and 1,227 agricultural unions
had been confirmed (TL, 12-13 March 1983). It also
came out that 817 motions for pardon had been submitted out of the 1,462 cases covered by the Decree

of 20 December 1982;   244 individuals had been pardoned so far while 24 cases had been rejected
(Kempara, TL, 21 March 1983).
     Kiszczak's Sejm report on public security was
basically an update of Stachura's December statement
(SSS, 22 March 1983, Cols. 9-21).   It was a paen
of victory by the spokesman of the security services over 'the counter-revolutionary forces, inspired and quite often directed and subsidised by
the diversionary espionage centres of the west'.
He also claimed success in breaking the crime wave
and the black market speculation which had developed
since 1980.   Kiszczak's political message was that
conspiratorial activities were now senseless and
unpatriotic;   the authorities would continue to normalise the situation and disarm opposition plans
for a general strike and a 'Front of Refusal'.   The
next day the Sejm debated the Three Year Plan and the
anti-inflation programme.   The most significant personnel change was Moczar's departure from political
life after 12 years as NIK chairman.   He was replaced by Division-General Tadeusz Hupałowski, whose
post of Administration and Territorial Economy
was taken over by Division-General Włodzimierz
Oliwa.   But the Deputies staged a mini revolt in
order to show their dissatisfaction with agricultural policy;   69 voted against and 81 abstained on
the dismissal of Jerzy Wojtecki as Minister of
Agriculture and his replacement by Stanisław Zięba,
the CC Agricultural Department Head (SSS, 23 March
1983, Col. 197).   Another appointment soon afterwards symbolised the new type of state-military
functionary favoured by Jaruzelski.   Mirosław
Wojchiechowski, a WAT engineering graduate, Military
Attaché in Washington, London and Stockholm and from
1976 director of Interpress, now became the new
chairman of the Radio and TV Committee.
     Jaruzelski told the vast (2,300 strong) national
conference of workers' aktyws in Warsaw on 30 March
that social support was needed for his economic recovery programme;   this was now the fundamental problem facing the country.   The workers complained,
however, that they were being made to bear the brunt
of austerity and the anti-inflation drive.   Doubts
were expressed whether social equality could be
reconciled with the efficient self-managing, self-
financing type of enterprise (TL, 31 March;   1-12
April 1983).   These criticisms and warnings were
assessed by the now habitual CC Secretariat meeting
with KW First Secretaries and by the Government
Presidium.   'A veritable concert of anguished

protests' had greeted the régime's 'first tentative attempt to regain a minimum of credibility without which, as the experience of the previous 16 months showed, it was incapable of surmounting the economic crisis which paralysed it and which daily increased its unpopularity' (Le Monde, editorial, 3-4 April 1983). One immediate consequence was that a whole stream of party and state spokesmen appeared on the mass media during the next six weeks to answer the workers' grievances. Jaruzelski now counted on Polish society's accepting the burial of the poli-tical-democratic hopes of 1980-1981. His premise was that he had limited repression; as economic austerity was inevitable it might as well be geared to a long-term programme for resolving the economic crisis. The result would be a continuation of what looked, to outsiders, like the post-1956 state-society stalemate - neither complete Sovietisation nor democratisation - but it would allow the Polish ship of state to lurch on as in the past. The standard Western and Polish opposition view that the authorities had manoeuvred themselves into, 'a spectacular civil-political stalemate by using force in December 1981', was, however, inaccurate. It was also poor analysis and mere pious aspiration to hope like the pseudonymous Garnisz that only a Magna Carta guaranteeing civil liberties and poli-tical pluralism could produce social agreement and economic improvement [63]. A small concession was the calling off of the anti-Western press campaign started in January with UPI and the BBC being al-lowed to reopen their agencies.

On 12 April the Politburo confirmed the Ideo-logical Documents to be submitted to the Twelfth Plenum which, although scheduled for mid-May, had to be postponed for a fortnight. The PRON National Provisional Council announced its Congress and ap-proved its draft programme and statute. The un-blocking of the political situation was paralleled by a ray of sunshine from GUS, which laundered the figures to show that industrial production in March increased by 7% compared with March 1982. The Politburo and Government Presidium in joint session on 19 April confirmed the slight economic improve-ment in the first quarter of 1983. The Council of State had by then pardoned and released 449 indi-viduals and rejected 58 pleas; all this allowed Urban to claim that only 215 political prisoners were left in Poland, not counting those under temporary arrest. On 28 April the Sejm passed the final draft of the Three Year Plan and confirmed a vast amount

of documentation amidst much fanfare.   As if to
divert attention away from the long-term economic
grind, the authorities   again attacked 30 odd ZLP
personalities for anti-socialist activities and
writings.   Wajda and his supporters also had film
production unit 'X' taken away from them.

The Politburo claimed to have mobilised $6\frac{1}{2}$
million Poles for its May Day celebrations, as
against a few thousand who rallied to the Underground'
counter-demonstrations.   The lie to this rhetorical
flourish was given by the intensity of the militia's
reaction, not so much on May Day as on 3 May.   On
2 May the Government Presidium met the PRON National
Council to finalise the draft bill on social consultation [64].   By early May 12,065 unions had been
registered and another 1,446 motions produced.   The
PRON Congress assembled 1,833 delegates in Warsaw's
vast Palace of Culture from 7 to 9 May who claimed
to represent an active membership of 450,000.   It
appealed to the nation to work with the authorities
so that the State of War could be lifted.
Dobraczyński was confirmed as the movement's Chairman, Orzechowski as its General Secretary and Czyrek
became the most prominent PZPR leader on its twelve
strong Presidium, which was elected by the 400
strong National Council and 60 strong Executive
Council (Polityka, 14 May 1983).   Jaruzelski suggested that the new process of National Understanding
which was being launched closed the chapters headed
August 1980 and December 1981.   The way was now
open for socialist-led reform.   He was convinced
that 'a long-term agreement with the Church' was
possible if it disciplined its contestatory priests
and did not allow the Papal Visit to be used for
purposes hostile to the PRL (Przemówienia 1983,
pp. 92-113).

The police detained Wałęsa in Warsaw after he
had drafted an Open Letter with opposition figures
demanding TU pluralism.   They prevented him from
meeting the Episcopal Council's Secretary.   These
public hardline measures failed to prevent an attack
by the Moscow Nowa Vremya (6 May 1983) on notable
Polish 'revisionists' like Rakowski, Wiatr and even
Nowe Drogi's deputy editor, Ludwik Krasucki.   However, Polityka (14 May 1983) replied in kind against
this full frontal blast by demonstrating that the
journal had relied on false sources.   The régime
sentenced its defecting ambassadors in the USA and
Japan to death in absentia.   It did likewise for
RFE Polish Section director, Zdzisław Najder, who
had decamped just before martial law.   The

Grzegorz Przemyk cas célèbre opened with the death
of the 19 year old student son of the opposition
writer, Barbara Sadowska, after he had been arrested
and beaten up by the militia in one of the main
streets of Warsaw.

On 12 May the Sejm attempted to allay discontent over the Government's agricultural and food
programme for the 1980s (SSS, VI Session, 35th Sitting).
The first regional TUs emerged in mid-May with the
Wrocław food-producing workers and the Lublin lorry
drivers while the shells of the first national ones
appeared with the teachers and the steelworkers.
The delicate political balance before the Twelfth
Plenum, which was finally set for 31 May, was upset
by Barcikowski's serious heart attack, as was the
work of the Government-Episcopal Commission preparing the Papal Visit on which he was a key member.
His political role in defending Jaruzelski's flexible
policies against the alleged Soviet-inspired attack
was assumed by CC Secretary and Politburo candidate
Mokrzyszczak, who visited Moscow to counteract
Ambassador Kociołek's intrigues in late May. The
stresses of running Poland's economy also provoked
Planning Chairman Gorywoda's heart attack.
Kiszczak met the PRON Executive Council and attacked
the Underground's foreign links and support. With
the ongoing Przemyk investigation in mind he revealed
unprecedented figures that 17% of all complaints of
police brutality had proved justified in 1982.
There had been 536 investigations against MO and
SB functionaries (96 for corruption, 124 for physical brutality and 31 for loss or unjustified use
of firearms). As a result 105 had been imprisoned,
97 had received suspended sentences and 207 had
been dismissed by the MSW (TL, 27 May 1983).

The Twelfth Plenum was preceded by speculation
that the hardline party apparat, led by Olszowski,
was making a last ditch effort with Soviet support
to sabotage the Papal Visit and the Economic Reform.
In spite of such gossip the key issue concerned the
respective power balances between the military and
civilian leaders after the lifting of the State of
War. The signs of leadership indecision and division and the obvious fact that Moscow had still not
arbitrated the issue were clear at the shortened
one day session on 31 May. Czyrek's Report confirmed Jaruzelski's centrist line. The PZPR was
rebuilding itself, the dialogue with the Church
continued and the Economic Reform had to be pushed
through; active opposition had to be outmanoeuvred
and defeated by political means. The key part of

his message was his attack on opportunist-revisionist as well as politically factional and demagogic attempts to prevent the PZPR's consolidation. All attempts to introduce the sort of pluralism demanded by Wałęsa, ex-branch unionists and the teachers into the new unions were rejected. Czyrek stepped up the attack on the political clergy and the pro-Solidarity intelligentsia, intimating that censorship would be tightened. CKKP chairman Urbański directed the party's ideological fire against revisionism while condemning attempts by dogmatists to challenge Jaruzelski's firmly centrist policies. He revealed that 60% of the 26,000 expulsions effected by control commissions in 1982 were for ideological-political deviations, as were 46% of the warning conversations. The CC passed resolutions lauding the Marxist classics and the Polish revolutionary tradition and deferred publication of the Kubiak Report because of the internal controversy over its contents (cf. Kubiak, Polityka, 23 April 1983). The key resolution confirmed the Ninth Congress line of 'policy struggle, understanding, socialist renewal' with a strong emphasis on 'the ideological and political strengthening of the party' [65].

Did this Plenum mark a Soviet veto on the permanent development of the Army-State produced by WRON to suit martial law conditions? Did the decision fall in favour of a gradual return to the traditional form of Leninist Party-State, albeit one in which Jaruzelski and the political officer group could maintain their positions on a permanent basis? The answer to the latter part of the question is undoubtedly yes; but the first issue remained obscure for a while. The continuation of martial law would have allowed the crystallisation of a more military form of communism. Its lifting in Summer 1983 certainly implied a return to classic Soviet methods and forms. But the Twelfth Plenum was also marked by more misinformation and political choreography than usual, indicating that a basic issue was in contention (cf. Bijak, Polityka, 11 June 1983). Olszowski's political fate was unquestionably in the balance. Jaruzelski and his supporters utilised the Soviet-sponsored 'Twardogłowi' offensive to introduce the harder ideological political line for the party fold but they maintained their tactically flexible policy towards Society and the Church. Jaruzelski summed up by stating that the stabilisation achieved so far 'was only the first step on a difficult laborious road. The question of the timespan for the complete overcoming of the crisis,

and the costs which we will pay for it, has not yet
been resolved. We are endeavouring to shorten this
time and to limit the costs'.
      The programme established by the suspension of
the State of War laid down that all associations
should either be dissolved or reactivated by the
end of June. Immediately after the Plenum
Jaruzelski's minions set about social groups
starting with the journalists. The First Congress
of the SD-PRL on 3 June claimed 5,375 members, 70%
of all journalists. Chairman Krzyżagorski carried
out the required samokrytyka condemning the policy
of the previous SDP leaders as 'political surrealism'
in the interests of Western and anti-Polish propaganda (TL, 4-5 June 1983). His promises of a return to discipline and committed party journalism
proved premature but gained time and residual autonomy for his profession. The film-makers had not
been normalised to anything like the same extent
and the authorities' first step was the forced resignation of Wajda and his presidium on 6 June.
They still fought a dogged rearguard action demanding the renewal of their League. Four film directors left rather than capitulate. On the 8th the
League of Polish Jurists (ZPP) reported that all
was in order. The régime continued its running
conflict with the ZLP. The CC Culture Department
told its representatives to change its presidium
and to accept the correct line by 15 June, when a
meeting was authorised. The officials hoped it
would be taken over by their collaborating writers'
aktyw. Szczepański and his supporters, however,
refused to capitulate and publicly demanded the
ZLP's reactivisation (Życie Warszawy, 14 June 1983).
The officials consequently called off the meeting
and threatened that the ZLP would have to be dissolved and rebuilt from scratch with 'healthy elements' (TL, 17 June 1983). Long drawn-out negotiations again postponed the inevitable until 19 August,
when the ZLP was dissolved, as was the Polish Pen
Club soon afterwards.
      The Summer 1983 political season was dominated
by the two related issues of the Papal Visit and the
lifting of the State of War. On 14 June the
Politburo assessed the work of the Twelfth Plenum and
the final preparations for the Papal Visit, which
is discussed in Chapter Six. The Church's main
defeat was its failure to force the régime to declare a General Amnesty. Zawadzki claimed that
there were only 202 political prisoners in Poland
and that another 450 were in preventive custody.

The mopping up of autonomous professional groups
continued with the surprisingly contestatory sculptors having their ZPAP dissolved on 23 June.
The second channel of Warsaw TV was closed down,
allegedly for economy reasons. This allowed
Wojciechowski to carry out a national reorganisation
and to weed out a few hundred more unreliables from
among his 12,000 workers. The régime took satisfaction from the registration of 15,218 enterprise
and two national unions by 20 July with another five
similar federations in the offing.

Jaruzelski and Olszowski had a final opportunity
to state their respective positions in Moscow during
the Communist Foreign Ministers' conference of 28
June. On his return, with the Order of Lenin in
the bag for his sixtieth birthday, Jaruzelski attempted to mobilise the PZPR youth aktyw at a huge national conference (4,000 participants) in Gdańsk on
2-3 July. Like Rakowski, he admitted that 'the
fundamental question is the rebuilding of full confidence and the party's links with society, above all
with the working class'; but he appealed to youth
to join in support of his system as 'ours will be
the victory' (Przemówienia 1983, pp. 161-162). On 5
July the Politburo met unprecedently together with the
Government Presidium, the Sejm-Presidium and the
Council of State to discuss 'the actual socio-political situation in the country and the tasks stemming
from it' (TL, 6 July 1983). This was obvious code
for the finalisation of the lifting of the State of
War. Another bit of tidying up concerned the Sejm
Committee's on Constitutional Responsibility recom-
mendation on 12 June that ex-Premier Jaroszewicz
and Planning Chief Wrzaszczyk should answer before
the State Tribunal for their catastrophic management.
Gierek and Babiuch were stated only to have political responsibility and were therefore exempt from
judicial sanctions. The lax incompetence of deputy
Premiers Pyka and Szydlak was not sufficient to
justify proceedings against them. This long-drawn
charade ended up with Jaroszewicz and Wrzaszczyk
eventually receiving a slap on the wrist from the
State Tribunal.

Another era ended with the replacement of the
redoubtable Soviet ambassador in Poland, Boris
Aristov, with Alexander Aksionov, the Premier of
Byelorussia. Michał Atlas, the CC Administrative
Department Head, confirmed that the authorities
would seek Special Legal Regulations to control the
opposition even after the lifting of martial law.
The latter was formally appealed for by the PRON

Executive Committee on 10 July and welcomed by the
Politburo on the 12th when it confirmed the drafts
of the regulations and of the amnesty. The former
were considered by the Sejm Committees on Justice
and Legislative and Internal Affairs. The specially
summoned Sejm session of 14 July approved the 1982
Budget Report, bills regulating the legal position
of the MSW and State Archives, the Press Regulations
Law (i.e. censorship) and the constitutional amendments incorporating PRON in place of the FJN,
guaranteeing the private peasant ownership of land
and the introduction of a new type of State of
Emergency to cover domestic contingencies (SSS, 38th
Session). This would supplement the existing provisions for a State of War which would now be applied to external threats. Another publicity preparation was the GUS communiqué on the first half
of 1983 which contrived comparisons with the first
half of 1982, claiming an 8.2% increase in industrial production and improvement in most economic
sectors - some by as much as 20-30% (TL, 20 July
1983). WRON approved the details of the lifting
of the State of War at its final meeting on 18 July.
It congratulated itself on having fulfilled its
historic mission. The Government set out its own
view of its historical record by publishing a most
extensive report on its most important achievements
between 13 December 1981 and 12 July 1983 (TL, 19
July 1983; Contemporary Poland, July 1983, pp.11-18).
Rather symbolically, as if to mark how quickly history had moved on, the now forgotten but not long
previously much reviled Jerzy Łukasiewicz, Gierek's
Ideology and mass media boss of the 1970s, died on
18 July at the early age of 52.
    On 20 July, attended by only 369 of the 460
Deputies, the Sejm passed the law on People's Councils and the four constitutional amendments. The
crucial proceedings, however, took place the following day, held intentionally on the eve of
Poland's National Day. The Council of State had
officially lifted the State of War in a Decree of
20 July and the Sejm confirmed this. Jaruzelski
summed up the achievements of 'the 585 long,
difficult days' of the State of War in controlling
the forces of anarchy and counter-revolution; but
he warned that they would be repressed just as
strongly after as before the lifting of martial
law [66]. He promised Socialist Renewal on the
basis of the Ninth Congress programme, Economic
Reform and Workers' Self-Management, while suggesting that the worst of the economic crisis had

passed. WRON was being dissolved and the Army was
returning to the rear lines but the military personnel who had become political and state functionaries 'would serve the country further in civilian
positions'. His somewhat low-tone speech concluded
with the habitual unconvincing appeal for national
unity and understanding (Jaruzelski, Przemówienia
1983, pp. 164-176). The controversial items before
the Sejm were the Special Legal Regulations for the
Period of Overcoming the Crisis up till 31 December
1985. These gave the Premier and Ministers, especially those of the Interior and Administration, a
whole battery of powers to regulate political,
economic and social life and to ensure public order.
Deputies Osmańczyk and Zabłocki criticised the limited character of the normalisation on offer (SSS,
39th Session, Cols. 144-147 & 151-154); but at the
end the regulations were accepted with only three
abstentions (Bukowski, Małcużyński and Reiff).
The other controversial matter was the partial and
conditional Amnesty Law, even though it passed unanimously. It was a total one for all women and the
under 21s and for various offences which had received up to three year sentences during martial law
[67]. Some heavier sentences were to be halved
(TL, 23-24 July 1983 for Amnesty Law and Special
Regulations). Any recidivity before the end of
1985 would result in the full sentence being applied.
The gravest offences, ranging from murder to economic
crimes and attempts to leave the country, were excluded. The top KPN, KOR and Solidarity leaders
were left out. Underground activists, as well as
those abroad, could benefit if they applied to the
authorities, revealed their activities and promised
to desist from them by 31 October 1983. Justice
Minister Zawadzki confirmed that the Amnesty would
cover about 650 political prisoners and 1,000 ordinary criminals. The convicted KPN leaders, the
Solidarity seven and the KOR figures against whom
proceedings were in train were excluded, but
Zawadzki stressed that Underground members would not
be prosecuted if they came out of hiding
(Rzeczpospolita, 23 July 1983).
The lifting of the State of War was largely
significant for the Amnesty. It was a psychological
milestone of sorts but it did not change the underlying political realities and the authorities' dis-
cretionary powers except for eroding the Underground
structures down to their basic hardcores. Opposition
individuals would not be eliminated physically as
in Stalinist times, but deputy Justice Minister Skóra

threatened automatic three year prison sentences for
participation in strikes or protests. The Criminal
Code and the Censorship Law were tightened in respect of strikes, protests and street demonstrations
by the Sejm on 28 July. It was not so much the
country which was normalised as the political system
'which shed its military vestment' [68]. Jaruzelski,
with his military commissioners and compliant state
administration,had rebuilt full power at the centre.
They now counted on time and geography eroding Polish
society's capacity to resist. Would this allow
them to reactivate such political instruments as the
PZPR, PRON and the new TUs as fully controlled and
effective agents of social mobilisation at some future
time?

Notes

1. Konstytucja PRL (Warsaw, KiW, 1976), p. 24. See inter-
    view with Justice Minister Zawadzki in Polityka, 20
    March 1982.
2. The First Sejm in the Stalinist period from 1952 to 1956
    passed 42 laws (31 in 1956) and confirmed 161 Council of
    State decrees. The 1957-1961 Sejm passed 174 Laws and
    confirmed 13 decrees (12 in 1957); but it then had only
    two decrees to confirm as against 189 Laws in the 1961-
    1972 period. See G. Sakwa, 'The Role of Parliament in
    a Communist System', unpublished London University Ph.D.
    Thesis, 1974, Table 15, p. 218.
3. 'Atak na Socjalizm i jego obrona', ND (November 1981),
    p. 191.
4. Biuro Prasowe Rządu; 300 niespokojnych dni & Przed 13
    grudnia (Warsaw, KiW, 1982). Compare the official
    Calendar of Events, TL, 31 December 1981, with the one
    in Le Monde, 15 December 1981.
5. These arguments were developed in great detail during
    the State of War, most notably in a cycle of pro-régime
    apologias entitled 'Interpretations' by the Party pub-
    lishing house. Cf. Jerzy Borowiecki, Solidarność.
    Fronty walki o władzę (Warsaw, KiW, 1982). Lesław
    Wojtasik, Podziemie polityczne (Warsaw, KiW, 1983).
    Edward Modzelewski, Import kontrrewolucji. Teoria i
    praktyka KSS-KOR (Warsaw, KiW, 1982). MON also joined
    in: Lesław Wojtasik, Elementy socjotechniki
    Solidarności (Warsaw, MON, 1982).
6. Jerzy Bielecki, 'Co wydarzyło się w Polsce od sierpnia
    1980 roku?' (Wydział Informacji PZPR, KiW, April 1982),
    pp. 15-16.
7. TL, 14 December 1982.
8. General Leon Dubicki interviewed in Der Spiegel, No. 53
    (December 1981).

9. Communist Affairs, Vol. I, No. 3 (July 1982), pp. 713-714.

10. See Ruane, The Polish Challenge, pp. 287-288.

11. Zbigniew Siedlecki, 'Porozumienie-mimo wszystko', TL, 19-20 December 1981.

12. Norbert Michta, 'Na zakręcie historii ...', TL, 2-3 January 1982.

13. M. Łopiński, M. Moskit & M. Wilk, Konspira. Rzecz o podziemnej Solidarności (Paris, Editions Spotkania, 1984), p. 27, Borusiewicz testimony.

14. M.F. Rakowski, Trudny dialog (Warsaw, KiW, 1983), pp. 92-108.

15. Konspira, p. 24.

16. The National Centre for Computer Technology was included for raiding even though it had been closed down in April! (ICPA, 1/82, p. 29).

17. DzU, No. 29, pos. 159. Cf. Feliks Prusak (ed.), Stan Wojenny w Polsce (Warsaw, Interpress, 1982), p. 133.

18. Survey (Autumn 1982), pp. 68-69. For internment memoirs see W. Kuczyński, Obóz (London, Aneks, 1983). T. Mazowiecki, Internowanie (London, Aneks, 1982).

19. For references, 'Poland' in Walker, Official Publications of the Soviet Union and Eastern Europe, pp. 200-201.

20. On these and foregoing aspects see chapters by Szydłowski and Prusak in Prusak, Stan Wojenny w Polsce.

21. The fullest documentation on repression under martial law is the TKK's 'Prawa człowieka i obywatela w PRL w okresie stanu wojennego' produced by the Polish Helsinki Committee in February 1983 (First 'Madrid Report').

22. Andrew Świdlicki, 'Mechanisms of repression in Poland during martial law', Polish Review, XXIX, No. 1/2 (1984), pp. 97-126.

23. ICPA, 1/82, of 10 January 1982, p. 18.

24. S. Gebethner, 'Stany szczególnego zagrożenia jako instytucja prawa konstytucyjnego', Państwo i Prawo, XXVII, No. 8 (August 1982), pp. 5-19.

25. J. Stembrowicz, 'Z problematyki stanu nadzwyczajnego w państwie burżuazyjno-demokratycznym', Studia Nauk Politycznych, 3/83 (1983), pp. 7-44.

26. Persky & Flam, The Solidarity Source-Book, p. 29.

27. Dawisha, Kremlin and the Prague Spring, pp. 327 ff.

28. Circular and oath in Communist Affairs, I, No. 4 (October 1982), pp. 808-810.

29. Communist Affairs (July 1982), pp. 718-719.

30. Świdlicki, 'Mechanisms of repression ...', pp. 100-101.

31. Jaruzelski, Przemówienia 1981-1982, pp. 427-428.

32. Dariusz Fikus, Foksal 81 (London, Aneks, 1984).

33. SSS, 8th Sejm, 3rd Session, 18th sitting of 25 January 1981; Jaruzelski Cols. 7-32; Małcużyński Cols. 72-78; Zabłocki Cols. 57-63; Osmańczyk Cols. 63-69.

34. ND (March 1982); Jaruzelski pp. 8-33; Orzechowski pp.
    85-87; Morawski pp. 62-67; Urbański pp. 76-79; Draft
    Declaration pp. 39-50; Resolution pp. 34-38.
35. ICPA, 4/82, of 5 March 1982, p. 3.
36. SSS, 19th sitting of 26-27 February 1982. Another five
    Deputies (Drożdż, Grygiel, Haensel, Hebda and a major
    1970s' figure, Stanisław Kowalczyk) had resigned at
    the previous sitting.
37. Rakowski, Trudny dialog, pp. 123-152.
38. SSS, 20th sitting of 25-26 March 1982; Wojtecki Cols.
    64-71; Czyrek Cols. 6-21; voting Cols. 185, 190.
39. VIII Plenum KC PZPR, 22-23 Kwietna 1982, ND supplement;
    Woźniak pp. 9-23; Obodowski pp. 34-35; Obiedziński pp.
    107-111; resolution pp. 119-123. See commentary in
    Polityka, 1 May 1982, p. 3.
40. Ibid., p. 126.
41. SSS, 4th Session, 21st sitting of 3-4 May; Szczepański
    Cols. 105-111; Zabłocki Cols. 28-34; Rakowski Cols.
    37-55.
42. IX Plenum PZPR, 15-16 lipca 1982r, ND supplement.
    Voting on the new appointments revealed a surprising
    amount of opposition to Jaruzelski's consolidation of
    the Politburo and Secretariat. Kubiak's resignation
    met with 6 votes against and 7 abstentions, while
    Olszowski's got 5 dissentients and 5 abstentions.
    Bejger only garnered 100 votes, Gorywoda 119, Kałkus
    148, Główczyk 163, but Woźniak got 167, within a
    dozen of the maximum. Significantly only 133 votes
    were found to support Baryła's co-option as a CC candi-
    date member. Kałkus expressed his views in Polityka,
    4 September 1982.
43. SSS, 24th sitting of 21 July; Jaruzelski Cols. 6-16;
    Rakowski Cols. 32-42; Olszowski vote, Col. 100.
44. Rakowski, Trudny dialog, pp. 240-268.
45. SSS, 26th sitting of 8-9 October 1982. Jaruzelski
    Cols. 166-184; Vote on TU Law Col. 97. Kultura
    (Paris, November 1982, p. 10) claims that 12 Deputies
    voted against (4 PZKS, 4 SD and 4 non-party, while
    Małcużyński was away in Rome).
46. Amongst the Government changes Planning Chairman Madej
    was replaced by Obodowski so that he could concentrate
    on relations with Comecon. The Economic Council was
    dissolved but Jaruzelski strengthened his team by ap-
    pointing Szalajda as deputy Premier for Industry and
    Technology. Tejchma's replacement at Culture by
    Żygulski marked the end of a notable political career
    at the top leadership levels for over two decades.
47. Ignacy Krasicki, 'KSS-KOR - fakty i wnioski', TL,
    22 September 1982.
48. Kępiński & Kilar, Kto Jest Kim.Inaczej, p. 420.

49. Hardly surprisingly only partial results were revealed. Interview with Dr. Lechosław Dębowski, TL, 22 September 1982.
50. X Plenum KC PZPR października 1982, ND supplement. The appointment of a 26 strong Maritime Commission headed by Bejger and the nomination of the phenomenally young Waldemar Świrgoń (born 1953) as a CC Secretary (132 votes/180) increasingly became matters for the political cognoscenti.
51. Rakowski, Trudny dialog, pp. 269-287.
52. Guetta, 'Quatre pièces maîtresses sur l'échiquier politique', Le Monde, 24 November 1982. Compare D. Passent, 'Ani wszystko ani nic', Polityka, 20 November 1982.
53. Jaruzelski, Przemówienia 1981-1982, pp. 492-503.
54. Ibid., pp. 504-510.
55. SSS, 29th sitting of 13 December; Jabłoński Cols. 8-18; Barcikowski Cols. 18-24; Zabłocki Cols. 37-41; Komender Cols. 46-55.
56. Translation of Special Regulations in Contemporary Poland, XVI, No. 1 (January 1983), pp. 41-51. See interview with Justice Minister Zawadzki, Polityka, 18 December 1982.
57. XI Plenum KC PZPR i NK ZSL, 20-21 stycznia 1983, ND supplement. Michałek, pp. 9-28; resolution, pp. 168-173.
58. Jaruzelski, Przemówienia 1983, pp. 15-25.
59. See Round Table discussion in Polityka, 12 February 1983.
60. 'Informacja Sekretariatu KC o działalności PZPR w roku 1982', TL, 11 February 1983.
61. Jaruzelski, Przemówienia 1983, pp. 15-25.
62. Ibid., pp. 48-65.
63. Casimir Garnisz, 'Polish Stalemate', Problems of Communism (May-June 1984), pp. 51-59.
64. See interview with Professor Janusz Reykowski, chairman of PRON's programme commission, Polityka, 7 May 1983.
65. XII Plenum KC PZPR, 31 maja 1983, ND supplement.
66. Contemporary Poland, XVI, No. 13/14 (July 1983), pp. 50-59. Sejm resolution, pp. 65-67.
67. S. Zawadzki, 'Amnestia', Polityka, 23 July 1983.
68. Guetta, 'La fin de l'État de Guerre en Pologne n'ouvre pa la voie à un compromis', Le Monde, 23 July 1983.

Chapter Five

MILITARY RULE AND THE REBUILDING OF THE PARTY

The varied reasons for the PZPR's political,
organisational and ideological weaknesses are well
known [1].   They are embedded in Poland's postwar
political development, socio-economic dynamics and
international situation.   The repercussions of social
crisis upon the party have also had dramatic consequences in terms of leadership, membership and
policy change [2].   The PZPR's crisis-ridden relationship with society has forced it to produce public programmatic responses, such as Kania's October
1980 Plenum speech, the Ninth Congress documents
and the Kubiak Report [3].   The PZPR's evolution
during the 1980-1981 crisis has already been examined
elsewhere [4].   But huge grey areas still remain.
We have only an impressionistic picture of such
uncharted areas as the joint PZPR-Solidarity membership, the Horizontal Movement, the Katowice Forum
and the life of reform-dominated provincial parties.
The general view is that the party had 'collapsed'
and lost its capacity to exercise its leading role.
Jaruzelski therefore replaced Kania in October 1980.
But this view is only half true.   The Ninth Congress effected two parallel, and somewhat contradictory, tendencies.   It produced new, uncompromised
and fairly cohesive political leadership at
Politburo and CC levels which was inherited by
Jaruzelski.   The central level decentralised and
shared power with the local municipal and KZ groups,
which had also been renewed to a sweeping extent
before the Congress.   The crucial result was that
fresher, ambitious and more combative party aktyws
were produced by the democratisation process at
every level.   The CPA gave them a strong policy
lead in the growing conflicts with Solidarity and
dissident party currents after the Ninth Congress.
The net effect was to rally the inner hardcore of

187

the party, which one can most tentatively estimate
as being about half a million strong. This was
the party 'spine' which Jaruzelski used to rebuild
the PZPR during martial law. But the reassertion
of the directing cores at the various levels was
matched by the dissolution of the 'outer ring' of
over two million members, as defined by Annie
Kriegel and Georges Lavau in their studies of the
French CP [5]. This dimension still remains relatively unexplored. We lack detailed case studies
which might provide authoritative answers to the
following questions. What was the nature and extent of the PZPR membership collapse? There is
considerable evidence for the thesis that the PZPR
was threatened with a loss of control, perhaps even
of presence, in the workplaces, but what did the
politicised, pro-Solidarity workers really want?
How did they react to the Fourth Plenum ukase 'to
define themselves'? Another controversial question,
which is a matter for delicate judgement, is whether the communist intelligentsia-professional
stratum really was on the verge of mounting a
serious challenge to the CPA by forcing it to respond to Solidarity workers' demands? My view is
that the demise of Horizontalism after the Ninth
Congress was more apparent than real. Political
life abhors a vacuum and under the right circumstances a successor form would have emerged in early
1982.

Whatever happened to the Party Membership?
     One of the main indicators concerning the above
broad issues is the size and composition of the PZPR
membership [6]. Global figures for the Summer 1980
to Ninth Congress period are reliable. They have to
be collated from different sources and cover slightly
overlapping periods though. The picture from the
Ninth Congress to the imposition of martial law,
and again from December 1981 to its lifting in July
1983, has intentionally been kept murky by the
authorities. The degree of surmise is consequently
greater, especially as the party's disorganisation
rendered its own internal returns unreliable. It
is also unclear how many PZPR members dropped out
or handed their cards in as against the clearer
category of those who were expelled or formally
deleted.

Table 4
Total PZPR membership (millions)

1970	1975	Feb. 1980	July 1980	Dec. 1980
2.32	2.44	3.08	3.15	3.01
July 1981	Dec. 1981	Dec. 1982	Dec. 1983	Dec. 1984
2.85	2.69	2.33	2.19	2.17

Sources: Figures collated from Small Statistical Yearbooks, ND and Ninth Congress material.

Table 4 shows how Gierek expanded the party membership in the late 1970s in an effort to anchor it in society. The PZPR then lost around a million members between its peak of 3.15 million in July 1980 and the plateau of 2.19 million round about which it stabilised in late 1983. The membership loss in the individual sub-periods is, however, our most important indicator of party trends. The Ninth Congress Report admitted that 305,858 had been deleted from party membership between 1 May 1980 and 30 June 1984, of whom 203,766 were workers (ND, August 1981, p. 90). 197,300 had just straightforwardly handed in their cards (6.3% of the party), of whom 72% were workers, and 8% peasants (ND, August 1980, p. 58). Only 7,399 were formally expelled from the party for radical or pro-Solidarity factional activity; this was mostly camouflaged by the cover of the anti-corruption drive. The CKKPs alone carried out 21,761 warning conversations in the 14 months before the Ninth Congress, which testifies to the PZPR's politicisation. The global effect was that PZPR membership at the time of the Congress was 2.85 million. This represented a net membership loss of 9.5% over the previous year, of whom 7/10ths were workers whose representation in the PZPR consequently fell from 46.4% to 44.7% (ND, August 1980, p. 95).

The above is relatively straightforward but membership statistics are part of the political minefield concerning the July to December 1981 subperiod. The officially laundered figure of a national loss of 159,000 is highly suspect (TL, 10 December 1981). Firstly, the admitted membership loss of 415,000 (13.2%) from Summer 1980 to martial law is internally inconsistent with the above (305,858 + 159,000 = 464,858). Secondly, local evidence suggests a huge PZPR membership loss, especially at workplace level, during the second half of 1981. PZPR membership in Nowa Huta declined

from 9,442 in June 1980 to 8,325 in March 1981,
while another 800 were deleted by the end of the
year (ND, January 1983, pp. 33 ff). WSK Świdnik
membership was 2,030 in January 1981, 1,579 in
December 1981 and a mere 1,301 at the end of 1982
(ND, February 1983, pp. 60 ff). The most dramatic
fall was caused by the PZPR onslaught on its joint
Solidarity members in Autumn 1981. The case of
the Szczygłowice coalmine near Rybnik was worsened
by the arrest of a Solidarity leader and a miners'
sit-in; it provided the famous instance of the
management being driven out 'on wheelbarrows'.
There the membership was 1,651 in August 1980, 1,390
in May 1981, but it had collapsed to 643 by Autumn
1981 (ND, August 1984, pp. 44-45). There were
about 1.4 million workers in the PZPR before the
crisis broke out. It is estimated that slightly
over half joined Solidarity [7]. This mass of
7-800,000 PZPR worker-members was disappointed by
the Ninth Congress. They were at risk, or seriously
disaffected, by the Fourth Plenum decisions. It
would therefore be unrealistic to expect that the
formal handing in of cards represented the full extent of workers' discontent with the PZPR in Autumn
1981. I suspect that much of the membership loss
reported in the early months of martial law had
effectively gone in the earlier period. This was
an additional reason for its imposition. Demands
for the workers' referenda and new electoral laws
for the Sejm and People's Councils, as well as the
basic conflict over managerial appointments and
workplace self-management, reflected this swelling
tide against the PZPR.

The controversy over whether the PZPR membership collapsed in the second half of 1981 may be
helped by looking at subsequent end-of-year figures.
Officially claimed PZPR membership was 2.33 million
at end 1982, 2.19 million at end 1983 and 2.18 million
at end 1984. The key figures are, however, that
PZPR membership decreased by 352,000 (13.8%) in
1982, of which half, 176,000, went from January to
March. Elsewhere it was admitted that 44,500 were
deleted in March alone; almost half a million left
between July 1981 and February 1982 (TL, 21 April
1982). The total membership figure of 2.35 million
in Spring 1982 suggests that either a third of a
million (half a million less 159,000) really went as
a result of the initial martial law verification, or
that the Autumn 1981 loss was nearer 300,000 (the
admitted 159,000 plus another 160,000; I arrive at
the latter figure by subtracting 176,000 from the

third of a million).   All this is confused and
inspired guesswork.   The official figures are themselves probably somewhat unreliable both because of
the inaccuracy of the party's internal procedures at
that time and the tactical political need to camouflage the real state of the party, especially just
before martial law.   On the other hand, the picture
of a 31% overall membership loss from 1980 to
1983 is borne out quite well.   The Gdańsk provincial
party should have been more affected than most: KW
First Secretary Bejger claimed that it had only
fallen from a total of 105,000 in July 1980 to
96,000 in June 1981;   this is credible enough, given
Fiszbach's policies and personal role at the time.
But the figure of 76,000 for May 1983 only implies
a 28% overall membership drop from the outset (ND,
May 1983, pp. 63 ff).   The evidence suggests the
apparent paradox that the membership decline was largest in percentage terms in rural provinces but greater   in   quantitative terms in the industrial ones.
   Membership   loss either by expulsion, deletion
of the handing in of cards is only one side of the
equation.   The other is the number of candidates,
the number confirmed as full members and the level
of recruitment of new candidates at any time.   Here
there is no doubt that the PZPR effectively ceased
to renew itself for well over two years after the
Ninth Congress.   The PZPR had an inflated complement of 291,000 candidates at end 1980, which had
shrunk to 172,000 at end 1981, 66,200 at end 1982,
41,700 at end 1983 and a questionable 57,200 at
end 1984.   These MRS 1984 and 1985 figures are
contradicted by conflicting pieces of local and other
evidence.   Again the picture is clear and the
figures are reliable until the Ninth Congress.
106,300 new candidates were recruited in the first
half of 1980, compared with only 28,600 from July
1980 to June 1981 (ND, August 1981, p. 58).   We
also know that 54,709 candidates were deleted from
April 1980 to end May 1981 (ND, August 1981, p. 90).
On paper this still left a potential stock of about
a quarter of a million 1980 intake candidates to
be confirmed into the party in 1981, but all the
evidence is that most of these dropped out.   The
picture becomes even murkier after that as recruitment statistics became part of the political conflict and the propaganda war.   According to a re-
putable party academic, Augustin Wajda, the PZPR
recruited only 11,000 new candidates during almost
the whole of martial law;   7,600 during 1982 and
3,400 in the first quarter of 1983 (ND, May 1984,

p. 74). After that membership recruitment picked
up slightly (TL, 23 January 1985). It is clear,
though, that the PZPR's main aims in 1982-1983 were
to consolidate the party membership ideologically
and qualitatively. Verification and the testing of
members' loyalty through the various martial law
traumas were designed to produce the reliable party
slimmed down to its 1970 size which could be expanded quantitatively when the political circumstances were judged to be right.

The overall conclusion which one can draw from
these unreliable and contradictory data is that, if
there were a membership collapse before December
1981, then it was mainly a workers' one; they represented over 70% of the loss while the peasant
outflow was about 10%. The white-collar profes-
sionals and intelligentsia only provided about 20%
of the membership loss. This accentuated their
already over-represented position within the party.
The working-class share, which had fallen to 42.7%
by early 1982 (Rzeczpospolita, 9 February 1982),
was only 38.8% of the party in late 1984 compared
with its 43.2% chunk in society (Życie Partii,
No. 17/1984). The second conclusion one can draw
is that the 1982-1983 verification, which really
should be regarded as starting after the Ninth Congress, together with the voluntary handing in of
cards, slimmed down the PZPR by about two-thirds of
a million, or 22-23%; this is somewhat less than
the 28% decline caused by Husak's purge of the
Czechoslovak CP between 1968 and 1970 [8]. On the
other hand, the PZPR membership loss taken from
the outset of the crisis was of Czechoslovak proportions, a decrease from 3.149 million in July 1980
to 2.19 million at end 1983 (31.6%).

The reason why over two-thirds of the membership loss was working class takes us into a sociological discussion of the bases of power in People's
Poland at all levels from that of the central organs
of the party-state to the industrial workplace. It
also involves a subsidiary discussion of the under-
developed and weak PZPR implantation in the peasant
countryside, which led to greater reliance on the ZSL
in this sector after 1981. On the other hand, the
central role of the university-educated professional
élite in running People's Poland, and in benefiting
most from post-1968 developments, has been obscured
by the critique produced by its radical wing; this
culminated in the DiP criticism of the party apparatus [9]. It had always shown itself in the general
liveliness and contestatory character of the Polish

creative-humanist intelligentsia after 1956. The
reader is directed to the works by Kolankiewicz,
Mason, Pravda, Szymanski, Touraine and Woodall listed
in the bibliography for examination of these and
related topics. Here I am not concerned primarily
with whether the university-educated professional
intelligentsia really formed the 'New Class' in
Gierek's Poland or whether a class struggle in
Maoist terms between it and the party apparatus, on
the one hand, and the workers and peasants on the
other broke out in 1980-1981. The crisis, as I
argued in the Introduction, resulted from the interplay of a wide range of factors such as leadership,
political and economic mistakes, the institutionalisation of meritocracy and qualified corruption,
the burying of ideologically directed Marxism-
Leninism except for its symbolism and vocabulary,
the disappointment of economic expectations and
the clogging up of socio-professional mobility.
PZPR rule in Poland has always had a largely in-
strumental basis [10]. It has never controlled
and reshaped Polish society or come to terms fully
with competing national, religious and even socio-
economic attitudes. The result was that all the
classic revolutionary ingredients diagnosed by de
Tocqueville came together in Poland; the crucial
psychological dimension was boosted fortuitously
by Wojtyła's election. The cognitive dissonance
which had made Poland such a civilised place in
comparative communist terms after 1956 now became
an unbearable clash between the ideal and reality,
between what was said and what was done. This
particularly affected the naïve, half educated
younger working class of Wałęsa's ilk. Their expectations had been built up and then disappointed
[11]. Both within and outside the PZPR they had
a purely extractive attitude towards the communist
state and a conditional attitude towards its authority. A process of political overload thus
overwhelmed the system. But one political analyst's
'overload' is another's 'Legitimacy Crisis' [12].
What is clear is that the values and interests of
both the established and contestatory groups should
not be taken purely at face value. The dispassionate separation of political slogan from political
fact in their ideological justifications and programmes is an indispensible exercise.

Was a new Party formed by the Ninth Congress?

The main apparent consequence of the Ninth
Congress and the Electoral Report campaign which

preceded it was that it produced the most sweeping
renewal and turnover of directing personnel at all
levels [13]. The renewal also produced a redis-
tribution of power, what Kolankiewicz called 'the
most fundamental change in the exercise of party
power since 1948' [14]. Previous CCs had been
dominated as of right by Politburo and Secretariat
members, KW First Secretaries, Ministers and even
deputy Ministers. This group had made up 60% of
the Eighth Congress CC but it was now reduced to a
mere 8.5% (Szeliga, Polityka, 25 July 1981). A
major separation of party, state and economic administration functions occurred which, along with
the decrease in the representation of influential
office holders, seemed to satisfy the party reformers' main demands. But, as any observer of university politics knows, the storming of a committee
often leads to real power moving elsewhere to informal caucuses of individuals. Other basic Ninth
Congress principles were that the full-time party
functionaries, who totalled 17,166, of whom 11,003
were political workers, in 1981 (ND, August 1981,
p. 99), should have a wholly service function in
relation to the party membership. The Congress
delegates also retained their mandates and acted
as an additional layer of party power supervising
the work of party committees. They were in fact
recalled in mid-term for the National Delegates
Conference of March 1984. The changes in party
life and procedures were institutionalised in the
new and expanded party statute, which had been
argued over vigorously within the party ever since
Autumn 1980. CC Secretary Kurowski summarised its
major principles as being that elected bodies at
all levels were superior to executives and secre-
tariats. The former should be elected democratically. Inner party democracy and an open, consultative, well informed party style would revitalise the PZPR's leading role. The process was to
be safeguarded by strengthened and autonomous control
commissions (TL, 20 July 1981). On paper the
statute attempted to create a balanced form of
democratic centralism which would heal the rift
between the PZPR's inner and outer membership rings.
Its aims were to produce a credible PZPR offering
institutional guarantees against deformations and
social crises.

Kolankiewicz considers that the PZPR vanished
from view after the Ninth Congress because its
programme and statute satisfied much of the demands
of the party reformers. But democratic structures

and methods, as any Labour Party ward member knows instinctively, without reading Michels or Ostrogorski on oligarchy, can lead to more flexible central control than bureaucratic bodies proper. What is surprising is that these procedures should not have been better utilised during Autumn 1981 to create an internal reform movement in favour of National Understanding and compromise with Solidarity. The answer lies in the absence of real democratic traditions and knowledge of how to work such mechanisms; but the key was that these reforms rallied the top rather than the bottom of the party; the inner cores of the party reformed more legitimate and self-confident party aktyws at every level who backed the growing policy of polarisation and confrontation with Solidarity. The party radicals had been conceded the external forms but had lost the power struggle within the party. They were disorientated by the course of events in Autumn 1981. The democratic statute, having served its tactical purpose, was suspended by the Politburo 'Instruction' of 10 December 1981 [15]. This restored the initiative to the directing committees and their presidia but it formally retained the recast framework. By then, however, the PZPR foundations had continued to disintegrate. There was no sign of its rebuilding the penetration of Polish society, which was the essential preliminary in Kania's strategy for reasserting the PZPR's leading role. The party's control of the industrial workplaces, on the contrary, was being challenged by the workers and seemed to be on the point of being lost.

The Ninth Congress programme and statute were amplified by the Plena in the run-up to martial law. The Second Plenum on 11 August 1981 established 12 CC Problem Commissions and another 4 were appointed subsequently. It also confirmed new standing orders guaranteeing the rights of the CC, Politburo and Secretariat. The Third Plenum of 2-3 September 1981 established the Kubiak Commission to look into the facts, circumstances and causes of social conflict in People's Poland. The Fourth Plenum of 16-18 October, as well as taking the key decisions to replace Kania with Jaruzelski and to ban party members from belonging to Solidarity, also established committees to work on the PZPR's perspective programme and a history of the Polish workers' movement. These internal organisational and procedural changes were to continue under martial law, as did the work of the committees established in Autumn 1981. This is why I outline the Ninth Congress

framework in this section; it provided the ideological and political reference point for martial
law.   But I stress again the crucial significance
of power and control of these slogans and procedures
by the central Leninist aktyw.   This necessitated
the repression of society, the reconquest of the
industrial workplaces and the internal shift to
the military within the élite during the State of War.
     There is a considerable amount of public opinion
poll and survey material which allows an unwontedly
full picture to be drawn of societal perceptions of
the PZPR during the crisis period.   A well known
OBOP poll of May 1981 showed that the PZPR ranked last
of 15 in terms of social confidence with 32%;
Solidarity's OBS poll of November 1981 demonstrated
that only 7% of Solidarity supporters had confidence
in it [16].   The 'Polacy 80' survey showed overwhelming (92%) support for greater social control
over the authorities.   Only 33% wanted the PZPR's
role in the administration to be strengthened, as
against 56% who opposed.   The 'Polacy 81' poll
showed that 60% wanted to limit the PZPR (including
46% of party members), while only 20% wanted to
strengthen it.   It also presented the astounding
finding that only a quarter favoured the PZPR's
leading role, while over half would have preferred
a system without it.   But the emphasis on Independent Social Movements to control and limit the PZPR
led to some strikingly naïve attitudes about political institutions and forces as compared with
Czechoslovak public opinion in 1968 [17].   All
this provided apparent evidence for the allegedly
'Self-Limiting' character of Solidarity.   In reality
it only covered up its leaders' failure to play the
only political game that was on offer with any
success.   But only 25% of Poles favoured the creation of new political parties (including 24% of PZPR
members) and only 20% (23% of Solidarity members)
favoured the idea that Solidarity itself should
create a parallel political party.   How the PZPR's
leading role could be transformed and retained as
a slimmed-down hegemonic one,and the political
mechanisms which were required to ensure that a
pluralist society could exercise social control over
the authorities without either replacing them or
causing permanent conflict, deadlock and anarchy,
was never seriously thought about by the Solidarity
worker leaders.   They preferred to hide their heads
in the sand in the comfortable belief that their
very existence sufficed to guarantee their desirable
goals.

'Polacy 81' showed the widespread appeal of
Solidarity to PZPR members of all occupational groups;
76% of PZPR skilled workers, 65% of middle cadres
and specialists, 55% of members with higher education
and highest level cadres, a third of all office and
administrative workers, but only 15.8% of peasants
and farm workers were estimated to have joined
Solidarity. What is crucial here is that the attitudes of the PZPR outer membership ring did not
diverge markedly from those of society as a whole
in 1981. Only 31% of members, as against 13% of
non-members, were strongly opposed to strikes.
What was odd was that PZPR members admitted to taking part in protests more often (21.6%) than the
societal sample (18.4%). As far as responsibility
for the crisis was concerned, 25.5% of PZPR members
blamed the Government, while only 8.7% blamed
Solidarity and 47% attributed joint responsibility.
The corresponding figures for non-members were 48%,
4% and 39%. There is therefore considerable evidence for the thesis that the split after the Eighth
Plenum in February 1981 was not between the PZPR
and Solidarity but between the inner leadership core
and the rest of society. Mason presents a convincing case that 'virtually the entire population demanded a qualitative transformation of the system';
the PZPR, in spite of undergoing 'the most substantial changes in its history, indeed in the history
of any CP', still remained the focus of popular
criticism of its 'power and privilege' [18]. All
this is true as far as the attitudes and expectations of 1981 are concerned. But the attempts to
establish a permanent institutionalised form of
Historical Compromise failed. There was no trust
on either side that the other could or wanted to
compromise. Solidarity can be criticised for its
refusal to accept that co-partnership meant taking
responsibility for the inevitable long-term austerity
programme which was essential if the economy were
to be rehabilitated. Wałęsa and his church-in-
fluenced advisers can also be faulted for their
Panglossian belief that they did not need to come
to terms with the régime as they were indestruc-
tible because of their mass support. Their failure
to consider how best they could be incorporated in
the system was punished by martial law; so was
Wałęsa's caution in not facing up to the régime at
Bydgoszcz and his political incompetence in not
finding allies within the PZPR outer membership
ring. The PZPR leadership can be condemned for
taking so long over its internal renewal, for not

delivering meaningful reforms in 1981 without social conflict and for not offering a genuine Social Contract to Solidarity in Autumn 1981. It finally opted for military-police repression to ensure that reform would be controlled from above and would not endanger the basic structures and values of its system. The communists had been a minority within the nation who had lived with the state-society split in various guises since 1944. With the wind of history in their sails and with Soviet support they had no qualms in imposing their own terms on society, even though they realised the long-term consequences.

The PZPR and Martial Law
      With martial law the leading role of the party was effectively frozen. It lost its control over the state and economic administrations. In the initial period real power moved from the Politburo to WRON and from the party to KOK and its provincial committees (WKOK). This stage was shortlived, though. The military moved formally into many key party and state positions. Jaruzelski adapted the PZPR Secretariat to his purposes very quickly. The debate as to whether the military supplanted or took over the PZPR's leading role and its apparatus is, however, largely superfluous. As was argued in earlier chapters,the key word should be 'symbiosis'. The PZPR's internal life resumed from early 1982 onwards. A new claque of displaced and disgruntled civilian party functionaries came into existence whose grumbles were expressed by fallen notables like Grabski later in 1982. Urban told Warsaw University political scientists in June 1982 that about 18,000 officers and NCOs had taken over medium to low level decision-making functions from discredited party apparatchiks. This may have been a high estimate but the lowest figure must have been 10-12,000. There is no doubt therefore that the PZPR was shunted to one side by martial law; the early period was dominated by the process of verifying and purging the PZPR membership and of creating the new ideological and programmatic lines to suit the slimmed-down party.
      With Jaruzelski's appointment as First Secretary the PZPR lost its traditional type of leader. The General gave priority to his roles as Premier and Military Commander in 1982. This meant that the main PZPR political spokesmen became supporters who ran the party for him. Previously second rank figures like the chairmen of the CKKP and CKR

played key roles under conditions very different
from those envisaged by the Ninth Congress reformers. A whole series of CC Secretaries like
Czyrek, Woźniak, Porębski, Główczyk, Gorywoda and
Świrgoń assisted the indispensible Barcikowski and
Mokrzyszczak as the General's agents for the party
at various times [19]. More specialised sectors
like Ideology were delegated to other CC Secretaries
like Orzechowski and then Bednarski. The first
major formulation of the PZPR's new role in the
changed circumstances of martial law came from the
main remaining independent party chieftain within
the power centres, Stefan Olszowski, in his gloss on
the Seventh Plenum: 'For communists it is clear
that the basic condition of overcoming the political
crisis in our country is the rebirth on the basis
of Marxism-Leninism of a once again ideologically
united party which will be cohesive in action as
well as the restoration and consolidation of its
links with the working class' [20]. Olszowski
presented a noticeably harder public line than
Jaruzelski on 'the anarchy and anti-communism' of
Solidarity. The 'class trunk' of the party had
not been shaken but Olszowski directed his fire
at ideological confusion and factional infighting
within it. Revisionism was,for him,a greater
threat than dogmatism. He defined the party's
tasks as the achievement of 'a clear and unequivocal
ideological and political line', supported by committed and morally pure PZPR members who had returned to Marxist-Leninist class principles.
     WRON's immediate party concern was the verifi-
cation of the PZPR membership. The 'Instruction'
sent to KW First Secretaries just before martial law
suspended the Ninth Congress statute and vested
power in the party committees. KWs were given the
right to dissolve or suspend any local party groups
whose ideological and party activity was deemed
contrary to the decisions of the central organs.
After 13 December this provided the basis for the
dissolution of a wide range of enterprise, university and other POPs. What this meant politically
was illustrated graphically by the dissolution of
the PZPR cell at Toruń University. All 350 of
its members were verified during January, although
296 had their membership confirmed straightaway and
a mere 18 were expelled and 17 deleted from the
party. It was clear that the Toruń provincial
PZPR Executive had won its long drawn-out conflict
with the University POP, which had been the hive
of Horizontalism and which was reformed in late

Military Rule

January (TL, 18 February 1982). Jaruzelski's closest
party aide at this time, Politburo member and CC
Secretary Barcikowski, supported by Politburo candidate and CC Secretary Mokrzyszczak and CKKP chairman
Jerzy Urbański, directed the internal verification
of the PZPR in early 1982. PZPR membership was
reported as having dropped by over 100,000 within
the first two months of martial law (Życie Partii,
3, March 1982); the proportions due to the purge
and to voluntary dropping out in protest were
unclear. It is true that the membership loss continued at an average rate of 30,000 per month thereafter throughout 1982; by end December it must have
stood at rather less than 2.33 million, an officially
admitted loss of 360,000 since 13 December 1981.
But the membership drain was perhaps not as vital
initially as the purge of PZPR activists and functionaries, who were adjudged to have been unreliable
during 1982, especially on PZPR committees. In
the first two months of martial law military men
supervised the replacement of various KW First Secretaries, 349 provincial and municipal Secretaries,
307 KZ Secretaries and 2,091 POP First Secretaries
plus over 2,000 members of KW and municipal committees. The GZP took a particular interest in subor-
dinating the CPA and professional apparat. The
process was facilitated by the appointment of General
Tadeusz Dziekan as Head of the CC Cadres Department. By June 1982 no less than 5,000 out of the
PZPR's 11,000 full-time political party workers had
been replaced, 3,500 having been shunted right out.
But, in contrast, only three CC members were dismissed. There was very little movement out of the
top two bodies, the only Politburo casualty being
Łabęcki. The General strengthened his position by
promoting Kałkus, Kiszczak, Woźniak and Bejger at
Politburo level. The introduction of his supporters
Gorywoda, Główczyk and Świrgoń into the CC Secretariat
was matched by Olszowski's departure in July 1982.
The only other liberal loss was Kubiak's departure
from the Secretariat. These personnel changes gave
the impression that in 1982 Poland was being ruled
by an Octovirate of three Generals (Jaruzelski,
Siwicki and Kiszczak), three party men (Barcikowski,
Czyrek and Olszowski, soon replaced by Messner) and
two deputy Premiers (Rakowski and Obodowski).
        The PZPR Secretariat was reported as meeting
on 19 December but no formal announcement of the
Politburo's doing so was made until the 22nd. Even
then it only rubber stamped the military's decisions.
The impression that the CPA had been shunted to one

200

side was heightened by media coverage of WRON's meetings and decisions and of the activities of the TGOs. According to Ross Johnson, WRON now 'formally substituted itself for the Party Politburo as Poland's supreme political leadership' [21]. It soon transpired that KOK was the real, the WRON only the symbolic, centre of power. KOK played the crucial role at the central level. All new laws had to be agreed between KOK's Secretary and the relevant Minister. It was indicative of the realities of power in the State of War that non-state bodies or groups no longer needed to be consulted; the drafts of Laws were to be worked out between the interested parties and MON, MSW, the Justice Ministry and the Bureau of the Council of Ministers (TL, 2-3 January 1982).

At the local level the real rulers of Poland, in the early months of martial law, with crucial organising and co-ordinating functions became the provincial Committees of National Defence (WKOKs) responsible to KOK. Headed by the Wojewoda, they were composed of deputy Governors, provincial PZPR First Secretaries, the provincial MO commander and the chief of the military provincial staff, who doubled up as the committee's deputy chairman (KOK deputy Secretary, Colonel Zdzisław Molina, TL, 2-3 January 1982). The KOK plenipotentaries in the region and other officials were summoned as required. About 2,000 military commissioners, backed up by between 5 and 8,000 soldiers, supervised the factories, posts, ports, services, the mass media and the administration in great detail. In May 1982 the system was consolidated. The commissioners in 1,064 localities and 1,059 enterprises were slimmed down to 528,covering 830 enterprises. At territorial level 3-4 strong Operational Groups covered about 5 villages apiece, the TGOs in towns were reduced in size from four to two, while strengthened Inspection Teams of 10-15 Officers were created to support the provincial commissioner [22]. Military commissioners were a novel institution in communist politics. Their functions were only repressive in the first instance. Their job was then to animate the party, state and economic bureaucracies, to check up on the competence, honesty and political reliability of all directing personnel and to arbitrate and push through all decisions which had previously been blocked. The parallels with the aims of the interwar military dominated Sanacja (Moral Renewal) Movement are striking instances of continuity in political

culture.   So too was the undoubtedly high degree of
trust reposed in the commissioners both by society
and by Solidarity supporters [23].   The martial law
experiment also did not last long enough, just for a
year, for the officers to get caught up in the usual
maws of corruption, bureaucracy and 'układy' (privileged relations with other key local worthies such
as the party and TU Secretaries, the MO commander and
enterprise directors).   The fascinating testimony
by Lieutenant-Colonel Włodzimierz Buchacz, military
commissioner for the town of Świętochłowice, shows
how such fair and decisive new brooms lubricated
the martial law system at local level.   They
unblocked the local bureaucratic log jam gaining
social confidence, in rural areas and small towns,
through real service to the community [24].   In
the large cities the repressive aim of breaking
workers' resistance was often coupled with the
resolution of technical problems through the application of military efficiency [25].

On the surface it looked as though an additional, and superior, level of military power had
been added to the party and state ones.   In practice
what occurred was a fused symbiosis marked by the
interchangeability of cadres typical of other communist crisis periods,like the Russian Civil War of
1918-1921 or the PPR takeover of power in Poland
itself.   The military's initial aims were to maintain security, order and labour discipline and to
suppress all opposition.   WKOKs also played an important role in verifying and dismissing officials.
But the detailed administrative work of running
Poland remained with the state administration.
Jaruzelski's role as Premier became the dominant one.
He used Janiszewski and the Bureau of the Council of
Ministers to great effect to oversee and co-ordinate
the policy-making process.   This arm of Government
was heavily preoccupied with public order and then
economic problems.

The party's impotence and marginality were illustrated by the fact that the Politburo's most important activity in January was its appeal for the
victims of the massive Vistula floods in the Płock
region (TL, 13 January 1982).   More significantly,
an ambitious hardline party chieftain, Żabiński, was
replaced as Katowice First Party Secretary by
Politburo member Zbigniew Messner;   the latter had
been a professor and then Rector of the Higher
Economics School (WSE) in Katowice.   He had been
brought to the fore by the crisis as chairman

of the Katowice Provincial People's Council (see
interview, Polityka, 22 May 1982). He was a close
Jaruzelski lieutenant who eventually became the
General's economic supremo and his Premier in 1985.
A spurious political balance was then claimed by
replacing the liberal Fiszbach in Gdańsk with
Stanisław Bejger, the Shipping Minister. Fiszbach
was neutralised further by being sent as Commercial
Attaché to Finland, taking Bejger's previous posi-
tion in Helsinki.

The military authorities allowed the PZPR provincial aktyws to meet from January to February in
order to assess the party's reactions to martial
law. The PZPR themes surfaced at the Warsaw City
Plenum of 8 January. Politburo member Siwak admitted, rather hysterically, that 90% of the Warsaw
party had either belonged to, or believed in,
Solidarity. Secretary Bolesławski's Report
stressed that it would take the PZPR many years to
verify and rebuild its membership and to regain
the social confidence which would allow it to exercise its leading role in full (TL, 9 January 1982).
CC Secretary Kubiak had difficulty in explaining to
the Kraków Party how the PZPR's Ninth Congress
democratisation could be balanced by the disciplined unity envisaged for it by Jaruzelski (TL, 1
February 1982). The same themes were amplified by
CKKP chairman, Urbański. The party's verification
from top to bottom was the essential prerequisite
for rebuilding its moral and ideological strength
and political unity. Without discipline and cohesiveness it could not exercise its leading role.
The PZPR's internal house cleaning went ahead with
the reminder that party control commissions had
considered 14,200 accusations against PZPR members
in directing positions between October 1980 and
December 1981 (TL, 30-31 January 1982). The CKKP's
current slogan for martial law was that 'the guilty
must be punished and the innocent cleared'; even under
martial law conditions, though attempts were made to
limit the centralist control of the December 'Instruction'. A Poznań academic cited Barcikowski as tell-
ing CC lecturers in early January that the Instruction was a temporary emergency measure. The statute should apply wherever possible. Cegła's case
was that verification without inner party democracy
would prove to be a 'political catastrophe' for the
party [26]. The Białystok KW First Secretary also
confirmed that the Instruction had been essential
under the emergency conditions of December 1981.
The party could now be consolidated in a more

balanced way and the statute should be applied in
a looser form (Zawodziński, <u>Polityka</u>, 3 April 1982).
The WSNS conference of 25-26 January on the
sources of the crisis started off a party debate
which eventually culminated in the Kubiak Report.
On 27 January the CC conference of KW Ideology and
Propaganda Secretaries heard Orzechowski's call to
battle for the Polish social consciousness.
Manoeuvring before the Seventh Plenum Siwak called
for an even sharper purge of the PZPR. The Plenum
itself, as noted in Chapter Four, confirmed WRON
decisions on martial law and the measures initiated
by the military for the organisational and ideological rebuilding of the PZPR. The Politburo's
'Tasks of party bodies and organisations' of 6 March
signalled the beginning of the drive against 'internal emigration' and party factionalism. The attitudes of PZPR members, especially those in directing
positions, were to be evaluated by the end of April.
KWs were given till the end of the month to liquidate
all 'the non-statutory organisations and programmes
which had infiltrated the party during 1981-1982'
(<u>TL</u>, 11 March 1982). This naturally applied most
of all to the radical and Horizontalist groups but
most had already been dealt with. The Katowice
Forum was finally dissolved by the Katowice KW in
late March [27]. Significantly, though, this
group, which could hardly raise its head publicly
in Summer 1981, was now praised for the political
activity of its members 'in a difficult period
for the party' (<u>Le Monde</u>, 28-29 March 1982).
At the PZPR's First Ideological-Theoretical
Conference on 2-3 April Jaruzelski defined Marxism-
Leninism as a creative and 'powerful weapon of the
party in the ideological conflict which is taking
place' (<u>Przemówienia 1981-1982</u>, p. 340). The major
party chieftains presented their theses on how the
PZPR's ideological front should be rebuilt. The
conference then broke up, in the now modish fashion,
into four problem commissions at which 86 participants spoke. Their chairmen summed up at the renewed plenary session: Główczyk on the general
regularities of building socialism, Barcikowski on
the party's leading role, Orzechowski on the ideological struggle and Olszowski on party propaganda
[28]. What a typical political officer thought of
these proceedings came out in the conference theses
of Colonel Docent Dr. Habilitated Czesław Staciwa,
a Departmental Head in the General Staff Academy.
His recipe was to educate the nation, as well as
PZPR members, in the Marxist-Leninist classics and

in current documents like the party programme.
He voiced the crucial importance of forming the
correct social consciousness (TL, 20 April 1982).
Party life still continued to be largely a
matter for the inner ring. New 'Tasks for party
committees and organisations arising out of the
resolutions of the PZPR Eighth Plenum' were set in
early May (TL, 10 May 1982). On 25 May, however,
the Politburo decided to mobilise the outer ring by
announcing gingerly that Report conferences at POP
and lower committee level would take place in the
Autumn; the provincial party aktyws were to meet
earlier in June in order to rally the faithful and
to prepare the ground.

A revealing indicator of how politics worked
under martial law was the replacement of the popular
First Party Secretary in Poznań, Edward Skrzypczak,
by Air Force Brigade-General Edward Łukasik on 28
May. Skrzypczak had collaborated with the party
reformers in 1981. He was a typical Ninth Congress
figure even though he was not elected to the CC.
He now wanted to prevent disturbances on the anniversary of the 1956 Poznań Uprising in late June by
turning it into an official celebration. The
Church would guarantee calm,as it had done the previous year. The leadership disagreed and Skrzypczak
lost his job; but it needed both Mokrzyszczak's
and Dziekan's presence to face down the KW's discontent (Le Monde, 4 June 1982). This departure of a
'radical', as in the earlier Żabiński-Fiszbach
changes, was occasioned by the CPA's need to balance
the more important replacement of the hardline Warsaw
City First Secretary, Kociołek. The longtime KW First
Secretary in Lublin, Władysław Kruk, was also replaced, soon afterwards, by Wiesław Skrzydło, the
UMC-S Rector and a noted academic politologue.

On 1 June the CC Secretariat assessed very
positively the measures which were in train designed
to rebuild the internal life and organisation of
the PZPR. The results of the verification of the
party membership between 13 December 1981 and 30
April 1982 were presented to the CC Internal Party
Commission headed by Mokrzyszczak on 8 June; the
subject was, however, too delicate for the findings
to be revealed directly to the public. A juxta-
posed report by the Chełm KW, the party's smallest,
did let slip that the provincial party had lost
2,600 members and candidates between August 1980
and December 1981, while subsequently another 900
members and candidates had been deleted and
another 380 had handed in their cards (TL, 9 June

198?). We also know that the Poznań party membership, one of the least affected, had shrunk from
125,210 in July 1980 to 109,421 in April 1982, a
12.6% drop. Its social composition, with the earlier figures in brackets, was now as follows: workers 48,579 (59,118), peasants 8,708 (9,560), white-
collar 40,030 (48,579), students 1,187 (1,797) and
women 28,708 (24,987) (Polityka, 17 April 1982,p.2).
Olszowski's parting shot, before being pushed
out of the CC Secretariat into the Foreign Ministry,
was to tell the Toruń KW, in his usual aggressive
manner, that Horizontalism and the opportunist-
revisionist current had been 'the main danger inside the PZPR' in 1981. This alternative power
centre to the CPA had attempted to push the party
towards Social Democracy and power sharing with
the Church and Solidarity. His comforting prognosis for the Soviet brand of Leninism was that the
year-long 'struggle for the Marxist-Leninist character, for the unity and cohesiveness of the party
ranks' would produce an 'ideological rebirth,
strengthening the leading role of the PZPR in the
process of building socialism in Poland' (TL, 8
June 1982). These themes were doubtless taken up
by the CC Ideological Commission on 13 June, the
Politburo accepted the draft Ideological Declaration
on 29 June, while the KW aktyws discussed the
problems of ideological work and youth in the run-up
to the Ninth Plenum. Not long afterwards CKKP
chairman, Urbański, signalled the beginning of a
trend away from verification and punishment within
the PZPR to prophylactic-educational work (TL, 5
July 1982). The purge of the Polish party had
therefore been far less extreme and vindictive
than that of the Czechoslovak CP in 1969-1972. The
military were not so much in control of their society
and party membership and also faced far more horrendous economic problems. The Ninth Congress
legacy and the Kubiak Commission reflected their
awareness of the contestatory character of the
Poles, the social ebullition since 1980 and a
genuine desire to utilise military rule for reform
purposes (Kubiak, Polityka, 23 April 1982).
An interesting picture of the state of the
PZPR at the end of 1982 was given by CC Organisation
Department Head, Kazimierz Cypryniak. Membership
totalled 2.327 million, having decreased by
779,000 (28%) since August 1980. This was 9% of
all Poles, 11.6% of those employed and 14.5% of
those in the state sector. The PZPR incorporated
12.6% of the working class, 3.7% of the peasants

and a staggering 31% of the intelligentsia (43.6% of all journalists but 17% of all doctors). Its working-class composition was now just under 40% (Tl, 16-17 July 1983). As we have seen, the top leadership and CPA levels began to function normally in the PZPR from early 1982 onwards. They carried out the membership verification and purges after rooting out all open internal opposition on the basis of the 'Instruction'. Life at the lower party levels, though, was not 'normalised' until much later; peculiar features persisted even after the lifting of martial law. During the State of War the key roles were played by the aktyws, which had been reconstituted by the Ninth Congress at all levels. A particularly important role had been played by the control commissions and not only in checking up on and verifying the general membership; as Cypryniak revealed, 86% of all party deletions were effected by the POPs. Control commissions together with committee members, in effect, became the party's hardcores. Firstly, they expelled or browbeat party members who attempted to organise opposition to martial law [29]. They then supported all WRON's initiatives in rebuilding the party, developing PRON and establishing the new workplace unions. But the party report conferences in early 1983 showed that there was more continuity of membership at the aktyw level than might have been expected. Even a radical party like Kraków was reported as having delegates that were 80% the same as in 1981. Kraków's Central District party had lost 4,334 members out of 25,500 but the sharpest loss was a thousand academics [30]. The party, in Jaruzelski's phrase, was the same Marxist-Leninist, working-class one as before but it was different in that its members had, miraculously, become more modest and ideologically motivated again as in good Gomułka's time. Such claims, about the PZPR's consolidation and moral renewal expressed by Mokrzyszczak, are difficult to verify; so is his assertion of full and lively discussion of all issues at Politburo level [31]. A major régime publicist, however, argued that the PZPR needed to take a realistic view of the shocks undergone by its members, especially of its committees and executives, of which about a fifth left as a result of martial law. Krasucki set out Jaruzelski's centrist consensus, avoiding both radical reformism on the 1981 model and hurrah-ideological conservatism, which was to be developed in full from the Twelfth Plenum onwards [32].

The Line of Struggle and Understanding

Communist policy since the Fourth Plenum in
October 1981 had been the two-pronged one of
struggle against irreconcilable enemies and of
achieving understanding with those who could be
won over to the new order [33]. This policy continued in various forms in the struggle against
the Solidarity Underground and in the military purge
of unreliable or revisionist elements in the PZPR,
state, administrative and economic sectors in 1982.
Jaruzelski's plan of battle, unveiled at the Seventh
Plenum in February 1982, was therefore repression,
re-establishment of social and economic discipline,
the rebuilding and consolidation of a new socialist
order and then, with economic rehabilitation, the
regaining of social support.

The PZPR had almost ceased functioning as a
ruling CP in early 1982 when it was effectively replaced by the WRON-KOK framework. Its leadership
organs and processes were gradually brought back to
life under Jaruzelski's military control, the
Secretariat, which he used for his own purposes
straightaway, and then the Politburo with the dissolution of WRON in December 1982. But the priority
as far as the general membership was concerned was
its ideological and personal quality and the consolidation and unity of the party. The quantitative aspect, the recruitment of new members to compensate for the unprecedented membership decline
from 3.15 million in Summer 1980 to 2.19 million in
1983 was therefore hardly broached until the mid-
1980s (Wajda and Malak, ND, May 1984, p. 3). A
modicum of middle and lower level activity had been
restored by the lifting of martial law. The
PZPR's recalcitrant outer membership ring and its
patchy social implementation, as well as a certain
amount of internal effervescence, remained the
long-term Achilles' Heel in the party's rebuilding
process. But the PZPR renewed itself ideologically
by returning to first principles in the classical
texts of Marx and Lenin and in its revolutionary
origins and traditions. The First Nationwide
Ideological-Theoretical Party Conference in April
1982 initiated the process of rebuilding a revised
theoretical base for the PZPR's leading role and for
its combative ideological character [34]. Gierek's
neglect of class struggle and his theoretically
cooler and more technocratic version of 'Developed
Socialism' were diagnosed as prime reasons for the
PZPR's collapse in 1980. The process culminated
with the National Delegates' Conference of March

1984. It approved the new PZPR Ideological Declaration after a two year long debate [35]. The debate in the PZPR press and journals was not particularly original. But one should not underestimate
its significance in producing the ideological motivation and raison d'être which is essential, for the
inner circles at least, of a ruling CP; as Lenin
said, there can be no revolutionary movement without
revolutionary theory. Professor Marian Orzechowski,
the CC Ideology Secretary from November 1981 to
November 1983, headed this campaign and the commission on the party's perspective programme. He also
typified the intelligent centrist Khrushchevite
reformism linked with a form of neo-dogmatic Marxist-
Leninism which characterised this period [36]. The
key battle was defined as being for the PZPR's correct political consciousness so that it could then
attack and change the nation's 'false social consciousness' [37]. Cynics would say that the struggle
had to be transferred to the higher ideological plans
as so little could be hoped for in the purely political and economic sectors! It was symptomatic,
though, that the attempt to introduce the term 'socialist pluralism' into the communist lexicon was countered by the official insistence that the PZPR's
priority was to achieve ideological and organisational cohesion [38].

From Army-State to Party-State to Communist Rechstaat?
    With the imposition of the State of War power
undoubtedly shifted from the PZPR Politburo to WRON
which publicised KOK decisions. A highly centralised
ad hoc military and party-state leadership centred
around Jaruzelski became the rulers of Poland. His
team was composed of military colleagues from MON,
which he headed from 1968 to 1983. He then strengthened his position as Commander in Chief by re-
vamping KOK. The most notable political Generals
assumed ministerial posts (Kiszczak, Siwicki,
Hupałowski, Piotrowski and Oliwa). Others assumed
direct control of CC Departments,like Dziekan over
Cadres until his death in November 1984. Czesław
Dęga headed the Foreign Department in order to
help CC Secretary Czyrek oversee Olszowski's doings
at the MSZ. Janiszewski became the equivalent of
Jaruzelski's Chef de Cabinet for the state apparatus;
his Government Bureau was much expanded.The slightly
older generation of Generals in political control
of the Army - Molczyk, Tuczapski and Urbanowicz - saw
their influence wane; that of GZP Head (1980-1985),
and now CC Secretary, Baryła, his GZP successor,

Szaciło, General Staff Chief Użycki and his deputy, Jasiński, waxed correspondingly. The grumbles of PZPR functionaries about military predominance and the weakening of the party's leading role, expressed openly by Grabski,were utilised by the Kremlin to prevent the Army-State,based on martial law conditions, from continuing past Summer 1983. It was rumoured that CPSU Secretary and Russian Nationalist leadership contender, Grigori Romanov, was less benevolently inclined towards Jaruzelski than the residual Brezhnev-Chernenko faction, who eventually co-opted Andropov and Gorbachov. Nevertheless Jaruzelski dominated the PZPR Politburo and Secretariat as well as WRON and KOK and the Council of Ministers during the State of War. He controlled the subsequent shift back to party influence and methods by placing his supporters in all key positions. Significant members of his leadership team have worked for him in both the CC Secretariat and the Government Presidium [39]. The most notable Politburo supporters were as follows: Zbigniew Messner (born 1929) oversaw the economy and became his Premier when Jaruzelski ceded the post after the October 1985 Sejm elections. CC Secretary, Józef Czyrek (born 1928), has been Jaruzelski's foreign policy supremo and adviser on General Political Questions. In the mid-1980s he certainly appeared to be Jaruzelski's Number Two and the best placed candidate for the succession, if the case were to arise. Barcikowski's influence in the Secretariat ended when he was kicked upstairs in late 1985; he effectively became Jaruzelski's deputy when the General became Chairman of the Council of State. Orzechowski also became Foreign Minister at the same time. Olszowski's long political career, which had always just fallen short of the top post, ended for good. Their influence in the Secretariat was taken over by Wrocław First Secretary, Tadeusz Porębski, who entered in November 1983, and Marian Woźniak, who relinquished the Warsaw City First Secretaryship in late 1985 in order to concentrate on his promising national role. Other Jaruzelski Secretaries - like Mokrzyszczak, Główczyk and Michałek - have been supplemented by younger entrants like Ideology Secretary Bednarski and Świrgoń, who moved on from Youth Questions to running PRON. The last somewhat autonomous Secretary, Security Chief Milewski, vanished quietly without trace in mid-1985. As well as promoting a whole host of political professors (Messner, Porębski, Orzechowski and Economic Reform Minister, Baka), Jaruzelski

also likes interesting political journalists within
his entourage. Rakowski was a heroic figure at
the outset in 1981, then a tragic one in 1982 and
a rather pathetic one after that, notably in his
confrontations with the Gdańsk Shipyard workers.
He was deputy Premier until October 1985 when he
became Sejm Marshal. He had already ceded the
influential editorship of Polityka to Jan Bijak in
September 1982. Media spokesmen like Major Wiesław
Górnicki had close access to the General's ear. So
did Government press spokesman, Jerzy Urban, whose
weekly press conferences for foreign journalists
were incredibly pugnacious and fascinating exposi-
tions of the Jaruzelski line, especially in 1982-
1983, after which he rather went off the boil.
The General apparently also liked to consult scin-
tillating pens like Kazimierz Koźniewski, the
editor of Tu i Teraz, and Krzystof Teodor Toeplitz.
KTT now writes mainly for Polityka, which declined
markedly in quality post 1982.

As suggested at the end of Chapter Two, military penetration of party-state positions was far
from wholesale. It was more significant in qualitative than quantitative terms except for 1982.
The WRON-KOK-military commissioner framework then
gave grounds for supposing that a new type of communist Army-State was in the making. But with the
suspension of martial law there was a clear reversion to the classic institutions and processes of
the Party-State. The main novum was the growth and
continued maintenance of the state administration.
This was animated and controlled by Jaruzelski and
the political officer hardcore in the early 1980s
and backed up by the security and judicial apparats.
With the decay of the PZPR's local and factory
influence in 1980-1982 power moved decisively from
the KW First Secretary to the Wojewoda, especially
in the ten or so run by military men. Another
similar development was Jaruzelski's greater use
of the Sejm than party bodies to publicise martial
law decisions in 1982-1983 [40].

The evidence is therefore unclear whether there
was any serious attempt by the Generals to use martial law conditions to transform Poland's Party-State
permanently into an Army-State. The final result
in Summer 1983 was that the two fused together in a
novel symbiosis. This would allow new permutations
between them in response to future socio-economic
developments and the play of the bureaucratic
pluralism of communist politics. But the authorities claimed that they were converting this new

reality into a communist Rechstaat; that is one
in which the power holders may be autonomous but
in which citizen-state relations are based on written
codified laws with guaranteeing institutions [41].
Such developments as the establishment of a High
Administrative Court in 1980, the concession of
the principle of judicial oversight over the administration, the setting up of State and Constitutional Tribunals and of a wide variety of control
bodies were all designed to constrain the unbridled
exercise of power [42]. The doyen of Polish
constitutional lawyers, Professor Sylwester
Zawadzki, Justice Minister from 1981 to 1983,
stressed 'the enormous changes' which were in train
in an interview to this author in Warsaw on 25
September 1984. One might perhaps ask whether the
notorious cases of illegality, such as Popiełuszko's
murder and the beating up and death of the Warsaw
student Przemyk, were exceptions to this underlying
process? What was perhaps significant was not
so much their occurrence under conditions of communist authoritarianism and police repression of
social contestation as the outcry which turned them
into cas célèbres putting the authorities on the
defensive. What is clear though is that Jaruzelski's
Patriotic Rebirth was a highly contested one. Predictably it was only a success within the communist
fold,but that is always the crucial factor in Soviet-
Leninist terms. PRON had not generated much autonomous support,but then neither did its FJN predecessor except in 1971. Minor parties have admittedly been given greater roles within the party
system. The ZSL chairman, deputy Premier and then
Sejm Marshal, Roman Malinowski, and the PAX and ChSS
leaders, Komender and Morawski, were close to
Jaruzelski, who spared no effort to build up their
prestige.
    Military rule in 1982-1983 rebuilt communist
power but failed to heal the state-society split.
It eventually broke organised opposition and re-
established its major institutions and cores of
directing personnel. The bulk of the soldiers went
back to barracks and to normal military duties in
late December 1982. They remained in reserve, to
be called upon again if necessary. The remaining
few hundred senior political officers, headed by
Jaruzelski, remained ensconced, comfortably, in
their party-state positions. Since 1983 the
Polish communist system has reverted to the traditional forms of Soviet-Leninist rule. The distinction between civilian and military functionaries

has become eroded with the passage of time, demonstrating the interchangeable character of the communist functionary class irrespective of original specialised provenance.

Notes

1. See M.K. Dziewanowski, The Communist Party of Poland (Cambridge, Mass., Harvard U.P., 2nd rev. edn., 1976). J.B. de Weydenthal, The Communists of Poland (Hoover Institution Press, Stanford, 1978).
2. J. Bielasiak, 'The party - permanent crisis' in A. Brumberg (ed.), Poland. Genesis of a revolution (New York, Vintage Books, 1983). Z. Kruszewski, 'The CP during the 1980-1981 democratisation of Poland' in Bielasiak & Simon, Polish Politics, pp. 241-267.
3. Cf. Taras, 'Official etiologies of Polish crises', op. cit.
4. Notably by Sanford, Polish Communism in Crisis. See Introduction, f.1, for the full references.
5. A. Kriegel, The French Communists. Profile of a people (Chicago U.P., 1972). G. Lavau, A quoi sert le PCF? (Paris, Fayard, 1981).
6. D.S. Mason, 'Membership of the Polish United Workers' Party', Polish Review, XXVI (1982), pp. 138-156.
7. Reliable estimates of dual PZPR-Solidarity membership are difficult to come by. Journalistic estimates of up to 1.7 million should be treated with extreme caution, Christian Science Monitor, 28 January 1981. Evidence drawn from 'Polacy 80' and a 1980 Łódź survey suggests that 35% of the PZPR, as against 37% of adult society, joined Solidarity. This would give a credible national PZPR figure of around one million. See D.S. Mason, Public Opinion and Political Change in Poland, 1980-1982 (Cambridge U.P., 1985), pp. 148-150.
8. G. Wightman & A. Brown, 'Changes in the levels of membership and social composition of the CP of Czechoslovakia', Soviet Studies, XXVII, No. 3 (July 1975), pp. 396-417. The January 1968 to December 1970 decline was 473,731 (28%), p. 414. Wightman demonstrates that membership was cut from 1.66 million in April 1969 to 1.38 million in April 1976 (16.8%); 'Membership of the CP of Czechoslovakia in the 1970s', Soviet Studies, XXXV, No. 2 (April 1983), p. 209.
9. M.F. Vale (ed.), Poland. Report on the State of the Nation based on a social and economic survey by the Experience and Future Group (London, Pluto Press, 1981). The DiP reaction to Martial Law, its Fourth Report, is in Kultura (Paris, July-August 1982), pp. 143-208.
10. Sanford, 'Polish People's Republic' in B.Szajkowski (ed.), Marxist Governments (London, Macmillan, 1981), Vol. I, pp. 556-570.

11. Bogdan Mieczkowski's inverse relationship between consumer satisfaction and the party's authority is no longer relevant in the 1980s: 'The relationship between consumption and politics in Poland', Soviet Studies, XXX, No. 2 (April 1978), pp. 262-269.
12. Cf. P. Lewis (ed.), Legitimation in Eastern Europe (London, Croom Helm, 1985).
13. Sanford, Polish Communism in Crisis, ch. 6.
14. G. Kolankiewicz, 'Renewal, Reform, or Retreat; the Polish Communist Party after the Extraordinary Ninth Congress', World Today, Vol. 37, No. 10 (October 1981), p. 369.
15. The statute is available in English translation in W.B. Simons & S. White (eds.), The Party-Statutes of the Communist World (The Hague, Martinus Nijhoff, 1984), pp. 323-361. Cf. G. Kolankiewicz, 'The limits to reform in a ruling communist party; the status of statutes', Unpublished ECPR conference paper, Freiburg, 1983.
16. D.S. Mason, 'Solidarity, the Régime and the Public', Soviet Studies, XXXV, No. 4 (October 1983), p. 538.
17. Cf. Jaroslav Piekalkiewicz, Public Opinion Polling in Czechoslovakia, 1968-1969 (New York, Praeger, 1972).
18. D.S. Mason, 'The Polish party in crisis, 1980-1982', Slavic Review, Vol. 43, No. 1 (May 1984), pp. 43-45. For the most comprehensive and authoritative examination of public opinion in this period, consult D.S. Mason, Public Opinion and Political Change, op. cit. The appendix outlining the major polls and surveys of 1980-1982 is particularly useful, pp. 249-252.
19. Sanford, 'Poland' in McCauley & Carter, Leadership and Succession ..., Table 3.5, p. 62.
20. S. Olszowski, 'Konsolidacja partii-warunkiem jej odrodzenie', ND, Nos. 1-2 (January-February 1982), pp. 5-15.
21. Johnson, East European Military Establishments, op. cit., p. xii.
22. Malcher, Poland's Politicised Army, pp. 186-187.
23. Mason, Public Opinion and Political Change in Poland, pp. 205 ff.
24. Interview, 'Ktoś z zewnątrz spoza układów', Polityka, 16 October 1982.
25. As in the case of Colonel Dr. Wacław Kołodziej, military commissioner for the Warsaw Transport System: 'Chyba jeszcze pozostanę', Polityka, 8 January 1983.
26. Józef Cegła, 'Grudzien, Luty i dalej ...', Polityka, 6 March 1982.
27. An interpellation in the Sejm by Rudolf Buchała to Premier Jaruzelski on the activities of one of its leaders, Wsiewołod Wolczew, deputy director of the Silesian Institute, seems to have gone unanswered. Text in SSS, 18th sitting of 25 January 1982, Interpellation Cols. 18-19.

28. I Ogólnopolska Partyjna Konferencja Ideologiczno-
    Teoretyczna (Warsaw, KiW, 1982).
29. Adam Czarniecki (deputy chairman, Warsaw Control Com-
    mission), 'Nie jesteśmy żandarmerią w partii', Polityka,
    29 January 1983.
30. Jan Rurański, 'Kraków jest jak pryzmat', Polityka,
    5 February 1983.
31. Kulisy, 113/1983.
32. Ludwik Krasucki, 'Nie taką samą', Polityka, 9 April 1983.
33. G. Sanford, 'Poland's recurring crises; an interpre-
    tation', World Today (January 1985), p. 9.
34. I Ogólnopolska Konferencja ..., op. cit.
35. '0 co walczymy? Dokąd zmierzamy?', ND supplement 2/1984,
    pp. 333-344.
36. See his critique of Adam Schaff's increasingly Euro-
    communist analyses contained in Communism at the Cross-
    roads.   M. Orzechowski, Spór o Marksistowską teorię
    rewolucji (Warsaw, KiW, 1984).
37. Round Table Discussion on Social Consciousness, ND
    (October 1983), pp. _92-126.
38. A long drawn-out debate took place around Professor
    Jan Wawrzyniak's doomed attempt to get the term ac-
    cepted.   Cf. ND (November-December 1983), pp. 144-146.
39. Consult Sanford, 'Poland', in McCauley & Carter,
    Leadership and Succession ...
40. Jolanta Strzelecka, 'The functioning of the Sejm since
    13 December 1981', Poland Watch, No. 7 (1985), pp.55-74.
41. In the post-Martial Law period Poland's state-society
    situation and economic problems seemed to parallel
    Yugoslavia's rather than Hungary's in many respects.
    Cf. A. Fisk, 'A Communist Rechstaat - Yugoslav consti-
    tutionalism', Government and Opposition, V, No. 1
    (1969-1970), pp. 41-53.
42. Hubert Izdebski, 'La jurisprudence de la Haute Cour
    Administrative Polonaise', Revue Internationale de Droit
    Comparé (1984), No. 3.

Chapter Six

THE ROMAN CATHOLIC CHURCH. NEARER TO ETERNITY THAN
TO SOLIDARITY

The reasons for Poland's intensely close identification with Roman Catholicism are ingrained in
the country's history since the adoption of
Christianity by Mieszko I in 966 AD. Poland's role,
and self-perception, as the bulkwark of Christianity
in Eastern Europe against the Mongols, Tartars and
Turks and as the bastion of Catholicism against
Protestant Germans and Orthodox Russians, developed
over the thousand years of her statehood. But the
loss of national independence in the nineteenth century gave the equation 'Polak-Katolik' (Pole =
Catholic) a deeper socio-psychological dimension.
The Church became the most important support of the
Polish language, culture, moral values and even
economic aspirations. As the state was controlled
by hostile partitioning powers the Poles formed
something close to a Roman Catholic, family based,
national counter-community which was particularly
strong in the peasant countryside. Although this
picture can be qualified for different regions and
social groups at various times, a tradition of quasi-
religious messianism and Romantic Nationalism was
also embedded by great writers such as Słowacki,
Krasiński and Mickiewicz [1]. These values, although
challenged by the positivist and realist 'Organic
Work' reaction to the failure of the 1863 insurrection, also crystallised the tradition of the 'Emigration' in Western Europe. The Roman Catholic
Church was given a privileged constitutional position
in the Interwar Republic, even though only about two-
thirds of the population were ethnically Polish and
Roman Catholic. There was no formal separation of
Church and State; the 1925 Concordat with the Vatican
allowed religious instruction in state schools.
Quite apart from any other considerations, People's
Poland therefore had to do this and to implement the

other secularisation measures which had already been
adopted in much of the rest of Europe [2]. The
secularisation of the Polish state in the immediate
postwar period should therefore be viewed in a different light from the subsequent Stalinist attempt to
reduce the Church to less than its religious-pastoral
mission and to subordinate it politically.

Since the Second World War Poland has as a result of the redrawing of frontiers, mass population
transfer and educational socialisation become an
extremely homogenous country ethnically and reli-
giously. Poland is now overwhelmingly a country
of baptised Roman Catholics, the Church claim for
the national average being 93% [3]. Estimates of
self-definition of believers range from 81% of
the urban and 90% of the rural population in 1966,
to 72.5% of the former and 83% of the latter in
1976, while 64% of a sample of middle level intelligentsia declared themselves to be believers [4].
Nowak's 1973 study presented a credible picture that
8% of the population were ardent believers, 55%
believers, 10% were undecided, 15% non-believers and
14% decidedly non-believers [5]. The key socio-
political indicator,though, is not the level of
formal affiliation but the degree of Catholic religious practice. Here we find that, unlike France,
there is no glaring distinction between practising
and dechristianised regions or social groups.
Peasants are clearly the most Catholic, while the
urban intelligentsia and the élites are the least so
inclined. The claims for astoundingly high levels,
for a modern European state, of attendance at mass
of the order of half to two-thirds and of confession
and communion, especially in the countryside, however, mask all sorts of distinctions, as Fiszman
has shown in his study of lower level rural school
teachers [6]. Recent studies show that 60% of
all Poles go to Sunday mass regularly; 84% take
communion, at least, once a year; while 85% declare themselves to be believers, 10% are agnostics
and 5% atheists [7].

The issues of the intensity of actual belief
or religiosity and the significance of participation
in religious life are dimensions concerned with the
private individual sphere of religious belief and
practice. The interpretation of the political consequences of such phenomena is, however, controversial.
A 1958 poll showed that 76% of non-believers, as compared with 66% of believers, declared themselves in
favour of socialism; the evidence is that the percentage increased up till the 1980s [8]. This

217

supports Kolankiewicz's and Taras' argument that
Poles draw a clear distinction between the general
ethical values of socialism which they support and
the party's materialist Marxist-Leninism.   Gomułka
believed that most 'believers do not tie their religious faith to political beliefs' (ND, June 1965,
p. 5).   The secularising effect of postwar socio-
economic change, especially urbanisation and mass
education, is also a dimension which analytically
can be considered separately from the PZPR's attempts
to inculcate the Marxist-Leninist world view.   But
recurring political conflicts and partisanship make
it difficult to consider traditional forms of
Church-State conflict in Poland over the building of
a modern secular society dispassionately.   The
determining factor has been that the very existence
of such a powerful autonomous social force as the
Church has presented an insuperable obstacle to
Poland's transformation into a totalitarian society.
The Roman Catholic Church has therefore inevitably
been the PZPR's main rival in interpreting the
country's history and destiny.   The Church is also
an organisational, as well as an ideological, competitor, which undermines the PZPR's claim to a
monopoly of political legitimacy and control.
   The Church in postwar Poland has been an im-
mensely powerful structure with deep social roots.
At times it has acted as a haven for discontented
social groups, while it has always been particularly
concerned with peasant interests.   It has revived
its latent historical role, developed in the Partition
and Second World War periods, of being the symbol
and the aggregator of national opposition to a hostile occupying power, as well as tapping the still
strong Polish resistance to state authority.
Kolankiewicz and Taras, however, endorsed Gierek's
thesis that religious belief or identification does
not necessarily imply a clash with socialist socio-
economic principles or prevent the citizen from
contributing to the common good.   Their argument,
that the Church acts as an opposition force, mainly
in a defensive way, out of 'consideration for practical politics', is a compelling one [9].   One can
also follow their analytical distinction between the
three levels of the Catholic Church.   Firstly,
there is the mass body of believers and worshippers.
Secondly, there is the Catholic intelligentsia,
which possesses a wide range of journals and discussion clubs.   Since 1956 the two régime-sponsored
Catholic political organisations, PAX and the more
intermediate Catholic Social Association (ChSS), not

to mention the wholly autonomous Znak and its PZKS
successor, have allowed it a significant legal foothold within the communist system.   Lastly, there
is the Church Establishment, which in practice means
the Primate, his advisers and the Episcopal Conference.   A full study of the Church's political
role would examine all three dimensions, something
which Szajkowski notably fails to do in his book
[10];   but, for our purposes here, one inevitably
has to concentrate on the leadership level, which
includes the influence of the Vatican, while the
social and intellectual levels have to be appraised
as factors in the Church's political outputs.

It is widely accepted that the Roman Catholic
Church is the most significant institution in Poland
next to the PZPR;   some would claim that it is even
more important.   But the Church's role really needs
to be examined under the following headings, which
are extremely tangled and difficult to separate out
successfully:

1.   Its eternal religious mission of preaching the
Christian Gospel and of ministering to the religious
needs of the faithful.
2.   Its very extensive pastoral and charitable mission of assisting the needy and sick as well as
individuals and families in distress.
3.   Its 'normal' relationship with the state involving the everyday regulation of questions arising out of the form, boundaries and consequences of
its existence, and of its activities in furthering
the above two missions.   This covers the stock West
European Church-State issues of religious education,
civil marriage and divorce, family life, contracep-
tion and abortion, the licensing of new Churches,
the appointment of new clergy and the forms and extent
of Church publishing, propaganda, recruitment and
seminary status.   These, elsewhere, have caused
conflicts since medieval times.
4.   For peculiarly Polish historical, social and
geo-political reasons the Polish Church has an almost symbiotic relationship with the national community.   Its role in relationship to the hostile
state has variously been described as being the
'Protector', 'Mediator' and more recently the
'Tribune' of society.   With the suppression and
banning of Solidarity it became the sole remaining
spokesman for civil society.   This function developed out of the Stalinist persecution of the early
1950s and the establishment of a Church-State ar-
rangement by Gomułka and Wyszyński in 1956, which,

although punctuated by conflicts and confrontation, has survived structurally until the present.

The consequence of the fourth factor has been that the Church has become a principal actor in Polish politics. The Church claims that it has always ascribed priority to its religious and pastoral missions; it has only become involved in politics in order to preserve and extend these functions. This seems to have been confirmed by its policy under Glemp when it did not tie itself irrevocably to Solidarity. Although it acted as the spokesman for the national-religious values of society, it was very careful, as in Wyszyński's time, not to get manoeuvred into any fundamental confrontation with the communist state.

The Roman Catholic Church has a massive and irreducible organisational structure [11]. The Church after Wyszyński's death in 198? was led by Cardinal Józef Glemp, the Primate of Poland and Archbishop of Gniezno and Warsaw. He chaired an Episcopal Conference of around 89 bishops which met, at least, quarterly. This body in turn elected a Main Council of nine on which Glemp and the Metropolitan Archbishops of Kraków, Cardinal Franciszek Macharski, of Wrocław, Henryk Gulbinowicz, and of Poznań, Jerzy Stroba, sat ex officio. So did Archbishop Bronisław Dąbrowski, who was re-elected for a fourth term as the Secretary of the Main Council in March 1984; not to be confused with his deputy, Bishop Jerzy Dąbrowski. These bodies supervised the work of the 27 dioceses and 7,469 parishes into which the Polish Church was divided in 1983. A total of 20,947 clergy, of whom 4,716 were monks, worked in these parishes. In addition another 9,603 monks resided in 45 monasteries, while there was an almost medieval figure of 27,429 nuns in 104 convents. Apart from these 58,000 men and women in the full-time service of the Church one would have to add the large number of ancillary and voluntary workers which the Church could draw on. Of the 14,498 churches in active use, 4,201 were chapels, while about 20,000 catechism points had been established after much controversy and conflict with the authorities [12]. The PAX daily Słowo Powszechne, the weekly Tygodnik Powszechny published in Kraków by Catholics closer to the hierarchy and independent monthlies like Więź in Warsaw and Znak in Kraków were supplemented by the ChSS Ład, after 1980. The Church also published a mass of diocesan bulletins and

devotional works. Through its parish pulpits it
had a crucially important non-censored form of
direct communication with both its faithful and
society in general.

Although there is a wide range of religious
practice in Poland and the authorities are scrupu-
lous in their respect for, and encouragement of,
the 33 registered non-Roman Catholic denominations,
they only totalled about two-thirds of a million
and had a mere 1,900 clergy and 1,381 religious
meeting places [13]. The Church's overwhelming
weight, therefore, gave it a formidable capacity
for exercising its pastoral and social work roles
and for penetrating every sector of society except
for the communist hardcore, which itself was not
wholly immune.

One of the basic facts of postwar Polish political life has therefore been that both the PZPR
and the Roman Catholic Church have had to accept
the permanent and irreducible character of the other.
Even at the height of the Stalinist persecution of
the early 1950s, when Wyszyński, 9 bishops and
several hundred priests were imprisoned, it is
doubtful whether the communist leaders really attempted to destroy the Church through persecution.
The Agreement of 14 April 1950 was the equivalent
of a concordat, replacing that of 1925 regulating
Church-State relations, and it was confirmed and
amplified in 1956 [14]. As neither side could hope
to extirpate the other a modus vivendi had to be
established. But the acceptance of peaceful co-
existence did not diminish the intensity of their
ideological and political competition for the minds
and support of the Polish nation. Continuous
skirmishing took place in order to push back the
other's jurisdiction. The grudgingly practical
modus vivendi was punctuated by 'growling sessions'
and confrontations provoked by specific disputes.
Stefan Wyszyński, who became Primate in 1948 in succession to August Hlond, accepted the communist
order and Soviet hegemony as a fact of life. After
1956 he supported Polish raison d'état in exchange
for an autonomous religious jurisdiction and the
communist state's confirmation of the Church's
promotion of its religious and pastoral missions [15].

The perennial problem has always been that it
is not clear what belongs to God and what to Caesar
[16]. At the October 1956 Eighth Plenum Gomułka
conceded that the Church could have religious and
pastoral freedom as long as it accepted communist
power in Poland and the Soviet alliance; it should

also take a patriotic 'Polish way' regarding Poland's
frontiers, independence and stable domestic evolution.
This established the post-October tradition that
the PZPR's domestic-nationalist wing would seek
Church assistance in revolutionary periods in order
to calm society down. The Church-State premise was
that the Episcopacy should distinguish between the
Soviet Stalinist plague and the milder Gomułka-
Gierek type of national-communist influenza. The
Church also had a realpolitik understanding of the
costs of national insurrection and Soviet invasion.
Wyszyński thundered in December 1956 that 'we have
had enough conflagrations in our Fatherland ... it
is high time they stopped mustering armies of heroes
and shedding blood on Polish soil' [17]. Gomułka
abandoned direct persecution and attempts to destroy
the Church. But the need for co-existence did not
eliminate the ideological struggle; it was now to
be carried on by political not police-administrative
means (ND, June 1957, p. 69). Direct anti-Church
activity carried out by the Association of Atheists
and Freethinkers through its journals Argumenty and
Fakty i Myśli, in which Leszek Kołakowski played a
prominent role, met with limited success. Gomułka
also made it clear that the Church would not be permitted to act as an anti-socialist, or even as an
independent, opposition [18]. Conflicts over the
exact frontiers of the Church-State relationship
(notably over the licensing of new churches, as in
Nowa Huta in 1961, over religious teaching in school
premises and over tax exemptions on Church property)
were built into this relationship. They recurred
with great regularity. These issues were rather
different from the major conflicts which blew up over
the celebration of Poland's Millenium in 1966, or
the Letter of the Polish to the German Bishops the
previous year, which raised the broader question of
whether the Party or the Church spoke for the nation.
After 1956 the PZPR attempted to secularise and
modernise society. The PZPR hoped along with
Minister of Education, Władysław Bieńkowski, that
socio-economic modernisation, urbanisation, material
prosperity and education would produce a secular
minded society which would undercut the bases of
religious belief; this seemed to be partly confirmed
up till the mid-1970s. Bieńkowski declared that
'only by fostering apathy can we prepare the way
for the reduction of the Church's influence ... the
decline of religion is not achieved by struggle with
it but by the problem declining'. Wyszyński countered this line in a 1959 sermon: 'An apathetic

nation is a nation without strength, without energy,
without hope. We do not want such a nation' [19].
Gomułka's grudging co-existence with the Church
was replaced by the fuller normalisation of Church-
State relations and the practice of a more positive
policy of understanding by Gierek. He downtoned
pragmatically the whole series of political and ideological controversies with the Church. His policy
stressed the unity of the nation. All citizens,
whatever their world ideological viewpoint, could
join together in building his brand of socialism in
Poland [20]. Poland's communist leaders needed
the support of the Church in order to stabilise
and legitimise their power after both 1956 and 1970.
Gierek attempted to incorporate a wider variety of
non-party people, including believers, in working
for the socialist cause. He therefore conceded
Church tax and property claims, but his real effort
was directed into negotiations with the Vatican.
These resulted in 1972 in the Holy See's recognising
Poland's Western frontier and in the regularisation
of the Church administration in the Western Territories at long last. In December 1977 Gierek paid
an official visit to Pope Paul VI after numerous
high level contacts with Cardinal Casaroli had led
to the establishment of informal diplomatic relations. But along with this normalisation the
Primate and his bishops increasingly supported
dissident protest groups [21]. These took advantage of Gierek's tolerant line and mushroomed after
the controversy over the constitutional amendments
and the mishandling of the food price increases in
1976. The new KOR opposition, influenced by Adam
Michnik's Kościół, Lewica, dialog, buried the postwar
leftwing ideological conflict with the Church.
The hierarchy responded, as in Wojtyła's support
of the Kraków students in 1977 after the police
killing of the student Pyjas. Gierek and Wyszyński
met in the Sejm for the first time on 29 October
1977. Although the authorities made further concessions over religious instruction the Church failed
to respond to pleas to dampen down the growing social
ferment [22]. All this led Tadeusz Grabski, the
Konin KW First Secretary, to attack Gierek openly
at a Plenum in 1978 for 'capitulationism' towards
the Church [23].
    The election of the Archbishop of Kraków,
Cardinal Karol Wojtyła, as Pope John Paul II was a
psychological turning point. It set off a national
outburst of joy. Politically it moved the undisputed leadership of the Polish Church away from

Wyszyński to an external source outside the direct
influence of the communist authorities. John Paul's
return visit to Poland from 2 to 10 June 1979 'was
a psychological earthquake, an opportunity for mass
political catharsis' [24]. An informed observer
of the Polish scene reported that Wojtyła's elevation
'was a trigger for the mechanisms which set the
events of August 1980 in train' [25]. The Slav
Pope restated the new Vatican Ostpolitik and staked
out the Catholic Church's claim to the moral and
spiritual leadership of the Poles [26]. By demonstrating its greater mobilising appeal than the PZPR
the Church accelerated the erosion of support for
the latter. The mass crowds and the sense of
national emotional unity, particularly among the
young and the opposition groups, led to the rebirth
of traditional Polish sentiments of political
idealism and even chiliasm. From feeling an
unwarranted inferiority complex until the early
1970s the Poles now went to the opposite extreme.
The atmosphere built up the feeling that will power
and national unity could work miracles; many Poles
during the Solidarity period gave the impression
that such psychological sentiments were sufficient
to polish off any mere political and economic disas-
ters; the same applied to some of their spokesmen
in the West.

Church, State and Solidarity: the failed mediation
        The Church hierarchy's reaction to the Workers'
Upsurge was one of habitual political caution laced
with general moral and spiritual support. In his
Jasna Góra sermon of 26 August, which was broadcast
on radio, Wyszyński was primarily concerned with
preventing the social outburst from getting out of
hand (Słowo Powszechne, 27 August 1980). The Main
Episcopal Council's communiqué of 27 August, however,
counterbalanced Wyszyński's patient explanation of
the effect of the social uprising on Polish raison
d'état; it set out fundamental demands, notably
the rights to religious freedom, worship and church
activity, to accurate information and debate, to a
fair wage, to own agricultural land and to organise
free associations, including TUs [27]. Wyszyński
influenced the Gdańsk workers' leaders in their
negotiations with Jagielski through Bishop Lech
Kaczmarek of Gdańsk and through various Catholic
intellectuals, notably his own personal adviser,
Professor Romuald Kukułowicz,who was assisted by
Andrzej Wielowieyski, Andrzej Święcicki, Tadeusz
Mazowiecki, the Więź editor, and Bogdan Cywiński.

The Roman Catholic Church

The main Church gains were the broadcasting of
Sunday mass and the resumption of the Joint Government-Episcopal Committee, which had met 7 times
after October 1956, before lapsing in 1967. This
now met on 24 September 1980 and monthly thereafter.
Such institutional contacts reflected the fact that
the Church now became a key political actor with
great influence over Solidarity and Polish society
and regular high-level contacts with the officials
of the weakened communist system.

The Church, in spite of its increased influence
and prestige,did not, however, have much direct
control over the spontaneous and mushrooming emergence
of Solidarity in the Autumn. Wyszyński's advice
was that Solidarity should primarily be a TU confederation on the interwar Polish pattern; it
should concern itself mainly with workers' socio-
economic interests and demands. He wanted the
situation to be stabilised on the basis of the Social
Agreements so that the economic situation could be
controlled. He used his influence to persuade the
Solidarity leaders to behave responsibly, although
he deplored communist obduracy on such issues as
the Registration Crisis. The Solidarity leaders
were profoundly Catholic; hence their adoption of
religous forms and ceremonies and deference to the
clergy which gave the Gdańsk Shipyard its particular symbolism. Wałęsa accepted the Primate as his
'Number One Adviser' and acknowledged his debt to
the Church: 'If it had not been for the Church
none of this would have happened. Apart from anything else I would not be what I am' [28].
Wyszyński received Wałęsa and the Solidarity
leaders on 10 November 1980. He admonished them to
think in broad national categories and to resist
the radical blandishments of KOR intellectuals and
other political advisers (Słowo Powszechne, 21
November 1980).

Although the Church helped to moderate Solidarity
demands and to prevent its transformation into a
political opposition, it failed to convince the PZPR
of the need to accept Solidarity and free TUs permanently. Nothing like a Party-Solidarity-Church
condominium emerged. The first two forces remained
locked in combat over recurring issues and social
outbursts during 1980-1981. This allowed the Church
to develop a mediating influence at both national
and local levels. It became involved directly in
defusing social conflicts, especially in January-
February 1981, notably at Bielsko-Biała. Its intellectuals played an important role in advising the

new Solidarity leadership and an even more influential role in establishing, gaining recognition for and guiding Rural Solidarity [29]. All this increased the Church's hold over society immeasurably. But the direct increase of the Church's toehold within the Government system was relatively small apart from the regular contacts with officials and the work of the Joint Commission.

Wyszyński's prime concern was always to prevent the social crisis from getting out of hand so that it would not threaten Poland's frontiers and cause grave human and material losses, as so often in her history. The Episcopal Council's call in early December 1980 against 'actions that could endanger our Fatherland' was directed by their press spokesman, Father Orszulik, against 'irresponsible' KOR and KPN attacks on Poland's socialist allies (Słowo Powszechne, 15 December 1980). The symbolic participation of the Church in public life and its ambiguous relations with both Solidarity and the communist state was highlighted by the presence of Macharski, Dąbrowski, Glemp and Kaczmarek at the unveiling of the Gdańsk Memorial in the form of three huge intertwined metal crosses on 16 December 1980. This ceremony provided a temporary religious-patriotic emotional surrogate for the tensions of the time. In early 1981 the Church then played an important role as a 'fireman' in dampening down a whole series of local outbursts. It is also possible that the critically ill Wyszyński's meeting with Premier Jaruzelski on 26 March 1981 ensured a peaceful outcome to the Bydgoszcz crisis (Życie Warszawy, 27 March 1981).

The Polish Church suffered two great blows in May 1981. On 13 May a Turkish terrorist, Ali Agca, attempted to murder the Pope in St. Peter's Square. This was a graphic reminder to the Poles of the uncertain and potentially violent character of their situation. The Polish Pope was 'not just a spiritual shepherd but the champion of national and social resistance' [30]. On 28 May Wyszyński died after a long illness, at the age of 79 after almost 33 years as Primate. His lying in state and ceremonial funeral were seen by perhaps half the nation on the mass media; it was attended by 36 Cardinals, by leading party-state representatives and by Solidarity representatives. For the Vatican, Cardinal Casaroli declared that Wyszyński's greatest passions had been 'the Church and Poland'. Official condolences hailed him as

'a great priest and patriot'. Solidarity declared
its gratitude for his support 'in the most difficult moments' and for 'laying out the great programme
of moral renewal of the nation long before the
events of last August' [31]. Wyszyński's successor
was his protégé and nominee, Józef Glemp (born 1929),
the Bishop of Warmia in Olsztyn since 1979. Glemp
had been Wyszyński's Personal Secretary and Chaplain
from 1967 onwards and a lecturer at the Warsaw
Theological Academy who worked on the revision of
Canon Law. Glemp initially lacked the old
Cardinal's authority, charisma and stature, which
had been developed in almost four decades of
standing up to and seeing communist leaders like
Bierut, Gomułka and Gierek come and go. But this
soft-spoken, ruddy-cheeked priest had all his predecessor's strength of character and a commonsense
intellect derived from his peasant origins. Everything indicated he would also develop a long and
determined reign.

Glemp confirmed that he would continue his
predecessor's policy of 'dialogue and co-operation';
he would respond to developments in a pragmatic
manner (Życie Warszawy, 10 July 1981). He felt
that the Church's role as a mediator arose because
the communist power refused to come to terms with
society; this caused all the recurrent conflicts
(interview in Polityka, 31 August 1981). He presumably said as much to Jaruzelski when they met on
10 July (TL, 13 July 1981). Glemp's concern with
the growing political polarisation and social
strife was expressed in both his homily at Jasna
Góra on 26 August and in his message to the
Solidarity Congress in Oliwa Cathedral on 5
September. The Main Episcopal Council on 13
August defended free TUs as the greatest gain of
1980-1981 and demanded access to the mass media
[32]. After his discussions of 16-21 October
with John Paul in the Vatican, Glemp supported the
concept of a Front of National Understanding (FPN)
at his meeting with Jaruzelski on 21 October. The
Solidarity KPP under Glemp's influence called for
industrial restraint just before the Jaruzelski-
Glemp-Wałęsa summit meeting of 4 November. But
the meeting only cleared the ground for further
substantive talks, which in the event never took
place [33]. With the suppression of the Żolibórz
Firemen's School sit-in, the situation worsened
dramatically. Glemp was pressed by Wałęsa to write
to the Sejm Deputies, in a letter dated 6 December,
warning them that the passing of the Emergency

Powers Bill might have tragic consequences and provoke a General Strike.   He also wrote in similar
terms to both Jaruzelski and Wałęsa on 8 December ap-
pealing for the resumption of the tripartite Govern-
ment-Church-Solidarity negotiations over the FPN.
The next day Glemp conferred with Wałęsa and the
Solidarity leaders before they left for the KPP
meeting in Gdańsk, which, presumably against the
Primate's advice, went ahead with the demands for
the national referendum and free elections.   At
the same time Jaruzelski met the heads of the three
Catholic political clubs in the Sejm - Reiff of
PAX, Morawski of the ChSS and Zabłocki of the PZKS.
These last-minute attempts to re-establish contacts
and a basis for mediation proved unavailing.   Reiff,
however, swung PAX away from the régime at the very
last minute before martial law,which he then opposed.
He was soon replaced as PAX leader by Żenon Komender,
who had attended the same Marianite School in
Warsaw - Bielany   as the General [34].
     The Church had done whatever it could to mode-
rate Solidarity and to restrain social passions but
its mediating efforts proved fruitless;   the gap
between the communist authorities and Solidarity was
unbridgeable.   The Church, however, was only a
tactical factor in Jaruzelski's calculations.   It
is symptomatic that he only mentioned it once publicly during 1981.   Even that was in his very
first speech as Premier when he called for Church
support for his 90 days' strike-free appeal [35].
At the end of the day when Solidarity radicalised
itself in the Autumn the Church became tactically
less important to the communist authorities and
was brushed aside with martial law.

The Church between the Party and Society
     Both Pope and Primate were politically ex-
perienced enough in communist realities not to have
been taken entirely by surprise by the imposition
of martial law.   As political realists,though,
they recognised very quickly that the military coup
spelt the end of the Solidarity experiment.   It
doomed the Church's efforts to negotiate a meaningful Social Accord.   Their first priority, as so
often in Wyszyński's time, was to minimise bloodshed
and to contain the confrontation between society
and the repressive forces of the communist system.
The Pope, speaking in Polish at his Sunday mass
broadcast over Vatican Radio, stressed that 'Polish
blood cannot be spilt, as too much has been spilt
already, especially during the War'.   This thought

was amplified by Glemp in a sermon at the Jesuit
Church in Warsaw that evening. He expressed his
understanding for the indignation caused by the
replacement of dialogue by 'summary coercion'.
He promised that the Church would do everything in
its power to assist the victims of repression; but
the most pressing need was to avoid civil war, to
prevent the eruption of a hopeless insurrection and
to save life (Le Monde, 15 December 1981). The
Primate avoided the outright condemnation of force
and of communism which Mindszenty had indulged in
in Hungary but neither did he approve the military's
actions. He proved himself a balanced, realistic
and judicious statesman who restrained his country-
men from an even greater misfortune. Glemp preserved the previous framework of Church-State relations and avoided the Church's being politically
isolated, as in Mindszenty's case.

On 15 December the Polish bishops condemned the
State of War 'as a blow to social expectations and
hopes at a moment when the resolution of unresolved
matters on the basis of national understanding was
under consideration. The moral feelings of society
have been deeply hurt' but 'the nation would not
step back and cannot give up the democratic renewal
which had been announced' (Le Monde, 19 December
1981). The Church line was therefore to avoid a
bloodbath, to condemn the abandonment of Social
Dialogue and to defend the victims of martial law.
Jaruzelski's war against the nation was not therefore sanctioned by the Church, although it saw no
reason to hinder the re-establishment of order and
of economic activity. The Polish bishops had made
it clear that the nation 'was terrorised by military force' but their demands, which were supported
by the Pope, for Wałęsa's release, the reinstatement
of Solidarity, the release of all internees and the
rapid lifting of martial law, soon turned out to
be mere whistling in the wind. The new authorities
were resolved to smash the opposition and to rebuild
the system on their own terms. This intention was
only camouflaged verbally in order to lessen resistance. The Church, therefore, faced the same
dilemmas which had plagued it since 1948. Over
three decades of experience in the strategy and
tactics of 'co-existence' and crisis meant that it
had little difficulty in following the middle road
pioneered by Wyszyński, of neither total opposition
nor surrender to the authorities. It would save
whatever could be saved from Solidarity's shipwreck,
defend its social and individual moral values and

deepen its role as the only remaining independent
spokesman for Polish society.

After the initial bloodshed and the threat of
national uprising had passed, the Church hierarchy
felt freer   to criticise WRON's repressive actions.
Early protests gained the clergy the right to visit
and to celebrate mass for interness [36].   On 28
December Glemp sent Jaruzelski the strong and well
publicised protest against the forced loyalty oaths
and resignations from Solidarity which the authorities were exacting [37].   By 6 January Cardinal
Macharski was condemning martial law 'as a great
evil'.   At their meeting in Warsaw on 9 January
1982, Jaruzelski and Glemp merely 'exchanged views
on the current situation and expressed intentions
directed to the normalisation of life in the country'
(TL, 11 January 1982).   The regular transmission of
Sunday mass was resumed from 17 January onwards,
although the authorities insisted on censoring the
sermons beforehand.   The Joint Government-Episcopal
Committee also met on 18 January, without much
meeting of minds [38].   In a Pastoral Letter of 19
January the bishops condemned repression, internment and the suppression of the right of workers
and students to organise themselves freely.   They
were particularly eloquent that limitation of human
freedom 'leads to protest, rebellion and even civil
war'.   As usual there was a division of labour between Pope and Primate which external observers
interpreted as a split in the Church camp.   Glemp's
softer line that priests should have nothing to do
with the new OKONs, but that lay Catholics might
try to influence them, was utilised by the authorities as sanctioning participation and resented by
the opposition [39].   Glemp's emphasis on the
Church's traditional pastoral role led to increased
support for poor families and the distribution of
food and clothes sent by the West at parish level.
Above all, the Primate's Committee for Assistance to
Internees established on 21 January set up five
sections which gave massive material, spiritual and
financial help to internees, other prisoners and
victims of martial law and their families [40].

The 183rd Episcopal Conference of 25-26 February
hammered out the Church's more developed line.   Glemp
and Macharski had just discussed this in a week-long
visit to John Paul in the Vatican.   The communiqué
appealed, as usual, for a new Social Agreement.   But
it was more outspoken in reiterating 'the basic civic
freedoms which recognise human dignity' and the need
for social control over public life.   Specific

demands were now stated more sharply and precisely.
Civil rights should be guaranteed by the Government,
which should open itself to social pressures. Martial law was denounced as 'a moral, social and
economic catastrophe'. But realistic and gradual
compromises could still heal the deep rifts in Polish
society within the limits of the country's geo-
political position [41]. By then Glemp realised
that his negotiations with the authorities for a
genuine political compromise, gaining the relegali-
sation of Solidarity in exchange for the departure
of the extremists, would prove fruitless. The
main lines of his new long-term strategy were that
the Church would 'speak the truth', defend persecuted
social groups and build up its standing and support
through such events as the Pope's visit for the
Częstochowa celebrations in the Summer (Le Monde,
10 March 1983).

The foregoing ideas were developed for the
bishops by prominent Catholic intellectuals such
as Stomma, Micewski, Wielowieyski, Turowicz and
Kukułowicz. They participated in the work of the
28 strong Primate's Social Council for Catholic
Laymen,which had been formed in November 1981 as a
'Think Tank' for Glemp. This body produced the
very comprehensive and much publicised ten-point
'Theses of the Primate's Social Council on the Question of Social Accord' on 5 April 1982. A copy
was sent to Jaruzelski but it was ignored pointedly
by the authorities, who remained committed solely
to their PRON conceptions [42]. Martial law was
denounced as a tragedy which would cause a national
decline if nothing were done. Some form of institutionalised power-sharing and self-management
within the limits set by the PZPR's hegemony and
the Soviet alliance was essential. Social peace
could only be ensured by ending martial law, re-
leasing internees and guaranteeing civil rights,
including free TUs. Solidarity had to be re-
legalised but it was accepted that it would play a
less political role. These well thought out proposals for ending the Polish deadlock went well beyond
the FPN ideas of Autumn 1981. They were, therefore, not considered acceptable by the authorities,
who had no intention of indulging in any serious
dialogue or compromise with society until they had
rebuilt their organisational structures and boosted
the ideological morale and unity of their supporters. The April Theses were amplified in May in
the 'Propositions of the Primate's Social Council
on Social and Economic Qustions' which were again

forwarded to the authorities, with little response.
This document criticised the harmful consequences of
centralised bureaucratic-directive control of the
economy, the preference for heavy industry at the
expense of housing and consumer goods and the mismanagement of agriculture and handicrafts. The
concluding presumption, as normal in these circles,
was that no political solution or economic reform
was possible without an agreement between the communist authorities and society.

The régime, however, had little to offer the
Church when it began its Ideological Counter-Offensive in April. On 25 April Jaruzelski and Glemp
therefore merely discussed the continuing 'complicated situation' (TL, 26 April 1982). It is highly
likely that Glemp gathered from this meeting that
Solidarity was finished. He drew the appropriate
conclusions well before anyone else. But in his
late April conversations with the Pope he went along
with Wojtyła's stress on the need to give Solidarity
and Polish society the Church's much needed support.

Solidarity activists feared that the Church
was transforming its relationship with the communist
state into a bipartite one,as before 1980. The
Episcopacy's loss of direction and self-confidence
at its June 1982 Conference [43] encouraged radical
priests such as Stanisław Małkowski to challenge
the Social Council Theses 'that reform of the communist system was possible'; such ideas merely
provided ammunition for 'the deceitful propaganda
of the system'. Church concessions represented
'the beginning of defeat for all liberation movements' [44]. Anka Kowalska, the KOR and Gdańsk
shipyard activist, also wrote to Glemp protesting
against what she considered was the Church's con-
donation of the crimes of martial law [45]. Glemp
and the Church hierarchy thus came under increasing
attack for allegedly betraying Solidarity; but
this was a small price to pay for maintaining their
position as a privileged interlocutor who had some
influence on Jaruzelski's decisions. The Pope,
however, was under no such constraint. His ILO
address in Geneva on 15 June was a call for 'a new
Solidarity without frontiers'; such external support was only of moral-psychological influence.
The Polish hierarchy, therefore, tried a new tack
in order to get out of their political doldrums.
They dangled an economic carrot before Jaruzelski
in June, in order to induce political concessions.
Their 'Memorandum on the Assistance Programme for
Private Agriculture and the Private Enterprise

Sector' was an extremely ambitious plan for mobilising Western economic assistance of the order of
$250 million per annum for a recovery programme for
Polish agriculture, domestic trade and handicrafts.
Discreet negotiations with the Polish and other
interested Governments continued throughout 1982.
Glemp relaunched the idea in the New Year. In the
event this very worthy idea, which was fostered by
Glemp himself, had no chance in 1982, although everyone was either too polite or too embarrassed to say
so outright.

As it became clear by mid-1982 that full normalisation and the lifting of the State of War was
not imminent, Church-State relations became dominated by the issue of the Pope's visit to Poland.
Glemp had discussed the question during his visits
to the Vatican in early February and late April.
John Paul wanted to return to Poland in August 1982
to celebrate the 600th Anniversary of the Black
Madonna in Częstochowa. All sides were aware of the
huge psychological and political significance of
such a visit. The régime shuddered at the thought
of John Paul's appearance under martial law conditions. It made some minor concessions as it
did not want to be seen to veto it openly. The
bishops, however, renewed their invitation for late
August on 8 June. This sparked off a series of
Church-State meetings and statements on the question
by John Paul, Glemp, Casaroli and Archbishop Poggi
on the Church side, and Czyrek and Adam Łopatka, the
new Minister for Religious Affairs, for the Government. The PZPR Politburo considered that 'the
visit should be prepared carefully from the organisational point of view. The appropriate socio-
political conditions are essential for this. They
depend on the progress of normalisation in Poland'
(TL, 14 June 1982). But the June street demonstrations stiffened Polish and Soviet communist doubts.
The long drawn-out negotiations could not change the
fact, however, that both sides could not agree on
terms. For the moment we still do not know if
the Church had demanded the actual lifting of martial
law as a precondition. If so, it was not satisfied
by Jaruzelski's concessions of 21 July. Jaruzelski
made it clear that peace and order had to be re-
established and that all opposition activity must
cease before John Paul could come. His Government
would do everything in its power to ensure that
this would come about by 1983 at the latest. Later
Glemp announced publicly that the Papal visit had
been postponed because of the tense domestic situation;

but the Black Madonna celebrations would be extended and the Pope's visit would take place within
their framework, come what may.

Church-State relations hardened in the aftermath
of this failure. Both the Pope and then Glemp,
in his Jasna Góra homily on 26 August, reiterated the
demands for creating the conditions for dialogue -
the lifting of martial law, a full amnesty, the release of all political detainees, the legalisation
of Solidarity, TUs and other social associations and
the setting of a date for the Papal visit [46].
Polish society's disappointment about the latter may
have contributed to the scale and intensity of the
riots which greeted the late August anniversary of
the signing of the Social Agreements. Calls for
calm by the bishops, read from the pulpit on 29
August, proved fruitless. The authorities' repressive reaction and the loss of life provoked an
unusually bitter outburst by Bishop Tokarczuk of
Przemyśl in his Częstochowa sermon: 'Brute force
solves nothing' but only makes the situation worse,
said the Bishop, calling on militiamen to refuse to
participate in such actions in future [47]. Hardly surprisingly Tokarczuk, and other radical
prelates like Gulbinowicz, came in for much official attack (Rzeczpospolita, 8 September 1982).
However, both sides intervened very quickly to
prevent the polemics from getting out of hand,
although they went their own way following their
own concerns.

The final abandonment of the Church's attempt
to mediate and its return to its more traditional
Tribune role as Guardian of the country's spiritual
values was signified by the de-legalisation of
Solidarity. A planned meeting between Jaruzelski
and Glemp was called off and the latter also postponed his trip to the Vatican [48]. The Primate
was apparently informed of the detail of the Law
and informal exchanges took place until the very
last moment. Jaruzelski promised to meet the
Church half way on all matters relating to its
pastoral mission (SSS, Sitting of 9 October 1982,
Cols. 166-184). He hoped that specific social and
economic matters could be resolved by the direct
sort of discussions which were now taking place
between the Primate's Social Council and the Government's Consultative Economic Council. The General
also confirmed his willingness to arrange the details of the Pope's Second Visit. Glemp responded
the following day by saying that, while structures
might disappear, Solidarity's ideals would survive.

John Paul, however, condemned the banning of
Solidarity more openly and bitterly as 'a violation
of the basic rights of man'. The Primate's considered reaction was that all hope of an understanding had now gone as the authorities 'had liquidated the most important factor in the dialogue'
(Le Monde, 19 October 1983).
In retrospect the Polish bishops can now be seen
to have allowed emotion to rule their heads in over-
ruling Glemp and in demanding Solidarity's reinstatement during 1982. This, to any detached political
analyst, was a lost cause; the State of War had been
imposed with the prime purpose of liquidating
Solidarity, although the authorities very cunningly
stretched the process out during 9 months, in order
to lessen opposition by maintaining the illusory
'torture of hope' that it might still be saved.
Solidarity supporters overlooked the fact that the
Church had its own primarily religious mission.
Wyszyński had always believed that the Church
should not tie itself to any party or sectional
interest; this applied to Solidarity, however close
that movement's social and national and even religious interests were to the Church. It now became
clear that the Church was 'nearer to Eternity than
to Solidarity' [49]. The result was that Glemp
was blamed personally for weakness and over-con-
ciliatoriness in relation to the communist authorities, both by some of his bishops and the lower
clergy. Glemp maintained the Wyszyński tradition
of steering the Church ahead of and of avoiding fundamental confrontations. He advised publicly against
the Solidarity call for an 8-hour strike on 10
November, 'the consequences of which could only be
great repression' (Le Monde, 2 November 1982). An
unpleasant by-product from now on was a spate of
snide remarks by the contestatory priests and
their supporters, especially the Paris-based Kultura,
about the Primate's literary, oratorical and intellectual talents. Phrases like 'Comrade Glemp' and
even 'the Science of Glempology' entered the Polish
lexicon.
The Church's main concern at this time, though,
was the canonisation ceremonies of Father Maximillian
Kolbe, a monk who had voluntarily given his life
in order to save that of another at the Oswięcim
death camp. Glemp had abandoned his trip to Rome
for these celebrations in his fruitless attempts to
prevent the banning of Solidarity. It would seem,
though, that Glemp managed to convince John Paul,
during his delayed ten-day trip to the Vatican from

25 October onwards, of the need to contain the
Church-State conflict, to swallow the legal demise
of Solidarity and to play 'the card of stabilisation' in order to maintain the Church's influence
(Guetta, Le Monde, 10 November 1982). The
General and the Primate agreed at their 8 November
meeting that the Pontiff could begin his pilgrimage
on 18 June 1983. They 'carried out a review of the
current situation in Poland and expressed their
mutual concern over the maintenance and strengthening of peace, social order and honest work' (TL,
9 November 1982). Glemp requested Wałęsa's release
and this symbolic measure of appeasement occurred a
week later.
     Jaruzelski's Church policy was attacked by
party hardliners. Grabski, among his other Open
Letter criticisms, demanded a harder policy towards
the Church: 'The party must oppose clerical inter-
ference in political life, ensure that the Church
does not become a political party on the side of
the opposition' (ICPA, 20/82, pp. 38-40).
Namiotkiewicz, the CC Ideology Department Head,
attempted to defuse such criticisms by promising
firm opposition to 'attempts to promote political
clericalism which is clearly anti-socialist in nature
and the trend towards the clericalisation of social
life in Poland' (Żołnierz Wolności, 5 November 1982).
These developments occurred against the background
of the PZPR's ideological reassertion and the more
determined activity of its lower level and police
officials against opposition supporters. The
security services started preparing a campaign
against 'extremist priests' in the New Year.
     Glemp unveiled what he termed 'a strategy of
peace, love and truth' in Lublin on 7 November.
The first two qualities were designed to lead to
negotiations and political compromises with the
authorities, the latter to defend the rights of
the Church and Society (Le Monde, 23 & 24 November
1982). The Church was not satisfied by the suspension of martial law. Glemp wrote to the Sejm
Marshal expressing the bishops' opposition to the
elastically formulated Special Regulations which
gave the authorities enlarged powers.
     The agenda of Church-State relations during
the first half of 1983 was inevitably dominated by
the negotiations over the Papal visit, for which
the Church held a national day of prayer on 2 February.
The main difficulties concerned the Papal itinerary.
The authorities refused to let him visit the Baltic
trouble spots. They also wanted to vet the Pope's

sermons and speeches beforehand. The Episcopacy, however, hurried the matter along by issuing its own formal invitation and itinerary unilaterally. The bishops demanded the full lifting of martial law and a complete amnesty in order to move towards social reconciliation (ICPA, 4/83, pp. 27-30). Jaruzelski, however, made it clear that it was up to both the Church and State to create the necessary conditions for the Papal visit together. He complained that 'a section of the clergy is engaging in actions which have nothing to do with religion' (Przemówienia 1983, pp. 19-20). The contrasting Church-State viewpoints were presented by Glemp and Jaruzelski at their meeting on 9 March. Their main concern was stated to be the 'further stabilisation of social life and economic regeneration'. The Papal visit was confirmed for 16-22 June. Both sides bound themselves to prepare the visit so that 'it would contribute to the beneficial development of the currently most important matters of the state and nation' (TL, 10 March 1983). Jabłoński issued his formal invitation as Head of State on 21 March. The three major unresolved issues concerned whether the Pope would be allowed to visit the KUL where he had been a lecturer, whether he would be permitted to meet opposition leaders, especially Wałęsa, and, most importantly, whether the Church could force the régime into proclaiming a full and general amnesty for all martial law victims. The Pope requested the latter in a letter to Jabłoński in early May. This was refused on the grounds that an amnesty could only be declared on the final lifting of martial law, which itself depended on full socio-political normalisation. An intense round of horse trading then took place which culminated in the agreement endorsed by Glemp and Jaruzelski at their 6 June meeting.

The Papal visit took place because all sides thought that they could profit from it. For Jaruzelski it signified that the Church accepted that it would have to live with the new political realities in Poland. The visit ended Poland's international isolation and was sold to the Soviet bloc as a symbol of normalisation (Łopatka, Polityka, 4 June 1983). Glemp and the Polish Episcopacy would have their prestige raised and their policy of extracting gradual and behind-the-scenes concessions from the régime sanctioned. The 192nd Plenary Conference on 4 May said as much by placing the visit in the context of the concessions, such as the lifting of martial law, the amnesty, the Act of

Obl'vion and the release of all political prisoners, which were expected to accompany it [50]. For the Polish national community it represented the great hope that martial law was finishing and that life would improve gradually. Paradoxically, the individual who might have been most dissatisfied with the specific, as against the symbolic, psychological and existential benefits of the visit might well have been John Paul himself. He had to accept the official condition that the lifting of martial law would follow and not precede his visit, if only by a short space. The other dissatisfied protagonist was the Solidarity underground. Its leaders knew that they were now being abandoned and shunted to the sidelines of history as a political force. Bujak declared that he would greet the Pope with joy along with the rest of the nation but that he did not expect any concrete results. The TKK called on its supporters not to demonstrate politically but to show their attachment to Solidarity's badges and slogans during the visit (ICPA, 12/83 & 13/83). The régime's fear of possible outbursts was to be shown in a massive police presence headed by deputy Minister of the Interior, Konrad Straszewski. In the event the Church stewards, in collaboration with the civil authorities, avoided any serious incidents.

Had the Church really betrayed Solidarity during 1982-1983? The charge that the Church had abandoned Solidarity in making its own deals with the authorities, time after time, was felt very keenly by some Solidarity activists. It was, however, expressed most bitterly by the Polish émigré press in the West, who directed their fire mainly against Glemp. They preserved the image of John Paul as their committed supporter, who was reluctantly moved along by a reactionary Church establishment in Poland and a cynical Vatican bureaucracy. The possibility that the Church hierarchy would develop a dialogue with the martial law authorities was perceived by analysts from the very outset [51]. As early as Spring 1982 the editors of the main émigré journal in the West considered that the Polish bishops had succumbed to the pressure of the military junta: 'The Church has its mission and its aims which do not always run parallel with those of Poland' [52]. The banning of Solidarity gave a bitter edge to the inquest on its failure. Klempski, in keeping with the new fashion, ostentatiously described himself as a 'Polak-Katolik'. Hinting that Glemp was 'a collaborator', he considered that

the Church's negotiations and bargains with the
régime, for which it had not received a social man-
date, was one of the main reasons for Solidarity's
defeat [53]. He claimed that the Church had struck
a secret deal with the régime over the Pope's visit,
was offensive about Glemp's literary and oratorical
style and taxed the Primate for his simple-minded
credulity towards the authorities [54]. The fullest
blast against Church policy, in relation to communism and the Polish crisis, came from the well known
French thinker, Alain Besançon, who castigated the
Polish Church for its 'Second Silence' towards the
crimes of martial law [55]. While all this indignation was being vented in the West Solidarity publicists in the Underground in Poland itself showed
far greater understanding for the Church's eternal
religious mission [56].

Pope John Paul was greeted at Warsaw Okęcie
airport at 5.0 p.m. on 16 June by Jabłoński,
Olszowski, Czyrek, Gucwa, Łopatka, and a whole host
of party political and Catholic grouping leaders
(Ozdowski, Komender, Morawski, Jankowski [PAX]
and Zabłocki), as well as by Glemp, Macharski, the
Polish bishops and even Cardinal Krol, Archbishop
of Philadelphia [57]. Jabłoński, in his welcome,
stressed the religious pastoral character of the
Pope's pilgrimage to the Black Madonna; their
'superior interests above socio-political divisions'
were Poland's independence, frontiers and the reforms
needed to ensure her harmonious domestic socio-
economic development. In reply the Pope declared
that his visit was to the whole of Poland, thus showing his dissatisfaction with the limits of his itinerary. After a triumphant drive through Warsaw
John Paul celebrated mass and set out the religious
themes of Solidarity, reconciliation, forgiveness
and the underlying political motifs which were to
characterise his visit. The most official part
of the visit took place on the morning of 17 June in
the Belweder Palace, the residence of the Head of
State. Jaruzelski welcomed him in terms of the
shared historical and national traditions, experiences
and interests which bound the Polish State and the
Roman Catholic Church together in a common community
of European culture and civilisation. All this
enabled them to work together for the common good.
He admitted the depth of social discontent but
claimed that the worst was now over; successive
stages of normalisation had occurred. The appropriate legal-humanitarian measures would accompany
the imminent lifting of the State of War. John Paul

str:ssed that the Social Renewal embodied in the
Social Agreements of 1980 were essential 'for maintaining Poland's good name in the world and also for
getting out of the crisis'. He recommended the
path of dialogue to Poland's rulers in settling
both their domestic and their international relations (TL, 18-19 June 1983). There then followed
two hours and twenty minutes of discussion between
Jaruzelski, Jabłoński, John Paul and Glemp in the
Pompeian Room, no less, of the Palace. According
to Urban, later the same day, the communist leaders
explained to their guest why martial law had been
necessary and that it was now in skeleton form as
there were only 147 political prisoners (TL, 18-19
June 1983).

The Pope's subsequent itinerary, following
visits to the Pawiak Prison Museum and the ex-Jewish
Ghetto and the celebration of a mass in a huge football stadium, took him to Kolbe's monastery at
Niepokalanów and then on to the main point of his
visit, the 600th anniversary celebrations at Jasna
Góra. From there the Pope visited Poznań, Katowice,
Wrocław and St. Anne's Mount near Opole before concluding the official part of the visit in his old
seat in Kraków and Nowa Huta. The Jagiellonian
University bestowed an honorary doctorate upon him
to place alongside the one from KUL, which a visiting delegation had had to present to him in Warsaw;
Lublin was after all excluded from his tour. The
Pope met Jaruzelski again for one and a half hours
in the Wawel. The following day, during a short
rest near to his birthplace in the Tatra foothills,
he received Wałęsa [58]. The 8-day visit finished
at Kraków Balice airport on the late afternoon of
the 23rd. The Pope was seen off by the whole bevy
of Church and State dignitaries, headed by Glemp
and Jabłoński,who had met him at the outset.

What was the effect, and were there any political results, of these days of supercharged emotion
and communally shared experience? The Pope had
once again demonstrated his capacity to draw huge
crowds of adoring and enthusiastic Poles and the
Church's intimate links with national life. He
had certainly acted as the spokesman for the nation's
moral and spiritual values and more; but the effect,
as usual with this great showman, was greater in
terms of political atmosphere than specific political concessions. The Pope transmitted the universal Christian message. At the same time he also
reiterated the legitimacy of the 1980-1981 aspirations. The end effect was designed to nudge the

nation towards the realistic Glemp view that
Solidarity's political game had been lost.   The
movement and Wałęsa should, at best, be relegated
to the sidelines.   By underscoring the moral
sanctity of Solidarity's and the nation's struggle
he kept hope open for the future; by accepting that
they had been defeated he opened up the way for a
return to the traditional Church-State entente pioneered by Wyszyński and Gomułka, except that the
Church was now more clearly the Tribune of society
than previously.   The 195th Episcopal Conference
in late August under Macharski's chairmanship, because of Glemp's illness, however, could only deplore
the authorities' refusal to profit from the Pope's
visit in order to effect a genuine national understanding [59].   The régime for its part did not
expect the Church to legitimise its power, but only
wanted it to accept its reality and to join with
it in dampening down violent resistance, social
unrest and any thoughts of Underground terrorism
(cf. Bijak, Polityka, 25 June 1983).   It soon showed
its political ingratitude in its ideological-political offensive against the Church, especially its
contestatory priests in the Autumn.

The State's Religious Policy
      The communist state abandoned the attempt to
inculcate a materialist Marxist-Leninist world out-
look in Polish society after 1956.   It had difficulty enough in even doing so to a minimum extent
in its own lower level membership ranks.   The
'Polacy 80' survey presented the rather extraordinary
finding that 80% of PZPR members were believing
Catholics and that 27% were practising ones.   The
issue of the religiosity of party members was one
of the most controversial problems of the 1980-1981
reform period.   The Ninth Congress line, confirmed
in the new statute, was that religious believers
could join the PZPR, irrespective of their world
view, as long as they gave priority to supporting
the PZPR's programme (Życie Partii, 2 September 1981).
A June 1983 IPPM-L poll of new PZPR candidates
found that only a third considered that party membership should entail giving up religious beliefs
and practices.   60% considered that an individual
could reconcile both with party membership under
Polish conditions.   The findings reflected the
inevitable cognitive dissonance which lubricated
life in this area; 63% also thought that party
members should have a materialist world view and
only 28% disagreed (ND, May 1984, p. 82).

The principles of the state's post-1980 religious policy were summed up in a book by Kazimierz Kąkol, the Minister of Religious Affairs from 1973 to 1980, which appeared in 1982 [60]. Kąkol argued that the communist state had to take a flexible and pragmatic line. It realised the historical and national-psychological reasons why the Roman Catholic Church was embedded so strongly in contemporary Polish society and culture. The state wanted to maintain permanent contacts and to establish 'constructive collaboration' with the Church, as had been done during his tenure of office. The Church could maintain its identity in its own sphere but it had to be led to accept the basic principles of the socialist system and the Polish raison d'état which Gomułka and Gierek had jointly recognised with Wyszyński. Differences, misunderstandings and conflicts which inevitably arose out of their differing standpoints and interests could be resolved by negotiation, as long as the above framework was recognised.

What Kąkol's gloss meant under martial law conditions was developed by his successor, the Poznań Professor of State Law, Adam Łopatka. Publicly, he emphasised the flourishing nature of Roman Catholic religious life, as well as that of the other religious denominations. He also documented how the 1952 Constitution protected the rights of religious belief and practice and how the state conceded full freedom for the latter in churches and their surroundings, cemeteries and in private dwellings. He attacked the misuse of this facility by some of the clergy since 1980, and the use of church buildings for political aims and meetings which masqueraded under charitable, cultural and educational purposes (ND, April 1983, pp. 15-25). Łopatka had, however, been much sharper in a private address to CC lecturers [61]. As the secularisation of Polish life was currently impossible he set out the state's more modest immediate aims as follows: the primary one was to liquidate all anti-socialist political activity by clerics and their religious supporters. He considered that about 5-10% of the Roman Catholic clergy and a dozen bishops were engaged actively in combating the socialist system; the régime could perhaps count on the positive support of 13-15% of the clergy. The policy was now to encourage the correct and neutrally non-engaged minority and to cut off all clerical links with the Solidarity Underground and its supporters. Łopatka explained that the policy of licensing increased church

building and of facilitating the Church's pastoral
and charitable work would, in the long run, enable
the Church leadership to exercise its non-political/
religious role in a manner which would calm Polish
society and be acceptable to the communist authorities. He discerned a major turning point in Church
policy under Glemp in early 1983 in the preparations
for the Papal visit: 'The Church has ceased to
consider itself as the supporting base for the movements combating law and order, security and the political system.' It had accepted that 'stabilisation
will take place on the basis of socialism and not
any other' [62].
   There was therefore a de facto return to the
pre-crisis pattern of Church-State relations in
early 1983. The communist leaders in the unofficial concordat with the Church over the Papal visit
accepted that the Church's social and religious
influence was irreversible for the moment. On the
other hand, a determined drive now took place to
ensure ideological purity within the PZPR itself.
A spate of articles appeared in Nowe Drogi defending
Historical Materialism from the depredations of
bourgeois-humanist and structuralist notions [63].
An offensive was mounted against Kołakowski and a
critical, although not too bitter, discussion of
West European Marxists like Gramsci and Althusser,
and soon-to-be-labelled-revisionists like Adam
Schaff, took place [64]. The theoretical relationship between Marxism and religion was aired with a
view to showing how the tolerance of religious belief
and practice by the communist state could be reconciled with the propagation of Marxist values [65].
Lenin's maxim that Church and State should be completely separate, but that it was inadmissible to
discriminate against citizens on grounds of religious belief, was cited repeatedly [66]. The conclusion was that 'the struggle against clericalism
has the character of a political struggle ... in our
conditions it is synonymous with the defence of the
appropriate character of religion and the Church'
[67]. Marxist-Leninist intellectuals were, however,
quick to attack the values expounded by John Paul
during his visit as hindering the PZPR's drive to
form a new social consciousness [68]. The more
positive aspect of the reaffirmation of Marxist-
Leninist materialist values, coupled with tolera-
tion and even alliance with believers in building
socialism, was sympathetic coverage of the social
teaching of the Roman Catholic Church and the re-
visions brought about by Popes John XXIII and

Paul VI [69]. But John Paul's conservatism on social
issues was held 'to discount the vital social aspirations of our society' (ND, September 1983,
pp. 135 ff.). It was accepted that the Pope was a
formidably intelligent and creative 'adversary of a
new type'. He had assimilated many aspects of
scientific-socialist thought during his life in
Poland. He had also developed a compelling
'Catholic vision of an ideal,utopian society' to
rival the Marxist-Leninist offer of a classless
society, whose credibility had been so tarnished by
the developments of the previous decade (ND, June
1984, p. 126). John Paul's argument was that the
Church, and not Marxism, had raised 'human labour
to the dignity of the highest humanist value,
creating human being' [70]. A lively discussion
on the possibility, and the limits, of a dialogue
between Marxists and Catholics and how it could aid
social integration continued throughout 1983
(Stefanowicz & Szczepański, Życie Warszawy, 1 January
1983; Kmita, Życie Warszawy, 23-24 April 1983).

Turbulent Priests, cautious Bishops and political
Soldiers
        As we have seen, Glemp's cautious line was
criticised by numerous pro-Solidarity inclined members of the lower clergy, as well as by some of his
bishops. These feelings were vented at a meeting
of the clergy of the Warsaw archdiocese on 7 December
1982 with Glemp. The Primate took a negative attitude towards the Polish Romantic tradition of national uprisings and placed himself, if the record
is to be trusted, in the Endek political-realist
tradition of accommodating oneself to realities [71].
Social protests and the struggle without a programme
of the Solidarity Underground could not be supported
by the Church (ICPA, 1/83, pp. 22-25). Father
Roman Indrzejczyk reproached Glemp for giving inter-
views which helped the régime, of not giving sufficient psychological support to Polish society in the
defeat of its ideals and of not leading demonstrations by the clergy against the ZOMO. The Curate
of Anin attacked him for sacrificing the truth and
for collaborating with the régime. Other priests
suggested that, although the Church had helped to
pacify society, there was no guarantee that the
régime would not now turn on it, especially in
the struggle for the hearts and minds of Poland's
youth. But Glemp had a pugnacious streak, even
though his health broke down and he had to enter
hospital in early August. He continued to annoy

the radicals through his remarks about KOR intellectuals and his disciplining of contestatory priests.
He forbade the fiery Father Małkowski from delivering
any more sermons and had Father Nowak transferred
to a less sensitive parish than Ursus. With the
worsening of Church-State relations from Autumn
1983 onwards, it is significant that only about 38%
of the clergy and perhaps 5 of the 80 odd bishops
voted in the People's Council's elections of June
1984 (Urban, TL, 20 June 1984). The authorities
were reported soon afterwards as having handed Glemp
a list of 67 clergy and 2 bishops whose activities
were considered unacceptable. The state used the
police to harass priests who went beyond their
purely pastoral-religious role and threatened new
laws against them. Sensitive cas célèbres such
as school strikes over the removal of crucifixes
blew up.

The quintessential turbulent radical priest
was the young and good looking Father Jerzy
Popiełuszko. His Church of St. Stanisław Kostka
in the Northern Warsaw suburb of Żolibórz became a
centre of Solidarity and grassroots Catholic opposition. He was also Chaplain to the Solidarity
stronghold in Huta Warszawa and became well known
to foreign journalists based in Warsaw. Along with
Father Jankowski, Wałęsa's parish priest, he benefited from the amnesty; he had been harassed and
detained by the police and procuracy at various times.
Popiełuszko was one of the opposition figures most
hated by the régime, as demonstrated by Jerzy
Urban's violent attack on him a month before his
death. The official press spokesman, writing under
the pseudonym of Jan Rem, called him the Savonarola
of anti-communism and a political fanatic who presided over 'séances of hatred' in his church [72].
The MSW contained a sub-department headed by Colonel
Adam Pietruszka which had long been detailed to
shadow his activities and, if possible, to intimidate or compromise him. When all these attempts
failed, Captain Grzegorz Piotrowski, with
Pietruszka's help, and probably on his instructions,
abducted and murdered him outside Toruń on 19
October 1984, after the failure of an earlier attempt a few days earlier. Although his body was
thrown in the River Vistula, his chauffeur escaped.
The whole bungled and immoral affair very quickly
became an open and dramatic crisis for the authorities. His funeral in early November occasioned
renewed tension and the usual symbolic demonstrations of grief. However, it did not spark off an

outburst, as perhaps might have been hoped by the
police and their anonymous hardline patrons. The
régime reacted quickly by arresting the three per-
petrators and Pietruszka [73]. It claimed, as
usual, that it was a hardline provocation directed
against Jaruzelski's more conciliatory policies
towards Church and society.

The trial in Bydgoszcz, between 27 December
1984 and 7 February 1985, which sentenced Pietruszka
and Piotrowski to 25 years' imprisonment, and
Lieutenants Pękała and Chmielewski to 15 and 14
years respectively, was an unprecedented event, although secret policemen had been tried and sentenced
for excesses in Eastern Europe in the de-Stalinisation
period. The trial threw much light on MSW methods
and mores; but it contained the responsibility at
the departmental level, headed by Pietruszka and his
immediate superior; Brigade-General Zenon Płatek,
was suspended, either for neglect or involvement,
and went into permanent oblivion. The trial's
latter stages occasioned much public indignation by
concentrating on the alleged moral responsibility
for his own death occasioned by the activities of
radical priests like Popiełuszko and his ilk!

The affair was almost certainly caused by ambitious, frustrated and over-zealous policemen being
encouraged by a hardline faction which wanted to
intimidate the opposition and to sabotage Jaruzelski's
democratisation policies, which were being unveiled
at the 17th Plenum; the exact links were not, and
probably never will be, revealed. Be that as it
may, the man directly responsible to the party for
these matters, CC Secretary and Politburo member,
Milewski,was sacked discreetly, but summarily, when
the affair had blown over, in mid-1985. Jaruzelski
immediately assumed party control over the MSW at
the 17th Plenum. He also introduced an ex-KW First
Secretary, Andrzej Gdula, as a deputy Minister to
scrutinise the MSW. The MSW Head, Army Corps-
General Kiszczak, kept a remarkably low profile during
all these proceedings. One can only assume that
the Popiełuszko murder was a re-run of the
Bydgoszcz crisis of March 1981. It was sparked off
by subterranean infighting between Army-State and
police apparats which provided the opportunity and
the atmosphere for independent action by Pietruszka
and the determined Piotrowski (Sunday Times, 3 February
1985). This time ,though, there was no major public
reaction, except a widespread feeling of grief and
anger; the military politicians very quickly brought
the grumbling and recalcitrant sections of the secret

police to heel [74]. Popie*uszko's church and
grave, however, remained as an opposition shrine.
As we have seen, the Catholic Church in Poland
has been involved in traditional forms of conflict
with the communist state over its constitutional
position, the role of its clergy, the licensing of
new churches and catechism points, and the limits of
its press, publishing and socio-intellectual life.
But the real oddity of the Polish Church is that it
has increasingly assumed a Tribune role in relation
to society. This was because, apart from 1976-
1981, it was the only institution which could publicly express traditional, national symbolism and
cloak it around its moral and religious values [75].
The recurrent movements of social discontent after
1956 came and went but it was always a potential
partner to the PZPR in the limited pluralism of the
Polish political system. What was unprecedented,
though, in the comparative communist experience, was
that socio-economic urbanisation, educational transformations and the emergence of a materialist, consumer and secularised society took place without
weakening the Church's political and religious
hold. These changes weakened the extent of personal, spiritual belief in the Church's ethics and
theology but not the commitment to the Church as a
national institution whose world view ran parallel
to that of society. Although the PZPR changed significantly in 1956, traditional national, peasant,
West European and anti-Russian traditions came to be
symbolised by the Church. Its functional position
always enabled it to outbid the state in this sphere,
without really trying, as was demonstrated by its
support over the Millenium celebrations of 1966.
Secondly, the pastoral and social work role of its
58,000 dedicated priests, monks and nuns made it a
formidable force capable of penetrating the whole of
society [76]. Its capacity for charitable assistance was given an additional boost by the huge
stream of Western and Polish emigration food, cloth-
ing and material gifts which were largely sent to it
for distribution during 1982-1983. Thirdly, its
Catholic intellectuals extended its influence among
the young, the workers and even the intelligentsia
during the 1970s, when it appeared that Revisionism
and Marxist-Reformism had exhausted their appeal.
Lastly, no institution, except Solidarity itself in
1980-1981, could compete with the Church in terms of
its heady and powerful symbolism and traditional
forms and structures of behaviour for bringing large
masses of people together in shared and exalted

feelings of communal solidarity. The practice
started with the 'Oasis Movement' and with the
fashion for pilgrimages during the 1970s; it ex-
ploded in the two Papal visits which brought millions of Poles together and, of course, in the large
workers' sit-ins of 1980-1981. In the 1980s it
also became fashionable to flaunt one's membership
or conversion to the Church,whose leaders, at least,
were on occasion embarrassed by flagrantly exhibi-
tionist behaviour.

The Church's Tribune function has to be explained by all three dimensions of Poland's historical inheritance, postwar socio-economic development
and the play of Church-Communist politics. The role
naturally reflects back on the dimension of secularisation and the intensity of actual religious belief and practice. This produces the impression
that Poland is a spiritually Roman Catholic country,
whereas it is merely a country which gives massive
support to the Roman Catholic Church as an institution. This view has been confirmed to me by
numerous clergy whose dissatisfaction with their
flock goes far beyond what might be expected by an
outsider. The opposition ideologists also claimed
that the 1970s saw a rebirth of civil society, but
this is a false claim. Polish civil society, although shattered by the Nazis during the war and then
persecuted by the Stalinists, was never brought under
a Soviet type of control by the PZPR; the tacit
recognition of this fact was the historical significance of 'October'. Hence the Church always
acted as the Tribune of an independent civil society
after 1956. The Church's role deepened during the
crisis period from the late 1970s onwards as an
umbrella for social groups, and as the articulator
of social demands for human and civil rights, an
autonomous educational system, respect for law and
the individual, the ending of political repression
and the pressure for a pluralist system in which the
PZPR would play a hegemonic, not a monopolistic,
role. But the Church is a timeless institution
and its religious message and pastoral functions
allowed it to withstand the shock of the military-
police dismantling of Solidarity and the other 1980-
1981 agents of civil society. This meant that the
population had nowhere else to turn; hence the apparent strength of the Church, which was manifested
again during the second Papal visit. Recognised as
a full political actor by the Jaruzelski régime, it
was able to influence the timing, and the nature, of
post-December 1981 decisions. The 'Silent Church'

The Roman Catholic Church

of the early 1950s had, willy-nilly, become a vocal
partner in Jaruzelski's corporate, military-dominated
party state.

Notes

1. Andrzej Walicki, Philosophy and Romantic Nationalism
   (Oxford, Clarendon Press, 1982).
2. Adriana Gozdecka, 'Udział prasy w reformie prawa
   małżeńskiego', Unpublished Master's thesis, Department
   of Journalism and Political Science, Warsaw University,
   1976.
3. Kościół Katolicki w Polsce (Poznań, Pallotinum, 1979),
   p. 21.
4. Adam Podgorecki, Polish Sociological Bulletin, No. 4
   (1976), p. 25.
5. Stefan Nowak, Polityka, 10 April 1976. For the urban
   working class, see Edward Ciupak, 'Katolicyzm
   Warszawiaków', Polityka, 27 January 1969. Cf.
   Władysław Piwowarski, Religijnośc miejska w rejonie
   uprzemysłowionym (Warsaw, 1977), p. 212.
6. J.R. Fiszman, Revolution and Tradition in People's
   Poland. Education and Socialisation (Princeton U.P.,
   1972), pp. 205-209.
7. Janusz Ziółkowski,chairman of the Polish Sociological
   Association, interviewed in Przegląd Katolicki, 8
   October 1985.
8. Albert Szymanski, Class Struggle in Socialist Poland
   (New York, Praeger, 1984), p. 93.
9. G. Kolankiewicz & R. Taras, 'Poland. Socialism for
   everyman' in A. Brown & J. Gray (eds.), Political Culture
   and Political Change in Communist States (London,
   Macmillan, 1977), p. 114.
10. Cf. my review of Szajkowski's Next to God ... Poland in
    Political Studies, XXXIII, No. 2 (June 1985), pp. 337-338.
11. Rocznik Polityczny i Gospodarczy 1981-1983 (Warsaw,
    PWE, 1984), p. 213. Peter Raina, Kościół w Polsce
    1981-1984 (London, Veritas, 1985), ch. 6. J. Proprzeczko,
    Polityka, 25 December 1982.
12. On the scale of the construction of church buildings,
    especially after 1980, see Adam Łopatka, 'Zasady polityki
    wyznaniowej w Polsce', ND, No. 4 (April 1982), p. 16.
13. Rocznik Polityczny i Gospodarczy 1984 (Warsaw, PWE, 1985),
    pp. 179-191.
14. For an English translation of the 1950 Agreement, see
    Hansjakob Stehle, The Indepdendent Satellite. Society
    and Politics in Poland since 1945 (New York, Praeger,
    1965), pp. 306-310.
15. The post-1976 amended version of the 1952 Constitution
    can be consulted in W.B. Simons (ed.), The Constitutions
    of the Communist World (Alphen aan van den Rijn,Sijthoff
    & Nordhoff,1980),Articles 67, 81, 82 & 95.

16. Cf. Zenon Rudny, 'Cesarzowi - co Cesarskie, Bogu - co Boskie', Polityka, 24 October 1983.
17. Stehle, Independent Satellite, p. 64.
18. III Zjazd PZPR, 10.iii-19.iii.1959r (Warsaw, KiW, 1959), pp. 114-115.
19. Stehle, Independent Satellite, p. 68.
20. II Krajowa Konferencja PZPR (Warsaw, KiW, 1978), p. 39.
21. The then Minister of Religion claims, however, that his meetings with Wyszyński showed that the Primate disliked the 'KORowcy' and disapproved of the 'social excesses' of June 1976; Kazimierz Kąkol, Kardynał Stefan Wyszyński jakim go znałem (Warsaw, IWZZ, 1985), pp. 29, 67.
22. Cf. Rakowski, Polityka, 25 March 1978. W. Mysłek, 'Państwo i Kościół', ND, No. 5 (May 1979), pp. 68-70.
23. See Vincent Chrypinski, 'Church and State in Poland' in Simon & Kanet, Background to Crisis, pp. 239-264.
24. Szajkowski, Next to God, p. 72.
25. Stewart Steven, The Poles (London, Macmillan, 1982),p.154.
26. For the Pope's speeches, Return to Poland. The Collected Speeches of John Paul II (London, Collins, 1979).
27. Raina, Kościół w Polsce, pp. 142-144.
28. M. Dobbs, K.S. Karol, & D. Trevisan, Poland, Solidarity, Walesa (London, Pergamon, 1981), p. 98.
29. Raina, Poland 1981, chs. 2, 3.
30. D. Singer, The Road to Gdansk (New York, Monthly Review Press, 1981), p. 191.
31. Raina, Poland 1981, pp. 199-200.
32. Raina, Kościół w Polsce, pp. 159-162.
33. Cf. G. Sanford, 'The Polish communist leadership and the onset of the State of War', Soviet Studies, XXXVI, No. 4 (October 1984), p. 506.
34. Jaruzelski was in the year above Komender,who has denied journalistic gossip that he was a close schoolboy chum of the General's; Kępiński & Kilar, Kto jest kim w Polsce. Inaczej, pp. 173-174.
35. Jaruzelski, Przemówienia 1981-1982, p. 13.
36. Raina, Jan Paweł II, Prymas i Episkopat Polski o stanie wojennym, pp. 56-57.
37. ICPA 3/82 of 19 February 1982, pp. 15-17.
38. Raina, Kościół w Polsce, pp. 173-174.
39. Józef Glemp, Przez Sprawiedliwośc ku miłości (Warsaw, 1982), p. 132.
40. ICPA 4/82 of 5 March 1982, pp. 9-10.
41. Ibid., pp. 6-8.
42. English translation in Szajkowski, Next to God, Appendix 3.
43. Raina, Kościół w Polsce, pp. 184-186.
44. Cited in Szajkowski, Next to God, p. 177.
45. ICPA 14/82 of 30 July 1982, pp. 14-16.
46. ICPA 16/82 of 3 September 1982, pp. 20-25.
47. ICPA 17/82 of 7 September 1982, pp. 11-14.

48. ICPA 19/82 of 22 October 1982, pp. 23-27.
49. Andrzej Ursynowski in ICPA 2/83 of 28 January 1983, pp. 22-25.
50. Raina, Kościół w Polsce, pp. 197-199.
51. Patrick Michel, 'L'Eglise; une situation paradoxale' in Pologne. L'Etat de Guerre (Paris, La Documentation Française, No. 435, 1982), p. 26.
52. Kultura (Paris, March 1982).
53. Tymoteusz Klempski, 'Widziane z bliska', Kultura (Paris, January 1983), pp. 13-18. Compare D. Passent, 'Z granatami na ptaki', Polityka, 11 June 1983.
54. Klempski, 'Pielgrzymka i pielgrzymstwo', Kultura (Paris, October 1983), p. 14.
55. Alain Besançon, 'Drugie milczenie Kościóła', Kultura (Paris, March 1983), pp. 3-12.
56. Maciej Poleski (pseud. Czesław Bielecki), 'Z uwag o dialogu z terrorystą', Kultura (Paris, October 1982), p. 26.
57. For details of the Papal visit, see Szajkowski, Next to God, pp. 221-227.
58. This was counterpoised by Vergilio Levi's article in Osservatore Romano, 25 June 1983, which let it be known that Wałęsa's political role was finished. The 'indiscretion' caused his immediate resignation as deputy editor. A nine-days' wonder ensued over whether John Paul had counselled Wałęsa to take 'a back seat'.
59. Raina, Kościół w Polsce, pp. 199-202.
60. Kazimierz Kąkol, Socjalizm, Państwo, Kościół (Warsaw, KiW, 1982).
61. Document and attendant question and answer session in Raina, Kościół w Polsce, pp. 40-62.
62. Ibid., p. 54.
63. Jacek Tittenbrun, 'Struktura jako kategoria materializmu historycznego', ND, 2/405 (February 1983), pp. 138-145.
64. ND, 5/408 (May 1983), pp. 158-161, for Ładosz on Schaff. Wacław Mejbaum, 'Przyczynek do dziejów antikomunizmu. Na marginesie "Głównych nurtów marksizmu" L.Kołakowskiego', ND, 2/405 (February 1983), pp. 146-155.
65. Stefan Opara, 'Marksizm a religia', ND,3/406 (March 1983), pp. 54-64.
66. W.I. Lenin, Socjalizm a religia (Warsaw, KiW, 1955), pp. 6-7.
67. Stanisław Markiewicz, 'Partia a religia', ND, 4/407 (April 1983), p. 35.
68. ND, 10/413 (October 1983), p. 98.
69. Beata Witkowska, 'Doktryny społeczne Jana XXIII i Pawla VI', ND, 5/408 (May 1983), pp. 140-148.
70. Stanisław Markiewicz, Ewolucja społecznej doktryny Kościóła (Warsaw, KiW, 1983), p. 275.
71. Zeszyty Historyczne, No. 64 (Paris, Instytut Literacki, 1983), pp. 206-218. Some of the accompanying comments suggest that the record was compiled by a critical priest.

251

72. Jan Rem (pseud.), 'Seanse nienawiści', Tu i Teraz, 19 September 1983.
73. Paul Lewis, 'Turbulent Priest; political implications of the Popiełuszko Affair', Politics, V, No. 2 (October 1985), pp. 33-39.
74. G. Sanford, 'Poland's recurring crises', World Today, op. cit., p. 10.
75. Ludwik Dembinsky, 'Les choix politiques des structures confessionelles en Pologne', Revue Française de Science Politique, XXIII, No. 3 (June 1973), pp. 537-549.
76. Tokarczuk's proposals for a radical extension of the Church's structures for extending its pastoral and social role elicited an interesting official response. This used the Vatican's Annuarium Statisticum Ecclesiae to demonstrate how well served, in comparative European terms, the Polish Church was in both its total number of churches and in the number of new religious buildings licensed since 1980 (about 1,400). See Jerzy Jarzeniec, 'Posługi Religijne', Polityka, 23 November 1985.

Chapter Seven

SOCIETY, WAŁĘSA AND THE SOLIDARITY UNDERGROUND

The full story of the political and social opposition and of the Civil Resistance Movement to martial
law still remains to be written [1]. Various aspects of the relations between the Jaruzelski régime
and Wałęsa and the Solidarity Underground have already been elucidated in this study. Why a national
uprising did not break out on its imposition is covered in Chapter Four, as are the various stages of
repression of opposition. This chapter therefore
just outlines the main lines of the opposition's
internal response to martial law in terms of political strategy, tactics and organisational development, the internal debate over its political aims,
programme and its reaction to the authorities' policies. The main analytical problem faced by the
Solidarity-KOR opposition from the outset was whether to prepare for a single General Strike à la
Sorel or whether to organise long-term social resistance. The issue of 'Single Outburst' versus
'Long March' conditioned views as to whether an
Underground State or Underground Society should be
worked for and the consequent degree of centralised
or decentralised leadership and organisation.

The Opposition's Underground Structures
About 20% of the Solidarity leadership escaped
internment at the outset. A few, such as Siła-
Nowicki and Stanisław Rusinek, were left at large
so that they could be used as intermediaries; their
December 1981 negotiations with the régime proved
fruitless, as did further preliminary exchanges
encouraged by the Church. Given the conditions discussed in Chapter Four, it is hardly surprising that
the Underground (which was the major opposition force
but not the sole one as Nationalist and Catholic
groupings also existed) never succeeded in creating

an efficient nationwide, hierarchically-based organisation [2]. Its main characteristic, inevitably, was the highly local, autonomous, spontaneous and decentralised nature of its constituent parts. Its first National Resistance Committee (OKO) was set up by a secret meeting of Solidarity activists on 13 January 1982 which appointed 'Mieszko' as its chairman. The general view was that conspiratorial structures and terrorist measures were unnecessary and dangerous as the State of War would be shortlived. What was required was a secret leadership body to stimulate and co-ordinate social opposition to martial law. The 'Appeal to the Public' demanded the ending of martial law, the release of all internees and for the régime to negotiate with the whole of the Solidarity leadership led by Wałęsa. It called on society to form secret and autonomous four strong Circles of Social Resistance (KOS) to assist internees and oppose repression (ICPA, 1/82, pp. 7-11). The Solidarity leaders therefore adopted the strategy of 'organising a mass, society-wide underground resistance movement' to force the régime to lift martial law and to negotiate an agreement with them on the basis of Solidarity's Oliwa Congress programme (Tygodnik Wojenny, 11 February 1982). The bulk of Solidarity leaders, given Polish national character, refused to submit to armed repression; only 3 out of 107 Solidarity KPP members did so at the outset. The opposition's main initial aims were to oppose the martial law authorities by all means from the switching off of lights right up to strike action, but excluding violent terrorism in order to avoid repression. Solidarity had to show that it had not been crushed. After the December confrontations, though, there was a lull until the Spring. The emphasis was on passive resistance to the régime's onslaught, the boycott of all official activity and 'collaborators' and the building up of the organisational and financial bases for an information campaign. In the first 3-4 months of 1982 the opposition Underground acted under the illusion that it could force the ending of martial law through passive resistance and non-co-operation and a widespread propaganda and publishing campaign. At the same time the political debate between its leaders, both internal and external, crystallised the strategy and tactics for the most active period of its existence between May and November 1982.

OKO was replaced on 22 April by the Provisional Co-ordinating Committee (TKK). Its original membership was Bujak, Frasyniuk, Lis and Hardek, the main

leaders at large, who represented Mazowsze, Lower
Silesia, Gdańsk and Małapolska. KPP member
Eugeniusz Szumiejko entered the TKK in May, Poznań
was represented in July, while Piotr Bednarz replaced
the arrested Frasyniuk and on his own capture his
place was taken by Józef Pinior. The TKK was the
Underground's first effective national leadership
body; its founding communiqué was its first comprehensive programmatic declaration under martial law.
The clandestine leaders stated that it was 'impossible
to resolve the problems which confront Poland without
the opening of negotiations between the power-holders
and society. We are determined to undertake all
forms of action and pressure to force the power-
holders to negotiate with the Solidarity leadership
led by Lech Wałęsa.' Its prior conditions were
the release of all those sentenced, interned or
arrested for martial law offences, the restoration
of human and civil rights and the acceptance of the
Theses of the Primate's Social Council as a basis
for negotiation. Their 'Statement on the Methods
and Forms of Action' stressed that the reconstruction
of the union's activities entailed more than moral
opposition. The three main efforts should be directed towards the formation of KOSs, the extension of
publishing activity and the creation of discussion
clubs to work out the movement's strategy and tactics. A General Strike was threatened if Solidarity
were de-legalised and a 15 minute strike and a one
minute stoppage of all traffic was called for midday
on 13 May. This challenge to the authorities 'at
the national level would be the proof and the demonstration of our Solidarity and our strength' (ICPA,
9/1982, pp. 3-5).
    The Underground's regional structure emerged
earliest in Gdańsk, Wrocław, Warsaw and Kraków, which
were its main strongholds during 1982. Bujak admitted that the police had smashed the union's structures in Łódź and Katowice (much of whose leadership
emigrated); Poznań and Szczecin had barely started
reconstruction. Bujak favoured 'Positional Struggle'
to create a counter-society independent of the régime.
He was against the movement's overcentralisation
which might lead to head-on conflicts with the régime.
He presented a nebulous picture of loosely connected
Underground structures with changing composition whose
propaganda and protest initiatives fed on the social
discontent fuelled by the cut in living standards
aggravated by the draconian price rises (Le Monde,
28 April 1982). The Underground reached its peak
during the second half of 1982 when the bulk of the

regional organisations were set up. Most styled
themselves Regional Co-ordinating Committees (RKK),
as in Warsaw, Gdańsk and Tarnów. They were largely
autonomous, although they backed the TKK's calls for
nationwide action. The Regional Committees, however,
had varied success in organising Secret Factory
Committees (TKZs) outside the hardcores of Solidarity
support in such enterprises as Ursus, Huta Warszawa,
the Lenin Shipyard and the Nowa Huta Lenin Steelworks.
The Gdańsk TKK's main task in Summer 1982 was to
attempt to extend its factory base (Solidarność
Gdańska, 1982, No. 5). The difficulties of building
up TZKs because of police repression and penetration,
the growing social fear of reprisals and even fatigue
at the growing pointlessness of continued resistance
led to attempts to return to the Inter-Factory Strike
Committees (MKSs) of Summer 1980. The first of
these, the Workers' Inter-Factory Solidarity Committee (MZKRS) of late April 1982, claimed to represent
63 Warsaw factories; it had a strong journal, the
CDN-based 'Głos Wolnego Robotnika'. The MZKRSs
formed fighting groups which freed Naroźniak after
his arrest and beating-up in Warsaw. Their leaders
were arrested in December 1982 and charged with carrying out KOR-inspired terrorist acts, as were the
Gdańsk leaders, caught soon afterwards. Another
resurgent form was the Horizontal principle. This
was expressed in the Inter-Regional Committees for
the Defence of Solidarity (MKOs),which by September
1982 claimed to represent 13 regions and which did
not always follow TKK decisions. At the margin
ephemeral extremist groups like 'Fighting Solidarity'
also emerged in embattled Lower Silesia, although
their influence was slight (Tygodnik Mazowsze, 1982,
No. 26). Overall the Underground was therefore a
haphazard mosaic of loosely connected and often
parallel organisations. These formed and reformed
depending upon the interplay between the Solidarity-
KOR hardcores, social discontent and state-police
repression.

The Underground's Tactics, Strategy and Programme
     A whole book based on the Underground's massive
domestic literary output as well as the discussion
which took place in key émigré journals like Kultura
and Aneks could be written about this fascinating
subject. Opposition sources claimed that about
1,500 regular publications appeared in Poland without
the censor's permission in the second half of 1982
(listed in Paris Kultura, Nos. 6/417 and 12/423 for
1982 and 5/428 for May 1983). The Underground press

(notably NOWA, Krąg and CDN) in addition published
a large number of works ranging from Orwell's 1984,
Wiktor Woroszylski's Dziennik Internowania to the
DiP's Fourth Report. The Underground naturally took
over Second World War resistance themes such as
Zakazane piosenki (Forbidden Songs). The contribu-
tors to its internal political debates, even interned
leaders like Kuroń and Michnik, appeared quickly and
were given widespread distribution [3]. Arguably
the opposition's greatest success in 1982, in spite
of the continual arrest of its writers, printers and
distributors, was its publication and propaganda
drive. Its supporters claimed that this was at
over twice the level attained under what they termed
were the similar conditions of the first year of
German occupation in 1939-1940.

The Poles developed a very specific tradition of
'Political Emigration' during the 19th century
Partitions, especially after the failure of the 1831
and 1863 Uprisings. This mixture of values and organisation re-emerged during the Second World War
and continued postwar in the early years of resistance to communist rule. Perhaps up to half a million Poles failed to return to Poland at the end of
the Second World War for a mixture of political,
economic and personal reasons. What concerns us
here is not so much the moribund successors to the
London Government-in-Exile as the post-1968 radical
opposition groups which formed under the impetus of
the expulsion of major academic figures in that
year - Kołakowski, Bauman, Brus and Hirszowicz.
They were also reinforced year by year by younger
members of the student 'commando' generation of 1968.
They rejuvenated the aging Emigracja. Régime propaganda denounced opposition activists in the West as
CIA agents animated by the two West German based
Polish language broadcasting stations, Radio Free
Europe and Radio Liberty. It made the most of
Solidarity's links with what it was pleased to call
the 'Western centres of ideological diversion' and
'information aggression' [4]. These were the two
radio stations, the established monthly journal of
the 'old Emigration', the Paris Kultura, and the
journal of the post-1968 opposition, Aneks, published
in Sweden. These groups were allegedly given their
theoretical programme by American political strate-
gists, notably Zbigniew Brzezinski, who played the
new card of Independent Social Movements rather than
the old one of National Independence. In the late
1970s he considered that Poland was the weakest link
in the Soviet Camp. Its destabilisation would be

America's ace in the Great Power conflict with the
USSR. The best means of doing this was to use the
Third Basket of the Helsinki Agreements to encourage
the post-1976 dissident and opposition groups.
Whether there was such a coherent US strategy in
providing what the Warsaw régime called 'propaganda
aggression' is a moot point; but the external sources
were certainly of great psychological, financial
and organisational-informational support for the
domestic opposition. They were also a most important additional arena for debating tactics, strategy
and programmatic aims during martial law. Régime
claims that RFE animated the Solidarity opposition
and produced its programme and tactics are self-
serving nonsense. It was, however, crucially important in transmitting the opposition's version of
events and its appeals, declarations and calls to
action back to the Poles in a rapid and accessible
form. Zygmunt Najder, the Head of RFE's Polish
Section, whom the authorities condemned to death
in absentia, denied that RFE was the tuba of the
Underground opposition but it inevitably played its
tunes. On the other hand, the level of its intellectual and political analysis was criticised by the
more sophisticated Kultura [5].
     The monthly journal Kultura was founded in Paris
in 1946. Under the editorship of Juliusz Mieroszewski
and Jerzy Giedrojc, it acted as the main source of
political and cultural debate for the Polish Emigration in Western Europe. Its intellectual level sur-
passed that of all the other journals of the Old
Emigration, especially in London, until the influence
of the Younger Emigration made itself felt from the
1970s onwards. Kultura, along with RFE, has always
been the Polish régime's main bogey. During martial
law Kultura and Aneks became the main centres of debate, publicity and co-ordination for the political
theorists and militants of the Solidarity Underground
as well as their varied Polish-speaking supporters
in the West. They published the statements of the
opposition chieftains plus the views of their own
commentators; the analyses contained therein provide
the best source for examining the debate over the
opposition's tactics and strategy under martial law
and for 'internationalising' the Polish Question in
order to gain the West's moral and material support.
The latter has traditionally been the main aim of
all Polish Emigrations since Napoleonic times.
Kultura may only have published 10,000 copies
monthly plus about 2,500 copies of an edited broad-
sheet for smuggling into Poland itself, but its

influence cannot be measured in purely statistical
terms [6]. The same applies to the bi-monthly
Aneks, which published 40 odd numbers by 1986.
Solidarity's fortnightly Information Bulletin (130
numbers by December 1985) published by the Solidarity
Co-ordination Bureau Abroad in Brussels was more in
the nature of a house magazine.
The first Solidarity political reactions to martial law were inevitably of a local or individual
character. Some Solidarity leaders, notably KPP
vice-chairman Krupiński, called for a General Strike
at the outset [7]. Zbigniew Janaś, in one of the
earliest political analyses, saw the Church as society's
sole support. He foresaw 'a spontaneous outbreak
of protest' and therefore viewed the opposition's
priority as to prepare for 'the proclamation of a
General Strike' (ICPA, 1/82, pp. 25-27). The 'Basic
Principles of Resistance' issued by an opposition
group in Rybnik-Katowice on 21 December advised supporters to protect leaders and organisers under cover
of strikes, to wear the police and the management
down through non-co-operation and obstructionism and
to eschew 'ill considered bravura' (ICPA, 1/82,
pp. 22-23). Wałęsa's first publicised reaction
smuggled out of detention was: 'Let us not allow
ourselves to be broken. Let us carry out strikes
in the larger enterprises and passive resistance in
the smaller ones. In the event of force being
applied by the Army, let us behave in such a way as
will prevent the spilling of blood. Being in
Solidarity together, and helping one another mutually,
we will demonstrate that our union continues to
exist and to be active' (Tygodnik Mazowsze, 1982,
No. 1-2). Wałęsa's reaction to force majeure was
that the régime (władza) 'never was, and never will
be honest. Consequently [we] do not take even a
step backwards' (ICPA, 2/82, p. 5).
The Solidarity leaders were, however, divided
in their assessments of the early martial law situation. Bujak and the majority were optimistic about
their level of social support. Their strategy was
therefore to go underground to organise peaceful
resistance. The pessimists were a minority led by
Viktor Kulerski, who had earlier been the most
prescient Solidarity leader on the possibility of
armed repression. He saw no point in going underground as the situation would last many years.
He emphasised 'long-term information activity' (ICPA,
2/82, pp. 26, 39). Bujak attributed the initial
success of the State of War to surprise, repression
and the restriction of civil liberties (ICPA, 3/82,

pp. 27-33). Kuroń's view on the need to organise
a General Strike was originally regarded as a typical exaggeration by the interned enfant terrible
of the opposition. Under martial law, however,
the KOR experience of strategy and organisation in
the pre-1980 period became very relevant. This increased the influence of the interned KOR leaders,
Kuroń and Michnik, and their ideas about the building of a political Underground movement capable of
long-term and all out opposition to the régime.
The workers' Solidarity leaders at large, like Bujak,
Lis and Frasyniuk, thought until the Spring that
martial law would prove shortlived. Their problem
was therefore not so much to build permanent Underground structures and to present a new Solidarity
programme as to organise widespread and continuing
social resistance to demonstrate Solidarity's capacity to force the authorities to end martial law and
to negotiate.

The internal Solidarity debate was fuelled by
Kuroń's 'Theses for getting out of a situation without issue' which predicted massive social discontent
because of the total economic disaster and the militarisation of society [8]. Even though communism
was going through a General Crisis the Kremlin would
not allow its system to collapse in Poland, but the
Poles, especially the young, would rebel under hopeless conditions sooner or later unless the opposition
showed them a different way out. Kuroń therefore
considered that 'a massive and well organised resistance is the only chance for the Poles to force the
authorities into a negotiated compromise to prevent
a social outburst or to head off Soviet intervention'. The opposition's informational activity and
street and factory protests should be extended;
'but our last chance for a compromise would be a
General Strike'. The opposition should therefore
demonstrate its strength through a variety of actions in order to encourage the partisans of compromise within the régime into an agreement. This
would guarantee the USSR's basic interests while
providing a national understanding which would prevent a national uprising as well as providing the
sole way out of the crisis. Kuroń's blast provoked
another major exchange over strategy between Bujak
and Kulerski in March. Bujak wanted to form 'an
alternative, decentralised, informal and invisible
union structure'. Kulerski argued that a peaceful,
legal organisation would be more advantageous to
the régime in coming to terms with the socio-economic
crisis than a violent Underground; this would

encourage them into the required political compromises (ICPA, 6/82, pp. 7-10). Bujak polemicised
with Kuroń's 'futile' suggestion that eventually
the opposition would need to organise a centralised
resistance movement to destroy the régime through a
General Strike. He favoured 'a decidedly decentralised movement, adopting different methods of action. Only such a diffuse and varied movement will
be elusive and difficult to suppress ... Positional
struggle would be both efficient and safe. Various
social groups and circles must build up a resistance
mechanism against the monopoly of the authorities'
(ICPA, 8/82, pp. 8-10). Kulerski, however, argued
'a Third Possibility'. Kuroń's alternative of
either compromise or revolution was a false one and
a nationwide secret organisation was impossible.
His recipe was for a multi-centred, decentralised
movement consisting of mutually independent and
loosely connected social resistance, informational
and assistance groups. Kulerski, rather optimis-
tically, foresaw an erosion of the régime's power
leading to gradual liberalisation, the restoration
of social influence and the rebirth of autonomous
social life. The opposition should therefore take
refuge in an Underground society not State. Kuroń's
reply to Bujak and Kulerski was 'that no self-defence
or any other social movement is possible under martial law'. The régime had to be resisted by all
means including violence but the first priority was
'to organise the movement's centre and information
network'. The nation would revolt because of the
economic disaster so 'a new mass movement is to
emerge underground' (ICPA, 11/82, pp. 8-14).
    Such demands from Kuroń, Lis, their Western
supporters and above all grassroots pressure in the
large Warsaw and Wrocław factories moved the Mazowsze
leadership of Bujak, Janaś, the Ursus Solidarity
leader, Romaszewski and Kulerski to begin preparations for a General Strike in June after the lessons
of the first round of major disturbances in May had
been digested. They feared that a spontaneous and
unplanned outbreak would be both dangerous and inef-
ficacious, so they called on their provisional factory committees to establish strike committees to
make preparations and to report back on workplace
support. The mid-June protests were particularly
strong in Wrocław. The TKK then called off its
offensive and all strikes and demonstrations in late
June for a month. It claimed that the street demonstrations showed that 'Solidarity is still a real
power'. Their Moratorium was proof of their

willingness to come to an agreement. Rejection 'would force the union to resume all sorts of pressure including a General Strike' (ICPA, 13/82, p.3). This met with a uniformly hardline official reaction. There was no question of negotiation with anti-socialist forces, although opposition figures could retire unpunished into private life (Bielecki, TL, 15 July 1982). Romaszewski still hoped, just before his arrest, that the social stalemate would produce 'a weak agreement'. If not, a General Strike would be necessary in the Autumn, although the desperate hope was that sit-in strikes and protests in August would be sufficient to force leadership changes in favour of compromise (Tygodnik Mazowsze, No. 16, 2 June 1982).

The Solidarity leaders were, however, very disappointed by Jaruzelski's concessions of 21 July which led to the release of 1,227 internees, leaving 637 in the camps. The TKK declarations of 28 July 1982 set out its 'Five Noes': The State of War was not abolished but extended indefinitely, not all internees and none of the 2,000 convicted had been released, there was nothing about Solidarity's reactivisation, no principles of authentic Social Accord and no specific detail on the Economic Reform. 'These five noes mean that society has been deprived of all hope ... the ever deepening gulf between the governors and the governed reduces dramatically the chances of overcoming the crisis' (ICPA, 15/82, pp. 3-4). 'The Underground Society', the Basic Principles for a Programmatic Declaration by the TKK, set out its mature strategy for the second half of 1982 (ICPA, 15/82, pp. 4-8). The initial decisions were to resume protest action as of 13 August and to hold a massive day of peaceful protest on the 31st. The 'Five Yeses' were Solidarity's re-establishment, the lifting of martial law, the return of civil liberties and the release of all internees and political prisoners. The TKK now wanted to organise a resistance movement to the régime within the framework of an underground society. As the military authorities had rejected all national agreement proposals it had become 'indispensible to prepare the population for a long drawn-out struggle'. Small action groups were to be formed in workplaces and living areas as components of the Underground society to oppose official organisations and their collaborators, to assist internees and other victims of martial law and their families and to carry out widespread publishing activity, as well as to boycott the official mass media and its propaganda. The

political aim was to 'exercise pressure on the power-
holders to oblige them really to accept the idea of
social understanding' (Tygodnik Mazowsze, No. 23,
1 August 1982). The same issue reported that decentralised Regional Co-ordination Centres existed in
Białystok, Bydgoszcz, Częstochowa, Lower Silesia,
Elbląg, Gdańsk, Kraków, the Carpathians, West
Pomerania, Szczecin, the East-Central region, Poznań,
Warmia and Mazuria. Wrocław was by far the strongest region with about 60% of its workplaces supporting Solidarity. The KOS were mainly urban phenomena, while Solidarity published about 250 titles
regularly, the average circulation being a few hundred,
but the highest claimed was up to 30,000. There
had also been 16 Radio Solidarity transmissions, 10
of them in Warsaw. The Solidarity consensus in the
Summer was to agree with the interned Poznań Professor
Leszek Nowak that General Uprising à la Kuroń was
premature and that an Underground Society was over-
due (ICPA, 14/82, pp. 30-32).

The domestic Solidarity leaders knew that August
was their last chance to demonstrate to the rulers
that the cost of continued social repression would
far outweigh those of a negotiated political settlement. In particular they wanted to overawe the
régime away from any thought of dissolving Solidarity.
August was the most serious and developed social
challenge to the authorities during the whole period
of martial law, although it fell short of expectations.
The realistic Bujak considered that the August events
would in a 'very considerable measure decide the
strategy which we will adopt in the next stage. The
effects will certainly not be obvious at once but
if August had passed off quietly this would have signified to the power-holders that the union and
society are broken and very weak' (Tygodnik Mazowsze,
No. 26, 1982). Bujak thought further that if the
Poles stood up to repression in August the radical
line of pressure would soon force the authorities
into trilateral negotiations with the Church and
Solidarity,including Wałęsa. But the breaking of
the August protests would 'signify that we are not
in any state to push through radical forms of resistance, that we must give up mass actions' and concentrate on long-term resistance under conditions of
a conspiratorial Underground'.

The TKK met on 5-7 September to hail the 31
August demonstrations as 'a moral victory for the
nation' which had demonstrated that it could not be
governed by force and that it was 'determined to
fight for the re-establishment of its rights'. It

reiterated its line on negotiations and fixed new
dates for protest against the régime. The TKK also
condemned the legal indictment of the KOR leaders
as a process designed 'to eliminate union militants
from social life for many years' (ICPA, 19/82,
pp. 18-22). Frasyniuk's gloss was that after the
'moral victory' of August Solidarity's main task was
now to organise its Underground structures and to
set about preparing the General Strike in earnest
(Solidarność Dolnośląska, No. 38, 1982). The emphasis on moral values is always the recourse of the
weak and defeated. It increasingly became a dominant theme in opposition discourse from now on.
On 6 September the TKK feared that spontaneous social
outbursts would give the authorities the pretext to
repress the opposition under conditions which were
favourable to it. It therefore called another
Moratorium for September while it prepared its
November actions (ICPA, 19/82, pp. 18-22). In
reality the TKK and the regional leaderships were
demoralised and hopelessly divided over the next
steps, particularly over how they should react to
Solidarity's imminent de-legalisation. The opposition leaders, in spite of putting a brave face on
it, and although encouraged by the mid-September
Wrocław and Nowa Huta disturbances, knew that the
August protests had been insufficient to save
Solidarity. The authorities now felt strong
enough to ban it as well as to start legal proceedings against the four KOR leaders plus Jan Józef
Lipski, who returned from medical treatment in
England. The 30 September commemoration was therefore localised to Gdańsk. It passed off quietly
as the militia did not intervene. Michnik's 'Appeal
to the International Community', issued from
Białołęka on 2 September, denounced the KOR indictment as the first step in a show trial. Kuroń,
on the other hand, had somewhat lost touch with
reality by now. He considered that 'national salvation can only be achieved on the basis of a programme supported by society which is organised inde-
pendently from the party and state authorities and
a programme accepted in a national referendum'
(Tygodnik Mazowsze, No. 21, 1982). The only advice
offered by Frasyniuk, just before the heavy blow of
his arrest, was to prepare 'for many years of persis-
tent struggle'. The immediate tactics were to
'gain partial concessions from the authorities by
various means of pressure' (ICPA, 21/82, pp. 23-25).
    On 9 October the TKK denounced the dissolution
of Solidarity and all other TUs as 'an unprecedented

act in the annals of civilised societies'. It
called for the boycott of the new 'façade unions';
this would constitute 'a sort of national referendum
by which the people would express themselves against
the policy of repression'. It also called for a 4
hour national strike on 10 November, the second anniversary of Solidarity's registration, and for a massive day of protest against its banning and against
economic misery. Secret strike committees should
be established in all workplaces to organise the
protest and to develop 'the union's future strategy'
(ICPA, 20/82, pp. 21-28). Their depression was,
however, compounded by the militarisation and effective suppression of the Gdańsk Shipyard strike by
the authorities and by the failure of the Nobel
Committee to award its Peace Prize to Wałęsa as expected, and almost demanded, by the Solidarity Underground; he received it the following year. The
renewed wave of disturbances in sympathy with the
Lenin Shipyard,notably in Wrocław,claimed another
life when a plainclothesman panicked and shot a
worker, Bogdan Włosik, in Nowa Huta. Wałęsa let
it be known, through his wife who visited him, that
he now supported 'all forms of protest'. He had
refused all régime offers to collaborate in the new
unions or to emigrate from Poland with his family.
But he still remained optimistic and believed in
Solidarity's ideals.

By Autumn 1982 the Jaruzelski régime had effectively won the battle for the banning of Solidarity
and had forced the Church to accept its conditions
for normalisation and the Papal visit. The Underground leaders, after Solidarity's de-legalisation,
were divided between two tactics. Mazowsze's
advisers considered that they lacked the strength
to carry out the decisive and widespread industrial
action necessary either to overthrow the existing
communist leadership or to force it to reactivate
Solidarity. They even considered that a long-term
boycott of the official unions would not succeed and
might rebound against them (KOS, No. 18, 1982).
Such perspectives were tantamount to accepting defeat. The TKK therefore decided to stake all on a
last effort to organise a national strike to force
the régime to concede free TUs, a real Economic
Reform and genuine workers' self-management
(Tygodnik Mazowsze, No. 31, 1982). The communiqué
of 20 October planned 'a new stage of the struggle'
based on a more long-term and determined form of
resistance. The TKK extended the strike on 10
November from 4 to 8 hours and called for a national

day of protest on the 11th to celebrate the regaining of independence in 1918. It appealed to all
social groups, including the peasants, to demonstrate
'the régime's total isolation' and its complete
responsibility for the socio-economic stalemate because of its refusal to negotiate an agreement.
Solidarity's de-legalisation was purely symbolic as
it had effectively been banned on 13 December.
The authorities would, however, be unable to dissolve the resistance movement, which would continue
to fight the dictatorship by boycotting its unions
(Tygodnik Mazowsze, No. 28, 1982). In the face of
Glemp's opposition to the strike call, the régime's
political and police counter-offensive and such
psychological blows as Bednarz's arrest, the strike
never really got off the ground.

Once again the Solidarity leadership had demonstrated appalling judgement and timing in calling
the first General Strike under martial law under the
worst psychological and political conditions. The
10 November strike failure was not compensated for
by the sporadic street confrontations with the police.
The Underground finally had to accept that it could
not force the authorities into negotiations through
social opposition and pressure. The steam was further taken out of the latter by Wałęsa's release and
the State-Church moves towards the suspension of martial law. The TKK therefore lost much of its political standing. Its role as the main opposition
spokesman was largely taken over by Wałęsa. But
the Underground, although a number of its militants
now abandoned clandestine activity, still remained
a strong informational and propaganda network with
considerable support in some workplaces. This
allowed it to pursue its own interests and to support the initiatives of Wałęsa and the Church in the
period of the suspension of martial law in 1983.

The TKK set out its considered reaction to the
10 November strike fiasco in its 'Conditions of
Truce' of 22 November 1982. It called off the
mid-December protests and reiterated its demands for
the release of internees and political prisoners and
the restoration of civil and TU liberties. The TKK
was ready 'to subordinate itself to the decisions of
Lech Wałęsa, who alone can define the conditions under
which the TKK, on his demand, could decide to dissolve itself' (ICPA, 22/82, pp. 9-10). Its accompanying declarations accepted that 'a completely
new political situation had been created'. The need
was now 'to work out new forms of struggle'. The
strategy of mobilising social protest against the

régime had failed and support would inevitably ebb
even further in 1983.

Sure of the Underground's support, Wałęsa wrote
to Jaruzelski on 4 December stating their argument
that the only way to achieve social stabilisation
was to implement the 1980 Social Agreements, to have
a General Amnesty for all the victims of martial law
and to return to TU pluralism: 'The working class
had not accepted the solutions which are currently
being applied and without it no understanding was
possible, although neither side had to ask for it
"on its knees"' (ICPA, 23/82, p. 27). Wałęsa was
ignored but he now became a major political actor.
His relations with the police, procuracy, Western
journalists and with the opposition focused world
attention on him. He was also the rallying point
for the demonstrations of his supporters in Gdańsk
throughout 1983.

The partial nature of the suspension of martial
law was foreseen by the Underground leaders, who as
early as 12 December declared that their struggle
would continue in their 'Aims of the Resistance'
(ICPA, 23/82, pp. 33-35). Three of the document's
signatories (Onyszkiewicz,Sobieraj and Tokarczuk)
were released but the remaining seven were accused
of conspiracy against the state and kept in confine-
ment. It repeated that Solidarity 'continued to
exist because of the will of its members',who would
continue the struggle for the Self-Managing Republic.

Bujak himself drew up the Underground's 'Balance
Sheet for the year' (ICPA, 23/82, pp. 38-48). The
Poles' success had been that, unlike the Czechoslovaks
and Hungarians, they had not fallen silent and had
preserved a modicum of independent cultural and
social life. Bujak did not consider 'any of the
direct actions - the strikes and the demonstrations
organised by the Underground - as being sufficiently
massive to say that there had been a victory, and
this included the demonstrations of 31 August, which
I assess as being too weak for a union of ten million members'. The July protests had been even
more inadequate, although they had been essential in
order to rally morale. But the August demonstrations
had been the last chance to save Solidarity. As
only 15,000, not 150,000, demonstrated the régime had
a tenfold easier task in de-legalising Solidarity.
The movement's successes had been to maintain its
honour and aspirations, the universal boycott of
the new unions and to demolish the myth of the omni-
competence of the security forces. New forms of
activity were now needed, not to overthrow the régime,

but to force it to implement reforms. 'The struggle
for the possibility of carrying an open action' was
the priority, although the Underground structures
should remain in place until all political prisoners
were released. Urban in the contrasting régime
prognosis felt that 1983 would see the failure of
attempts to create alternative societies and the
dying away of confrontation as political stabilisation set in [9].

Wałęsa contra the Régime

The doings of 'an ordinary citizen', the ex-
chairman of the Solidarity TU, continued to make
headlines in the Western press. It would, however,
be too tedious to chronicle his travels and relations
with the security forces in full. Wałęsa was put
back on the payroll in the Lenin Shipyard in late
January, but he did not resume his job as an elec-
trician until April. The TKK, now composed of
Bujak, Lis, Hardek, Szumiejko and Józef Pinior
(vice the arrested Bednarz), in its Programmatic
Declaration of 22 January still considered that its
strongest weapon was 'the inevitable General Strike'.
It would be helped along by social boycotts and the
struggle within the workplaces over the new unions
(ICPA, 2/83, pp. 8-9). In sum, the Underground
should 'formulate a minimum social programme which
would bring together all demands and take account
of the limitations stemming from political realities, both national and international'. Wałęsa
shared the TKK's objectives but 'at the moment a
General Strike is not part of my programme, although
I might decide one day that such a method is necessary' (Le Monde, 30-31 January 1983). Wałęsa was,
however, shaken by the political trials of Anna
Walentynowicz (15 months suspended), Edward Bałuka
(5 years),the MRKS activists and the Kwidzyń internment camp 'mutineers' in March. He told Western
journalists that the authorities were 'dishonest'
and that he would be 'firmer' towards them. Armed
resistance was impossible but he now supported
'demonstrations, hunger strikes as well as strikes'
(Le Monde, 12 March 1983). He therefore backed the
renewed wave of 13 March demonstrations in Gdańsk,
Warsaw and Wrocław. It is not clear how Wałęsa reconciled this, at his meeting with Glemp in Warsaw
on 19 March, with the Primate's desire for social
calm before the Papal visit. The authorities
tolerated Wałęsa's meeting with opposition figures
in Siła-Nowicki's flat the same day. They counteracted his activities by stepping up their investigation

of alleged financial irregularities in the Gdańsk
Solidarity organisation,which gave them an excuse
to tie him down to Gdańsk.
  'Solidarity is alive and cannot be destroyed.
It is vigorous and well anchored in the factories,'
declared the TKK defiantly on 23 March (ICPA, 7/83,
pp. 10-11). Its call for 'independent celebrations'
on May Day and 3 May was supported by Wałęsa in his
press conference of 20 March. Wałęsa, however, went
considerably further. He evaded police surveillance
and met the TKK in secret on the weekend of 9-11
April. Their communiqué stated that 'they had
discussed the current situation of the country in
detail and co-ordinated their positions' (Le Monde,
13 April 1983). The meeting was an open act of
defiance which confirmed the unity between Wałęsa
and the TKK on the Papal visit. The TKK welcomed
it in the hope that it would reaffirm the movement's
'values and ideological fundamentals'; 'Solidarity
was, and will be, a spiritual revolution aiming to
create new values' in the building of a stable democracy in Poland (ICPA, 8/83, p. 13). The Gdańsk
police reacted by interrogating Wałęsa, strengthening their surveillance over him and in dispersing
crowds of supporters who attempted to meet around
St. Brigid's and St. Anne's Churches.
  Wałęsa told Western journalists, in an impromptu
news conference in his flat, after being turned back
at Olsztyn by the militia in his attempt to get to
Warsaw for the Ghetto Uprising anniversary, that the
authorities were 'arrogant' and 'ill willed'.
Solidarity had a peaceful and realistic programme;
'it was a moral force without whose participation
Poland could not get out of the crisis'. His key
theme was that 'we do not want to overthrow the
Government. We do not want to push the party aside.
We do not want to undermine our country's alliances.
What we want is to improve workers' living conditions within the framework of TU pluralism'. That
is why he supported the TKK's call for protest.
May Day would find him on the streets (Le Monde,
22 April 1983). All this activity led to Wałęsa's
being hailed in the West and denounced in the East.
'Decidedly M. Wałęsa is not only a charismatic tribune but a talented political man' (Le Monde, 22
April 1983).
  The May Day and 3 May protests were the most
significant since the suspension of martial law, but
smaller and more localised than the previous year.
The militia detained Wałęsa in Warsaw on 6 April and
prevented him from meeting the Episcopal Council's

Secretary.   He was escorted back to Gdańsk and
effectively confined to his flat for a while.
Wałęsa had, however, earlier drafted an Open Letter
to the Sejm.   This called for a return to TU
pluralism, opposed the forcible dragooning of workers into a single factory union and demanded the
release of all arrested union militants.   The
security forces, however, continued their protracted
cat and mouse game with Wałęsa by questioning him
whenever he seemed set to leave Gdańsk.   All this
was very low key compared to the events of the previous year.   The return to normality was demonstrated by the Grzegorz Przemyk cas célèbre.   His death
after being arrested by the militia on 16 May opened
up a typically intense and long drawn-out affair.
It ended up with a rather odd verdict clearing
militiamen but imprisoning an ambulance crew (ICPA,
10/83, pp. 16-18;   11/83, pp. 19-21).
      One of the main issues in the weeks before the
Papal visit, involving a considerable struggle of
wills, was whether Wałęsa would be allowed to meet
the Pontiff.   The authorities refused to give him
leave from the shipyard.   They threatened to arrest
him if he left Gdańsk without their permission.   The
question was left hanging until the Pope arrived.
The opposition did not, however, expect that the
régime would make any concessions as a result of the
visit.   Bujak stated that his movement would only
give up its struggle if TU pluralism were conceded
[10].   He considered that the TKK's meeting with
Wałęsa and the Open Letter had been 'a great political action';   Wałęsa merited praise as he 'had
completely different possibilities from the Underground and he makes excellent use of them'
(Tygodnik Mazowsze, 28 May 1983).   The TKK confirmed
its position that the Poles should greet the Pope
with joy and flaunt their Solidarity allegiance but
avoid any provocation which might mar the visit.
Bujak warned against excessive optimism.   There would
be no immediate results from the visit.   'The
struggle which is being carried on by our union demands time;   not only weeks and months but years.   We
have a long road before us and many of us will go to
prison.   I only expect from the visit that it will
help people to last out and not to abandon future
struggles' (ICPA, 12/83, June 1983). The visit, as
described in Chapter Six, took place amidst much
excitement and emotion but without any outbursts.
John Paul must have told Wałęsa gently, at their
meeting in a Tatras hotel on the last day of the
visit, that his major political role was over now

270

that martial law was being lifted. He certainly
advised him to avoid strikes and demonstrations which
might be used as pretext for applying the Special
Regulations. Levi's resignation and the furore
around his article only showed how sensitive the
issue was if stated too bluntly. Wałęsa himself was,
however, either too stupid or too thick skinned to
recognise this. He regaled Western journalists
on 26 June with his usual whistling in the wind about
the continuing struggle to force the authorities to
negotiate and to return to the Social Agreements and
TU pluralism. He admitted that he might now take
'a back seat' if this were necessary,but his wife
and claque of supporters confirmed that he remained
the unofficial leader of Poland's workers.

The authorities' determination to continue on
their chosen road was demonstrated in early July
by the rejection of the KPN leaders' appeal against
their sentences. The lifting of the State of War
was also replaced by such a battery of Special
Regulations that Wałęsa considered that they were
tougher than martial law itself. On 3 July the
TKK dismissed the end of the State of War as 'a
gesture deprived of any serious political meaning'
(ICPA, 14/83, p. 3). The Solidarity Co-ordinating
Bureau Abroad stated on 22 July that 'the extraordinary legislation of martial law had been per-
petuated, that Polish society's resistance had not
been broken, that no real "normalisation" had occurred and that the struggle for the liberation
of political prisoners would continue' (ICPA, 15/83,
pp. 11-12). In their full reaction to the end of
martial law on 28 July the TKK called on its supporters 'to demonstrate on 31 August our fidelity
to the ideals of August 1980 and to bear witness
that Solidarity lives'. Branches should organise
protests suited to local conditions but should participate in a national boycott of public transport.
'The Poles would continue their struggle for the
Social Agreements, Free TUs, the right to strike and
freedom for political prisoners.' The Special Regulations 'extinguished all rights to liberty of
opinion and independent activity'. The TKK rejected the amnesty's condition that Underground
members should give up their struggle and return to
private life by 31 October. The lifting of martial
law was merely 'a propaganda gesture' and an attempt
to mislead Polish society and public opinion in
order to obtain credit facilities and the raising of
economic sanctions (ICPA, 16/83, p. 14). In sum,
the opposition hardcores would continue their struggle

Wałęsa and the Underground

alt^hough with less open social support and under
much less favourable conditions than in the late
1970s.

Notes

1. So far authoritative assessments only of the pre-martial
    law roles of Solidarity and KOR, written by participants,
    have appeared. Jerzy Holzer, Solidarność 1980-1981.
    Geneza i Historia (Paris, Instytut Literacki, 1984).
    Jan Józef Lipski, KOR (London, Aneks, 1983).
2. The changing kaleidoscope of varied structures is
    chronicled by Michał Kołodziej, 'Podziemne struktury
    NSZZ Solidarność 13.xii.1981-13.xii.1984', Zeszyty
    Historyczne, No. 72 (Paris, 1985), pp. 65-90. The
    taped interviews with seven major opposition figures -
    Bogdan Borusiewicz, Zbigniew Bujak, Władysław Frasyniuk,
    Aleksander Hall, Tadeusz Jedynak, Bogdan Lis and
    Eugeniusz Szumiejko - give an indispensible insight
    into opposition views, motivations and assessments of
    the various stages of the Underground struggle.
    M. Lopiński, M. Moskit & M. Wilk, Konspira. Rzecz
    o podziemnej Solidarności (Paris, Spotkania, 1984).
3. Convenient collections of their writings have been pub-
    lished in the West. Jacek Kuroń, Polityka i
    Odpowiedzialność (London, Aneks, 1984). Adam Michnik,
    Szanse Polskiej Demokracji. Artykuły i Eseje (London,
    Aneks, 1984).
4. Lesław Wojtasik, Podziemie polityczne (Warsaw, KiW,
    1983), p. 11.
5. Tomasz Mianowicz, 'O Wolnej Europie bez mitologii',
    Kultura, 7/418 (Paris, July 1982).
6. Persky & Flam, Solidarity Sourcebook, p. 243.
7. 'Poland. Keeping dissent alive', Newsweek, 22 February
    1982.
8. J. Kuroń, 'Tezy o wyjściu z sytuacji bez wyjścia',
    Aneks, No. 27 (1982).
9. J. Urban, 'Wiosna Nasza', Tu i Teraz, 5 January 1983.
10. On the internal debate within the Underground, Tomasz
    Mianowicz, 'Konspiracja, podziemie, opór społeczny',
    Kultura, 4/427 (Paris, April 1983), pp. 138-143.
    Maciej Poleski, 'Program i Organizacja', Kultura,
    5/428 (Paris, May 1983), pp. 3-21. One of the main
    sources is Aneks, Nos. 28 to 38.

CONCLUSION: THE POLISH RONDO CONTINUES

The reasons for social discontent in Poland are many and varied. A whole generation was affected indelibly and politicised by the 1980-1982 Events. But these psychological aspects of social consciousness and political culture need to be counterpoised by the unpredictable factor of straightforward economic and consumer discontent. After 1980 frustrated expectations were replaced by real economic hardship, especially among the old. The young have been dubbed 'the lost generation' in terms of lost life chances, notably in housing and consumption, since 1978. As has been argued, the Polish Crisis was aggravated by a prevalent egalitarianism which levelled up aspirations in the 1970s and worsened the Socialist State's Distribution Crisis. A hardcore of permanent oppositionists was also created by the 1980-1982 Events who could be neither eliminated by Stalinist means nor reintegrated into the system. The consequence has been the periodic cycle of opposition activity and régime legal sanctions, as in the 2-3 year sentences on Frasyniuk, Lis and Michnik in 1985. On the other hand, the Roman Catholic Church, although often dampening down social outbursts, by its very existence guarantees that the communist régime is condemned to living with an uncontrolled society and that the state-society stand-off will continue. Lastly, as a result of the foregoing, Polish social groups remain fairly autonomous. The discontents of workers, peasants and intellectuals are bound to continue to have a destabilising effect on the system.

It is the oldest debate in Poland's political history since the seventeenth century, whether such a situation is best resolved by strong but benevolent authoritarianism or whether the answer is decentralisation and democratisation. This study has examined how the Polish communist system halted and repressed the Solidarity experience. Step by protracted step, and with varying degrees of success, Jaruzelski then rebuilt the foundations of CP rule at the various levels of the administration, the outer-party membership ring, PRON and the factories. The Army-State structures of martial law have been replaced gradually by more normal Soviet Party-State mechanisms but the Jaruzelski cohort of political officers have remained as general political functionaries. The main political milestones since the lifting of martial law have been the People's Council elections, the General Amnesty, Popiełuszko's murder and the

Conclusion

re-establishment of national TUs topped by the OOZ
during 1984, the Sejm election of October 1985 and
the preparations for the PZPR Tenth Congress announced for late July 1986.   All of these marked a gradual, if contested, return to the Soviet type of
normality.

In postwar Poland elections have often been important barometers of a communist régime's standing
with the nation and of its control capacities.
The elections to the provincial and lower-level
People's Council of 17 June 1984 were the first open
test of the régime's mobilising power.   The results,
claimed as 'a relative success' by the PRON Secretary-
General,showed both the extent of régime stabilisation and of national dissatisfaction.   Turnout in
the key provincial elections was just under 75%
and between 66.8% and 78% for the municipal and communal ones (State Electoral Commission Bulletin, TL,
20 June 1984).   The abstention rate was thus unpre-
cedentedly high for a communist election, as even in
1957 it had been 94.1%.   In addition, 85 mainly
rural districts in East Poland failed even to achieve
the 50% turnout for the election to be valid and had
to have repeat ballots.

The sweeping amnesty of 21 July 1984, on the fortieth anniversary of the PRL, resolved the most
thorny problem left over from the State of War (TL,
22 July 1984).   It released all solely 'political prisoners' (630 out of 652) and closed the file on
Jaroszewicz and Wrzaszczyk.   Almost 35,000 individuals were released, 1,569 of whom were held for
non-criminal and another 347 for public order offences (TL, 21 September 1984).   But the amnesty
laid down that the opposition militants should now
refrain from all activities deemed illegal by the
authorities.   Despite this legal armlock some
(Frasyniuk, Lis, Pinior) soon became involved in
demonstrations and were sentenced to short prison
terms.   The amnesty was both a consequence and a
condition of normalisation.   It could not remove
the causes of social discontent or prevent future
contestation and repression.   But, as it was so
surprisingly full, it, for the moment, removed a
running sore from Polish political life.

The Sejm election of 15 October 1985 again showed
both the successes and the failures of the Jaruzelski
régime in extending its hold over Polish society.
Officially a national turnout of just over 78% was
claimed, although the opposition considered that it
was nearer 65%.   Although candidate selection had
been controlled through the PRON framework, the

voter had the usual Polish opportunity to signal
discontent with individuals.   It is significant
that on the National List of Fifty the least popular
individuals, in order, were Rakowski (96.33%),
Barcikowski, Gucwa, Kiszczak, Czyrek and Jaruzelski
(State Electoral Commission Bulletin, TL, 16 October
1985).   The cyclist Ryszard Szurkowski got the most
votes (98.12%).   In the 74 multi-member constituen-
cies 410 'favoured' candidates, all of whom were
elected, faced duels with, for the most part fairly
similar, counter-candidates.   Differential rates of
individual support were again possible, signalling
areas of most opposition.   Five favoured candidates
got under 90%.   The lowest was 82.81% in Nowa Huta,
while Stanisław Kania, who was most provocatively
parachuted into Gdańsk, got 88% and his opponent
with 8.45% received the highest personal vote for
a counter-candidate.   These individual distinctions
were, however, much less important than the key
battle over turnout.   The opposition called for a
boycott while the régime attempted, but failed, to
get a much better result than in the local elections.
Predictably the most disaffected areas were the
Solidarity industrial working-class strongholds.
It was admitted officially that turnout was only
65.81% in Gdańsk and 68-71% in Nowa Huta, Łódź,Lublin
and Warsaw, as compared with the highest turnout of
88% in Bydgoszcz.
   In 1984-1986 the Polish Rondo was continuing as
normal, although a significant hardening of political
atmosphere occurred even in this short period.   Official discourse in 1985 returned to an even deader
language than in the 1960s.   Concerned with arti-
ficial and stage-managed events like Peace Congresses,
it gave increasing coverage to Soviet developments
and the speeches of the Soviet leaders and to a
strident denunciation of Reagan's nuclear and Cold
War policies.   The PZPR Theses for the Tenth Congress published in March 1986 made it clear that
the 1980-1981 Crisis and martial law were now
past history.   They moved straight on to defining
the new political and socio-economic tasks for 1986-
1990 with barely an opening paragraph on past controversies which were now proclaimed to be dead.
The Theses promised to increase GNP by 16-19%, industrial goods consumption by 17%, foodstuffs by
12%, to bring inflation down to below 10% by 1990
(sic!) and to increase the number of new dwellings
by 10-20%.   This wholly technocratic document
à la Gorbachev, along with the other Congress preparations, indicated that leadership stability at

the top levels would be counterbalanced by a healthy degree of turnover at Central Committee and middle levels. All the dreams of 1980-1981 were thus buried. The Jaruzelski régime now looked forward to over a decade of stability during which it would apply an eclectic mixture of reforms drawn from the experience of all its socialist neighbours, from the USSR to Yugoslavia. The Tenth Congress was to be a Congress of Victors for the system irrespective of the fate of personalities, some of whom, like Olszowski, had already been retired or moved to honorific positions, like Barcikowski in December 1985. The draft programme for the Tenth Congress was an uncompromisingly orthodox Marxist-Leninist reassertion of the Leading Role of the PZPR, the Dictatorship of the Proletariat and of the building of socialism through various stages adapted to Polish conditions.

The gradual strengthening of the communist system and the slow, irregular and insufficient pace of economic improvement, however high the prices, ensured that the dialogue of the deaf between the revamped state, the Roman Catholic Church, the residual contestatory forces and social groups would continue. Crisis is built into the relationship but this does not mean that disaster will occur, however often it is threatened. As in Mikołaj Rej's sixteenth-century dialogue between Squire and Priest, the same conversation in Poland always seems to end up on the same note. So now the air was full of key words such as 'crisis', 'stalemate', 'dilemmas' and 'dialogue'. And yet most Poles lived reasonably well, enriched themselves as well as they could and their cultural life, although much impoverished, was still the envy of their hardline neighbours. In 1986 Jaruzelski seemed to have won the gamble undertaken in December 1981. The great question was whether Polish society would reassert itself as in the past, even after another generation? Or would the reconstructed and more determined communist system this time succeed in grinding it into the Soviet mould? One never knows, but the post-1956 experience suggests that, short of external cataclysms, the Polish Rondo will continue.*

* I am much indebted to Mrs. Anne Merriman for her painstaking and skilful typing of the whole of this study and for her extensive assistance in preparing the final text.

SELECT BIBLIOGRAPHY

Books, official publications and some key articles

Adelman, J. (ed.)   Communist Armies in Politics (Boulder,
                       Col., Westview Press, 1982)
Anderson, R.   'Soviet decision-making in Poland',
                       Problems of Communism, XXXI, No. 3
                       (March-April 1982), pp. 22-36.
Andrusiewicz, A.   SD w systemie politycznym Polski
                       Ludowej (Warsaw, PWN, 1984).
Ascherson, N.   The Polish August (Harmondsworth,
                       Penguin, 1981).
Ash, T.G.   The Polish Revolution. Solidarity
                       1980-1981 (London, Jonathan Cape, 1983).
Baka, W.   Polska reforma gospodarcza (Warsaw, PWE,
                       1982).
Bauman, Z.   'Bez precedensu', Aneks, No. 32 (1983),
                       pp. 21-43.
Bednarski, H. &   'Kilka uwag o ideologicznej pracy partii',
Nowak, W.   ND, 3/406 (March 1983), pp. 132-140.
Bejger, S.   'Zespalanie sił społecznych. Z
                       doświadczeń Gdańskiej organizacji
                       partyjnej', ND, 5/408 (May 1983),
                       pp. 63-73.
Berberiusz, E.   'Niemożliwe uczynić możliwym' (inter-
                       view with Tadeusz Mazowiecki) in Kultura,
                       5/428 (Paris, May 1983), pp. 77-87.
Besançon, A.   'Drugie milczenie Kościoła', Kultura,
                       3/426 (Paris, March 1983), pp. 3-12.
Beskid, L.   'Sprawiedliwy czy Egalitarny?', Polityka,
                       20 March 1982.
Bielasiak, J. &   Polish Politics. Edge of the Abyss
Simon, M. (eds.)   (New York, Praeger, 1984).
Bielecki, J.   Co wydarzyło się w Polsce od sierpnia
                       1980 roku? (Warsaw, Wydzial Informacji
                       KC PZPR, KiW, 1982).
Biuro Prasowe Rządu   300 niespokojnych dni (Warsaw, KiW,
                       1983).
                       Przed 13 grudnia (Warsaw, KiW, 1982).
Blazyca, G.   'Poland's economy under military manage-
                       ment', World Today, XXXX, No. 2
                       (February 1984).
                       'The Polish economy under martial
                       law', Soviet Studies, XXXVII, No. 3
                       (July 1985), pp. 428-436.
Blumstajn, S.   Je rentre au pays (Paris, Calmann-Lévy,
                       1984).
Bocheński, A.   Kryzys Polski i kryzys ludzkości (Warsaw,
                       PiW, 1982).

Bibliography

Borowiecki, J.   Solidarność. Fronty walki o władzę
                         (Warsaw, KiW, 1982).
Bromke, A.   Poland. The protracted crisis (Oakville,
                         Mosaic Press, 1983).
                         'Socialism with a martial face', World
                         Today, XXXVIII, No. 7-8 (July-August
                         1982), pp. 428-436.
Brumberg, A. (ed.)   Poland. Genesis of a revolution (New
                         York, Random House, 1983).
Chęciński, M.   'Ludowe Wojsko Polskie; przed i po marcu
                         1968r', Zeszyty Historyczne, No. 44
                         (Paris, 1978).
                         'Poland's military burden', Problems
                         of Communism, XXXII, No. 3 (May-June
                         1983), pp. 31-44.
Ciepły, S. &   Gorycz-rozsądek-nadzieja (Kraków,
Kleszcz, H. (eds.)   KAW, 1985).
Colton, T.   Commissars, Commanders and Civilian
                         Authority. The structure of Soviet
                         military politics (Cambridge, Mass.,
                         Harvard U.P., 1981).
Cywiński, B.   Doświadczenie Polskie (Paris, Spotkania,
                         1984).
Czyrek, J.   'Droga Manifestu Lipcowego', ND, 7/410
                         (July 1983), pp. 5-14.
Doświadczenie i   Raport Czwarty. Polska wobec Stanu
Przyszłość   Wojennego in Kultura, 7-8/419 (Paris,
                         July-August 1982), pp. 143-208.
Ehrlich, S.   Oblicza pluralizmów (Warsaw, PWN,
                         1984).
Erazmus, E.   Spór o kształt partii (Warsaw, KiW, 1983).
Fikus, D.   Foksal 81 (London, Aneks, 1984).
Głowacki, J.   Moc truchleje (London, Paris, 1982).
Garnisz, C.   'Polish stalemate', Problems of Communism,
                         XXXIII, No. 3 (May-June 1984), pp. 51-59.
Heller, M.   Sous le regard de Moscou (Paris, Calmann-
                         Lévy, 1982).
Herspring, D.R. &   Civil-Military Relations in Communist States
Volgyes, I. (eds.)   (Boulder, Col., Westview Press, 1978).
Holloway, D.   The Warsaw Pact. Alliance in transition
                         (London, Macmillan, 1984).
Holzer, J.   Solidarność 1980-1981. Geneza i Historia
                         (Paris, Instytut Literacki, 1984).
Jaruzelski, W.   Przemówienia 1981-1982 (Warsaw, KiW, 1983).
                         Przemówienia 1983 (Warsaw, KiW, 1984).
                         Przemówienia 1984 (Warsaw, KiW, 1985).
Jasiewicz, K.   'Przemiany świadomosci społecznej Polaków
                         1979-1983', Aneks, No. 32 (1983),
                         pp. 125-139.
Jędrychowski, S.   'Drogą prób i błędów', ND, 2/405 (February
                         1983), pp. 82-98.

Bibliography

Johnson, A.R., Dean, R.W. & Alexiev, A.	East European Military Establishments. The Northern Tier (New York, Crane-Russak, 1980).
Jones, C.	Soviet Influence in Eastern Europe. Political autonomy and the Warsaw Pact (New York, Praeger, 1981).
Kąkol, K.	Kościół w Polsce (Warsaw, KiW, 1985). Kardynał Stefan Wyszyński jakim go znałem (Warsaw, IWZZ, 1985).
Kałuszka, J. & Szymański, P.	Związki Zawodowe, Strajki, Negocjacje (Warsaw, MAW, 1982).
Kemp-Welch, A.	The Birth of Solidarity. The Gdańsk negotiations 1980 (London, Macmillan, 1983).
Kepiński, A. & Kilar, Z.	Kto jest kim w Polsce. Inaczej (Warsaw, Czytelnik, 1985).
Kiszczak, C.	'Realizm w ocenie pozwala być optymistą', Polityka, 17 July 1982.
Kołakowski, L.	Czy diabeł może być zbawiony i 27 innych kazań (London, Aneks, 1983). 'Winni (Solidarność) i niewinni (PZPR)', Aneks, No. 37 (1985), pp. 12-25.
Kolankiewicz, G.	'Renewal, Reform or Retreat. The Polish CP after the Extraordinary Ninth Congress', World Today, XXXVIII, No. 19 (October 1981), pp. 369-375.
Kolkowicz, R.	The Soviet Military and the Communist Party (Princeton U.P., 1967).
Kołodziej, M.	'Podziemne struktury NSZZ Solidarność, 13.xii.1981-13.xii.1984', Zeszyty Historyczne, No. 72 (Paris, 1985), pp. 65-90.
Komisja Planowania przy Radzie Ministrów	Warianty koncepcji Narodowego Planu Społeczno-Gospodarczego do 1985 roku, i wstępne założenia na lata 1986-1990 Rzeczpospolita (August 1982).
Konsultacyjna Rada Gospodarcza	'Sytuacja gospodarcza kraju w roku 1982', Życie Gospodarcze, 15 May 1983).
Korbonski, A.	'The Polish Army' in Adelman, Communist Armies in Politics, op. cit. 'Soviet policy toward Poland' in S.M. Terry (ed.), Soviet Policy in Eastern Europe (New Haven, Yale U.P., 1984), pp. 61-92.
Korbonski, A. & Terry, S.M.	'The military as a political actor in Poland' in R. Kolkowicz & A. Korbonski (eds.), Soldiers, Peasants and Bureaucrats (London, George Allen & Unwin, 1982).
Kraszewski, J.	'Wokół sporów o charakter partii', ND, 7-8/398-9 (July-August 1982), pp.51-64.

Bibliography

Kuczyński, W.   Obóz (London, Aneks, 1983).
                       'Solidarni i niepokonani', Aneks,
                       No. 29-30 (1983), pp. 9-21.
                       'Bilans gospodarczej reanimacji 1982-1984',
                       Aneks, No. 38 (1985), pp. 82-121.
                       'Kwestia krwi', Aneks, No. 37 (1985),
                       pp. 116-133.
Kuroń, J.   Polityka i odpowiedzialność (London,
                       Aneks, 1985).
                       'Tezy o wyjściu z sytuacji bez wyjścia',
                       Aneks, No. 27(1982).
Kuśmierek, J.   Stan Polski (Paris, Instytut Literacki,
                       1983).
Ładosz, J.   'Zródła i charakter naszego kryzysu',
                       ND, 1-2/392-393 (January-February 1982),
                       pp. 128-141.
Lamentowicz, W.   'Adaptation through political crisis in
                       Poland', Journal of Peace Research, XIX,
                       No. 2 (1982), pp. 117-131.
Ławrowski, A.   Od nadziei do rozczarowań. Zachód
                       wobec spraw polskich w latach
                       1969-1983 (Warsaw, MON, 1983).
Lewis, P.   Legitimation in Eastern Europe (London,
                       Croom Helm, 1985).
                       'The PZPR leadership and political de-
                       velopments in Poland', Soviet Studies,
                       XXXVII, No. 3 (July 1985), pp. 437-439.
                       'Turbulent Priest; political implica-
                       tions of the Popiełuszko affair',
                       Politics, V, No. 2 (October 1985),
                       pp. 33-39.
Liebiedziński, W.   'Marksizm a budownictwo socjalistyczne',
                       ND, 4/407 (April 1983), pp. 113-124.
Lipski, J.J.   KOR (London, Aneks, 1983).   Also pub-
                       lished in English translation by the
                       University of California Press, 1986.
Łopatka, A.   'Zasady polityki wyznaniowej w PRL',
                       ND, 4/407 (April 1982), pp. 14-25.
Lopiński, M.,   Konspira - rzecz o podziemnej
Moskit, M. &   Solidarności (Paris, Spotkania,
Wilk, M.   1984).
Macdonald, O.   'The Polish Vortex and Solidarity' in
                       Tariq Ali (ed.), The Stalinist Legacy
                       (London, Penguin, 1984).
Malcher, G.   Poland's Politicised Army. Communists
                       in uniform (New York, Praeger, 1984).
Malia, M.   'Poland. The Winter War', New York
                       Review of Books, 18 March 1982.
Malinowski, R.   'Nie mówimy ku pokrzepieniu serc',
                       Polityka, 24 July 1982.

Bibliography

Manteuffel, R.   Rolnictwo polskie w reformie (Warsaw,
                        LSW, 1984).
Markiewicz, S.   Ewolucja społecznej doktryny Kościoła
                        (Warsaw, KiW, 1983).
Markiewicz, W.   Konflikt społeczny w Polsce (Warsaw,
                        KAW, 1984).
Mason, D.S.   'Solidarity, the Régime and the Public',
                        Soviet Studies, XXXV, No. 4 (October
                        1983), pp. 533-545.
                        'The Polish Party in crisis, 1980-1982',
                        Slavic Review, Vol. 43, No. 1 (May 1984),
                        pp. 30-45.
                        Public Opinion and Political Change in
                        Poland, 1980-1982 (Cambridge U.P., 1985).
Mazowiecki, T.   Internowanie (London, Aneks, 1982).
Messner, Z.   'Z zewnątrz i od środka', Polityka,
                        22 May 1982.
Michnik, A.   Kościół, Lewica, dialog (Paris,
                        Instytut Literacki, 1977).
                        Szanse Polskiej Demokracji, Artykuły
                        i Eseje (London, Aneks, 1984).
                        'Polska Wojna', Aneks, No. 27 (1982),
                        pp. 9-21.
                        'List z Kurkowej', Aneks, No. 38 (1985),
                        pp. 3-27.
                        'KOR, szkoła wolności', Zeszyty
                        Historyczne, No. 68 (Paris, 1984).
                        'My ludzie Solidarności', Aneks, No. 37
                        (1985), pp. 38-53.
                        'We are all hostages', Telos, No. 51
                        (Spring 1982), pp. 173-182.
Mianowicz, T.   'Polityczny ruch oporu', Kultura, 3/426
                        (Paris, March 1983), pp. 89-94.
                        'Konspiracja, podziemie, opór społeczny',
                        Kultura, 4/427 (Paris, April 1983),
                        pp. 138-143.
Miłosz, C.   'O podboju', Aneks, No. 29-30 (1983),
                        pp. 3-8.
Miniur, K.   'Działaliśmy w trudnym czasie', ND,
                        1/404 (January 1983), pp. 33-44.
Mink, G. (ed.)   Pologne. L'État de Guerre (Paris, La
                        Documentation Française, No. 435, 12
                        March 1982).
Misztal, B. (ed.)   Poland after Solidarity (New Brunswick,
                        Transaction Books, 1985).
Modzelewski, E.   Import kontrrewolucji. Teoria i praktyka
                        KSS-KOR (Warsaw, KiW, 1982).
MSZ   Polityka Stanów Zjednoczonych wobec
                        Polski w świetle faktów i dokumentów
                        1980-1983 (Warsaw, Interpress, 1984).
Muszyński, J.   Dyktatura Proletariatu (Warsaw, PWN, 1981).

Bibliography

Narkiewicz, O.   Eastern Europe, 1968-1984 (London,
                      Croom Helm, 1986).
Nelson, D. (ed.)   Soviet Allies. The Warsaw Pact and the
                      issue of reliability (Boulder, Col.,
                      Westview Press, 1984).
Nowak, J.   'Jak Węgrzy wychodzili z kryzysu',
                      Polityka, 24 April 1982.
Nowakowski, M.   Raport o Stanie Wojennym (Paris,
                      Instytut Literacki, 1982). Trans. as
                      The Canary and other Tales of Martial
                      Law (London, Hamill Press, 1983).
Olszowski, S.   'Konsolidacja partii - warunkiem jej
                      odrodzenia', ND, 1-2, 392/393 (January-
                      February 1982), pp. 5-15.
                      'Bieżące i perspektywiczne zadania
                      Frontu Ideologicznego Partii', ND,
                      4/395 (April 1982), pp. 10-35.
Opałko, S.   'Zgodnie z linią historycznego Zjazdu',
                      ND, 11-12/414-415 (November-December
                      1983), pp. 5-12.
Orton, L.   'The Western Press and Jaruzelski's War',
                      East European Quarterly, XVIII, No. 3
                      (Autumn 1984).
Orzechowski, M.   Spór o marksistowską teorię rewolucji
                      (Warsaw, KiW, 1984).
                      'Wizje społeczeństwa socjalistycznego',
                      Polityka, 11 December 1982.
                      'Spór o marksistowską teorię rewolucji',
                      ND, 8/411 (August 1983), pp. 5-28.
Passent, D.   'Z granatami na ptaki', Polityka, 11
                      June 1983.
Pełnomocnik Rządu   Raport o reformie gospodarczej (Warsaw,
do Spraw Reformy   Rzeczpospolita supplement, August
Gospodarczej   1984).
Persky, S. &   The Solidarity Sourcebook (Vancouver,
Flam, H. (eds.)   New Star Books, 1982).
Plikus, M. (ed.)   Mała kronika Ludowego Wojska Polskiego
                      (Warsaw, MON, 1975).
Podemski, S.   'Sprawiedliwość - liczby i tendencje',
                      Polityka, 16 October 1982.
'Polacy 80'   Polacy 80. Wyniki badań ankietowanych
                      (W. Adamski et al., IFiS PAN, Warsaw,
                      1981).
'Polacy 81'   Polacy 81. Postrzeganie kryzysu i
                      konfliktu (W. Adamski et al., IFiS PAN,
                      Warsaw, 1982).
Pomian, G. (ed.)   Polska Solidarność (Paris, Instytut
                      Literacki, 1982).
Pomian, K.   Pologne. Défi à l'impossible (Paris,
                      Editions Ouvrières, 1982).

Bibliography

Pomian-Srednicki, M.   Religious Change in Contemporary Poland
                        (London, Routledge & Kegan Paul, 1982).
Pool, I. de Sola   Satellite Generals. A study of military
                        élites in the Soviet sphere (Stanford
                        U.P., 1955).
Popiełuszko, J.   Kazania patriotyczne (Paris, Libella,
                        1984).
Prusak, F. (ed.)   Stan Wojenny w Polsce (Warsaw, KiW,
                        1982).
PZPR   IX Nadzwyczajny Zjazd PZPR, 14-20 lipca
                        1981r. Podstawowe Dokumenty i Materiały
                        (Warsaw, KiW, 1981).
                        VII Plenum KC PZPR, 24-25 lutego 1982r,
                        ND, 3/394 (March 1982).
                        VIII Plenum KC PZPR, 22-23 kwietnia
                        1982r, ND supplement.
                        IX Plenum KC PZPR, 15-16 lipca 1982r,
                        ND supplement.
                        X Plenum KC PZPR, 27-28 października
                        1982r, ND supplement.
                        XI Plenum KC PZPR i NK SZL, 20-21
                        stycznia 1983, ND supplement.
                        XII Plenum KC PZPR, 31 maja 1983, ND
                        supplement.
                        XIII Plenum KC PZPR, 14-15 października
                        1983, ND supplement
                        Sprawozdanie z prac komisji KC PZPR
                        powołanej dla wyjaśnienia przyczyn i
                        przebiegu konfliktów społecznych w
                        dziejach Polski Ludowej, ND supplement
                        ('Kubiak Report').
                        Krajowa Konferencja Delegatów PZPR,
                        16-18 marca 1984, ND supplement, 2/2984
                        Part I.
                        I Ogólnopolska Partyjna Konferencja
                        Ideologiczno-Teoretyczna(Warsaw, KiW,
                        1982).
                        O co walczymy? Dokąd zmierzamy?, ND
                        supplement, 1/1984, pp. 333-344.
Raina, P.   Independent Social Movements in Poland
                        (London, Orbis, 1981).
                        Poland 1981. Towards Social Renewal
                        (London, George Allen & Unwin, 1985).
                        Jan Paweł II, Prymas i Episkopat Polski
                        o stanie wojennym (London, OPiM, 1982).
                        Kościół w Polsce (London, Veritas, 1984).
Rajkiewicz, A.   'Co można a co trzeba', Polityka, 19
                        June 1982.
Rakowski, M.F.   Partnerstwo (Warsaw, KiW, 1982).
                        Trudny dialog (Warsaw, KiW, 1983).
                        Czasy nadziei i rozczarowań (Warsaw,
                        Czytelnik, 1985).

Bibliography

Rakowski, M.F.   'Most nie jest zerwany', Polityka,
                 20 February 1982.
                 Interview with Oriana Fallaci, The Times,
                 23 February 1983.
Revesz, L.   'Die Polnische Volksarmee' in P. Gostony
                 (ed.), Zur Geschichte der Europäischen
                 Volksarmeen (Bonn, Hohwacht, 1976).
Reykowski, J.   'Rozwiązanie konfliktu', Polityka,
                 1 January 1983.
Rogowski, W.   Spor o przetrwanie (Warsaw, KiW, 1983).
Rupnik, J.   'The Polish Army and the Crisis of the
                 Party-State', Communist Affairs, I, No. 3
                 (July 1982), pp. 700-704.
Rybicki, M.   'Zmiany konstytucjne w Polsce Ludowej',
                 Studia Prawnicze, 4/78 (1983), pp. 3-35.
Ryszka, F.   'Porównania', Polityka, 6 March 1982.
Sadykiewicz, M. 'Jaruzelski's War', Survey, XXVI, No. 3
                 (Summer, 1982), pp. 18-26.
Sanford, G.   Polish Communism in Crisis (London,
                 Croom Helm, 1983).
                 'The Statute of the Polish United
                 Workers', trans. and intro. in W.B.
                 Simons & S. White (eds.), The Party
                 Statutes of the Communist World (The
                 Hague, Martinus Nijhoff, 1984).
                 'The Polish Communist Leadership and the
                 onset of the State of War', Soviet
                 Studies, XXXVI, No. 4 (October 1984),
                 pp. 494-512.
                 'Poland's recurring crises; an inter-
                 pretation', World Today, XXXI, No. 1
                 (January 1985), pp. 8-11.
                 'Interpreting the Polish Crisis', Soviet
                 Studies, XXXVI, No. 4 (Autumn 1985),
                 pp. 541-543.
                 'Poland' in M. McCauley & S. Carter (eds.),
                 Leadership and Succession in the Soviet
                 Union, Eastern Europe and China (London,
                 Macmillan, 1986), pp. 40-63.
Smolar, A.   'Między ugodą a powstaniem', Aneks, No.
                 28 (1982).
Sokolewicz, W.   'Konstytucja społeczeństwa i społeczna
                 rzeczywistość', Państwo i Prawo, XXXVII,
                 No. 7 (July 1982), pp. 3-15.
Staniszkis, J.   'Martial Law in Poland', Telos, No. 54
                 (Winter 1982-1983), pp. 87-100.
                 Poland's Self-Limiting Revolution
                 (Princeton U.P., 1984).
Stembrowicz, J. 'Z problematyki stanu nadzwyczajnego w
                 państwie burżuazyjno-demokratycznym',
                 Studia Nauk Politycznych, 3/63 (1983),
                 pp. 7-44.

Bibliography

Switak, I.	'Lessons from Poland', Telos, No. 52 (Summer, 1982), pp. 194-199.
Szaciło, T.	'Cel, stan i perspektywy polityczne obywatelskiego ruchu odrodzenia narodowego', ND, 4/395 (April 1982), pp. 119-129.
Szajkowski, B.	Next to God ... Poland (London, Frances Pinter, 1983).
Szawłowski, R.	Prawo człowieka a Polska (London, Polonia, 1982).
Szczepański, B.	Kryzys - i co dalej? (Warsaw, KAW, 1982).
Szczypiorski, A.	Z notatnika stanu wojennego (London, Polonia, 1983).
Szymanski, A.	Class Struggle in Socialist Poland (New York, Praeger, 1984).
Taras, R.	Ideology in a Socialist State. Poland 1956-1983 (London, Macmillan, 1984). 'Official etiologies of Polish crises: changing historiographies and factional struggles', Soviet Studies, XXXVIII, No. 1 (January 1986), pp. 53-68.
Toeplitz, K.	'Co było, co jest, co być musi', Polityka, 20 February 1982. 'Od sloganów do konkretów', Polityka, 13 November 1982.
Topolski, J.	'Fakty czy mity?', Polityka, 13 November 1982.
Touraine, A. et al.	Solidarity. Analysis of a Social Movement (Cambridge U.P., 1983).
Turbacz, M.	'Kościół a komunizm w Polsce', Kultura, 4/451 (Paris, April 1985), pp. 151-159.
Turowski, K.	'Czy narodowi polskiemu grozi upadek?', Kultura, 12/323 (Paris, December 1982), pp. 78-86.
Urbański, J.	'Odzyskiwanie społecznego zaufania', ND, 11/402 (November 1982), pp. 26-37.
Various	Kto jest kim w Polsce 1984 (Warsaw, Interpress, 1984).
Wajda, A.	'Polityczne jutro PZPR', ND, 7-8/398-399 (July-August 1982), pp. 26-32.
Wajszczuk, I.	'Poszukiwanie tożsamości. WSK Świdnik, 1980-1982 - zapis wydarzeń', ND, 2/405 (February 1983), pp. 60-70.
Warner, E.	The Military in Contemporary Soviet Politics (New York, Praeger, 1977).
Weydenthal, J., Porter, B. & Devlin, K.	The Polish Drama 1980-1982 (Lexington, D.C., Heath, 1983).
Woodall, J. (ed.)	Policy and Politics in Contemporary Poland (London, Frances Pinter, 1981).

Individuals mentioned in main text only.

Index

Index